REWARDS

Reading Excellence: Word Attack & Rate Development Strategies

D0879349

Reading Strategies
~ Applied to ~
# Social Studies Passages

Teacher's Guide

Anita L. Archer, Ph.D.
Mary M. Gleason, Ph.D.
Vicky Vachon, Ph.D.

Assisted by Beth Cooper

SOPRIS WEST EDUCATIONAL SERVICES
A CAMBIUM LEARNING COMPANY

BOSTON, MA • LONGMONT, CO

Cover photograph of Great Wall of China ©R. Ian Lloyd, Masterfile
Cover photograph of ship ©Doug Logan, Istockphoto
Cover photograph of Earth from space ©Bill Brooks, Masterfile
Cover photographs of Gandhi and immigrants ©2003 www.clipart.com

ISBN 13 Digit: 978-1-57035-802-9
ISBN 10 Digit: 1-57035-802-8
ISBN 1-57035-804-4 (TG and SB Set)

9 10 11 12 HPS 13 12 11 10

Printed in the United States of America
Published and Distributed by

Sopris West™
EDUCATIONAL SERVICES

A Cambium Learning Company

4093 Specialty Place ▪ Longmont, Colorado 80504
(303) 651-2829 ▪ www.sopriswest.com

24053/136/6-10

CONTENTS

ABOUT THE AUTHORS

Anita L. Archer, Ph.D.

Dr. Anita Archer serves as an educational consultant to school districts on effective instruction, classroom management, language arts instruction, and study skills instruction. She has taught elementary and middle school students and is the recipient of eight Outstanding Educator awards. She has been a faculty member at San Diego State University, the University of Oregon, and the University of Washington. Dr. Archer is nationally known for her presentations and publications on instructional procedures and design. She has authored many other curriculum and training materials as well as chapters and books.

Mary M. Gleason, Ph.D.

Dr. Mary Gleason is an educational consultant to school districts on implementation of literacy programs. Previously, Dr. Gleason was Director of Training for the National Institute for Direct Instruction (NIFDI). She began her career by teaching for eight years in general and special education classrooms. For 20 years as a professor at the University of Oregon, she designed and taught more than 40 college courses, including supervision and coaching, instructional design, methods courses for special education and general education, and technology in education courses. She is the author or coauthor of many journal articles, books, and curriculum materials. Her research focuses on academic interventions for students with learning disabilities.

Vicky Vachon, Ph.D.

Dr. Vicky Vachon is an educational consultant to school districts in the United States and Canada. She began her career as a classroom teacher in 1971. In 1983, she completed a master's degree in education at the University of Oregon. Upon returning to Canada, she worked as a teacher for the Toronto Board of Education. She was assigned to a multidisciplinary assessment team at the Child Development Clinic, Hospital for Sick Children, for nine years. In 1995, Dr. Vachon returned to the University of Oregon to complete a doctoral degree in special education. Her doctoral dissertation was about the effects of mastery of multisyllabic word reading component skills and the effects of context on the word and text reading skills of middle school students with reading deficiencies. She is a project director for the National Institute for Direct instruction, overseeing the usage of language arts and math curricula in several schools.

INTRODUCTION

What is REWARDS Plus?

REWARDS Plus is a specialized reading program designed for middle school and high school struggling readers. REWARDS Plus expands on the strategies introduced in the original REWARDS program. While most students make tremendous gains in decoding long words and in building fluency from participating in the REWARDS program, additional practice is often needed to "cement" these skills, to increase transfer to content area reading, and to move secondary students closer to grade level. REWARDS Plus has two application books, one that applies the reading strategies to social studies articles and the other with application to science articles. Either or both of these books can be used as a follow-up of the REWARDS program, and they can be used in either order. When the term REWARDS Plus is used in this Teacher's Guide, we will be referring to the application to social studies book.

Each of the 15 Application Lessons in REWARDS Plus requires two to three instructional periods, and each lesson is built around a captivating social studies article on such topics as the Greek origins of contemporary theater, kanji (characters in written Asian languages), and the mystery of Easter Island. REWARDS Plus structures each Application Lesson as follows:

- **Before** reading the passages, students use the REWARDS strategies to determine the pronunciation of difficult words. In addition, they are introduced to the meanings of critical vocabulary and are provided with background knowledge required for passage comprehension.
- **During** passage reading, students are asked questions to build their literal and inferential comprehension.
- **After** passage reading, repeated readings are used to build fluency. Students are also taught strategies for answering multiple-choice and short-answer items commonly found in assignments and tests. Finally, students are taught strategies for writing summaries and extended responses to writing prompts.

What are the goals of REWARDS Plus: Reading Strategies Applied to Social Studies Passages?

REWARDS Plus is designed to take middle and high school students closer to grade-level expectations. As a result of participation in this program, students will:

- Accurately read more multisyllabic words found in science, social studies, and health textbooks as well as other classroom materials.
- Be able to preview content-area chapters to gain an idea of their content.
- Read content-area passages not only accurately, but fluently.
- Experience increased comprehension as their accuracy and fluency increases.
- Accurately complete challenging multiple-choice items, justifying their answers.
- Accurately respond to short-answer questions, incorporating wording from the question into the answer.
- Write coherent summaries of, and extended responses to, reading passages.
- Have more confidence in their reading and writing abilities.

Which students should participate in REWARDS Plus?

REWARDS Plus is designed for struggling readers in middle school and high school (sixth through twelfth grade) who have completed the original REWARDS program and would benefit from continued decoding and fluency practice with greater focus on vocabulary, comprehension, and writing.

Where should students be placed in the program?

REWARDS Plus has two possible entry points. Students may enter at the beginning of the Review Lessons or at the beginning of the Application Lessons. If students have recently completed the REWARDS program successfully, they should begin REWARDS Plus with the Application Lessons. However, if students completed REWARDS in the previous year or semester—or if students did not demonstrate mastery of the *REWARDS* decoding strategies—they should begin *REWARDS Plus* by completing the six Review Lessons at the beginning of the program.

In what types of settings has REWARDS Plus *been taught?*

REWARDS Plus has been field-tested in a number of middle and high school settings. It could be used in special reading classes, in remedial or special education settings, or in literacy tutoring programs. *REWARDS Plus* is also appropriate as a part of intensive intervention programs after school, during the summer, or during interim sessions.

What are the components of REWARDS Plus?

1. *Teacher's Guide.* The *Teacher's Guide* consists of four sections:

   a. **Introduction**
      This section provides information about the *REWARDS Plus* program and how it is implemented. The Introduction should be read carefully before the program is implemented.

   b. **Review Lessons**
      Six Review Lessons are found at the beginning of the program. These lessons should be taught if students completed the *REWARDS* program in the previous year or semester, or did not demonstrate mastery at the end of *REWARDS*. These lessons review the critical preskills needed for the decoding strategies, provide guided and independent practice of the decoding strategies, and provide generalization practice through reading sentences. The sentences in the application to social studies book are different from those in the application to science book.

   c. **Application Lessons**
      Fifteen Application Lessons, each requiring two to three instructional periods, strengthen and expand the skills taught in the original *REWARDS* program.

   d. **Additional Materials**
      In the back of the *Teacher's Guide*, you will find:

- Blackline masters for Review and Application Lesson overhead transparencies.*
- Blackline masters for each strategy, plus a Prefixes, Suffixes, and Vowel Combinations Reference Chart, so that students can insert copies of the strategies and the chart into their notebooks (Appendix A).*
- Additional practice activities for vocabulary words that are introduced in each of the Application Lessons (Appendix B).*
- A Fluency Graph (Appendix C).*
- An outline for an optional incentive/grading program that could be used to provide feedback and encouragement (Appendix D).
- A pronunciation guide for the unique words introduced in the Application Lessons (Appendix E).
- An Activity A word list for the Application Lessons (Appendix F).

2. *Student Book.* The *Student Book* contains the stimuli used in the Review and Application Lessons for various teacher-directed and practice activities. All student materials needed for the program are found in the *Student Book*.

What is the content of the REWARDS Plus *Review Lessons?*

The *REWARDS Plus* Review Lessons review the flexible strategies for decoding long words that were introduced in *REWARDS*. These strategies involve peeling off prefixes and suffixes, segmenting the rest of the word into decodable "chunks" using the vowels, saying the word parts, saying the whole word, and making sure the word is a real word.

The ability to decode long words is critical for several reasons. First, word recognition is highly related to comprehension and is one of the greatest challenges facing struggling readers. Poor decoding skills, particularly as applied to long words, account for much of the gap between the reading proficiencies of lower and higher readers. In addition, the number of novel long words that students must read increases significantly in middle and high school textbooks. It is estimated that average students, from fifth grade on, will encounter approximately 10,000 new words in print each year. These longer words are also likely to carry most of the meaning in content area textbooks. (A complete review

---

* A complete set of transparencies may also be purchased separately.

Overt Strategy

1. Circle the prefixes.
2. Circle the suffixes.
3. Underline the vowels.
4. Say the parts of the word.
5. Say the whole word.
6. Make it a real word.

Example:

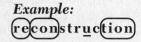

Covert Strategy

1. Look for prefixes, suffixes, and vowels.
2. Say the parts of the word.
3. Say the whole word.
4. Make it a real word.

of related research is found in the *REWARDS Teacher's Guide*.)

The steps in the Overt and Covert Strategies presented in *REWARDS* are shown above.

Students receive practice in the necessary preskills for these strategies (e.g., pronunciation of affixes and vowels) and the actual strategies in the six Review Lessons. Each activity found in the Review Lessons is briefly described here and on the following pages.

1. **Vowel Combinations.** Students review the common sounds (major sounds) for high frequency vowel combinations (**ay**, **ai**, **au**, **er**, **ir**, **ur**, **ar**, **a–e**, **o–e**, **i–e**, **e–e**, **u–e**, **oi**, **oy**, **or**, **ee**, **oa**, **ou**) and the major and minor sounds for **ow** (low, down), **oo** (moon, book), and **ea** (meat, thread). After the vowel combinations are presented, they are reviewed in subsequent Review Lessons to ensure accurate and quick recognition. The Vowel Combinations Chart below lists all the vowel combinations that are reviewed and presents a key word to clarify the pronunciation.

2. **Vowel Conversions.** Students are reminded that when they encounter a single vowel letter in a word, they should first try the short sound (referred to as the *sound* of the letter). If the resulting word is not a recognizable word, they should then say the long sound (referred to as the *name* of the letter). In this activity, students practice saying the sound and then the name for the letters **a**, **i**, **o**, **u**, and **e**.

3. **Prefixes and Suffixes.** About 80% of multisyllabic words have one or more affix. Thus, the ability to quickly identify and pronounce prefixes (e.g., **re**, **un**, **dis**) and suffixes (e.g., **tion**, **al**, **able**) facilitates the accurate, fluent decoding of longer words. Prefixes and suffixes have four characteristics: a specific pronunciation, a specific spelling, a specific meaning, and attachment to a root word. Thus, affixes assist us in decoding and spelling the word

Vowel Combinations Chart

(Shown in the order that they are introduced in the Review Lessons. See Appendix A for vowel combination reference chart grouped by type.)

Vowel Combination	Key Word	Vowel Combination	Key Word
ay	say	oi	void
ai	rain	oy	boy
au	sauce	or	torn
er	her	ee	deep
ir	bird	oa	foam
ur	turn	ou	loud
ar	farm	ow	low, down
a–e	make	oo	moon, book
o–e	hope	ea	meat, thread
i–e	side		
e–e	Pete		
u–e	use		

and, if the root word is known, assist us with word meaning.

However, in many cases the root word is not familiar to us. For example, the root may be an archaic form or has meaning in another language, such as Greek or Latin. In other situations, peeling off the affixes leaves a part that is an unfamiliar root word. In these instances, affixes may be helpful only with decoding and spelling because the affix does not carry a familiar meaning that is easily identifiable. Though these elements may not technically be acting as prefixes and suffixes within a specific word, they are still tremendously useful decoding elements.

In this activity, students review the pronunciation of prefixes and suffixes, practice saying these affixes, and review previously introduced affixes, the goal being accurate and quick pronunciation. The charts on this page and page 5 list affixes that are reviewed and their meanings.

4. **Strategy Instruction.** In this activity, the teacher demonstrates each step in the *REWARDS* Overt Strategy and guides students in applying the strategy steps to decode multisyllabic words.

5. **Strategy Practice.** In each Review Lesson, students practice using the Overt Strategy. Students circle prefixes and suffixes, underline the vowels in the rest of the word, and read the word by parts, thus applying the strategy with less teacher assistance.

6. **Independent Strategy Practice.** In Review Lessons 3–6, students shift to the Covert Strategy. Without circling and underlining, students read the word parts to themselves, then read each word aloud.

7. **Sentence Reading.** Sentence-reading activities are included to promote generalization of the *REWARDS* strategies to daily reading. In this activity, students read sentences laden with multisyllabic words that students had already read.

What is the content of REWARDS Plus Application Lessons?

1. **Passages.** The social studies passages were specifically written for *REWARDS Plus* to meet a number of requirements. First, the articles needed to be well-written, cohesive, interesting, and representative of

Prefixes Shown in the Order of Introduction

(Shown in the order that they are introduced in the Review Lessons. See Appendix A for an alphabetized reference chart.)

Prefix	Key Word	Meaning
dis	discover	away, apart; negative
mis	mistaken	wrong; not
ab	abdomen	from; away; off; not
ad	advertise	to, toward; against
in	insert	in, into; not; really
im	immediate	in, into; not
com	compare	with; together; really
be	belong	really; by; to make
pre	prevent	before
de	depart	away from; down; negative
re	return	again, back; really
pro	protect	in favor of; before; forward
con	continue	with; together; really
per	permit	through; really
un	uncover	not; reversal of; remove
a	above	in, on, at; not, without
ex	example	out, away
en	entail	in; within; on

Suffixes Shown in the Order of Introduction

(Shown in the order that they are introduced in the Review Lessons. See Appendix A for an alphabetized reference chart.)

Suffix	Key Word	Meaning
s	birds	more than one, verb marker
ing	running	when you do something; quality, state
ed	landed	in the past; quality
ness	kindness	that which is; state, quality
less	useless	without; not
ic	frantic	like; related to
ate	regulate	to make, act; having the quality of
ish	selfish	like, related to; to make
ist	artist	one who
ism	realism	state, quality; act
est	biggest	the most
ful	careful	full of
or	tailor	one who; that which
er	farmer	more; one who; that which
al	final	related to, like
tion	action	state, quality; act
sion	mission	state, quality; act
ion	million	state, quality; act
tive	attentive	one who; quality of
sive	expensive	one who; quality of
y	industry	having the quality of; in the manner of; small
ly	safely	how something is
ary	military	related to
ity	oddity	quality; state
ant	dormant	one who performs; thing that promotes; being
ent	consistent	one who performs; thing that promotes; being
ment	argument	that which; quality, act
ance	disturbance	action, process; quality or state
ence	essence	action, process; quality or state
ous	nervous	having the quality of
cious	precious	having the quality of
tious	cautious	having the quality of
cial	special	related to; like
tial	partial	related to; like
age	courage	that which is; state
ture	picture	state, quality; that which
able	disposable	able to be
ible	reversible	able to be
le	cradle	———

text commonly found in social studies books. Next, the articles needed to require little specialized background knowledge beyond that which could be easily introduced as a part of the lesson. Finally, specifications were followed for long words, readability, and passage length. The passages contain many multisyllabic words and have a readability range from eighth to ninth grade reading level. Because the pronunciations of all the difficult words are pretaught, the students experience a significantly lower readability. The passages vary in length from 567 words to 696 words.

2. **Lesson Activities.** Each of the fifteen Application Lessons contains the same activities divided into reading interventions that occur before, during, and after reading of the passage. These research-based interventions are summarized in the chart at the bottom of the page.

BEFORE PASSAGE READING

Before students read the passage, they are taught the pronunciation of the difficult words and their meanings. In addition, students preview the article and learn background information on the passage content.

3. **Vocabulary.** To increase students' decoding accuracy, fluency, and comprehension, the most difficult words are taught before the passages are read. Three instructional practices are used: *tell*, *strategy*, and *word families*. First, the teacher *tells* students the pronunciation of a set of difficult words that are proper names, irregular words, or words of foreign origin. For the second set of words, students use a *REWARDS* *strategy* to determine the pronunciation. For the third set of words, students are presented with groups of related words (*word families*) such as the family **apply**, **applicant**, and **application**. Students use the decoding strategies to determine the pronunciation of the words.

The meaning of each word is also presented along with the pronunciation. A short definition that corresponds to the use of the word in the passage (not necessarily the most common definition) is provided, coupled with the part of speech. Teachers are welcome to provide additional information concerning the definitions including examples, illustrations, and oral sentences that illustrate the word, depending on the background knowledge of students. You may wish to select 5 to 10 words from the lists for very explicit instruction. Select words that students might encounter in many of their classes and could incorporate into their written and spoken vocabulary (e.g., from Application Lesson 5—**occupation**, **disobedience**, **participate**). The following steps would be useful for those words.

Before Passage Reading Interventions	▪ Introduce the pronunciation of difficult words.
	   ▪ Tell students the pronunciation of irregular words.
	   ▪ Guide students in using their *REWARDS* strategies on regular words.
	▪ Teach the meanings of critical vocabulary.
	▪ Dictate spelling words.
	▪ Introduce critical background knowledge.
	▪ Preview the passage prior to reading.

During Passage Reading Interventions	▪ Guide students in reading the passage. ▪ Ask students questions to check their understanding and to model active thinking during reading.

After Passage Reading Interventions	▪ Engage students in repeated reading activities to increase fluency.
	▪ Guide students in answering multiple-choice questions and short answer questions on the article's content.
	▪ Provide engaging vocabulary practice including activities such as:
	   ▪ Yes/No/Why
	   ▪ Completion Activities
	▪ Guide students in planning, writing, and editing expository summaries and extended responses.

Explicit Vocabulary Instruction

Step 1: Introduce the pronunciation of the word and the definition.

Read the word. "obsolete"

Read the definition. "No longer used."

Step 2: Rephrase the definition, asking students to complete a statement.

When something is no longer used, it is _____. "obsolete"

Step 3: Check students' understanding by asking questions.

What causes something to become obsolete?

Are electric can openers obsolete? Why or why not?

Are record players obsolete? Why or why not?

Tell your partner examples of things that are obsolete.

A reproducible vocabulary activity is provided for each lesson (see Appendix B). These optional activities could be completed as a class activity, as a partner activity, or as an independent student activity either in class or as a homework assignment.

4. **Spelling.** Many students who have poor decoding skills also have low spelling knowledge and are intimidated by longer words. In this activity, the teacher dictates a lesson word, and then students say and write the parts of the word. Students then compare their spelling to the correct spelling of the word, cross out any misspellings, and rewrite those words.

5. **Background Knowledge.** As we are aware in our own reading, our comprehension is highly related to our background knowledge of the topic. This is very evident with students you are teaching. For this reason, a short background knowledge paragraph is presented before each selection. One of three methods can be used to read this section: read it to students, have students read it together, or call on individual students. This section is accompanied by a timeline and related graphic. The teacher should carefully examine these with their students and preview the content of the article by examining the title and the headings.

DURING PASSAGE READING

After students have been introduced to the words and background knowledge and have previewed the article, they read the related social studies article and are asked literal and inferential questions during the reading. Select the passage-reading procedure that best fits the reading proficiency of your students and the size of the group. Every effort should be made to not embarrass students, since many may have a history of reading difficulties and may be uncomfortable reading in front of the whole group, particularly with no prior practice.

If you are teaching a ***small group*** with students who ***are having difficulty, use Option A***. Have students read *one* paragraph silently. Then, call on one student to orally read a paragraph or a portion of the paragraph to the class. Call on students in random order, varying the amount that each student reads.

If you are teaching a ***small group*** with students who ***are not having difficulty, use Option B***. Have students read the entire selection silently, rereading it if they finish before their classmates. Then, call on one student to orally read a paragraph or a portion of a paragraph to the class. Call on students in random order, varying the amount that each student reads.

If you are teaching a ***large group*** with students who ***are having difficulty, use Option C***. Have students, paired with partners, read a paragraph silently. Then, have students read the paragraph to their partner. Alternate partner reading turns. In a large group, the use of partner reading increases the amount of practice each student receives and creates a safer venue for desired practice.

If you are teaching a ***large group*** with students who ***are not having difficulty, use Option D***. Have students read the article silently, rereading the article if their peers have not finished. Pair students with partners. Then, have students read the passage with their partners, alternating paragraphs.

AFTER PASSAGE READING

After students have read the passage, they work on building their passage-reading fluency. In addition, they learn comprehension strategies for answering multiple-choice and short-answer questions and writing strategies for producing summaries and extended responses.

6. **Passage Reading—Fluency.** A number of studies have determined that students' oral reading fluency is correlated with reading comprehension. As students read words more fluently with automaticity, they can turn their attention from decoding to comprehension.

The oral reading rate goals listed below represent the number of words read correctly in one minute at different reading levels (not grade levels).

Reading Level	Words Read Correctly in One Minute
Grades 6–8	150–180 words per minute
Grades 9–12	180–200 words per minute

Oral reading fluency can be increased through repeated readings of passages for which students already have a high level of accuracy. After practicing the passage for the purpose of accuracy, students use a repeated reading procedure to increase their reading fluency. First, students do a "Cold Timing" in which they whisper-read for one minute as the teacher times them. The reading is then practiced one or two more times, having students attempt to beat their Cold Timing. Next, students pair with partners, exchange books, listen to their partners read for one minute, and record their partner's errors and number of correct words read on the "Hot Timing." At the close of this activity, students graph their own number of correctly read words on the Cold Timing and Hot Timing. A Fluency Graph is found on the last page of the *Student Book*. An additional, reproducible copy is found in Appendix C.

7. **Comprehension Questions—Multiple Choice.** On classroom tests as well as on state and district standards tests, students' knowledge is often measured using multiple-choice items. In *REWARDS Plus,* each lesson contains four challenging multiple-choice items including vocabulary, cause/effect, compare/contrast, and main idea items. The distracters include plausible (though incorrect) answers, details drawn from the passage (though irrelevant to the question), and inferences not based on details found in the article.

Students are taught a strategy for completing these types of items: to read the multiple-choice item, to read all of the choices, to think about why each choice might be correct or incorrect, and finally, to select the best answer. While the strategy is simple, the critical thinking skills necessary to answer challenging multiple-choice items are very demanding and are enhanced through interactive practice. In this exercise, students complete an item and then discuss it with classmates, sharing their answers and rationales.

8. **Comprehension Questions—Short Answer.** Another commonly requested type of response is to reply to short-answer questions in which the answer is either found in the article or known by the student. The secret to these items is using some of the wording from the question in the written answer. Students complete two of these items in most Application Lessons.

9. **Expository Writing—Summary.** Writing a summary is not only an excellent activity for teaching the structure of expository writing, but is also a powerful comprehension strategy for homing in on the most critical information. Students are taught a six-step writing strategy and how to apply it to writing a summary. First, they *list* the most important details from the article. Next, they review the list, *cross out* irrelevant details, and *connect* details that could combine easily into one sentence. Then, students *number* the details in a logical order. Finally, students *write* and *edit* their summaries and evaluate them against a rubric. This writing strategy is carefully modeled and practiced with students to ensure coherent, well-written products.

10. **Expository Writing—Extended Response.** The writing strategy taught for summaries is also applied to writing prompts that require students to state and support their opinions or positions. Here, students are taught to write a topic sentence and then to give at least three reasons to support their opinions or positions. Each of the reasons is explained in the extended response, resulting in an elaborated paragraph.

How are REWARDS Plus *lessons designed in the* Teacher's Guide?

Each lesson contains a set of activities. The activities for the Review Lessons are similar each day, as are the activities for the Application Lessons. For each activity, two "lesson plans" are given. First, there is a general description of the activity. Next, there is a teacher script that includes the wording a teacher could use when teaching the lesson. Please read the lessons prior to instruction, including the activity procedures and the scripts. You may then choose to follow the general procedure or the script, maintaining the essence of the activity in either case.

How can I actively involve my students in the instruction?

Student achievement is highly related to opportunities to respond. When students must constantly say, write, or do things in a lesson, they are much more likely to be attentive and to learn from the resulting practice. The Best Practices for Eliciting Responses Chart below outlines some of the procedures you may wish to use to involve all students in the lessons.

How much time do the lessons take?

The amount of time to complete each lesson varies greatly depending on the size of the group, the competency of students, and the pace of the teacher.

Best Practices for Eliciting Responses Chart

Type of Response	Best Practice
Group Says Answer *(A group response can be used when the wording is short and the same for all students.)*	**If students are looking at the teacher.** **T:** Asks a question. **T:** Raises his/her hand to signal thinking time. **S:** Think of the answer. **T:** Says "Everyone" and lowers hand to signal end of thinking time. **S:** Say the answer. **If students are looking at their work.** **T:** Asks a question or gives a directive. **T:** Gives the students thinking time. **S:** Think of the answer. **T:** Signals audibly (e.g., voice signal, such as "Everyone"). **S:** Respond.
Student Partners Say Answer	**The teacher assigns a response partner to each student and the numbers 1 and 2.** **T:** Asks a question or gives a directive. **T:** Asks Partner 1 to respond ("Ones, tell your partner . . ."). **S:** Tells the answer to his/her partner. **T:** Monitors the class. **T:** Gives feedback to each group.
Individual Student Says Answer	**T:** Asks a question. **T:** Raises his/her hand to signal thinking time. Gives eye contact to all students to encourage formulation of an answer. **S:** Think of answer. **T:** Calls on one student. **S:** Gives an answer.
Students Write Answer	**T:** Gives a directive or asks a question. Tells students to put down their pencils and look up when they are done. **S:** Write a response. **T:** Monitors students. **T:** Gives feedback to students.

Generally, each Review Lesson requires one instructional period (45–50 minutes). Because of the extensive vocabulary instruction, fluency building, comprehension items, and writing activities, each Application Lesson requires two to three instructional periods of 45–50 minutes. If parts of lessons are not completed during an instructional period, the teacher may wish to review the lesson's content and complete it the next day.

How can I measure my students' progress?

Use the procedures outlined in Appendix G at the back of this *Teacher's Guide*. These procedures include directions for pre/post fluency and writing measures.

Review Lesson 1

Materials Needed:

- *Student Book:* Review Lesson 1
- Review Overhead Transparency A
- Appendix A Reproducible 1: *REWARDS* Strategies for Reading Long Words
- Appendix A Reproducible 2: Prefixes, Suffixes, and Vowel Combinations Reference Chart
- Paper or cardboard to use when covering the overhead transparency
- Washable overhead transparency pen

Text Treatment Notes:

- Black text signifies teacher script (exact wording to say to students).
- Green text in parentheses signifies directions or prompts for the teacher.
- Green text signifies answers or examples of answers.
- Green graphics treatment signifies reproduction of Overhead information.
- Green text and green graphics treatment do not appear in the *Student Book*.

PREPARATION

- Write the following words on a chalkboard or overhead transparency:

  intentionally
  unconventionality
  inventiveness

- Photocopy and distribute Appendix A Reproducibles 1 and 2 (*REWARDS* Strategies for Reading Long Words and Prefixes, Suffixes, and Vowel Combinations Reference Chart). Have students place the copies in their notebooks or in folders for later reference.

INTRODUCTION

1. In the next few days, we are going to review strategies for reading longer words that you learned in the *REWARDS* program. You will remember how to figure out words such as (point to each word on a chalkboard or the overhead) **intentionally**, **unconventionality**, and **inventiveness**.
2. First, we are going to review the skills you need to read longer words. Then, we will practice reading longer words in sentences and in some of our classroom books.

ACTIVITY A
Vowel Combinations

ACTIVITY PROCEDURE

(See the *Student Book,* page 1.)

In this activity, students review the sound to say when they see a combination of letters. Have students point to the letters in their *Student Books.* Tell students the sound as it is pronounced in the key word. Have students practice saying the sounds.

1. Open your *Student Book* to **Review Lesson 1**, page 1. Find **Activity A**. We are going to review some sounds. You learned all of them in the *REWARDS* program, but you may need a short review.
2. Look at the first line of letter combinations. Point to the letters **a - y**. The sound of these letters is usually /ā/. What sound?_
3. Point to the letters **a - i**. The sound of these letters is usually /ā/. What sound?_
4. Point to the letters **a - u**. The sound of these letters is usually /aw/. What sound?_
5. Look at the second line of letter combinations. Point to the letters **e - r**. The sound of these letters is usually /er/. What sound?_
6. Point to the letters **i - r**. The sound of these letters is usually /er/. What sound?_
7. Point to the letters **u - r**. The sound of these letters is usually /er/. What sound?_
8. Point to the letters **a - r**. The sound of these letters is usually /ar/. What sound?_
9. Go back to the beginning of the first line. Say the sounds again. What sound?_ Next sound?_ Next sound?_
10. (Continue Step 9 until students have reviewed all sounds in the two lines.)

ACTIVITY B
Vowel Conversions

ACTIVITY PROCEDURE

(See the *Student Book*, page 1.)

In this activity, students review how to switch between saying the *sound* and saying the *name* for a particular vowel letter. They review that when they see a vowel letter in a long word, they should first say the sound. If it doesn't make a real word, they will say the name. Have students point to the letter while you tell them the sound, and have them repeat the sound. Then, have students point to the same letter while you tell them the name, and have students repeat the name. Have students practice saying the sound, then the name for each letter.

1. Find **Activity B**. When you are reading words and see these letters, first try the sound. If it doesn't make a real word, then try the name.
2. Point to the first letter. The sound is /ă/. What sound?_ The name is **a**. What name?_
3. Point to the next letter. The sound is /ĭ/. What sound?_ The name is **i**. What name?_
4. Point to the next letter. The sound is /ŏ/. What sound?_ The name is **o**. What name?_
5. First letter again. What sound?_ What name?_
6. Next letter. What sound?_ What name?_
7. Next letter. What sound?_ What name?_

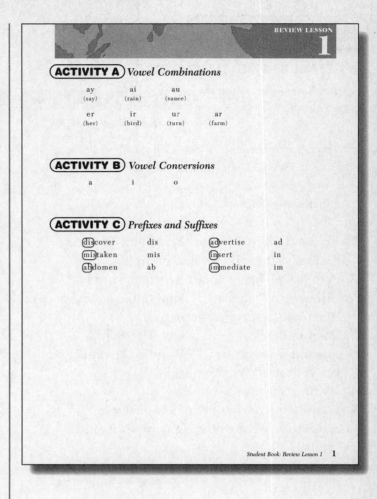

ACTIVITY A *Vowel Combinations*

ay	ai	au	
(say)	(rain)	(sauce)	
er	ir	ur	ar
(her)	(bird)	(turn)	(farm)

ACTIVITY B *Vowel Conversions*

a   i   o

ACTIVITY C *Prefixes and Suffixes*

discover	dis	advertise	ad
mistaken	mis	insert	in
abdomen	ab	immediate	im

Student Book: Review Lesson 1   **1**

ACTIVITY C

Prefixes and Suffixes

ACTIVITY PROCEDURE

(See the *Student Book,* page 1.)

In this activity, students review identifying and pronouncing prefixes and suffixes. In this lesson, have students first point to the words, then the circled prefixes, while you pronounce them. Ask students to repeat the words and prefixes after you.

1. Find **Activity C**. Now, we are going to review prefixes. Where do we find prefixes?_
2. Point to the first column. The first word is **discover**. What word?_ Point to the circled prefix. The prefix is /dis/. What prefix?_
3. Point to the next word below. The word is **mistaken**. What word?_ Point to the prefix. The prefix is /mis/. What prefix?_
4. (Repeat with **abdomen** and /ab/.)
5. Point to the third column. The first word is **advertise**. What word?_ The prefix is /ad/. What prefix?_
6. (Repeat with **insert** and /in/ and **immediate** and /im/.)
7. Find the second column. It has prefixes only. Read the prefixes. What prefix?_ Next?_ Next?_
8. Find the last column. What prefix?_ Next?_ Next?_

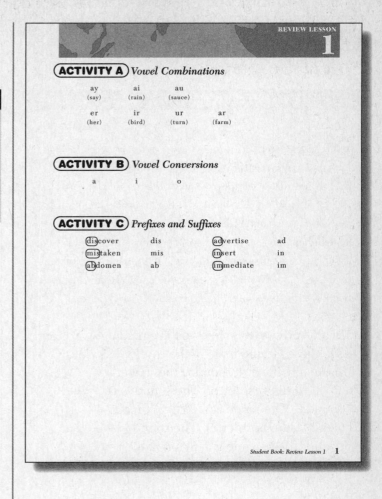

ACTIVITY D
Strategy Instruction

ACTIVITY PROCEDURE

(See the *Student Book*, page 2.)

In this activity, students practice using all their skills for figuring out longer words. First, use three words to show students how to use the strategy. Then, work with students to apply the strategy to the remaining words. For each word, ask students if the word has prefixes, then circle them. Underline the vowels and have students say the sounds. Finally, have students say the word, first part by part, and then as a whole word.

 Use Overhead A: Activity D

1. Turn to page 2. Find **Activity D**.
2. We are going to review the *REWARDS* strategy for figuring out longer words.
3. Look up here. Watch me use the *REWARDS* strategy. (Point to the word **abstract** in Line #1.)
4. First, I circle prefixes. (Circle **ab**. Point to the prefix and ask . . .) What prefix?_
5. Next, I underline the vowels in the rest of the word. (Underline **a** in **str<u>a</u>ct**. Point to the vowel and ask . . .) What sound?_
6. Next, I say the parts in the word. (Loop under each part and say the parts: **ab str<u>a</u>ct**.)
7. Next, we say the whole word. Remember to make it a real word. What word?_
8. (Repeat Steps 4–7 with **insist** and **impact**.)
9. Let's read some more words.
10. (Point to the word **distraught**.) Does the word have a prefix?_ (If the answer is "yes," circle the prefix and ask . . .) What prefix?_
11. (Underline the vowels in the rest of the word and ask . . .) What sound?_
12. Say the word by parts. (Loop under each part and ask . . .) What part?_ What part?_
13. (Run your finger under the whole word.) What word?_
14. (Repeat Steps 10–13 with **misfit** and **admit**.)

Note: You may wish to provide additional practice by having students read a line to the group or to a partner.

ACTIVITY D *Strategy Instruction*

1. abstract   insist   impact
2. distraught   misfit   admit

ACTIVITY E *Strategy Practice*

1. birthday   (mis)play   (dis)card
2. maintain   (dis)band   (in)distinct
3. modern   (ad)dict   (im)print
4. (ab)surd   (in)sert   railway

ACTIVITY F *Sentence Reading*

1. If you have a ticket, they will admit you to the theater.
2. You maintain a machine by taking care of it.
3. My mother hopes to discard all her old clothes.
4. The play's plot was absurd, so the actors must disband.
5. The markings on the bird were indistinct.
6. My sister must learn to not be a misfit.
7. Marcos will insist on buying a new car this year.
8. His abstract paintings had an impact.
9. My bad day left me feeling distraught.
10. Jasmine left an imprint of her hand in the sand.

ACTIVITY E
Strategy Practice

ACTIVITY PROCEDURE

(See the *Student Book*, page 2.)

In this activity, students practice using the strategy themselves for figuring out longer words. Have students circle prefixes and underline the vowels. Assist students in checking their work, then reading each word, first part by part, and then as a whole word.

 Use Overhead A: Activity E

1. Find **Activity E**.
2. Now, it's your turn. For each word, circle prefixes and underline the vowels in the rest of the word. Be careful. Remember that some words have no prefixes, and some words have one or more prefixes. Look up when you are done._
3. (Show the overhead transparency.) Now, check and fix any mistakes._
4. (When students are done checking, assist students in reading each word on the overhead transparency, beginning with the first word in Line #1.) Look up here._
5. (Loop under each word part in **birth day**.) What part?_ What part?_
6. (Run your finger under the whole word.) What word?_
7. (Repeat Steps 4–6 with all words in Activity E.)

Note: You may wish to provide additional practice by having students read a line to the group or to a partner.

ACTIVITY D *Strategy Instruction*

1. abstract   insist   impact
2. distraught   misfit   admit

ACTIVITY E *Strategy Practice*

1. birthday   misplay   discard
2. maintain   disband   indistinct
3. modern   addict   imprint
4. absurd   insert   railway

ACTIVITY F *Sentence Reading*

1. If you have a ticket, they will admit you to the theater.
2. You maintain a machine by taking care of it.
3. My mother hopes to discard all her old clothes.
4. The play's plot was absurd, so the actors must disband.
5. The markings on the bird were indistinct.
6. My sister must learn to not be a misfit.
7. Marcos will insist on buying a new car this year.
8. His abstract paintings had an impact.
9. My bad day left me feeling distraught.
10. Jasmine left an imprint of her hand in the sand.

ACTIVITY F

Sentence Reading

ACTIVITY PROCEDURE

(See the _Student Book_, page 2.)

In this activity, students use the strategy for figuring out longer words in the context of sentences that contain words they have already practiced. Have students read a sentence to themselves. Then, choose from several options of having students read the sentence together, to partners, or individually to the class.

Note: If you are teaching older students for whom "thumbs-up" is inappropriate, have students look at you when they can read the sentence.

1. Find **Sentence #1** in **Activity F.** These sentences include words that we practiced today. Read the first sentence to yourself. When you can read all the words in the sentence, put your thumb up.

2. (When students can read the sentence, use one of the following options:

   a. Ask students to read the sentence together [i.e., choral reading].

   b. Have students read the sentence to their partners. Then, call on one student to read the sentence to the group.

   c. Ask one student to read the sentence to the group.)

3. (Repeat these procedures with the remaining sentences. Be sure that you give ample thinking time for each sentence.)

REVIEW LESSON

1

ACTIVITY D _Strategy Instruction_

1. abstract   insist   impact
2. distraught   misfit   admit

ACTIVITY E _Strategy Practice_

1. birthday   misplay   discard
2. maintain   disband   indistinct
3. modern   addict   imprint
4. absurd   insert   railway

ACTIVITY F _Sentence Reading_

1. If you have a ticket, they will admit you to the theater.
2. You maintain a machine by taking care of it.
3. My mother hopes to discard all her old clothes.
4. The play's plot was absurd, so the actors must disband.
5. The markings on the bird were indistinct.
6. My sister must learn to not be a misfit.
7. Marcos will insist on buying a new car this year.
8. His abstract paintings had an impact.
9. My bad day left me feeling distraught.
10. Jasmine left an imprint of her hand in the sand.

2 _REWARDS Plus: Reading Strategies Applied to Social Studies Passages_

Review Lesson 2

Materials Needed:

- *Student Book:* Review Lesson 2
- Review Overhead Transparency B
- Paper or cardboard to use when covering the overhead transparency
- Washable overhead transparency pen

Text Treatment Notes:

- Black text signifies teacher script (exact wording to say to students).
- Green text in parentheses signifies directions or prompts for the teacher.
- Green text signifies answers or examples of answers.
- Green graphics treatment signifies reproduction of Overhead information.
- Green text and green graphics treatment do not appear in the *Student Book*.

ACTIVITY A

Vowel Combinations

ACTIVITY PROCEDURE

(See the *Student Book*, page 3.)

In this activity, students review the sounds to say when they see combinations of letters. First, have students point to each combination of letters, and tell students the sound as it is pronounced in the key word. Then, have students practice all the sounds from this and the previous lesson.

1. Open your *Student Book* to **Review Lesson 2**, page 3. Find **Activity A**. We are going to review some sounds. You learned all of them in the *REWARDS* program, but you may need a short review.

2. Look at the line of letter combinations. Point to the letters **a—e**. The sound of these letters is usually /ā/. What sound?_

3. Point to the letters **o—e**. The sound of these letters is usually /ō/. What sound?_

4. Point to the letters **i—e**. The sound of these letters is usually /ī/. What sound?_

5. Point to the letters **e—e**. The sound of these letters is usually /ē/. What sound?_

6. Point to the letters **u—e**. The sound of these letters is usually /ū/. What sound?_

7. Go back to the beginning of the line. Say the sounds again. What sound?_ Next sound?_ Next sound?_ Next sound?_ Next sound?_

8. Point to the letters **e - r** in **Line #1**. What sound?_ Next sound?_ Next sound?_ Next sound?_ Next sound?_

9. (Repeat Step 8 for letters in Lines #2–4.)

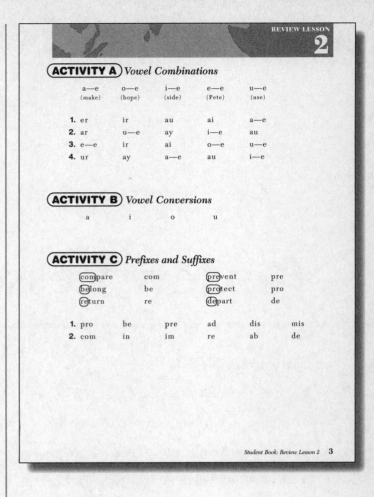

ACTIVITY B
Vowel Conversions

ACTIVITY PROCEDURE

(See the *Student Book,* page 3.)

Have students point to the letter while you tell them the sound, and have them repeat the sound. Then, have students point to the same letter while you tell them the name, and have students repeat the name. Have students practice saying the sound, then the name for each letter.

1. Find **Activity B**. When you are reading words and see these letters, first try the sound. If it doesn't make a real word, then try the name.
2. Point to the first letter. The sound is /ă/. What sound?_ The name is **a**. What name?_
3. Point to the next letter. The sound is /ĭ/. What sound?_ The name is **i**. What name?_
4. Point to the next letter. The sound is /ŏ/. What sound?_ The name is **o**. What name?_
5. Point to the next letter. The sound is /ŭ/. What sound?_ The name is **u**. What name?_
6. First letter again. What sound?_ What name?_
7. Next letter. What sound?_ What name?_
8. (Repeat Step 7 for the remaining letters.)

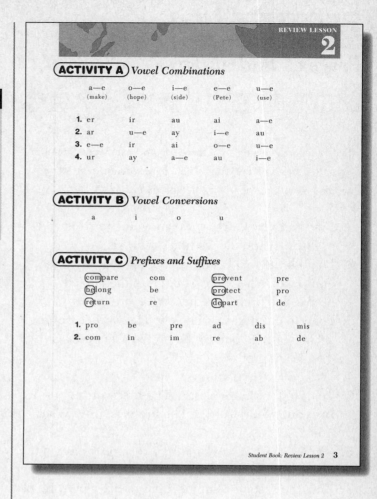

ACTIVITY C

Prefixes and suffixes

ACTIVITY PROCEDURE

(See the *Student Book,* page 3.)

Tell students the words, then the circled prefixes. Have students repeat the words and prefixes. Then, have students practice saying the new and previously learned prefixes.

1. Find **Activity C**. Now, we are going to review prefixes. Where do we find prefixes?_
2. Point to the first column. The first word is **compare**. What word?_ Point to the circled prefix. The prefix is /com/. What prefix?_
3. Point to the next word below. The word is **belong**. What word?_ Point to the prefix. The prefix is /be/. What prefix?_
4. (Repeat with **return** and /re/.)
5. Point to the third column. The first word is **prevent**. What word?_ The prefix is /pre/. What prefix?_
6. (Repeat with **protect** and /pro/ and **depart** and /de/.)
7. Find the second column. It has prefixes only. Read the prefixes. What prefix?_ Next?_ Next?_
8. Find the last column. What prefix?_ Next?_ Next?_
9. Point to the first prefix in **Line #1**. What prefix?_ Next?_ Next?_ Next?_ Next?_ Next?_
10. (Repeat Step 9 for prefixes in Line #2.)

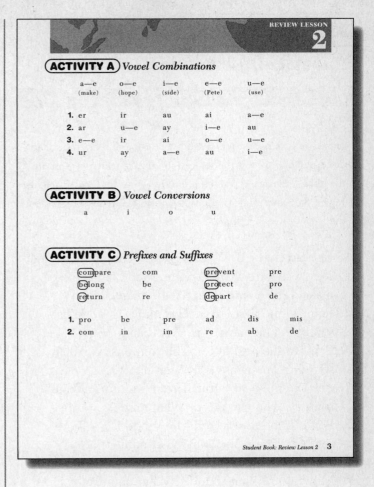

ACTIVITY D

Strategy Instruction

ACTIVITY PROCEDURE

(See the *Student Book*, page 4.)

First, use three words to show students how to use the strategy for figuring out longer words. Then, work with students to apply the strategy to the remaining words. For each word, ask students if the word has prefixes, then circle them. Underline the vowels, and have students say the sounds. Finally, have students say the word, first part by part, and then as a whole word.

 Use Overhead B: Activity D

1. Turn to page 4. Find **Activity D**.
2. We are going to review the *REWARDS* strategy for figuring out longer words.
3. Look up here. Watch me use the strategy. (Point to the word **beside**.)
4. First, I circle prefixes. (Circle **be**. Point to the prefix and ask . . .) What prefix?_
5. Next, I underline the vowels in the rest of the word. (Underline and connect the **i** and **e** in **side**. Point to the vowel and ask . . .) What sound?_
6. Next, I say the parts in the word. (Loop under each part and say the parts: **be side**.)
7. Next, we say the whole word. Remember, it must be a real word. What word?_
8. (Repeat Steps 4–7 with **readjust** and **prepay**.)
9. Let's read some more words.
10. (Point to the word **combine**.) Does the word have a prefix?_ (If the answer is "yes," circle the prefix and ask . . .) What prefix?_
11. (Underline the vowels in the rest of the word and ask . . .) What sound?_
12. Say the word by parts. (Loop under each part and ask . . .) What part?_ What part?_
13. (Run your finger under the whole word.) What word?_
14. (Repeat Steps 10–13 with **provide** and **defraud**.)

Note: You may wish to provide additional practice by having students read a line to the group or to a partner.

REVIEW LESSON 2

ACTIVITY D Strategy Instruction

1. beside   readjust   prepay
2. combine   provide   defraud

ACTIVITY E Strategy Practice

1. backbone   reprint   costume
2. mistake   promote   prescribe
3. obsolete   propose   sunstroke
4. decode   holiday   subscribe

ACTIVITY F Sentence Reading

1. On my holiday, I will go by railway.
2. If you do a really good job, we will promote you.
3. Dr. Smith will readjust your backbone.
4. Dr. Smith will prescribe pills and provide a splint.
5. Dr. Smith will also help you with sunstroke.
6. It is a mistake to defraud people of their money.
7. Can you decode all the words in the reprint?
8. Do you subscribe to *USA TODAY*?
9. You will need to prepay for the holiday trip.
10. What costume do you propose to wear?

4   *REWARDS Plus: Reading Strategies Applied to Social Studies Passages*

ACTIVITY E
Strategy Practice

ACTIVITY PROCEDURE

(See the *Student Book,* page 4.)

Have students circle prefixes and underline the vowels. Assist students in checking their work, then reading each word, first part by part, and then as a whole word.

 Use Overhead B: Activity E

1. Find **Activity E**.
2. Now, it's your turn. For each word, circle prefixes and underline the vowels in the rest of the word. Look up when you are done._
3. (Show the overhead transparency.) Now, check and fix any mistakes._
4. (When students are done checking, assist students in reading each word on the overhead transparency, beginning with the first word in Line #1.) Look up here._ (Loop under each word part in **back bone**.) What part?_ What part?_ (Run your finger under the whole word.) What word?_
5. (Repeat Steps 2–4 with all words in Activity E.)

Note: You may wish to provide additional practice by having students read a line to the group or to a partner.

ACTIVITY D *Strategy Instruction*

1. beside	readjust	prepay
2. combine	provide	defraud

ACTIVITY E *Strategy Practice*

1. backbone	reprint	costume
2. mistake	promote	prescribe
3. obsolete	propose	sunstroke
4. decode	holiday	subscribe

ACTIVITY F *Sentence Reading*

1. On my holiday, I will go by railway.
2. If you do a really good job, we will promote you.
3. Dr. Smith will readjust your backbone.
4. Dr. Smith will prescribe pills and provide a splint.
5. Dr. Smith will also help you with sunstroke.
6. It is a mistake to defraud people of their money.
7. Can you decode all the words in the reprint?
8. Do you subscribe to *USA TODAY*?
9. You will need to prepay for the holiday trip.
10. What costume do you propose to wear?

ACTIVITY F
Sentence Reading

ACTIVITY PROCEDURE

(See the *Student Book*, page 4.)

Have students read a sentence to themselves. Then, choose from several options of having students read the sentence together, to partners, or individually to the class.

Note: If you are teaching older students for whom "thumbs-up" is inappropriate, have students look at you when they can read the sentence.

1. Find **Sentence #1** in **Activity F.**_ These sentences include words that we practiced today. Read the first sentence to yourself. When you can read all the words in the sentence, put your thumb up._

2. (When students can read the sentence, use one of the following options:
   a. Ask students to read the sentence together [i.e., choral reading].
   b. Have students read the sentence to their partners. Then, call on one student to read the sentence to the group.
   c. Ask one student to read the sentence to the group.)

3. (Repeat these procedures with the remaining sentences. Be sure that you give ample thinking time for each sentence.)

ACTIVITY D *Strategy Instruction*

1. beside   readjust   prepay
2. combine   provide   defraud

ACTIVITY E *Strategy Practice*

1. backbone   reprint   costume
2. mistake   promote   prescribe
3. obsolete   propose   sunstroke
4. decode   holiday   subscribe

ACTIVITY F *Sentence Reading*

1. On my holiday, I will go by railway.
2. If you do a really good job, we will promote you.
3. Dr. Smith will readjust your backbone.
4. Dr. Smith will prescribe pills and provide a splint.
5. Dr. Smith will also help you with sunstroke.
6. It is a mistake to defraud people of their money.
7. Can you decode all the words in the reprint?
8. Do you subscribe to *USA TODAY*?
9. You will need to prepay for the holiday trip.
10. What costume do you propose to wear?

4   *REWARDS Plus: Reading Strategies Applied to Social Studies Passages*

Review Lesson 3

Materials Needed:

- *Student Book:* Review Lesson 3
- Review Overhead Transparency C
- Paper or cardboard to use when covering the overhead transparency
- Washable overhead transparency pen

Text Treatment Notes:

- Black text signifies teacher script (exact wording to say to students).
- Green text in parentheses signifies directions or prompts for the teacher.
- Green text signifies answers or examples of answers.
- Green graphics treatment signifies reproduction of Overhead information.
- Green text and green graphics treatment do not appear in the *Student Book*.

ACTIVITY A

Vowel Combinations

ACTIVITY PROCEDURE

(See the *Student Book*, page 5.)

In this activity, students review the sounds to say when they see combinations of letters. First, have students point to each combination of letters, and tell students the sound as it is pronounced in the key word. Then, have students practice all the sounds from this and the previous lessons.

1. Open your *Student Book* to **Review Lesson 3**, page 5. Find **Activity A**. We are going to review some sounds. You learned all of them in the *REWARDS* program, but you may need a short review.

2. Look at the first line of letter combinations. Point to the letters **o - i**. The sound of these letters is usually /oy/. What sound?_

3. Point to the letters **o - y**. The sound of these letters is usually /oy/. What sound?_

4. Point to the letters **o - r**. The sound of these letters is usually /or/. What sound?_

5. Look at the second line of letter combinations. Point to the letters **e - e**. The sound of these letters is usually /ē/. What sound?_

6. Point to the letters **o - a**. The sound of these letters is usually /ō/. What sound?_

7. Point to the letters **o - u**. The sound of these letters is usually /ou/. What sound?_

8. Go back to the beginning of the first line of letter combinations. Say the sounds again. What sound?_ Next sound?_ Next sound?_ Next sound?_ Next sound?_ Next sound?_

9. Point to the letters **e - r** in **Line #1**. What sound?_ Next sound?_ Next sound?_ Next sound?_ Next sound?_

10. (Repeat Step 9 for letters in Lines #2–4.)

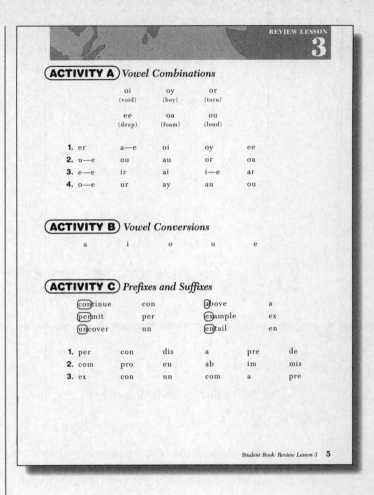

ACTIVITY A *Vowel Combinations*

oi	oy	or
(void)	(boy)	(torn)
ee	oa	ou
(deep)	(foam)	(loud)

1.	er	a—e	oi	oy	ee
2.	u—e	ou	au	or	oa
3.	e—e	ir	ai	i—e	ar
4.	o—e	ur	ay	au	ou

ACTIVITY B *Vowel Conversions*

a   i   o   u   e

ACTIVITY C *Prefixes and Suffixes*

(con)tinue	con	(a)bove	a
(per)mit	per	(ex)ample	ex
(un)cover	un	(en)tail	en

1.	per	con	dis	a	pre	de
2.	com	pro	en	ab	im	mis
3.	ex	con	un	com	a	pre

Student Book: Review Lesson 3 **5**

ACTIVITY B
Vowel Conversions

ACTIVITY PROCEDURE

(See the *Student Book,* page 5.)

Have students point to the letter while you tell them the sound, and have them repeat the sound. Then, have students point to the same letter while you tell them the name, and have students repeat the name. Have students practice saying the sound and then the name for each letter.

1. Find **Activity B**. When you are reading words and see these letters, what should you try first, the sound or the name?_ If it doesn't make a real word, what should you try?

2. Point to the first letter. The sound is /ă/. What sound?_ The name is **a**. What name?_

3. Point to the next letter. The sound is /ĭ/. What sound?_ The name is **i**. What name?_

4. Point to the next letter. The sound is /ŏ/. What sound?_ The name is **o**. What name?_

5. Point to the next letter. The sound is /ŭ/. What sound?_ The name is **u**. What name?_

6. Point to the next letter. The sound is /ĕ/. What sound?_ The name is **e**. What name?_

7. First letter again. What sound?_ What name?_

8. Next letter. What sound?_ What name?_

9. (Repeat Step 8 for the remaining letters.)

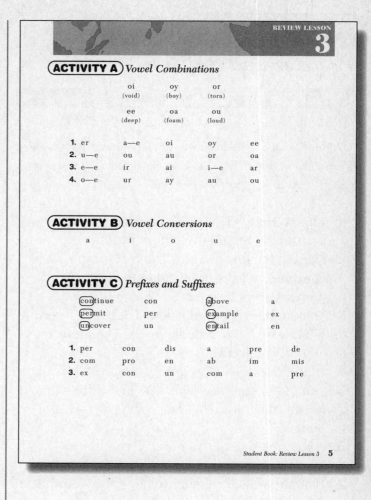

ACTIVITY C
Prefixes and Suffixes

ACTIVITY PROCEDURE

(See the Student Book, page 5.)

Tell students the words, then the circled prefixes. Have students repeat the words and prefixes. Then, have students practice saying the new and previously learned prefixes.

1. Find **Activity C**. Now, we are going to review prefixes. Where do we find prefixes?_
2. Point to the first column. The first word is **continue**. What word?_ Point to the circled prefix. The prefix is /con/. What prefix?_
3. Point to the next word below. The word is **permit**. What word?_ Point to the prefix. The prefix is /per/. What prefix?_
4. (Repeat with **uncover** and /un/.)
5. Point to the third column. The first word is **above**. What word?_ The prefix is /ŭ/. What prefix?_
6. (Repeat with **example** and /ex/ and **entail** and /en/.)
7. Find the second column. It has prefixes only. Read the prefixes. What prefix?_ Next?_ Next?_
8. Find the last column. What prefix?_ Next?_ Next?_
9. Point to the first prefix in **Line #1**. What prefix?_ Next?_ Next?_ Next?_ Next?_ Next?_
10. (Repeat Step 9 for prefixes in Lines #2–3.)

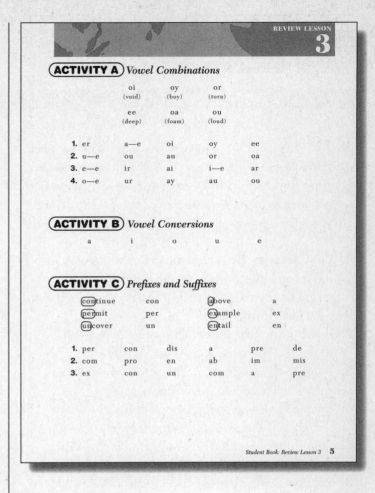

ACTIVITY D

Strategy Practice

ACTIVITY PROCEDURE

(See the *Student Book*, page 6.)

In this activity, have students apply the strategy for figuring out longer words by themselves. Have students circle prefixes and underline the vowels. Have students say the word part by part to themselves and then as a whole word aloud.

 Use Overhead C: Activity D

1. Turn to page 6. Find **Activity D**.
2. Circle prefixes and underline the vowels. Look up when you are done._
3. (Show the overhead transparency.) Now, check and fix any mistakes._
4. Go back to the first word._ Sound out the word to yourself. Put your thumb up when you can read the word. Be sure that it is a real word._ What word?_
5. (Continue Step 4 with all words in Activity D.)

Note: You may wish to provide additional practice by having students read a line to the group or to a partner.

ACTIVITY D *Strategy Practice*

1. perturb   uncurl   confess
2. afraid   expert   engrave

ACTIVITY E *Independent Strategy Practice*

1. misinform	disagree	spellbound
2. sweepstake	reproduce	protect
3. turmoil	bemoan	discontent
4. imperfect	boycott	reconstruct

ACTIVITY F *Sentence Reading*

1. Mr. Lin was discontent even after winning the sweepstakes.
2. I confess that the mistake will perturb me.
3. Can you reproduce the reprint?
4. We will reconstruct the house this summer.
5. Can you provide an expert who will not misinform us?
6. You should protect yourself from sunstroke.
7. Sometimes you disagree even with an expert.
8. The addict has an imperfect life.
9. The chance to win the sweepstakes held him spellbound.
10. Don't be afraid to decode words like **reconstruct** and **discontent**.

ACTIVITY E
Independent Strategy Practice

ACTIVITY PROCEDURE

(See the *Student Book*, page 6.)

In this activity, students independently practice using the covert strategy for figuring out longer words. They no longer use overt tasks, such as circling prefixes or underlining vowels. Have students look carefully at each word, locate prefixes and vowels, and figure out the word for themselves. Then, have students say the word aloud.

 Use Overhead C: Activity E

Note 1: If students have difficulty decoding a word, demonstrate the strategy on the overhead.

1. Find **Activity E**.
2. Find **Line #1**. Without circling and underlining, look carefully for prefixes. Look for vowels in the rest of the word. If you have difficulty figuring out the word, use your pencil. Put your thumb up when you can say the first word._ (Give ample thinking time.)
3. (When students have decoded the word, ask . . .) What word?_
4. Next word. Put your thumb up when you can say the word._ (Give ample thinking time.) What word?_
5. (Repeat Step 4 for the remaining words in Activity E.)

Note 2: You may wish to provide additional practice by having students read a line to the group or to a partner.

ACTIVITY D *Strategy Practice*

1. perturb   uncurl   confess
2. afraid   expert   engrave

ACTIVITY E *Independent Strategy Practice*

1. misinform   disagree   spellbound
2. sweepstake   reproduce   protect
3. turmoil   bemoan   discontent
4. imperfect   boycott   reconstruct

ACTIVITY F *Sentence Reading*

1. Mr. Lin was discontent even after winning the sweepstakes.
2. I confess that the mistake will perturb me.
3. Can you reproduce the reprint?
4. We will reconstruct the house this summer.
5. Can you provide an expert who will not misinform us?
6. You should protect yourself from sunstroke.
7. Sometimes you disagree even with an expert.
8. The addict has an imperfect life.
9. The chance to win the sweepstakes held him spellbound.
10. Don't be afraid to decode words like **reconstruct** and **discontent**.

ACTIVITY F

Sentence Reading

ACTIVITY PROCEDURE

(See the *Student Book,* page 6.)

Have students read a sentence to themselves. Then, choose from several options of having students read the sentence together, to partners, or individually to the class.

1. Find **Sentence #1** in **Activity F.** These sentences include words that we practiced today. Read the first sentence to yourself. When you can read all the words in the sentence, put your thumb up.

2. (When students can read the sentence, use one of the following options:
   a. Ask students to read the sentence together [i.e., choral reading].
   b. Have students read the sentence to their partners. Then, call on one student to read the sentence to the group.
   c. Ask one student to read the sentence to the group.)

3. (Repeat these procedures with the remaining sentences. Be sure that you give ample thinking time for each sentence.)

ACTIVITY D *Strategy Practice*

1. perturb   uncurl   confess
2. afraid   expert   engrave

ACTIVITY E *Independent Strategy Practice*

1. misinform	disagree	spellbound
2. sweepstake	reproduce	protect
3. turmoil	bemoan	discontent
4. imperfect	boycott	reconstruct

ACTIVITY F *Sentence Reading*

1. Mr. Lin was discontent even after winning the sweepstakes.
2. I confess that the mistake will perturb me.
3. Can you reproduce the reprint?
4. We will reconstruct the house this summer.
5. Can you provide an expert who will not misinform us?
6. You should protect yourself from sunstroke.
7. Sometimes you disagree even with an expert.
8. The addict has an imperfect life.
9. The chance to win the sweepstakes held him spellbound.
10. Don't be afraid to decode words like **reconstruct** and **discontent.**

Review Lesson 4

Materials Needed:

- *Student Book:* Review Lesson 4
- Review Overhead Transparency D
- Paper or cardboard to use when covering the overhead transparency
- Washable overhead transparency pen

Text Treatment Notes:

- Black text signifies teacher script (exact wording to say to students).
- Green text in parentheses signifies directions or prompts for the teacher.
- Green text signifies answers or examples of answers.
- Green graphics treatment signifies reproduction of Overhead information.
- Green text and green graphics treatment do not appear in the *Student Book*.

ACTIVITY A

Vowel Combinations

ACTIVITY PROCEDURE

(See the *Student Book,* page 7.)

In this activity, students review that sometimes a letter combination has two sounds. They review that when they see this letter combination in a word or word part, they should try the first sound they have learned. If the word doesn't sound right, they should try the second sound they have learned. Have students point to the letter combination. Tell them the sound as it is pronounced in the first key word. Then, tell students what sound to try if the word doesn't sound right. Have students practice what they would say first and what they would say second. Have students practice this sound and sounds from previous lessons. Whenever they come to a boxed letter combination, they should say both sounds.

1. Open your *Student Book* to **Review Lesson 4**, page 7. Find **Activity A**. We are going to review two sounds for these letters. You learned them in the *REWARDS* program, but you may need a short review.

2. Look at the letter combination with word examples. Point to the letters **o - w**. The sound of these letters is usually /ō/, as in **low**. What sound?_ If the word doesn't sound right, try /ou/, as in **down**. What sound?_

3. Let's review. What sound would you try first? /ō/ What would you try next? (/ou/)

Note: Whenever you come to boxed letters, ask, "What sound would you try first? What sound would you try next?"

4. Point to the letters **o - u** in **Line #1**. What sound?_ Boxed letters. What sound would you try first?_ What sound would you try next?_ Next sound?_

5. (Continue Step 4 for all remaining letters in Lines #1–4.)

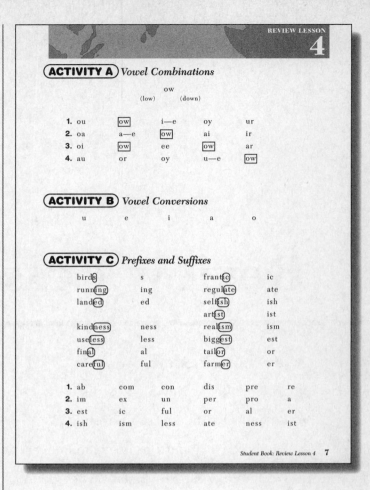

ACTIVITY B
Vowel Conversions

ACTIVITY PROCEDURE

(See the *Student Book,* page 7.)

Have students practice saying the sound and then the name for each letter.

1. Find **Activity B**. When you are reading words and see these letters, what should you try first, the sound or the name?_ If it doesn't make a real word, what should you try?_
2. Point to the first letter. What sound?_ What name? _
3. Point to the next letter. What sound?_ What name?_
4. Point to the next letter. What sound?_ What name?_
5. Point to the next letter. What sound?_ What name?_
6. Point to the next letter. What sound?_ What name?_
7. First letter again. What sound?_ What name?_
8. Next letter. What sound?_ What name?_
9. (Repeat Step 8 for the remaining letters.)

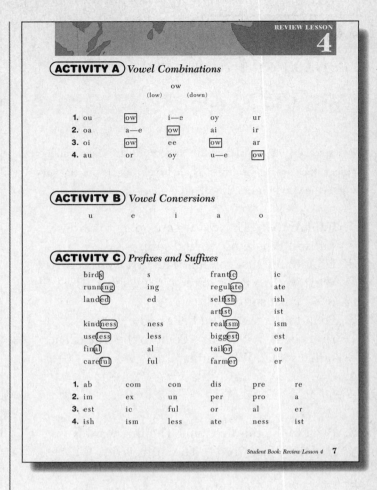

ACTIVITY C
Prefixes and Suffixes

ACTIVITY PROCEDURE

(See the *Student Book,* page 7.)

Tell students the words, then the circled suffixes. Have students repeat the words and suffixes. Then, have students practice saying the new and previously learned prefixes and suffixes.

1. Find **Activity C**. Now, we are going to review suffixes. Where do we find suffixes?_

2. Point to the first column. The first word is **birds**. What word?_ Point to the circled suffix. The suffix is /s/. What suffix?_

3. Point to the next word below. The word is **running**. What word?_ Point to the suffix. The suffix is /ing/. What suffix?_

4. (Repeat with **landed** and /ed/, **kindness** and /ness/, **useless** and /less/, **final** and /al/, and **careful** and /ful/.)

5. Point to the third column. The first word is **frantic**. What word?_ The suffix is /ic/. What suffix?_

6. (Repeat with **regulate** and /ate/, **selfish** and /ish/, **artist** and /ist/, **realism** and /ism/, **biggest** and /est/, **tailor** and /or/, and **farmer** and /er/.)

7. Find the second column. It has suffixes only. Read the suffixes. What suffix?_ Next?_ Next?_ Next?_ Next?_ Next?_ Next?_

8. Find the last column. What suffix?_ Next?_ Next?_ Next?_ Next?_ Next?_ Next?_ Next?_ Next?_

9. Point to the first prefix in **Line #1**. What prefix?_ Next?_ Next?_ Next?_ Next?_ Next?_

10. (Repeat Step 9 for prefixes and suffixes in Lines #2–4.)

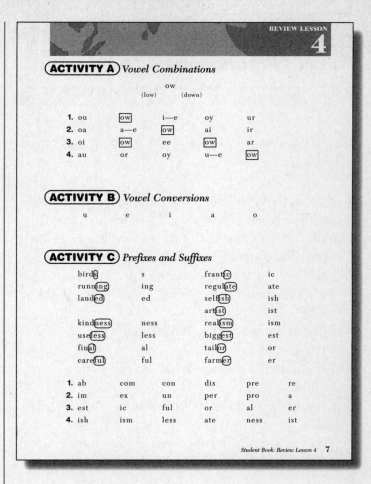

ACTIVITY D

Strategy Practice

ACTIVITY PROCEDURE

(See the *Student Book*, page 8.)

In this activity, have students apply the strategy for figuring out longer words by themselves. Have students circle prefixes and suffixes and underline the vowels. Have students say the word part by part to themselves and then as a whole word aloud.

 Use Overhead D: Activity D

1. Turn to page 8. Find **Activity D**.
2. Circle prefixes and suffixes and underline the vowels. Be careful. Remember that some words have no prefixes or suffixes, and some words have one or more prefixes or suffixes. Look up when you are done. _
3. (Show the overhead transparency.) Now, check and fix any mistakes._
4. Go back to the first word._ Sound out the word to yourself. Put your thumb up when you can read the word. Be sure that it is a real word._ What word?_
5. (Continue Step 4 with all words in Activity D.)

Note 1: If students have difficulty finding all the suffixes, remind them to start at the end of the word and work backward.

Note 2: You may wish to provide additional practice by having students read a line to the group or to a partner.

ACTIVITY D *Strategy Practice*

1. regardless	softness	unfortunate
2. programmer	slowest	historical
3. organism	inventor	personal

ACTIVITY E *Independent Strategy Practice*

1. abnormal	respectful	proposal
2. exaggerate	exhaust	untruthful
3. careless	unfaithful	astonish
4. alarmist	energetic	exclude

ACTIVITY F *Sentence Reading*

1. The programmer was exhausted from all the turmoil.
2. Everyone is respectful to the well-known inventor.
3. It is unfortunate that the respected inventor's proposal will not work.
4. It is a historical fact that some experts exaggerate.
5. Samuel's personal proposal was astonishing.
6. Regardless of the fact that some experts are untruthful and unfaithful, most would not defraud.
7. Because of her abnormal backbone, Vanessa must not be careless or too energetic.
8. Jason was discontent and bemoaned his job on the railway.
9. The tricks will astonish you and leave you spellbound.
10. We should not exclude anyone from winning the sweepstakes.

8   *REWARDS Plus: Reading Strategies Applied to Social Studies Passages*

ACTIVITY E

Independent Strategy Practice

ACTIVITY PROCEDURE

(See the *Student Book,* page 8.)

In this activity, students independently practice using the covert strategy for figuring out longer words. They no longer use overt tasks, such as circling prefixes and suffixes or underlining vowels. Have students look carefully at each word, locate prefixes, suffixes, and vowels, and figure out the word by themselves. Then, have students say the word aloud.

 Use Overhead D: Activity E

Note 1: If students have difficulty decoding a word, demonstrate the strategy on the overhead.

1. Find **Activity E**.
2. Find **Line #1**. Without circling and underlining, look carefully for prefixes and suffixes. Look for vowels in the rest of the word. If you have difficulty figuring out the word, use your pencil. Put your thumb up when you can say the first word._ (Give ample thinking time.)
3. (When students have decoded the word, ask . . .) What word?_
4. Next word. Put your thumb up when you can say the word._ (Give ample thinking time.) What word?_
5. (Repeat Step 4 for the remaining words in Activity E.)

Note 2: You may wish to provide additional practice by having students read a line to the group or to a partner.

ACTIVITY D *Strategy Practice*

1. regardless   softness   unfortunate
2. programmer   slowest   historical
3. organism   inventor   personal

ACTIVITY E *Independent Strategy Practice*

1. abnormal   respectful   proposal
2. exaggerate   exhaust   untruthful
3. careless   unfaithful   astonish
4. alarmist   energetic   exclude

ACTIVITY F *Sentence Reading*

1. The programmer was exhausted from all the turmoil.
2. Everyone is respectful to the well-known inventor.
3. It is unfortunate that the respected inventor's proposal will not work.
4. It is a historical fact that some experts exaggerate.
5. Samuel's personal proposal was astonishing.
6. Regardless of the fact that some experts are untruthful and unfaithful, most would not defraud.
7. Because of her abnormal backbone, Vanessa must not be careless or too energetic.
8. Jason was discontent and bemoaned his job on the railway.
9. The tricks will astonish you and leave you spellbound.
10. We should not exclude anyone from winning the sweepstakes.

ACTIVITY F

Sentence Reading

ACTIVITY PROCEDURE

(See the *Student Book,* page 8.)

Have students read a sentence to themselves. Then, choose from several options of having students read the sentence together, to partners, or individually to the class.

1. Find **Sentence #1** in **Activity F.** These sentences include words that we practiced today. Read the first sentence to yourself. When you can read all the words in the sentence, put your thumb up.

2. (When students can read the sentence, use one of the following options:

   a. Ask students to read the sentence together [i.e., choral reading].

   b. Have students read the sentence to their partners. Then, call on one student to read the sentence to the group.

   c. Ask one student to read the sentence to the group.)

3. (Repeat these procedures with the remaining sentences. Be sure that you give ample thinking time for each sentence.)

ACTIVITY D *Strategy Practice*

1. regardless   softness   unfortunate
2. programmer   slowest   historical
3. organism   inventor   personal

ACTIVITY E *Independent Strategy Practice*

1. abnormal	respectful	proposal
2. exaggerate	exhaust	untruthful
3. careless	unfaithful	astonish
4. alarmist	energetic	exclude

ACTIVITY F *Sentence Reading*

1. The programmer was exhausted from all the turmoil.
2. Everyone is respectful to the well-known inventor.
3. It is unfortunate that the respected inventor's proposal will not work.
4. It is a historical fact that some experts exaggerate.
5. Samuel's personal proposal was astonishing.
6. Regardless of the fact that some experts are untruthful and unfaithful, most would not defraud.
7. Beeause of her abnormal backbone, Vanessa must not be careless or too energetic.
8. Jason was discontent and bemoaned his job on the railway.
9. The tricks will astonish you and leave you spellbound.
10. We should not exclude anyone from winning the sweepstakes.

Review Lesson 5

Materials Needed:

- *Student Book:* Review Lesson 5
- Review Overhead Transparency E
- Paper or cardboard to use when covering the overhead transparency
- Washable overhead transparency pen

Text Treatment Notes:

- Black text signifies teacher script (exact wording to say to students).
- Green text in parentheses signifies directions or prompts for the teacher.
- Green text signifies answers or examples of answers.
- Green graphics treatment signifies reproduction of Overhead information.
- Green text and green graphics treatment do not appear in the *Student Book.*

ACTIVITY A
Vowel Combinations

ACTIVITY PROCEDURE

(See the *Student Book,* page 9.)

In this activity, students review the two sounds of another letter combination. Have students point to the letter combination. Tell them the sound as it is pronounced in the first key word. Then, tell students what sound to try if the word doesn't sound right. Have students practice what they would say first and what they would say second. Have students practice this sound and sounds from previous lessons. Remind them to try both sounds when they see boxed letters.

1. Open your *Student Book* to **Review Lesson 5**, page 9. Find **Activity A**. We are going to review two sounds for these letters. You learned them in the *REWARDS* program, but you may need a short review.

2. Look at the letter combination with word examples. Point to the letters **o - o**. The sound of these letters is usually /o͞o/, as in **moon**. What sound?_ If the word doesn't sound right, try /o͝o/, as in **book**. What sound?_

3. Let's review. What sound would you try first? /o͞o/ What would you try next? /o͝o/

Note: Whenever you come to boxed letters, ask, "What sound would you try first? What sound would you try next?"

4. Point to the boxed letters **o - w** in **Line #1**. What sound would you try first?_ What sound would you try next?_ Next sound?_ Next sound?_

5. (Continue Step 4 for all remaining letters in Lines #1–4.)

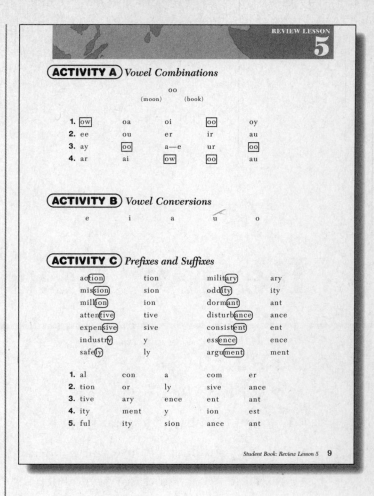

ACTIVITY B
Vowel Conversions

ACTIVITY PROCEDURE

(See the *Student Book,* page 9.)

Have students practice saying the sound and then the name for each letter.

1. Find **Activity B**. When you are reading words and see these letters, what should you try first, the sound or the name?_ If it doesn't make a real word, what should you try?_
2. Point to the first letter. What sound?_ What name?_
3. Point to the next letter. What sound?_ What name?_
4. Point to the next letter. What sound?_ What name?_
5. Point to the next letter. What sound?_ What name?_
6. Point to the next letter. What sound?_ What name?_
7. First letter again. What sound?_ What name?_
8. Next letter. What sound?_ What name?_
9. (Repeat Step 8 for the remaining letters.)

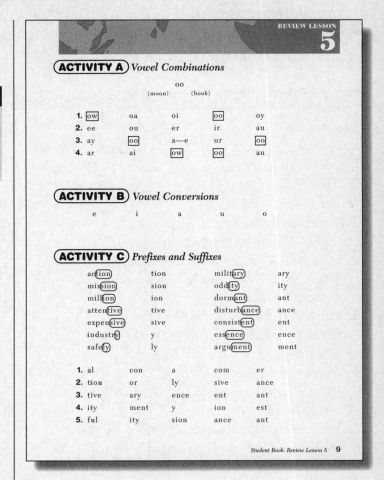

ACTIVITY C
Prefixes and Suffixes

ACTIVITY PROCEDURE

(See the *Student Book,* page 9.)

Tell students the words, then the circled suffixes. Have students repeat the words and suffixes. Then, have students practice saying the new and previously learned prefixes and suffixes.

1. Find **Activity C**. Now, we are going to review suffixes. Where do we find suffixes?_

2. Point to the first column. The first word is **action**. What word?_ Point to the circled suffix. The suffix is /tion/. What suffix?_

3. Point to the next word below. The word is **mission**. What word?_ Point to the suffix. The suffix is /sion/. What suffix?_

4. (Repeat with **million** and /ion/, **attentive** and /tive/, **expensive** and /sive/, **industry** and /y/, and **safely** and /ly/.)

5. Point to the third column. The first word is **military**. What word?_ The suffix is /ary/. What suffix?_

6. (Repeat with **oddity** and /ity/, **dormant** and /ant/, **disturbance** and /ance/, **consistent** and /ent/, **essence** and /ence/, and **argument** and /ment/.)

7. Find the second column. It has suffixes only. Read the suffixes. What suffix?_ Next?_ Next?_ Next?_ Next?_ Next?_ Next?_

8. Find the last column. What suffix?_ Next?_ Next?_ Next?_ Next?_ Next?_ Next?_

9. Point to **Line #1**. It has a mix of prefixes and suffixes. Point to the first suffix. What suffix?_ Next?_ Next?_ Next?_ Next?_

10. (Repeat Step 9 for suffixes in Lines #2–5.)

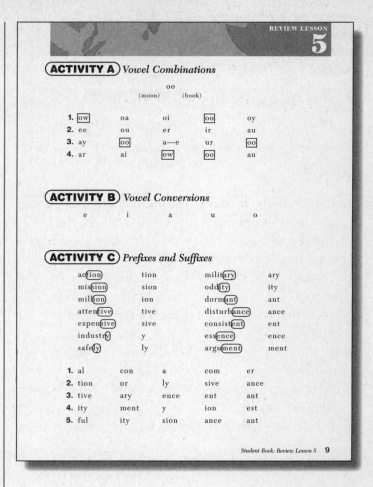

ACTIVITY D
Strategy Practice

ACTIVITY PROCEDURE

(See the *Student Book,* page 10.)

In this activity, have students apply the strategy for figuring out longer words by themselves. Have students circle prefixes and suffixes and underline the vowels. Have students say the word part by part to themselves and then as a whole word aloud.

 Use Overhead E: Activity D

1. Turn to page 10. Find **Activity D**.
2. Circle prefixes and suffixes and underline the vowels. Look up when you are done._
3. (Show the overhead transparency.) Now, check and fix any mistakes._
4. Go back to the first word._ Sound out the word to yourself. Put your thumb up when you can read the word. Be sure that it is a real word._ What word?_
5. (Continue Step 4 with all words in Activity D.)

Note: You may wish to provide additional practice by having students read a line to the group or to a partner.

REVIEW LESSON
5

ACTIVITY D *Strategy Practice*

1. advertisement   delightful   disinfectant
2. intentionally   property   expressionless
3. personality   admittance   incoherence

ACTIVITY E *Independent Strategy Practice*

1. perfectionist   independently   dictionary
2. contaminate   precautionary   deductive
3. inconsistently   excitement   repulsive
4. opinion   hoodwink   imperfect

ACTIVITY F *Sentence Reading*

1. The imperfect dictionary had many mistakes.
2. An advertisement should not intentionally misinform people.
3. A perfectionist will be discontent in a job with people who are unfaithful and disrespectful.
4. As a precautionary step, we should not contaminate our water.
5. Your classmates might disagree with your opinion.
6. We were delighted by the excitement of the energetic teacher.
7. Peter independently made a proposal for admittance to the club.
8. Unfortunately, the art was inconsistently reproduced when reprinted.
9. The energetic team members had delightful personalities.
10. Her statements were untruthful and disrespectful.

10   *REWARDS Plus: Reading Strategies Applied to Social Studies Passages*

ACTIVITY E

Independent Strategy Practice

ACTIVITY PROCEDURE

(See the *Student Book*, page 10.)

Have students look carefully at each word, locate prefixes, suffixes, and vowels, and figure out the word by themselves. Then, have students say the word aloud.

 Use Overhead E: Activity E

Note 1: If students have difficulty decoding a word, demonstrate the strategy on the overhead.

1. Find **Activity E**.
2. Find **Line #1**. Without circling and underlining, look carefully for prefixes and suffixes. Look for vowels in the rest of the word. Put your thumb up when you can say the first word._ (Give ample thinking time.)
3. (When students have decoded the word, ask . . .) What word?_
4. Next word. Put your thumb up when you can say the word._ (Give ample thinking time.) What word?_
5. (Repeat Step 4 for the remaining words in Activity E.)

Note 2: You may wish to provide additional practice by having students read a line to the group or to a partner.

REVIEW LESSON 5

ACTIVITY D *Strategy Practice*

1. advertisement   delightful   disinfectant
2. intentionally   property   expressionless
3. personality   admittance   incoherence

ACTIVITY E *Independent Strategy Practice*

1. perfectionist   independently   dictionary
2. contaminate   precautionary   deductive
3. inconsistently   excitement   repulsive
4. opinion   hoodwink   imperfect

ACTIVITY F *Sentence Reading*

1. The imperfect dictionary had many mistakes.
2. An advertisement should not intentionally misinform people.
3. A perfectionist will be discontent in a job with people who are unfaithful and disrespectful.
4. As a precautionary step, we should not contaminate our water.
5. Your classmates might disagree with your opinion.
6. We were delighted by the excitement of the energetic teacher.
7. Peter independently made a proposal for admittance to the club.
8. Unfortunately, the art was inconsistently reproduced when reprinted.
9. The energetic team members had delightful personalities.
10. Her statements were untruthful and disrespectful.

10   *REWARDS Plus: Reading Strategies Applied to Social Studies Passages*

ACTIVITY F
Sentence Reading

ACTIVITY PROCEDURE

(See the *Student Book,* page 10.)

Have students read a sentence to themselves. Then, choose from several options of having students read the sentence together, to partners, or individually to the class.

1. Find **Sentence #1** in **Activity F.** These sentences include words that we practiced today. Read the first sentence to yourself. When you can read all the words in the sentence, put your thumb up.

2. (When students can read the sentence, use one of the following options:

   a. Ask students to read the sentence together [i.e., choral reading].

   b. Have students read the sentence to their partners. Then, call on one student to read the sentence to the group.

   c. Ask one student to read the sentence to the group.)

3. (Repeat these procedures with the remaining sentences. Be sure that you give ample thinking time for each sentence.)

REVIEW LESSON
5

ACTIVITY D *Strategy Practice*

1. advertisement   delightful   disinfectant
2. intentionally   property   expressionless
3. personality   admittance   incoherence

ACTIVITY E *Independent Strategy Practice*

1. perfectionist   independently   dictionary
2. contaminate   precautionary   deductive
3. inconsistently   excitement   repulsive
4. opinion   hoodwink   imperfect

ACTIVITY F *Sentence Reading*

1. The imperfect dictionary had many mistakes.
2. An advertisement should not intentionally misinform people.
3. A perfectionist will be discontent in a job with people who are unfaithful and disrespectful.
4. As a precautionary step, we should not contaminate our water.
5. Your classmates might disagree with your opinion.
6. We were delighted by the excitement of the energetic teacher.
7. Peter independently made a proposal for admittance to the club.
8. Unfortunately, the art was inconsistently reproduced when reprinted.
9. The energetic team members had delightful personalities.
10. Her statements were untruthful and disrespectful.

Review Lesson 6

Materials Needed:

- *Student Book:* Review Lesson 6
- Review Overhead Transparency F
- Paper or cardboard to use when covering the overhead transparency
- Washable overhead transparency pen

Text Treatment Notes:

- Black text signifies teacher script (exact wording to say to students).
- Green text in parentheses signifies directions or prompts for the teacher.
- Green text signifies answers or examples of answers.
- Green graphics treatment signifies reproduction of Overhead information.
- Green text and green graphics treatment do not appear in the *Student Book*.

ACTIVITY A
Vowel Combinations

ACTIVITY PROCEDURE

(See the *Student Book,* page 11.)

In this activity, students review the two sounds of another letter combination. Have students point to the letter combination. Tell them the sound as it is pronounced in the first key word. Then, tell students what sound to try if the word doesn't sound right. Have students practice what they would say first and what they would say second. Have students practice this sound and sounds from previous lessons. Remind them to try both sounds when they see boxed letters.

1. Open your *Student Book* to **Review Lesson 6**, page 11. Find **Activity A**. We are going to review two sounds for these letters. You learned them in the *REWARDS* program, but you may need a short review.
2. Look at the letter combination with word examples. Point to the letters **e - a**. The sound of these letters is usually /ē/, as in **meat**. What sound?_ If the word doesn't sound right, try /ĕ/, as in **thread**. What sound?_
3. Let's review. What sound would you try first? /ē/ What would you try next? /ĕ/

Note: Whenever you come to boxed letters, ask, "What sound would you try first? What sound would you try next?"

4. Point to the boxed letters **o - o** in **Line #1**. What sound would you try first?_ What sound would you try next?_ Boxed letters. What sound would you try first?_ What sound would you try next?_
5. (Continue Step 4 for all remaining letters in Lines #1–4.)

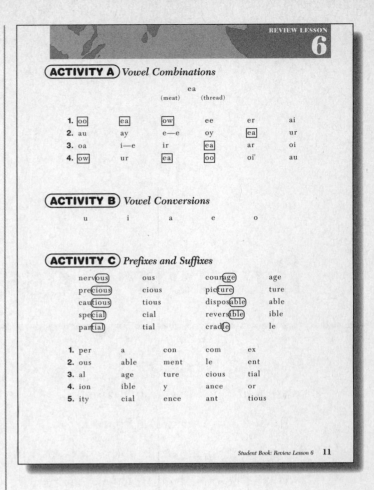

ACTIVITY B
Vowel Conversions

ACTIVITY PROCEDURE

(See the *Student Book,* page 11.)

Have students review saying the sound, then the name for each letter.

1. Find **Activity B**. When you are reading words and see these letters, what should you try first, the sound or the name?_ If it doesn't make a real word, what should you try?_
2. Point to the first letter. What sound?_ What name?_
3. Point to the next letter. What sound?_ What name?_
4. Point to the next letter. What sound?_ What name?_
5. Point to the next letter. What sound?_ What name?_
6. Point to the next letter. What sound?_ What name?_

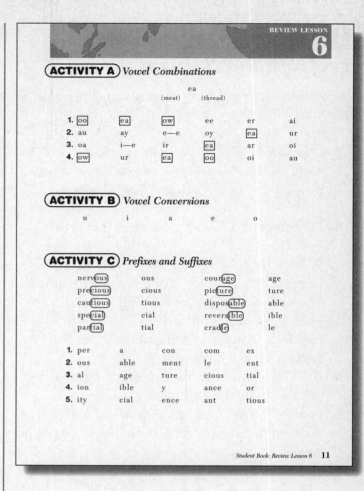

ACTIVITY A *Vowel Combinations*

			ea			
			(meat)	(thread)		
1.	oo	ea	ow	ee	er	ai
2.	au	ay	e—e	oy	ea	ur
3.	oa	i—e	ir	ea	ar	oi
4.	ow	ur	ea	oo	oi	au

ACTIVITY B *Vowel Conversions*

u	i	a	e	o

ACTIVITY C *Prefixes and Suffixes*

nervous	ous	courage	age
precious	cious	picture	ture
cautious	tious	disposable	able
special	cial	reversible	ible
partial	tial	cradle	le

1. per	a	con	com	ex
2. ous	able	ment	le	ent
3. al	age	ture	cious	tial
4. ion	ible	y	ance	or
5. ity	cial	ence	ant	tious

Student Book: Review Lesson 6 **11**

ACTIVITY C
Prefixes and Suffixes

ACTIVITY PROCEDURE

(See the *Student Book,* page 11.)

Tell students the words, then the circled suffixes. Have students repeat the words and suffixes. Then, have students practice saying the new and previously learned prefixes and suffixes.

1. Find **Activity C**. Now, we are going to review suffixes.
2. Point to the first column. The first word is **nervous**. What word?_ Point to the circled suffix. The suffix is /ous/. What suffix?_
3. Point to the next word below. The word is **precious**. What word?_ Point to the suffix. The suffix is /cious/. What suffix?_
4. (Repeat with **cautious** and /tious/, **special** and /cial/, and **partial** and /tial/.)
5. Point to the third column of words. The first word is **courage**. What word?_ The suffix is /age/. What suffix?_
6. (Repeat with **picture** and /ture/, **disposable** and /able/, **reversible** and /ible/, and **cradle** and /le/.)
7. Find the second column. It has suffixes only. Read the suffixes. What suffix?_ Next?_ Next?_ Next?_ Next?_
8. Find the last column. What suffix?_ Next?_ Next?_ Next?_ Next?_
9. Point to the first prefix in Line #1. What prefix?_ Next?_ Next?_ Next?_ Next?_
10. (Repeat for prefixes and suffixes in Lines #2–5).

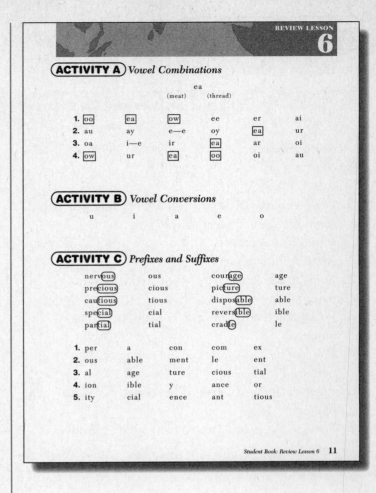

ACTIVITY D

Strategy Practice

ACTIVITY PROCEDURE

(See the *Student Book*, page 12.)

Have students circle prefixes and suffixes and underline the vowels. Have students say the word part by part to themselves and then as a whole word aloud.

 Use Overhead F: Activity D

1. Turn to page 12. Find **Activity D**.
2. Circle prefixes and suffixes and underline the vowels. Look up when you are done._
3. (Show the overhead transparency.) Now, check and fix any mistakes._
4. Go back to the first word._ Sound out the word to yourself. Put your thumb up when you can read the word. Be sure that it is a real word._ What word?_
5. (Continue Step 4 with all words in Activity D.)

Note: You may wish to provide additional practice by having students read a line to the group or to a partner.

REVIEW LESSON 6

ACTIVITY D *Strategy Practice*

1. official   substantial   delicious
2. pretentious   impressionable   incombustible
3. conjecture   inconspicuous   disadvantage

ACTIVITY E *Independent Strategy Practice*

1. administrative   performance   threadbare
2. circumstantial   investigation   professionalism
3. precipitation   environmentally   communication
4. unconventional   consolidate   misconception

ACTIVITY F *Sentence Reading*

1. In an attempt to reduce the size of the federal government, administrative departments will be consolidated.
2. Devon did not find his companion's sarcastic comments entertaining.
3. The written communication contained a number of misconceptions.
4. The children watching the evening performance were inconspicuous.
5. Consistency and professionalism are qualities needed in all occupations.
6. The defendant could not submit the circumstantial evidence from the investigation.
7. All corporations thrive on effective organization and environmentally safe conditions.
8. Historically, our population has always been environmentally concerned.
9. Most impressionable children do not act independently.
10. While the instructor's methods were unconventional, the results were tremendous.

12   *REWARDS Plus: Reading Strategies Applied to Social Studies Passages*

ACTIVITY E

Independent Strategy Practice

ACTIVITY PROCEDURE

(See the *Student Book*, page 12.)

Have students look carefully at each word, locate prefixes, suffixes, and vowels, and figure out the word by themselves. Then, have students say the word aloud.

 Use Overhead F: Activity E

Note 1: If students have difficulty decoding a word, demonstrate the strategy on the overhead.

1. Find **Activity E**.
2. Find **Line #1**. Put your thumb up when you can say the first word._ (Give ample thinking time.)
3. (When students have decoded the word, ask . . .) What word?_
4. Next word. Put your thumb up when you can say the word._ (Give ample thinking time.) What word?_
5. (Repeat Step 4 for the remaining words in Activity E.)

Note 2: You may wish to provide additional practice by having students read a line to the group or to a partner.

REVIEW LESSON 6

ACTIVITY D *Strategy Practice*

1. official   substantial   delicious
2. pretentious   impressionable   incombustible
3. conjecture   inconspicuous   disadvantage

ACTIVITY E *Independent Strategy Practice*

1. administrative   performance   threadbare
2. circumstantial   investigation   professionalism
3. precipitation   environmentally communication
4. unconventional   consolidate   misconception

ACTIVITY F *Sentence Reading*

1. In an attempt to reduce the size of the federal government, administrative departments will be consolidated.
2. Devon did not find his companion's sarcastic comments entertaining.
3. The written communication contained a number of misconceptions.
4. The children watching the evening performance were inconspicuous.
5. Consistency and professionalism are qualities needed in all occupations.
6. The defendant could not submit the circumstantial evidence from the investigation.
7. All corporations thrive on effective organization and environmentally safe conditions.
8. Historically, our population has always been environmentally concerned.
9. Most impressionable children do not act independently.
10. While the instructor's methods were unconventional, the results were tremendous.

12   *REWARDS Plus: Reading Strategies Applied to Social Studies Passages*

ACTIVITY F
Sentence Reading

ACTIVITY PROCEDURE

(See the *Student Book*, page 12.)

Have students read a sentence to themselves. Then, choose from several options of having students read the sentence together, to partners, or individually to the class.

1. Find **Sentence #1** in **Activity F.**_ These sentences include words that we practiced today as well as words we have not practiced. Read the first sentence to yourself. When you can read all the words in the sentence, put your thumb up._

2. (When students can read the sentence, use one of the following options:
   a. Ask students to read the sentence together [i.e., choral reading].
   b. Have students read the sentence to their partners. Then, call on one student to read the sentence to the group.
   c. Ask one student to read the sentence to the group.)

3. (Repeat these procedures with the remaining sentences. Be sure that you give ample thinking time for each sentence.)

Note: The sentences in this Review Lesson are very similar to the sentences in Lesson 20 of the *REWARDS* program. These sentences contain words that were—and were not—practiced in *REWARDS Plus* Review Lessons. If your students had difficulty with these sentences, you may want to reteach Lessons 13–20 from the original *REWARDS* program before going on to the Application Lessons in *REWARDS Plus*.

REVIEW LESSON
6

ACTIVITY D *Strategy Practice*

1. offi(cial)   substan(tial)   (de)li(cious)
2. (pre)(en)(tious)   (im)(pres)(sion)(ible)   (in)(com)(bust)(ible)
3. (con)(jec)(ture)   (in)(con)(spic)(uous)   (dis)(ad)(vant)(age)

ACTIVITY E *Independent Strategy Practice*

1. administrative   performance   threadbare
2. circumstantial   investigation   professionalism
3. precipitation   environmentally communication
4. unconventional   consolidate   misconception

ACTIVITY F *Sentence Reading*

1. In an attempt to reduce the size of the federal government, administrative departments will be consolidated.
2. Devon did not find his companion's sarcastic comments entertaining.
3. The written communication contained a number of misconceptions.
4. The children watching the evening performance were inconspicuous.
5. Consistency and professionalism are qualities needed in all occupations.
6. The defendant could not submit the circumstantial evidence from the investigation.
7. All corporations thrive on effective organization and environmentally safe conditions.
8. Historically, our population has always been environmentally concerned.
9. Most impressionable children do not act independently.
10. While the instructor's methods were unconventional, the results were tremendous.

12   *REWARDS Plus: Reading Strategies Applied to Social Studies Passages*

Application Lesson 1

Materials Needed:

- *Student Book:* Application Lesson 1
- Application Overhead Transparencies 1–4
- Application Overhead Transparency 61
- Appendix A Reproducible 1: *REWARDS* Strategies for Reading Long Words*
- Appendix A Reproducible 2: Prefixes, Suffixes, and Vowel Combinations Reference Chart*
- Appendix B Optional Vocabulary Activities: Application Lesson 1
- Paper or cardboard to use when covering the overhead transparency
- Paper or cardboard for each student to use during spelling dictation
- Washable overhead transparency pen

* If you did not teach the Review Lessons, copy and distribute Appendix A Reproducibles 1 and 2 to students. Have them place these in a notebook or a folder for future reference.

Text Treatment Notes:

- Black text signifies teacher script (exact wording to say to students).
- Green text in parentheses signifies directions or prompts for the teacher.
- Green text signifies answers or examples of answers.
- Green graphics treatment signifies reproduction of Overhead information.
- Green text and green graphics treatment do not appear in the *Student Book.*

ACTIVITY A
Vocabulary

ACTIVITY PROCEDURE, List 1

(See the *Student Book*, page 13.)

Tell students each word in the list. Then, have students repeat the word and read the definition aloud. For each definition, provide any additional information that may be necessary. Then, have students practice reading the words themselves.

Note A.1-1: See Appendix E, Pronunciation Guide for Unique Words, for correct pronunciations of uncommon vocabulary words.

Note A.1-2: If you wish to emphasize the part of speech, have students say the part of speech before reading the definition.

Use Overhead 1: Activity A
List 1: Tell

1. (Show the top half of Overhead 1.) Before we read the passage, let's read the difficult words. (Point to **Thrace**.) The first word is **Thrace**. What word?_ Now, read the definition._
2. (Point to **Thracians**.) The next word is **Thracians**. What word?_ Now, read the definition._
3. (Pronounce each word in List 1, and then have students repeat each word and read the definition.)
4. Open your *Student Book* to **Application Lesson 1**, page 13._
5. Find **Activity A**, **List 1**, in your book._ Let's read the words again. First word._ Next word._ (Continue for all words in List 1.)

ACTIVITY PROCEDURE, List 2

(See the *Student Book*, page 13.)

The second list of words can be read using the part-by-part strategy. Have students circle prefixes and suffixes, then underline the vowels. Using the overhead transparency, assist students in checking their work. Next, have students figure out each word to themselves, then say it aloud. Have them read the definition aloud.

Note A.2-1: Provide additional information for any definitions as needed.

Note A.2-2: If you wish to emphasize the part of speech, have students say the part of speech before reading the definition.

Note A.2-3: If you are teaching older students for whom "thumbs-up" is inappropriate, have students look at you when they can read the word.

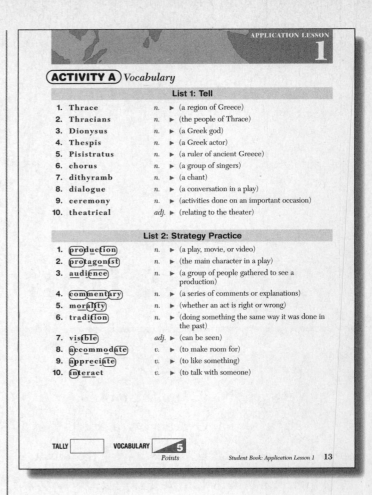

ACTIVITY A *Vocabulary*

List 1: Tell

1.	Thrace	n. ►	(a region of Greece)
2.	Thracians	n. ►	(the people of Thrace)
3.	Dionysus	n. ►	(a Greek god)
4.	Thespis	n. ►	(a Greek actor)
5.	Pisistratus	n. ►	(a ruler of ancient Greece)
6.	chorus	n. ►	(a group of singers)
7.	dithyramb	n. ►	(a chant)
8.	dialogue	n. ►	(a conversation in a play)
9.	ceremony	n. ►	(activities done on an important occasion)
10.	theatrical	adj. ►	(relating to the theater)

List 2: Strategy Practice

1.	production	n. ►	(a play, movie, or video)
2.	protagonist	n. ►	(the main character in a play)
3.	audience	n. ►	(a group of people gathered to see a production)
4.	commentary	n. ►	(a series of comments or explanations)
5.	morality	n. ►	(whether an act is right or wrong)
6.	tradition	n. ►	(doing something the same way it was done in the past)
7.	visible	adj. ►	(can be seen)
8.	accommodate	v. ►	(to make room for)
9.	appreciate	v. ►	(to like something)
10.	interact	v. ►	(to talk with someone)

TALLY [ ] VOCABULARY **5** Points

Student Book: Application Lesson 1 **13**

Use Overhead 1: Activity A
List 2: Strategy Practice

1. Find **List 2**. For each word, circle the prefixes and suffixes, and underline the vowels. Look up when you are done._
2. (Show the bottom half of Overhead 1.) Before you check your work on List 2, look at item #8. (Point to the third example.) When you completed the *REWARDS* program, you learned to recognize many prefixes and suffixes, but there are many more. (Point to the **ac** that is circled.) From now on, you can also circle **ac**. The prefix is /ac/. Say it._ Look at item #9. (Point to the third example and the **ap** that is circled.) You can also circle **ap**. The prefix is /ap/. Say it._ Now, go back to item #1. Check and fix any mistakes._
3. Go back to the first word again._ Sound out the word to yourself. Put your thumb up when you can read the word. Be sure that it is a real word._ What word?_ Now, read the definition._
4. (Continue Step 3 with all remaining words in List 2.)

Note A.2-4: You may wish to provide additional practice by having students read words to a partner.

ACTIVITY PROCEDURE, List 1 and 2

(See the *Student Book,* page 13.)

Tell students to look in List 1 or List 2 for a word you are thinking about. Have them circle the number of the word and tell you the word. Explain to students to make a tally mark for each correct word in the Tally box, and then enter the number of tally marks as points in the blank half of the Vocabulary box.

1. For this activity, I will tell you about words I am thinking about. You will have a short time to find those words in either List 1 or List 2, circle the number of that word, and then tell me the word I'm thinking about. Find the Tally box at the bottom of page 13. For every word that you correctly identify, make a tally mark in the Tally box. If you don't identify the correct word, don't do anything.

2. I am thinking of a word. Circle the number of the appropriate word.
   - If something can be seen, it is this. (Wait.) What word? **visible**
   - When we make room for people, we do this for them. (Wait.) What word? **accommodate**
   - Newscasters often give this on a certain subject. (Wait.) What word? **commentary**
   - This character is played by an actor. (Wait.) What word? **protagonist**
   - Most countries celebrate holidays that are full of, or steeped in, this. (Wait.) What word? **tradition**

3. Count all the tally marks, and enter that number as points in the blank half of the Vocabulary box.

ACTIVITY PROCEDURE, List 3

(See the *Student Book,* page 14.)

The words in the third list are related. Have students use the *REWARDS* Strategies to figure out the first word in each family. Have them read the definition and then read the other two words in the family.

Note A.3-1: Provide additional information for any definitions as needed.

Note A.3-2: If you wish to emphasize the part of speech, have students say the part of speech before reading the definition.

Note A.3-3: If you are teaching older students for whom "thumbs-up" is inappropriate, have students look at you when they can read the word.

List 3: Word Families

Family 1	religion	n.	▶ (a set of beliefs or moral principles)
	religious	adj.	
	religiously	adv.	
Family 2	compete	v.	▶ (to strive against others; to try to win)
	competition	n.	
	competitive	adj.	
Family 3	politics	n.	▶ (activities related to the government)
	political	adj.	
	politically	adv.	
Family 4	tragedy	n.	▶ (a play with a sad ending)
	tragic	adj.	
	tragically	adv.	
Family 5	comedy	n.	▶ (a play that is funny)
	comedic	adj.	
	comedian	n.	

ACTIVITY B *Spelling Dictation*

1. politics	4. compete
2. political	5. competitive
3. politically	6. competition

SPELLING **6** Points

14　REWARDS Plus: Reading Strategies Applied to Social Studies Passages

---

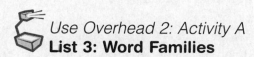

Use Overhead 2: Activity A
List 3: Word Families

1. Turn to page 14. Find **Family 1** in **List 3**. Figure out the first word. Use your pencil if you wish. Put your thumb up when you know the word._ What word?_ Read the definition._

2. Look at the next word in Family 1. Figure out the word._ What word?_

3. Next word. Figure out the word._ What word?_

4. (Repeat Steps 1–3 for all word families in List 3.)

Note A.3-4: You may wish to provide additional practice by having students read a word family to the group or to a partner.

Note A.3-5: Additional vocabulary practice activities are provided in Appendix B of the Teacher's Guide. These activities are optional and can be assigned during class, for homework, or as small group, in-class activities.

ACTIVITY B
Spelling Dictation

ACTIVITY PROCEDURE

(See the *Student Book,* page 14.)

For each word, tell students the word, then have students say the parts of the word to themselves while they write the word. Then, have students enter the number of correctly spelled words as points in the blank half of the Spelling box.

Note B-1: Distribute a piece of light cardboard to students so they can cover their page during spelling dictation. Students can also use the cardboard as a bookmark to quickly locate pages at the beginning of lessons.

 Use Overhead 2: Activity B

1. Find **Activity B**.
2. The first word is **politics**. What word?_ Say the parts in **politics** to yourself as you write the word. (Pause and monitor.)
3. (Show **politics** on the overhead.) Check **politics**. If you misspelled it, cross it out and write it correctly.
4. The second word is **political**. What word?_ Say the parts in **political** to yourself as you write the word. (Pause and monitor.)
5. (Show **political** on the overhead.) Check **political**. If you misspelled it, cross it out and write it correctly.
6. (Repeat the procedures for the words **politically**, **compete**, **competitive**, and **competition**.)
7. Count the number of words you spelled correctly, and record that number as points in the blank half of the Spelling box at the bottom of the page.

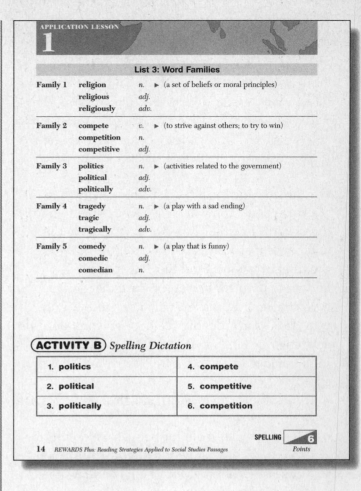

ACTIVITY C
Background Knowledge

ACTIVITY PROCEDURE

(See the *Student Book*, page 15.)

Read the Background Knowledge paragraph using one of three methods: read it to students, have students read it together, or call on individual students to read. Examine the timeline and the related graphic together. Then, preview the passage together by examining the title and the headings. Have students tell partners two things the passage will tell about.

1. Turn to page 15. Let's read the paragraph. (Read or ask students to read. Then examine the timeline and graphic together.)
2. Now, let's turn the page and preview the passage. Read the title._ What is the whole passage going to tell about?_
3. Now, let's read the headings. Read the first heading._ Read the next heading._ (Continue until students have read all headings.)
4. Turn to your partner. Without looking, tell two things this passage will tell about._

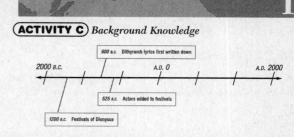

ACTIVITY C *Background Knowledge*

2000 B.C. | 600 B.C. Dithyramb lyrics first written down | A.D. 0 | A.D. 2000

525 B.C. Actors added to festivals

1200 B.C. Festivals of Dionysus

Many things that we experience today began thousands of years ago in another country. This article tells us about the development of theater in ancient Greece between 1200 B.C. and 525 B.C. During that period of time, the Greek civilization thrived around the Mediterranean Sea. The Greek people produced amazing cultural accomplishments in art and literature that continue to influence us today.

Map of Ancient Greece

ACTIVITY D

Passage Reading and Comprehension

ACTIVITY PROCEDURE

(See the *Student Book,* pages 16–17.)

Have students work on reading accuracy by selecting a passage-reading option that best fits your students.

Passage Reading: Accuracy

(Select a passage-reading procedure that matches the size of your group and the competency of your students.

Option A

If you are teaching a small group of students who are having difficulty, use Option A:

Have students read one paragraph silently. Then, call on one student to orally read a paragraph or a portion of the paragraph to the class. Call on students in random order, varying the amount that each student reads.

Option B

If you are teaching a small group with students who are not having difficulty, use Option B:

Have students read the entire article silently, rereading it if they finish before their classmates. Then, call on one student to orally read a paragraph or a portion of a paragraph to the class. Call on students in random order, varying the amount that each student reads.

Option C

If you are teaching a large group with students who are having difficulty, use Option C:

Have students read one paragraph silently. Then, have students read the paragraph to a partner. Alternate partner-reading turns.

Option D

If you are teaching a large group with students who are not having difficulty, use Option D:

Have students read the entire article silently, rereading it if they finish before their classmates. Then, have students read the passage with their partners, alternating on each paragraph.)

APPLICATION LESSON

1

ACTIVITY D *Passage Reading and Comprehension*

Greek Theater

13   When you think of theater, you might imagine a play performed at your
27   school, an evening at the opera, or even a Broadway musical. But theater was
     born 2500 years ago in Greece. Theater began there as a religious ceremony. (#1)

40   **The Cult of Dionysus**
44   Around 1200 B.C., in northern Greece, there was a region known as Thrace.
57   In spring festivals and rituals, the Thracians worshipped Dionysus, the Greek
68   god of fertility. The worshippers used dancing, feasting, storytelling, and animal
79   sacrifice to tell the god's stories and legends. When the beliefs in Dionysus
92   began to spread southward to different tribes in Greece, the ceremonies became
104   more formal and symbolic. By 600 B.C., these rituals were part of spring
117   festivities throughout Greece. The storytellers wore masks and chanted their
127   stories in choruses. The choruses did not sing like ours do today. They used a
142   rhythmic, chanting form of speech known as the *dithyramb*. (#2)

151   **Rituals Become Theater**
154   In about 600 B.C., the lyrics to the dithyrambs were written down for the first
169   time. About 75 years later, a man named Thespis added an actor who interacted
183   with the chorus. Now the actor (also known as a *thespian*) would interact with
197   the chorus, taking turns chanting the lyrics. When Thespis added a second actor,
210   theater was born. Now the two actors related directly to each other, using
223   dialogue and action to tell the story. The chorus added commentary and insight
236   to what was occurring between the actors. (#3)

243   **Drama Competitions**
245   In 534 B.C., Pisistratus ruled Athens, the greatest city-state in Greece. He
258   changed the Dionysian festival to a drama competition. This became a highly
270   competitive and popular annual event. Wealthy people in the city would fund
282   productions. In return, they would not have to pay taxes to the city that year. The
298   drama competitions would take place over several whole days in the spring. (#4)

310   **Amphitheaters**
311   Athens, as well as other major Greek cities, built large theaters to
323   accommodate this increasingly popular pastime. The amphitheaters were built

16   *REWARDS Plus: Reading Strategies Applied to Social Studies Passages*

Passage Reading: Comprehension Questions

(You may wish to ask the following questions as the passage is being read. Numbers corresponding to the questions are indicated at the point at which they could be asked.)

#1 How does the original Greek theater differ from a school play?
Began as a religious ceremony.

#2 How did the Dionysian festival change over time?
Ideas: Spread across Greece; became more formal and symbolic; choruses that chanted were added.

#3 How did choruses change to theater?
Actors were added who interacted with the chorus and each other.

#4 Why did the Dionysian festivals become more popular?
Became competitive.

332 into hillsides, so that people sat on tiered seats, looking downward at the stage.
346 The stage was a raised platform, which helped make the actors visible. Between
359 the raised stage and the audience was the orchestra, a platform on which the
373 chorus was positioned. (#5)

376 **Tragedy**
377 As theater became more and more popular, its forms began to change.
389 Between 600 and 500 B.C., the dithyramb evolved into the tragic play. Tragedies
402 were written as a sort of morality play, which shows the right and wrong paths in
418 life. In a tragedy, the main character (also known as the *protagonist*) is faced
432 with difficult decisions, circumstances, or obstacles. The protagonist suffers
441 throughout the story. This theatrical form enabled the playwrights to teach
452 lessons to the audience about how to live properly, how to respect the gods, and
467 how to behave in society. (#6)

472 **Comedy**
473 Comedic plays also became popular with theatrical audiences. The comedies
483 focused on the humor in society. The people in Athens and other Greek cities
497 especially appreciated the use of satire. Satirical plays poked fun at common
509 aspects of city life, including culture, religion, and politics. Many of the comedic
522 stories the Greeks used are still used today. (#7)

530 **Epilogue**
531 Although many Greek plays and theatrical traditions survive today, theater in
542 ancient Greece began to decline around 400 B.C., after the deaths of some of the
557 greatest playwrights. Shortly thereafter, Greece went to war with neighboring
567 states, eventually falling to Alexander the Great and his armies. But the forms
580 and practices of Greek theater spread into other cultures. Because of Greek
592 theater, we enjoy many kinds of theater today. (#8)
600

ACTIVITY E *Fluency Building*

Cold Timing		Practice 1	

Practice 2		Hot Timing	

Student Book: Application Lesson 1 **17**

#5 What were some of the possible limitations of the Greek amphitheaters?
Ideas: Theaters were outdoors; no sound systems, which made it difficult to hear the actors; many of the seats were far from the stage.

#6 What was the major purpose of the tragedies written for Greek audiences?
To teach people lessons about right and wrong actions.

What are some possible lessons that might be taught?
Answers will vary.

#7 If a play was a satire, what would the play attempt to do?
Make fun of some aspect of life.

#8 What events led to the decline of Greek theater?
The deaths of many of the great playwrights; changes of government following wars.

ACTIVITY E
Fluency Building

ACTIVITY PROCEDURE

(See the *Student Book,* page 17.)

In this activity, students will be using a repeated reading procedure of the Activity D article to increase their reading fluency. First, have students do a Cold Timing, in which they whisper-read for one minute as you time them. Have them record in their books the number of correct words they read. Then, have students repeat with one or two practice readings to attempt to beat their Cold Timing. Finally, students exchange books in preparation for a Hot Timing. Have students listen to a partner read for one minute, underlining any word errors, and have them determine the number of correct words their partner read. When both students have completed their Hot Timing, they return each other's books and complete their own Fluency Graphs by indicating the number of words they read correctly in the one-minute Cold Timing and the one-minute Hot Timing.

Note E-1: When assigning partners for this activity, have the stronger reader read first. As a result, the other reader will have one additional practice opportunity.

1. Now, it's time for fluency building.
2. Find the beginning of the passage again. (Pause.)
3. Whisper-read. See how many words you can read in one minute. Begin._ (Time students for one minute.) Stop._ Circle the last word that you read._ Count the number of words you read in one minute. (Assist students in determining the number of words by counting from the number at the beginning of the line to the circled word._) In your book, find **Cold Timing** in **Activity E** at the bottom of page 17._ Record the number of words you read._
4. Let's practice again. Return to the beginning of the article. Remember to whisper-read. See if you can beat your Cold Timing. Begin._ (Time students for one minute.) Stop._ Put a box around the last word that you read._ Count the number of words you read in one minute._ Find **Practice 1**._ Record the number of words you read._
5. **Optional** Let's practice one more time before the Hot Timing. Return to the beginning of the article. Remember to whisper-read. See if you can beat your Cold Timing. Begin._ (Time students for one minute.) Stop._ Put a box around the last word that you read._ Count the number of words you read in

one minute._ Find **Practice 2**._ Record the number of words you read._

6. Please exchange books with your partner._ Partner 1, you are going to read first. Partner 2, you are going to listen carefully to your partner as he or she reads. If your partner makes a mistake or leaves out a word, underline that word. Ones, get ready to read quietly to your partner. Begin._ **(Time students for one minute.)** Stop._ Twos, cross out the last word that your partner read._ Twos, determine the number of words your partner read in one minute._ Find **Hot Timing**._ Record the number of words your partner read._

7. Partner 2, you are going to read next. Partner 1, you are going to listen carefully to your partner as he or she reads. If your partner makes a mistake or leaves out a word, underline that word. Twos, get ready to read quietly to your partner. Begin._ **(Time students for one minute.)** Stop._ Ones, cross out the last word that your partner read._ Ones, determine the number of words your partner read in one minute._ Record the number of words your partner read after **Hot Timing**._

8. Exchange books._ Turn to the Fluency Graph on the last page of your book. First, put a dot and a "C" next to the number that shows how many words you read correctly for your Cold Timing._ Then, put a dot and an "H" next to the number of words you read correctly for your Hot Timing._

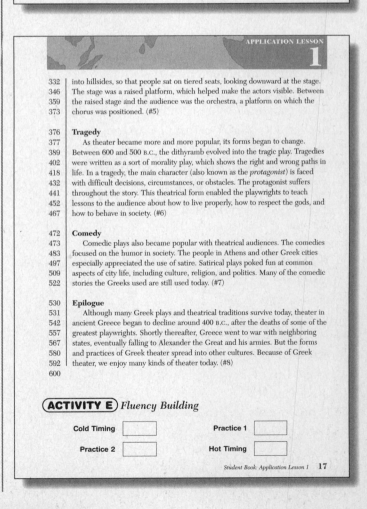

ACTIVITY D *Passage Reading and Comprehension*

Greek Theater

When you think of theater, you might imagine a play performed at your
13 school, an evening at the opera, or even a Broadway musical. But theater was
27 born 2500 years ago in Greece. Theater began there as a religious ceremony. (#1)

40 **The Cult of Dionysus**
44   Around 1200 B.C., in northern Greece, there was a region known as Thrace.
57 In spring festivals and rituals, the Thracians worshipped Dionysus, the Greek
68 god of fertility. The worshippers used dancing, feasting, storytelling, and animal
79 sacrifice to tell the god's stories and legends. When the beliefs in Dionysus
92 began to spread southward to different tribes in Greece, the ceremonies became
104 more formal and symbolic. By 600 B.C., these rituals were part of spring
117 festivities throughout Greece. The storytellers wore masks and chanted their
127 stories in choruses. The choruses did not sing like ours do today. They used a
142 rhythmic, chanting form of speech known as the *dithyramb*. (#2)

151 **Rituals Become Theater**
154   In about 600 B.C., the lyrics to the dithyrambs were written down for the first
169 time. About 75 years later, a man named Thespis added an actor who interacted
183 with the chorus. Now the actor (also known as a *thespian*) would interact with
197 the chorus, taking turns chanting the lyrics. When Thespis added a second actor,
210 theater was born. Now the two actors related directly to each other, using
223 dialogue and action to tell the story. The chorus added commentary and insight
236 to what was occurring between the actors. (#3)

243 **Drama Competitions**
245   In 534 B.C., Pisistratus ruled Athens, the greatest city-state in Greece. He
258 changed the Dionysian festival to a drama competition. This became a highly
270 competitive and popular annual event. Wealthy people in the city would fund
282 productions. In return, they would not have to pay taxes to the city that year. The
298 drama competitions would take place over several whole days in the spring. (#4)

310 **Amphitheaters**
311   Athens, as well as other major Greek cities, built large theaters to
323 accommodate this increasingly popular pastime. The amphitheaters were built

16 REWARDS Plus: Reading Strategies Applied to Social Studies Passages

332 into hillsides, so that people sat on tiered seats, looking downward at the stage.
346 The stage was a raised platform, which helped make the actors visible. Between
359 the raised stage and the audience was the orchestra, a platform on which the
373 chorus was positioned. (#5)

376 **Tragedy**
377   As theater became more and more popular, its forms began to change.
389 Between 600 and 500 B.C., the dithyramb evolved into the tragic play. Tragedies
402 were written as a sort of morality play, which shows the right and wrong paths in
418 life. In a tragedy, the main character (also known as the *protagonist*) is faced
432 with difficult decisions, circumstances, or obstacles. The protagonist suffers
441 throughout the story. This theatrical form enabled the playwrights to teach
452 lessons to the audience about how to live properly, how to respect the gods, and
467 how to behave in society. (#6)

472 **Comedy**
473   Comedic plays also became popular with theatrical audiences. The comedies
483 focused on the humor in society. The people in Athens and other Greek cities
497 especially appreciated the use of satire. Satirical plays poked fun at common
509 aspects of city life, including culture, religion, and politics. Many of the comedic
522 stories the Greeks used are still used today. (#7)

530 **Epilogue**
531   Although many Greek plays and theatrical traditions survive today, theater in
542 ancient Greece began to decline around 400 B.C., after the deaths of some of the
557 greatest playwrights. Shortly thereafter, Greece went to war with neighboring
567 states, eventually falling to Alexander the Great and his armies. But the forms
580 and practices of Greek theater spread into other cultures. Because of Greek
592 theater, we enjoy many kinds of theater today. (#8)
600

ACTIVITY E *Fluency Building*

Cold Timing		Practice 1	
Practice 2		Hot Timing	

Student Book: Application Lesson 1 **17**

ACTIVITY F

Comprehension Questions— Multiple Choice

ACTIVITY PROCEDURE

(See the *Student Book*, page 18.)

Have students read each step in the Multiple Choice Strategy. Model item #1 for students. Lead your students through item #2, proceeding step-by-step. Have students complete the remaining items and provide them with feedback on their answers.

Note F-1: The correct Multiple Choice answers are circled.

Multiple Choice Comprehension

1. Turn to page 18. Find **Activity F.** Often in school you take multiple-choice tests. Today, we are going to learn and practice a strategy for doing multiple-choice items.

2. Read **Step 1.** To be sure you understand the item, you may wish to read it more than one time.

3. Read **Step 2.** It is important to **not** make your selection before you have considered all the choices.

4. Read **Step 3.** This is the most critical step in the strategy. For each choice, you must really think about why the choice might be correct or incorrect. It may be necessary to look back in the article.

5. Read **Step 4.** After you have really thought about each choice, you can select the best answer.

6. My turn to do the first item. First, I read the item: **What words from the article are synonyms?** Synonyms are words that mean the same. Now, I have to read each of the choices and think about why the choice might be correct or incorrect.

7. I read choice **a**: **comedy** and **tragedy**. A **comedy** is funny and a **tragedy** is serious. These are not the same. This cannot be the correct choice.

8. I read choice **b**: **actor** and **thespian**. An **actor** acts in a play. Another name for an actor is **thespian**. This might be the correct choice.

9. I read choice **c**: **drama competition** and **production**. In a **drama competition**, the *best* drama would be the winner. This is not the same as the broader term, **production**. A production would not need to be competitive. This is not the correct choice.

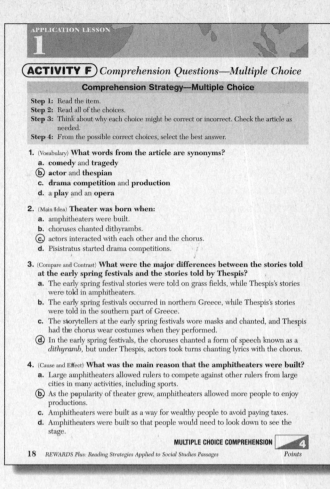

10. I read choice **d**: a **play** and an **opera**. A **play** and an **opera** are both examples of productions, but they are not the same. In an opera, the lines are sung.

11. I have thought about all the choices. I ask myself, "Which is the best answer?" I circle choice **b**.

12. Let's do one together. Read item #2.

13. Read choice **a.** Think about why this choice might be correct or incorrect. (Pause. Then, call on individual students.) (**Possible answer:** Theater was started **before** amphitheaters were built.)

14. Read choice **b.** Think about why this choice might be correct or incorrect. (Pause. Then, call on individual students.) (**Possible answer:** When choruses chanted, it was still not what we would call theater.)

15. Read choice **c.** Think about why this choice might be correct or incorrect. (Pause. Then, call on individual students.) (**Possible answer:** This is a possible correct choice, because theater came about when actors and choruses began to interact.)

16. Read choice **d.** Think about why this choice might be correct or incorrect. (Pause. Then, call on individual students.) (**Possible answer:** Theater occurred before the competitions began.)

17. Which is the best answer?_ Circle it._
18. Use the Multiple Choice Strategy to complete item #3. Be ready to explain why you selected your answer. (Wait while students complete the item. Call on individual students. Ask them why they chose their answer and why they eliminated the other choices. Encourage discussion.)
19. (Repeat Step 18 with item #4.)
20. Count the number of items you got correct, and record that number as points in the blank half of the Multiple Choice Comprehension box._

ACTIVITY F *Comprehension Questions—Multiple Choice*

Comprehension Strategy—Multiple Choice

Step 1: Read the item.
Step 2: Read all of the choices.
Step 3: Think about why each choice might be correct or incorrect. Check the article as needed.
Step 4: From the possible correct choices, select the best answer.

1. (Vocabulary) **What words from the article are synonyms?**
   a. **comedy** and **tragedy**
   b. **actor** and **thespian**
   c. **drama competition** and **production**
   d. a **play** and an **opera**

2. (Main Idea) **Theater was born when:**
   a. amphitheaters were built.
   b. choruses chanted dithyrambs.
   c. actors interacted with each other and the chorus.
   d. Pisistratus started drama competitions.

3. (Compare and Contrast) **What were the major differences between the stories told at the early spring festivals and the stories told by Thespis?**
   a. The early spring festival stories were told on grass fields, while Thespis's stories were told in amphitheaters.
   b. The early spring festivals occurred in northern Greece, while Thespis's stories were told in the southern part of Greece.
   c. The storytellers at the early spring festivals wore masks and chanted, and Thespis had the chorus wear costumes when they performed.
   d. In the early spring festivals, the choruses chanted a form of speech known as a *dithyramb*, but under Thespis, actors took turns chanting lyrics with the chorus.

4. (Cause and Effect) **What was the main reason that the amphitheaters were built?**
   a. Large amphitheaters allowed rulers to compete against other rulers from large cities in many activities, including sports.
   b. As the popularity of theater grew, amphitheaters allowed more people to enjoy productions.
   c. Amphitheaters were built as a way for wealthy people to avoid paying taxes.
   d. Amphitheaters were built so that people would need to look down to see the stage.

MULTIPLE CHOICE COMPREHENSION 4

18   *REWARDS Plus: Reading Strategies Applied to Social Studies Passages*   *Points*

ACTIVITY G

Expository Writing—Summary

ACTIVITY PROCEDURE

(See the *Student Book*, pages 19–20.)

Have students read the prompt. Point out the topic that Beth wrote in her plan. Explain how Beth reread the article and made a **LIST** of important details. Have students read Beth's details. Explain that less-important details should be **CROSSED OUT**, and have them cross out the same detail as Beth. Next, explain how ideas can be **CONNECTED** into one sentence, and have students connect ideas as Beth did in her plan. Have students **NUMBER** their details in the same manner as Beth. Finally, have students read Beth's summary.

Use Overhead 3
Example Summary Plan

1. Turn to page 19.＿ Oftentimes, you are asked to write a summary of material you have read, or heard in a lecture or movie. Today, we are going to see how Beth, another student, applied a strategy to writing a summary. Beginning tomorrow, you will be writing similar summaries.

2. Read the prompt.＿ Next, Beth wrote the topic of the summary in her plan. Read the topic.＿ Then, she followed the steps in the Summary Writing Strategy to write her summary.

3. Read **Step 1**.＿ In the Example Plan, Beth read each paragraph in the article and wrote one or two important details in her notes. In some cases, there may not be an important detail in a paragraph. Let's read her **list** of important details.

4. Read **Step 2**.＿ Next, Beth reread her details and **crossed out** any less-important details. What detail did she cross out?＿ Why do you think this detail was eliminated?＿ Cross out the same detail on your paper.＿

5. Read **Step 3**.＿ In a summary, you want to combine ideas into one sentence so that the summary is not too long. Beth **connected** "began as a religious ceremony" and "honored the Greek god Dionysus." These ideas can easily be combined into one sentence. Notice that she did not connect all of the ideas. She wanted both short and long sentences. Please draw brackets on your paper to connect the ideas that Beth connected.＿

ACTIVITY G *Expository Writing—Summary*

Writing Strategy—Summary

Step 1: LIST (List the details that are important enough to include in the summary.)
Step 2: CROSS OUT (Reread the details. Cross out any that you decide not to include.)
Step 3: CONNECT (Connect any details that could go into one sentence.)
Step 4: NUMBER (Number the details in a logical order.)
Step 5: WRITE (Write your summary.)
Step 6: EDIT (Revise and proofread your summary.)

Prompt: Write a summary of the information you read in the *Greek Theater* article.

Example Summary Plan

Planning Box
(topic) *Greek Theater*
① { (detail) – *began as a religious ceremony* / (detail) – *honored the Greek god Dionysus*
(detail) – ~~*beliefs in Dionysus began to spread southward*~~
② (detail) – *choruses chanted lyrics*
③ (detail) – *actors joined the choruses*
④ { (detail) – *the Dionysus festival in Athens became a drama competition* / (detail) – *amphitheaters were built*
⑤ { (detail) – *performed tragedies that taught lessons* / (detail) – *performed comedies that made fun of life*
⑥ (detail) – *declined when playwrights died and the government changed*

Directions: Write your summary on a separate piece of paper.

Example Summary

The roots of modern theater can be found in early Greek theater. Greek theater began as a religious ceremony that honored the Greek god Dionysus. At first, choruses chanted lyrics. When actors were added to interact with the chorus, theater was born. Later, the Dionysus festival in Athens became a drama competition, and amphitheaters were built to accommodate the event. Both tragedies, which taught lessons, and comedies, which made fun of life, were performed. Greek theater declined when the great playwrights died and the government changed.

Rubric— Summary	Student or Partner Rating	Teacher Rating
1. Did the author state the topic and the main idea in the first sentence?	(Yes) Fix up	Yes No
2. Did the author focus on important details?	(Yes) Fix up	Yes No
3. Did the author combine details in some of the sentences?	(Yes) Fix up	Yes No
4. Is the summary easy to understand?	(Yes) Fix up	Yes No
5. Did the author correctly spell words, particularly the words found in the article?	(Yes) Fix up	Yes No
6. Did the author use correct capitalization, capitalizing the first word in the sentence and proper names of people, places, and things?	(Yes) Fix up	Yes No
7. Did the author use correct punctuation, including a period at the end of each sentence?	(Yes) Fix up	Yes No

WRITING
7
Points

6. Read **Step 4**._ Beth then **numbered** the details in the order they would appear in her summary. In this case, the numbers are in the same order as her list, but that is not always necessary. Number your paper as Beth did._

7. Read **Step 5**._ Beth then **wrote** the sentences in her summary. Her first sentence introduces the topic and the main idea of the summary. The remaining sentences give important details.

Use Overhead 4
Example Summary

8. Read **Step 6**._ Beth reread and **edited** her summary. Turn to page 20. Let's read her summary.

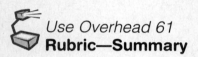

Use Overhead 61
Rubric—Summary

9. In the following lessons, you will be writing summaries and other types of responses to written prompts. The questions in this rubric define attributes of well-written summaries. We'll use these questions to evaluate Beth's paragraph and to determine what she needs to edit.

10. Read question #1._ Now, reread Beth's first sentence and determine whether or not she stated the topic and the main idea. Circle "Yes" if she did. Circle "Fix up" if she didn't._ What did you circle?_

11. Read question #2._ Reexamine Beth's summary to determine if she included important details. Then, circle "Yes" or "Fix up."_ What did you circle?_

12. Complete the ratings for the remaining questions. Remember to read each question, and then look at the Example Summary to make sure the criteria have been met.

13. Let's compare your ratings with my ratings of this summary. (Compare your ratings with students' ratings. Tell them that Beth should work on improving any items circled "Fix up." Direct students to add the number of questions that were answered "Yes" by both you and them, and then enter that number as points in the blank half of the Writing box below the rubric.)

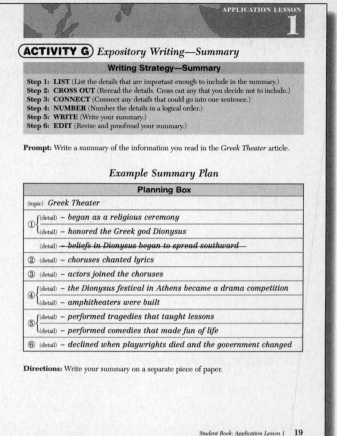

APPLICATION LESSON

1

ACTIVITY G *Expository Writing—Summary*

Writing Strategy—Summary

Step 1: **LIST** (List the details that are important enough to include in the summary.)
Step 2: **CROSS OUT** (Reread the details. Cross out any that you decide not to include.)
Step 3: **CONNECT** (Connect any details that could go into one sentence.)
Step 4: **NUMBER** (Number the details in a logical order.)
Step 5: **WRITE** (Write your summary.)
Step 6: **EDIT** (Revise and proofread your summary.)

Prompt: Write a summary of the information you read in the *Greek Theater* article.

Example Summary Plan

Planning Box

(topic) *Greek Theater*

① (detail) – *began as a religious ceremony*
    (detail) – *honored the Greek god Dionysus*
    (detail) – *beliefs in Dionysus began to spread southward*
② (detail) – *choruses chanted lyrics*
③ (detail) – *actors joined the choruses*
④ (detail) – *the Dionysus festival in Athens became a drama competition*
    (detail) – *amphitheaters were built*
⑤ (detail) – *performed tragedies that taught lessons*
    (detail) – *performed comedies that made fun of life*
⑥ (detail) – *declined when playwrights died and the government changed*

Directions: Write your summary on a separate piece of paper.

Student Book: Application Lesson 1 **19**

APPLICATION LESSON

1

Example Summary

The roots of modern theater can be found in early Greek theater. Greek theater began as a religious ceremony that honored the Greek god Dionysus. At first, choruses chanted lyrics. When actors were added to interact with the chorus, theater was born. Later, the Dionysus festival in Athens became a drama competition, and amphitheaters were built to accommodate the event. Both tragedies, which taught lessons, and comedies, which made fun of life, were performed. Greek theater declined when the great playwrights died and the government changed.

Rubric— Summary	Student or Partner Rating	Teacher Rating
1. Did the author state the topic and the main idea in the first sentence?	(Yes) Fix up	Yes No
2. Did the author focus on important details?	(Yes) Fix up	Yes No
3. Did the author combine details in some of the sentences?	(Yes) Fix up	Yes No
4. Is the summary easy to understand?	(Yes) Fix up	Yes No
5. Did the author correctly spell words, particularly the words found in the article?	(Yes) Fix up	Yes No
6. Did the author use correct capitalization, capitalizing the first word in the sentence and proper names of people, places, and things?	(Yes) Fix up	Yes No
7. Did the author use correct punctuation, including a period at the end of each sentence?	(Yes) Fix up	Yes No

WRITING
7
Points

Application Lesson 2

Materials Needed:

- *Student Book:* Application Lesson 2
- Application Overhead Transparencies 5–8
- Application Overhead Transparency 61
- Appendix A Reproducible 3: Comprehension Strategy—Multiple Choice
- Appendix B Optional Vocabulary Activities: Application Lesson 2
- Paper or cardboard to use when covering the overhead transparency
- Paper or cardboard for each student to use during spelling dictation
- Washable overhead transparency pen

Text Treatment Notes:

- Black text signifies teacher script (exact wording to say to students).
- Green text in parentheses signifies directions or prompts for the teacher.
- Green text signifies answers or examples of answers.
- Green graphics treatment signifies reproduction of Overhead information.
- Green text and green graphics treatment do not appear in the *Student Book*.

ACTIVITY A
Vocabulary

ACTIVITY PROCEDURE, List 1

(See the *Student Book,* page 21.)

Tell students each word in the list. Then, have students repeat the word and read the definition aloud. For each definition, provide any additional information that may be necessary. Then, have students practice reading the words themselves.

Note A.1-1: See Appendix E, Pronunciation Guide for Unique Words, for correct pronunciations of uncommon vocabulary words.

Note A.1-2: If you wish to emphasize the part of speech, have students say the part of speech before reading the definition.

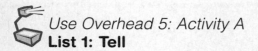

Use Overhead 5: Activity A
List 1: Tell

1. (Show the top half of Overhead 5.) Before we read the passage, let's read the difficult words. (Point to **Marco Polo**.) These first words are **Marco Polo**. What words?_ Now, read the definition._
2. (Point to **Italy**.) The next word is **Italy**. What word?_ Now, read the definition._
3. (Pronounce each word in List 1, and then have students repeat each word and read the definition.)
4. Open your *Student Book* to **Application Lesson 2**, page 21._
5. Find **Activity A, List 1**, in your book._ Let's read the words again. First word._ Next word._ (Continue for all words in List 1.)

ACTIVITY PROCEDURE, List 2

(See the *Student Book,* page 21.)

The second list of words can be read using the part-by-part strategy. Have students circle prefixes and suffixes, then underline the vowels. Using the overhead transparency, assist students in checking their work. Next, have students figure out each word to themselves, then say it aloud. Have them read the definition aloud.

Note A.2-1: Provide additional information for any definitions as needed.

Note A.2-2: If you wish to emphasize the part of speech, have students say the part of speech before reading the definition.

Note A.2-3: If you are teaching older students for whom "thumbs-up" is inappropriate, have students look at you when they can read the word.

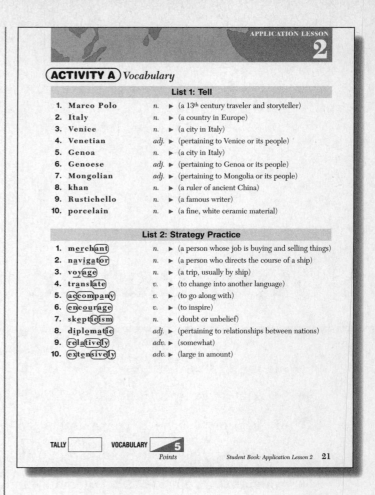

ACTIVITY A *Vocabulary*

List 1: Tell

1.	Marco Polo	*n.* ▶	(a 13th century traveler and storyteller)
2.	Italy	*n.* ▶	(a country in Europe)
3.	Venice	*n.* ▶	(a city in Italy)
4.	Venetian	*adj.* ▶	(pertaining to Venice or its people)
5.	Genoa	*n.* ▶	(a city in Italy)
6.	Genoese	*adj.* ▶	(pertaining to Genoa or its people)
7.	Mongolian	*adj.* ▶	(pertaining to Mongolia or its people)
8.	khan	*n.* ▶	(a ruler of ancient China)
9.	Rustichello	*n.* ▶	(a famous writer)
10.	porcelain	*n.* ▶	(a fine, white ceramic material)

List 2: Strategy Practice

1.	merchant	*n.* ▶	(a person whose job is buying and selling things)
2.	navigator	*n.* ▶	(a person who directs the course of a ship)
3.	voyage	*n.* ▶	(a trip, usually by ship)
4.	translate	*v.* ▶	(to change into another language)
5.	accompany	*v.* ▶	(to go along with)
6.	encourage	*v.* ▶	(to inspire)
7.	skepticism	*n.* ▶	(doubt or unbelief)
8.	diplomatic	*adj.* ▶	(pertaining to relationships between nations)
9.	relatively	*adv.* ▶	(somewhat)
10.	extensively	*adv.* ▶	(large in amount)

TALLY [ ] VOCABULARY [5] *Points*

Student Book: Application Lesson 2 **21**

Use Overhead 5: Activity A
List 2: Strategy Practice

1. Find **List 2**. For each word, circle the prefixes and suffixes, and underline the vowels. Look up when you are done._
2. (Show the bottom half of Overhead 5.) Before you check your work on List 2, look at item #4. (Point to the second example and the **trans** that is circled.) From now on, you can also circle **trans**. The prefix is /trans/. Say it._ Look at item #5. (Point to the first example and the **ac** that is circled.) Remember, you can also circle **ac**. What prefix?_ Now, go back to item #1. Check and fix any mistakes._
3. Go back to the first word again._ Sound out the word to yourself. Put your thumb up when you can read the word. Be sure that it is a real word._ What word?_ Now, read the definition._
4. (Continue Step 3 with all remaining words in List 2.)

Note A.2-4: You may wish to provide additional practice by having students read words to a partner.

ACTIVITY PROCEDURE, List 1 and 2

(See the *Student Book*, page 21.)

Tell students to look in List 1 or List 2 for a word you are thinking about. Have them circle the number of the word and tell you the word. Explain to students to make a tally mark for each correct word in the Tally box, and then enter the number of tally marks as points in the blank half of the Vocabulary box.

1. For this activity, I will tell you about words I am thinking about. You will have a short time to find those words in either List 1 or List 2, circle the number of that word, and then tell me the word I'm thinking about. Find the Tally box at the bottom of page 21. For every word that you correctly identify, make a tally mark in the Tally box. If you don't identify the correct word, don't do anything.

2. I am thinking of a word. Circle the number of the appropriate word.

   - If you are always doubting what you hear, you are full of this. (Wait.) What word? **skepticism**
   - When you inspire someone to act or think in a certain way, you do this. (Wait.) What word? **encourage**
   - When you go along with your friends to a movie, you do this. (Wait.) What word? **accompany**
   - This person on a ship is possibly the second most important crew member. (Wait.) What word? **navigator**
   - Nations try to find these types of solutions to their disagreements. (Wait.) What word? **diplomatic**

3. Count all the tally marks, and enter that number as points in the blank half of the Vocabulary box.

ACTIVITY PROCEDURE, List 3

(See the *Student Book*, page 22.)

The words in the third list are related. Have students use the *REWARDS* Strategies to figure out the first word in each family. Have them read the definition and then read the other two words in the family.

Note A.3-1: Provide additional information for any definitions as needed.

Note A.3-2: If you wish to emphasize the part of speech, have students say the part of speech before reading the definition.

Note A.3-3: If you are teaching older students for whom "thumbs-up" is inappropriate, have students look at you when they can read the word.

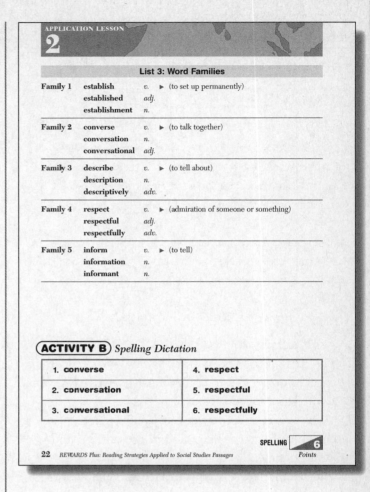

List 3: Word Families

Family 1	establish	v.	► (to set up permanently)
	established	adj.	
	establishment	n.	
Family 2	converse	v.	► (to talk together)
	conversation	n.	
	conversational	adj.	
Family 3	describe	v.	► (to tell about)
	description	n.	
	descriptively	adv.	
Family 4	respect	v.	► (admiration of someone or something)
	respectful	adj.	
	respectfully	adv.	
Family 5	inform	v.	► (to tell)
	information	n.	
	informant	n.	

ACTIVITY B *Spelling Dictation*

1. converse	4. respect
2. conversation	5. respectful
3. conversational	6. respectfully

SPELLING ► **6**

22 *REWARDS Plus: Reading Strategies Applied to Social Studies Passages*   Points

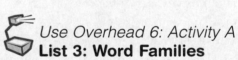

Use Overhead 6: Activity A
List 3: Word Families

1. Turn to page 22. Find **Family 1** in **List 3**. Figure out the first word. Use your pencil if you wish. Put your thumb up when you know the word._ What word?_ Read the definition._

2. Look at the next word in Family 1. Figure out the word._ What word?_

3. Next word. Figure out the word._ What word?_

4. (Repeat Steps 1–3 for all word families in List 3.)

Note A.3-4: You may wish to provide additional practice by having students read a word family to the group or to a partner.

Note A.3-5: Additional vocabulary practice activities are provided in Appendix B of the Teacher's Guide. These activities are optional and can be assigned during class, for homework, or as small group, in-class activities.

ACTIVITY B
Spelling Dictation

ACTIVITY PROCEDURE

(See the *Student Book,* page 22.)

For each word, tell students the word, then have students say
the parts of the word to themselves while they write the word.
Then, have students enter the number of correctly spelled
words as points in the blank half of the Spelling box.

Note B-1: Distribute a piece of light cardboard to students so they can cover
their page during spelling dictation. Students can also use the cardboard as a
bookmark to quickly locate pages at the beginning of lessons.

 Use Overhead 6: Activity B

1. Find **Activity B**.
2. The first word is **converse**. What word?_ Say the
   parts in **converse** to yourself as you write the word.
   (Pause and monitor.)
3. (Show **converse** on the overhead.) Check
   converse. If you misspelled it, cross it out and
   write it correctly.
4. The second word is **conversation**. What word?_
   Say the parts in **conversation** to yourself as you
   write the word. (Pause and monitor.)
5. (Show **conversation** on the overhead.) Check
   conversation. If you misspelled it, cross it out and
   write it correctly.
6. (Repeat the procedures for the words
   conversational, **respect**, **respectful**, and
   respectfully.)
7. Count the number of words you spelled correctly,
   and record that number as points in the blank half
   of the Spelling box at the bottom of the page.

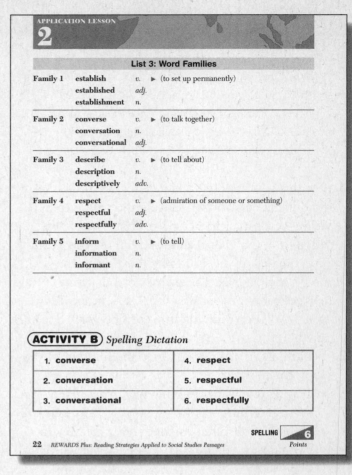

ACTIVITY C
Background Knowledge

ACTIVITY PROCEDURE

(See the *Student Book,* page 23.)

Read the Background Knowledge paragraphs using one of three methods: read them to students, have students read them together, or call on individual students to read. Examine the timeline and the related graphic together. Then, preview the passage together by examining the title and the headings. Have students tell partners two things the passage will tell about.

1. Turn to page 23. Let's read the two paragraphs. (Read or ask students to read. Then examine the timeline and graphic together.)
2. Now, let's turn the page and preview the passage. Read the title._ What is the whole passage going to tell about?_
3. Now, let's read the headings. Read the first heading._ Read the next heading._ (Continue until students have read all headings.)
4. Turn to your partner. Without looking, tell two things this passage will tell about._

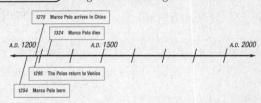

ACTIVITY C *Background Knowledge*

Since 100 B.C., a network of overland trade routes was developed to carry goods between Europe and Asia. These trade routes were called the "Silk Road" because of the valuable Chinese cloth that was transported on them. Trade continued on the Silk Road until ocean routes surpassed land routes in the 15th and 16th centuries A.D.

In this article, you will meet Marco Polo, who traveled with his father to China via the Silk Road. It is through his storytelling that we have learned a great deal about ancient China.

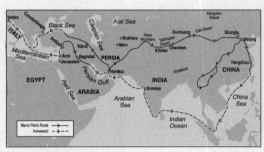

Map of Marco Polo's Route

Student Book: Application Lesson 2 **23**

ACTIVITY D
Passage Reading and Comprehension

ACTIVITY PROCEDURE

(See the *Student Book*, pages 24–25.)

Have students work on reading accuracy by selecting a passage-reading option that best fits your students.

Passage Reading: Accuracy

(Select a passage-reading procedure that matches the size of your group and the competency of your students.

Option A

If you are teaching a small group of students who are having difficulty, use Option A:

Have students read one paragraph silently. Then, call on one student to orally read a paragraph or a portion of the paragraph to the class. Call on students in random order, varying the amount that each student reads.

Option B

If you are teaching a small group with students who are not having difficulty, use Option B:

Have students read the entire article silently, rereading it if they finish before their classmates. Then, call on one student to orally read a paragraph or a portion of a paragraph to the class. Call on students in random order, varying the amount that each student reads.

Option C

If you are teaching a large group with students who are having difficulty, use Option C:

Have students read one paragraph silently. Then, have students read the paragraph to a partner. Alternate partner-reading turns.

Option D

If you are teaching a large group with students who are not having difficulty, use Option D:

Have students read the entire article silently, rereading it if they finish before their classmates. Then, have students read the passage with their partners, alternating on each paragraph.)

ACTIVITY D *Passage Reading and Comprehension*

Marco Polo

16	Born in Italy in the middle of the 13th century, Marco Polo was part of a
27	wealthy merchant family. His father and uncle had already been trading
37	extensively with Middle Eastern countries. They traded silk, porcelain, and
51	other exotic goods over the Silk Road. The Silk Road was a trading route
64	established between China and Rome. As a result, the Polos traveled a great
80	deal. Marco did not meet his father until he was 15 or 16, when his father
95	returned to Venice after many years of travel. This time, when he left again, he
	took young Marco with him. (#1)

Voyages to China

100	
103	The travelers set out overland rather than risk the sea route. They traveled
116	through what are now Armenia and Iran, through central Asia, across the
128	mountains, and across the Gobi Desert. In 1275, they arrived at the summer
141	court of Kublai Khan, near present-day Beijing, China. The khan, the ruler of
155	the area, warmly welcomed them, and he hired the Polos into his service. (#2)
168	Marco and his family spent the next 17 years working for Kublai Khan in
182	China. The khan had a special fondness for Marco's storytelling and
193	conversation. Marco was sent on diplomatic missions all over the empire. Each
205	time he returned to the khan, Marco had new stories and descriptions of the
219	lands and people he had seen. He was a highly respected diplomat and may
233	even have held a governing post in the city of Yangzhou. (#3)

A Wish to Return Home

244	
249	The Polos made several requests to the khan that they should be allowed to
263	return to Europe. But they were denied these requests because Kublai Khan
275	was so fond of his Italian visitors. But finally, in 1292, he allowed them to
290	accompany a Mongolian prinicess who would be traveling to Persia by sea. Once
303	she had arrived safely, the Polos traveled back to Venice. They returned home in
317	1295. People flocked to hear Marco Polo's accounts of his travels, and they
330	called him *il milione*—the man with a million stories. (#4)

A Fortunate Meeting

340	
343	Soon after his return to Venice, Marco got involved in the Venetian navy. He
357	was taken prisoner by the Genoese during a battle in the Mediterranean Sea.

Passage Reading: Comprehension Questions

(You may wish to ask the following questions as the passage is being read. Numbers corresponding to the questions are indicated at the point at which they could be asked.)

#1 How would Marco Polo's father's life set the stage for Marco's adventures?

Ideas: Had already traveled a great deal; was probably familiar with trade routes and people along the way.

#2 Why do you think the khan hired the Polos?

Ideas: The khan wanted to benefit from the Polos' knowledge of trade; the Polos had skills the khan could benefit from, such as knowledge of European languages; the khan liked the adventuresome Polos.

#3 What evidence is given that the khan trusted Marco Polo?

Ideas: Marco Polo represented the khan to other nations; Marco was given a position in the government; they worked together for a long time.

Line	Text
370	He was sent to a prison in Genoa. In prison, he met Rustichello, a relatively
385	famous writer of romances and tales of chivalry. Rustichello was enchanted with
397	Marco Polo's tales of his travels in the Far East and agreed to write down the
413	stories. When the book was published, it became extremely popular and was
425	translated into several languages. (#5)
429	Marco Polo was released from prison and returned to Venice. He died there
442	in 1324. But his book continued to tell his stories of travels in China. It became
458	a sort of handbook for merchants and navigators. Christopher Columbus had a
470	copy that was printed in Latin, which he often referred to while planning his
484	western route to Eastern countries. (#6)
489	**Skepticism**
490	As popularity of Marco Polo's book grew, so did questions about its
502	truthfulness. Maybe people felt that the stories were simply too fabulous to be
515	believed. But Marco maintained that they were true right up until his death. On
529	his deathbed, when encouraged to retract the "fables" he had spread, Marco
541	replied by saying that he had not told half of what he had seen—he was afraid it
559	would not be believed. Since his death, scholars have been able to verify much
573	of the information that Marco Polo collected, earning him a place as one of the
588	greatest travelers in the world. (#7)
593	

ACTIVITY E *Fluency Building*

Cold Timing [ ] Practice 1 [ ]

Practice 2 [ ] Hot Timing [ ]

Student Book: Application Lesson 2 **25**

ACTIVITY E
Fluency Building
ACTIVITY PROCEDURE

(See the *Student Book*, page 25.)

In this activity, students will be using a repeated reading procedure of the Activity D article to increase their reading fluency. First, have students do a Cold Timing, in which they whisper-read for one minute as you time them. Have them record in their books the number of correct words they read. Then, have students repeat with one or two practice readings to attempt to beat their Cold Timing. Finally, students exchange books in preparation for a Hot Timing. Have students listen to a partner read for one minute, underlining any word errors, and have them determine the number of correct words their partner read. When both students have completed their Hot Timing, they return each other's books and complete their own Fluency Graphs by indicating the number of words they read correctly in the one-minute Cold Timing and the one-minute Hot Timing.

Note E-1: When assigning partners for this activity, have the stronger reader read first. As a result, the other reader will have one additional practice opportunity.

1. Now, it's time for fluency building.
2. Find the beginning of the passage again. (Pause.)
3. Whisper-read. See how many words you can read in one minute. Begin._ (Time students for one minute.) Stop._ Circle the last word that you read._ Count the number of words you read in one minute. (Assist students in determining the number of words by counting from the number at the beginning of the line to the circled word._) In your book, find **Cold Timing** in **Activity E** at the bottom of page 25. Record the number of words you read._
4. Let's practice again. Return to the beginning of the article. Remember to whisper-read. See if you can beat your Cold Timing. Begin._ (Time students for one minute.) Stop._ Put a box around the last word that you read._ Count the number of words you read in one minute._ Find **Practice 1**._ Record the number of words you read._
5. **Optional** Let's practice one more time before the Hot Timing. Return to the beginning of the article. Remember to whisper-read. See if you can beat your Cold Timing. Begin._ (Time students for one minute.) Stop._ Put a box around the last word that you read._ Count the number of words you read in

---

#4 Why was Marco Polo given the nickname "*il milione*"?
Marco told many stories of his adventures; he was referred to as "the man with a million stories."

#5 Why might Marco Polo's time in prison be considered a fortunate occurrence?
Marco Polo met Rustichello, a famous writer, who recorded and later published Marco Polo's tales.

#6 In what ways could you say that Marco Polo lived beyond his death?
People read about his adventures long after his death; individuals such as Christopher Columbus learned from his teachings.

#7 What ended the skepticism about the truthfulness of Marco Polo's stories?
Scholars verified much of the information in his stories.

one minute.‗ Find **Practice 2**.‗ Record the number of words you read.‗

6. Please exchange books with your partner.‗ Partner 1, you are going to read first. Partner 2, you are going to listen carefully to your partner as he or she reads. If your partner makes a mistake or leaves out a word, underline that word. Ones, get ready to read quietly to your partner. Begin.‗ (Time students for one minute.) Stop.‗ Twos, cross out the last word that your partner read.‗ Twos, determine the number of words your partner read in one minute.‗ Find **Hot Timing**.‗ Record the number of words your partner read.‗

7. Partner 2, you are going to read next. Partner 1, you are going to listen carefully to your partner as he or she reads. If your partner makes a mistake or leaves out a word, underline that word. Twos, get ready to read quietly to your partner. Begin.‗ (Time students for one minute.) Stop.‗ Ones, cross out the last word that your partner read.‗ Ones, determine the number of words your partner read in one minute.‗ Record the number of words your partner read after **Hot Timing**.‗

8. Exchange books.‗ Turn to the Fluency Graph on the last page of your book. First, put a dot and a "C" next to the number that shows how many words you read correctly for your Cold Timing.‗ Then, put a dot and an "H" next to the number of words you read correctly for your Hot Timing.‗

ACTIVITY D *Passage Reading and Comprehension*

Marco Polo

16	Born in Italy in the middle of the 13th century, Marco Polo was part of a
27	wealthy merchant family. His father and uncle had already been trading
37	extensively with Middle Eastern countries. They traded silk, porcelain, and
51	other exotic goods over the Silk Road. The Silk Road was a trading route
64	established between China and Rome. As a result, the Polos traveled a great
80	deal. Marco did not meet his father until he was 15 or 16, when his father
95	returned to Venice after many years of travel. This time, when he left again, he
	took young Marco with him. (#1)

100	**Voyages to China**
103	The travelers set out overland rather than risk the sea route. They traveled
116	through what are now Armenia and Iran, through central Asia, across the
128	mountains, and across the Gobi Desert. In 1275, they arrived at the summer
141	court of Kublai Khan, near present-day Beijing, China. The khan, the ruler of
155	the area, warmly welcomed them, and he hired the Polos into his service. (#2)
168	Marco and his family spent the next 17 years working for Kublai Khan in
182	China. The khan had a special fondness for Marco's storytelling and
193	conversation. Marco was sent on diplomatic missions all over the empire. Each
205	time he returned to the khan, Marco had new stories and descriptions of the
219	lands and people he had seen. He was a highly respected diplomat and may
233	even have held a governing post in the city of Yangzhou. (#3)

244	**A Wish to Return Home**
249	The Polos made several requests to the khan that they should be allowed to
263	return to Europe. But they were denied these requests because Kublai Khan
275	was so fond of his Italian visitors. But finally, in 1292, he allowed them to
290	accompany a Mongolian princess who would be traveling to Persia by sea. Once
303	she had arrived safely, the Polos traveled back to Venice. They returned home in
317	1295. People flocked to hear Marco Polo's accounts of his travels, and they
330	called him *il milione*—the man with a million stories. (#4)

340	**A Fortunate Meeting**
343	Soon after his return to Venice, Marco got involved in the Venetian navy. He
357	was taken prisoner by the Genoese during a battle in the Mediterranean Sea.

370	He was sent to a prison in Genoa. In prison, he met Rustichello, a relatively
385	famous writer of romances and tales of chivalry. Rustichello was enchanted with
397	Marco Polo's tales of his travels in the Far East and agreed to write down the
413	stories. When the book was published, it became extremely popular and was
425	translated into several languages. (#5)
429	Marco Polo was released from prison and returned to Venice. He died there
442	in 1324. But his book continued to tell his stories of travels in China. It became
458	a sort of handbook for merchants and navigators. Christopher Columbus had a
470	copy that was printed in Latin, which he often referred to while planning his
484	western route to Eastern countries. (#6)

489	**Skepticism**
490	As popularity of Marco Polo's book grew, so did questions about its
502	truthfulness. Maybe people felt that the stories were simply too fabulous to be
515	believed. But Marco maintained that they were true right up until his death. On
529	his deathbed, when encouraged to retract the "fables" he had spread, Marco
541	replied by saying that he had not told half of what he had seen—he was afraid it
559	would not be believed. Since his death, scholars have been able to verify much
573	of the information that Marco Polo collected, earning him a place as one of the
588	greatest travelers in the world. (#7)
593	

ACTIVITY E *Fluency Building*

Cold Timing	_____	Practice 1	_____
Practice 2	_____	Hot Timing	_____

ACTIVITY F

Comprehension Questions— Multiple Choice

ACTIVITY PROCEDURE

(See the *Student Book*, page 26.)

Review the steps in the Multiple Choice Strategy. Have students complete one multiple-choice item. Have students share their answers and the rationale for their answers. Proceed item by item, emphasizing the rationale for the *best* answer. Have students record points for each correct item.

Note F-1: The correct Multiple Choice answers are circled.

Multiple Choice Comprehension

1. Turn to page 26. Find **Activity F**._ Let's review the steps in the Multiple Choice Strategy.

2. Read **Step 1**._

3. Read **Step 2**._

4. Read **Step 3**._

5. Read **Step 4**._

6. Finish item #1. Be ready to explain why you selected your answer._ (Wait while students complete the item. Call on individual students. Ask them why they chose their answer and why they eliminated the other choices. Encourage discussion.)

7. (Repeat Step 6 with items #2, #3, and #4.)

8. Count the number of items you got correct, and record that number as points in the blank half of the Multiple Choice Comprehension box._

9. (Distribute Appendix A Reproducible 3: Comprehension Strategy—Multiple Choice. Have students place this in a notebook or a folder for future reference.)

ACTIVITY F *Comprehension Questions—Multiple Choice*

Comprehension Strategy—Multiple Choice

Step 1: Read the item.
Step 2: Read all of the choices.
Step 3: Think about why each choice might be correct or incorrect. Check the article as needed.
Step 4: From the possible correct choices, select the best answer.

1. (Vocabulary) **Read these sentences from the passage: "Marco was sent on diplomatic *missions* all over the empire. Each time he returned to the khan, Marco had new stories and descriptions of the lands and people he had seen." Based on the wording of those sentences, what does the word *missions* mean?**
   a. Places used by missionaries for religious work.
   b. Tasks that a person is sent to perform.
   c. Books containing stories of adventurers.
   d. A group of diplomats assigned to a foreign country.

2. (Main Idea) **If the article needed a new title, which would be best?**
   a. *The Traveler*
   b. *The Prisoner*
   c. *Father and Son*
   d. *The Diplomat*

3. (Cause and Effect) **Why was it beneficial for Marco to have met Rustichello in prison?**
   a. Rustichello enjoyed Marco's stories, which made Marco feel better.
   b. Rustichello joined Marco on his journeys to China.
   c. Rustichello used details from Marco's travels in his romances.
   d. Rustichello wrote down Marco's stories, which later became a book.

4. (Compare and Contrast) **What did Marco Polo and Rustichello have in common?**
   a. They both wrote books.
   b. They both were imprisoned.
   c. They both loved adventures
   d. They both enjoyed travel to China.

MULTIPLE CHOICE COMPREHENSION *Points*

ACTIVITY G
Expository Writing—Summary

ACTIVITY PROCEDURE

(See the *Student Book*, pages 27–28.)

Have students read the prompt and record the topic of the summary. Next, have them **LIST** details in the Planning Box by referring back to the article. Encourage students to record notes rather than form complete sentences. When they are done with their lists, have them compare their lists of critical details with those of other classmates and the Example Summary Plan.

1. Turn to page 27._ Today, we are going to use the Summary Writing Strategy.
2. Read the prompt._ Write the topic "**Marco Polo**" in the Planning Box.
3. Read **Step 1** of the Summary Writing Strategy._ Now, reread the article and write **important** details in your plan on page 27. You may wish to write one important idea from each paragraph._ (Monitor carefully as students record details.)
4. Compare your details to your partner's list._

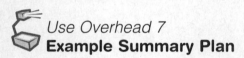

Use Overhead 7
Example Summary Plan

5. Let's read the list of details on the overhead. Your list should have some of the same ideas, but it does not need to be exactly the same._ If you want to fix up your list, do that now._

ACTIVITY PROCEDURE

Next, have students complete the additional steps in the Summary Writing Strategy. Have them reread their lists and **CROSS OUT** any weak or unimportant details. Then, have students **CONNECT** details that could go together in one sentence, **NUMBER** their ideas in a logical order, and **WRITE** their summaries on a separate piece of paper. When they are done, have them **EDIT** their paragraphs, revising for clarity and proofreading for errors in spelling, capitalization, and punctuation.

Have students read their summaries to their partners. Then, read the Example Summary.

Have students read each of the attributes on the rubric, examine their summaries, and circle either "Yes" or "Fix up." Give students time to make changes in their summaries.

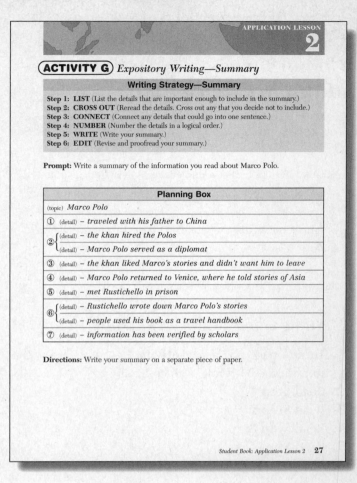

ACTIVITY G *Expository Writing—Summary*

Writing Strategy—Summary

Step 1: **LIST** (List the details that are important enough to include in the summary.)
Step 2: **CROSS OUT** (Reread the details. Cross out any that you decide not to include.)
Step 3: **CONNECT** (Connect any details that could go into one sentence.)
Step 4: **NUMBER** (Number the details in a logical order.)
Step 5: **WRITE** (Write your summary.)
Step 6: **EDIT** (Revise and proofread your summary.)

Prompt: Write a summary of the information you read about Marco Polo.

Planning Box
(topic) *Marco Polo*
① (detail) – *traveled with his father to China*
② (detail) – *the khan hired the Polos* / (detail) – *Marco Polo served as a diplomat*
③ (detail) – *the khan liked Marco's stories and didn't want him to leave*
④ (detail) – *Marco Polo returned to Venice, where he told stories of Asia*
⑤ (detail) – *met Rustichello in prison*
⑥ (detail) – *Rustichello wrote down Marco Polo's stories* / (detail) – *people used his book as a travel handbook*
⑦ (detail) – *information has been verified by scholars*

Directions: Write your summary on a separate piece of paper.

Student Book: Application Lesson 2 **27**

Optional: During or after the class session, fill in the third column of the rubric chart and assign points to the student summaries.

Optional: Have students date their writing and place the sample in a folder. Thus, students will be able to look back at their summaries and extended responses and literally see their writing improvement.

6. Read **Step 2.**_ If you have any less-important or unimportant details, cross them out now._ What details did you eliminate and why? (Call on individual students.)
7. Read **Step 3.**_ In a summary, you want to combine ideas into one sentence so that the summary is not too long. Look at your list. What ideas might you combine into one sentence? (Call on individual students._) Please draw brackets on your list to connect ideas._ (Monitor carefully.)
8. Read **Step 4.**_ Now, number the ideas in a logical order. If you have two or more connected ideas, give them only one number._ (Monitor.)

9. Read **Step 5.__** Write your summary on a separate piece of paper. Be sure that your first sentence tells the topic and the main idea.__ The rest of your sentences should include important details. (Monitor.)

10. Read **Step 6.__** Reread your summary. Check to be sure your summary is easy to understand. Fix any errors you find in spelling, capitalization, and punctuation.__ (Monitor.)

11. Read your summary to your partner.

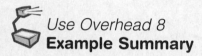

Use Overhead 8
Example Summary

12. Look at the overhead. Let's read this Example Summary. Yours doesn't need to be exactly the same, but it should be similar.

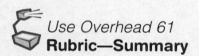

Use Overhead 61
Rubric—Summary

13. Turn to page 28. Today, you will be evaluating your own summary. You will use the questions in this rubric to determine what you need to edit.

14. Read the question for attribute 1.__ Reread your first sentence, and look for the topic and main idea. Circle "Yes" if you have it, or circle "Fix up" if you need to revise it.__ If you need to improve your first sentence, you will work on it later.

15. Read the question for attribute 2.__ Reread the rest of your sentences, and determine if you included important details. Circle "Yes" or "Fix up."__ If you circled "Fix up," work on it later.

16. Complete the ratings for the remaining questions. Remember to read each question, and then look at your summary to make sure the criteria have been met.

17. (When the evaluation is complete, give students adequate time to make any necessary changes to their summaries. Have students enter their points in the blank half of the Writing box below the rubric.)

Rubric— Summary	Student or Partner Rating		Teacher Rating	
1. Did the author state the topic and the main idea in the first sentence?	Yes	Fix up	Yes	No
2. Did the author focus on important details?	Yes	Fix up	Yes	No
3. Did the author combine details in some of the sentences?	Yes	Fix up	Yes	No
4. Is the summary easy to understand?	Yes	Fix up	Yes	No
5. Did the author correctly spell words, particularly the words found in the article?	Yes	Fix up	Yes	No
6. Did the author use correct capitalization, capitalizing the first word in the sentence and proper names of people, places, and things?	Yes	Fix up	Yes	No
7. Did the author use correct punctuation, including a period at the end of each sentence?	Yes	Fix up	Yes	No

WRITING 7
Points

28 REWARDS Plus: Reading Strategies Applied to Social Studies Passages

Application Lesson 3

Materials Needed:

- *Student Book:* Application Lesson 3
- Application Overhead Transparencies 9–12
- Application Overhead Transparency 61
- Appendix A Reproducible 4: Writing Strategy—Summary
- Appendix B Optional Vocabulary Activities: Application Lesson 3
- Paper or cardboard to use when covering the overhead transparency
- Paper or cardboard for each student to use during spelling dictation
- Washable overhead transparency pen

Text Treatment Notes:

- Black text signifies teacher script (exact wording to say to students).
- Green text in parentheses signifies directions or prompts for the teacher.
- Green text signifies answers or examples of answers.
- Green graphics treatment signifies reproduction of Overhead information.
- Green text and green graphics treatment do not appear in the *Student Book.*

ACTIVITY A
Vocabulary

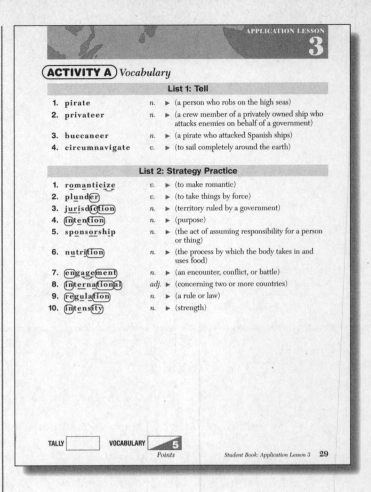

ACTIVITY A *Vocabulary*

List 1: Tell			
1. pirate	n.	▶	(a person who robs on the high seas)
2. privateer	n.	▶	(a crew member of a privately owned ship who attacks enemies on behalf of a government)
3. buccaneer	n.	▶	(a pirate who attacked Spanish ships)
4. circumnavigate	v.	▶	(to sail completely around the earth)

List 2: Strategy Practice			
1. romanticize	v.	▶	(to make romantic)
2. plunder	v.	▶	(to take things by force)
3. jurisdiction	n.	▶	(territory ruled by a government)
4. intention	n.	▶	(purpose)
5. sponsorship	n.	▶	(the act of assuming responsibility for a person or thing)
6. nutrition	n.	▶	(the process by which the body takes in and uses food)
7. engagement	n.	▶	(an encounter, conflict, or battle)
8. international	adj.	▶	(concerning two or more countries)
9. regulation	n.	▶	(a rule or law)
10. intensity	n.	▶	(strength)

TALLY   VOCABULARY **5** *Points*

Student Book: Application Lesson 3   **29**

ACTIVITY PROCEDURE, List 1

(See the *Student Book,* page 29.)

Tell students each word in the list. Then, have students repeat the word and read the definition aloud. For each definition, provide any additional information that may be necessary. Then, have students practice reading the words themselves.

Note A.1-1: See Appendix E, Pronunciation Guide for Unique Words, for correct pronunciations of uncommon vocabulary words.

Note A.1-2: If you wish to emphasize the part of speech, have students say the part of speech before reading the definition.

Use Overhead 9: Activity A
List 1: Tell

1. (Show the top half of Overhead 9.) Before we read the passage, let's read the difficult words. (Point to **pirate**.) The first word is **pirate**. What word?_ Now, read the definition._
2. (Point to **privateer**.) The next word is **privateer**. What word?_ Now, read the definition._
3. (Pronounce each word in List 1, and then have students repeat each word and read the definition.)
4. Open your *Student Book* to **Application Lesson 3**, page 29._
5. Find **Activity A**, **List 1**, in your book._ Let's read the words again. First word._ Next word._ (Continue for all words in List 1.)

ACTIVITY PROCEDURE, List 2

(See the *Student Book,* page 29.)

The second list of words can be read using the part-by-part strategy. Have students circle prefixes and suffixes, then underline the vowels. Using the overhead transparency, assist students in checking their work. Next, have students figure out each word to themselves, then say it aloud. Have them read the definition aloud.

Note A.2-1: Provide additional information for any definitions as needed.

Note A.2-2: If you wish to emphasize the part of speech, have students say the part of speech before reading the definition.

Note A.2-3: If you are teaching older students for whom "thumbs-up" is inappropriate, have students look at you when they can read the word.

Use Overhead 9: Activity A
List 2: Strategy Practice

1. Find **List 2**. For each word, circle the prefixes and suffixes, and underline the vowels. Look up when you are done._
2. (Show the bottom half of Overhead 9.) Before you check your work on List 2, look at item #1. (Point to the second example and the **ize** that is circled.) From now on, you can also circle **ize**. The suffix is /ize/. Say it._ Look at item #5. (Point to the second example and the **ship** that is circled.) From now on, you can also circle **ship**. The suffix is /ship/. Say it._ Now, go back to item #1. Check and fix any mistakes._
3. Go back to the first word again._ Sound out the word to yourself. Put your thumb up when you can read the word. Be sure that it is a real word._ What word?_ Now, read the definition._
4. (Continue Step 3 with all remaining words in List 2.)

Note A.2-4: You may wish to provide additional practice by having students read words to a partner.

ACTIVITY PROCEDURE, List 1 and 2

(See the *Student Book,* page 29.)

Tell students to look in List 1 or List 2 for a word you are think-ing about. Have them circle the number of the word and tell you the word. Explain to students to make a tally mark for each correct word in the Tally box, and then enter the number of tally marks as points in the blank half of the Vocabulary box.

1. Remember, the words I'm thinking about will be in either List 1 or List 2. For every word you correctly identify, circle the number of that word. If the word is correct, make a tally mark in the Tally box at the bottom of page 29. If you don't identify the correct word, don't do anything.
2. I am thinking of a word. Circle the number of the appropriate word.
   - These types of laws or customs are recognized in two or more countries. (Wait.) What word? **international**
   - In historical battles, armies that took things by force were said to do this. (Wait.) What word? **plunder**
   - If we wanted to figure out a person's purpose for doing something, we would ask about this. (Wait.) What word? **intention**
   - Eating a healthy diet leads to this being good. (Wait.) What word? **nutrition**
   - Any territory ruled by a government is under this. (Wait.) What word? **jurisdiction**
3. Count all the tally marks, and enter that number as points in the blank half of the Vocabulary box.

ACTIVITY PROCEDURE, List 3

(See the *Student Book,* page 30.)

The words in the third list are related. Have students use the *REWARDS* Strategies to figure out the first word in each family. Have them read the definition and then read the other two words in the family.

Note A.3-1: Provide additional information for any definitions as needed.

Note A.3-2: If you wish to emphasize the part of speech, have students say the part of speech before reading the definition.

Note A.3-3: If you are teaching older students for whom "thumbs-up" is inap-propriate, have students look at you when they can read the word.

List 3: Word Families

Family 1	inspire	v.	▶	(to influence; to fill with courage)
	inspiration	n.		
	inspirational	adj.		
Family 2	class	n.	▶	(a grouping of things together that are alike)
	classify	v.		
	classification	n.		
Family 3	theory	n.	▶	(an idea that explains an event)
	theoretical	adj.		
	theoretically	adv.		
Family 4	adventure	n.	▶	(a thrilling or exciting experience)
	adventurous	adj.		
	adventuresome	adj.		
Family 5	democracy	n.	▶	(a government run by the people)
	democratic	adj.		
	democratically	adv.		

ACTIVITY B *Spelling Dictation*

1. inspire	4. democracy
2. inspiration	5. democratic
3. inspirational	6. democratically

SPELLING 6 Points

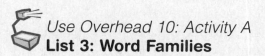

Use Overhead 10: Activity A
List 3: Word Families

1. Turn to page 30. Find **Family 1** in **List 3**. Figure out the first word. Use your pencil if you wish. Put your thumb up when you know the word._ What word?_ Read the definition._
2. Look at the next word in Family 1. Figure out the word._ What word?_
3. Next word. Figure out the word._ What word?_
4. (Repeat Steps 1–3 for all word families in List 3.)

Note A.3-4: You may wish to provide additional practice by having students read a word family to the group or to a partner.

Note A.3-5: Additional vocabulary practice activities are provided in Appendix B of the Teacher's Guide. These activities are optional and can be assigned during class, for homework, or as small group, in-class activities.

ACTIVITY B

Spelling Dictation

ACTIVITY PROCEDURE

(See the *Student Book,* page 30.)

For each word, tell students the word, then have students say the parts of the word to themselves while they write the word. Then, have students enter the number of correctly spelled words as points in the blank half of the Spelling box.

Note B-1: Distribute a piece of light cardboard to students so they can cover their page during spelling dictation. Students can also use the cardboard as a bookmark to quickly locate pages at the beginning of lessons.

 Use Overhead 10: Activity B

1. Find **Activity B**.
2. The first word is **inspire**. What word?_ Say the parts in **inspire** to yourself as you write the word. (Pause and monitor.)
3. (Show **inspire** on the overhead.) Check **inspire**. If you misspelled it, cross it out and write it correctly.
4. The second word is **inspiration**. What word?_ Say the parts in **inspiration** to yourself as you write the word. (Pause and monitor.)
5. (Show **inspiration** on the overhead.) Check **inspiration**. If you misspelled it, cross it out and write it correctly.
6. (Repeat the procedures for the words **inspirational**, **democracy**, **democratic**, and **democratically**.)
7. Count the number of words you spelled correctly, and record that number as points in the blank half of the Spelling box at the bottom of the page.

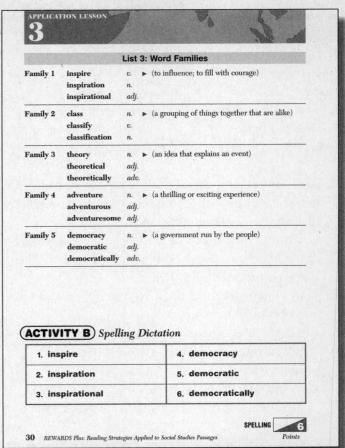

APPLICATION LESSON
3

List 3: Word Families

Family 1	inspire	v.	▶ (to influence; to fill with courage)
	inspiration	n.	
	inspirational	adj.	
Family 2	class	n.	▶ (a grouping of things together that are alike)
	classify	v.	
	classification	n.	
Family 3	theory	n.	▶ (an idea that explains an event)
	theoretical	adj.	
	theoretically	adv.	
Family 4	adventure	n.	▶ (a thrilling or exciting experience)
	adventurous	adj.	
	adventuresome	adj.	
Family 5	democracy	n.	▶ (a government run by the people)
	democratic	adj.	
	democratically	adv.	

ACTIVITY B *Spelling Dictation*

1. inspire	4. democracy
2. inspiration	5. democratic
3. inspirational	6. democratically

SPELLING [6]
Points

ACTIVITY C
Background Knowledge

ACTIVITY PROCEDURE

(See the *Student Book,* page 31.)

Read the Background Knowledge paragraph using one of three methods: read it to students, have students read it together, or call on individual students to read. Examine the timeline and the related graphic together. Then, preview the passage together by examining the title and the headings. Have students tell partners two things the passage will tell about.

1. Turn to page 31. Let's read the paragraph. (Read or ask students to read. Then examine the timeline and graphic together.)
2. Now, let's turn the page and preview the passage. Read the title._ What is the whole passage going to tell about?_
3. Now, let's read the headings. Read the first heading._ Read the next heading._ (Continue until students have read all headings.)
4. Turn to your partner. Without looking, tell two things this passage will tell about._

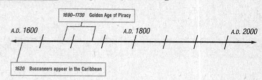

ACTIVITY C *Background Knowledge*

1690–1730   Golden Age of Piracy

A.D. 1600   A.D. 1800   A.D. 2000

1620   Buccaneers appear in the Caribbean

In this article, you will be reading about the Golden Age of Piracy in the 17th and 18th centuries. During this time, many ships sailed from Europe to the New World (North and South America) to obtain land and resources, such as gold. When the ships returned to Europe, they were often laden with valuable cargo, including gold. Pirates desiring these goods had little difficulty attacking the merchant ships because the navies of Spain and England had little presence in the seas off the coast of Florida, in the Caribbean, and off the shores of South America. Because of conflicts between Spain and England, some acts of piracy were supported even by the governments.

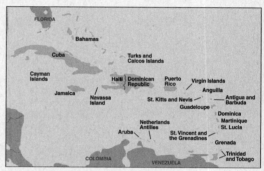

Map of the Caribbean

FLORIDA
Bahamas
Cuba
Turks and Calcos Islands
Cayman Islands
Jamaica
Haiti | Dominican Republic
Puerto Rico
Virgin Islands
Anguilla
Navassa Island
St. Kitts and Nevis
Antigua and Barbuda
Guadeloupe
Dominica
Martinique
St. Lucia
Netherlands Antilles
Aruba
St. Vincent and the Grenadines
Grenada
Trinidad and Tobago
COLOMBIA
VENEZUELA

Student Book: Application Lesson 3   **31**

ACTIVITY D

Passage Reading and Comprehension

ACTIVITY PROCEDURE

(See the *Student Book*, pages 32–33.)

Have students work on reading accuracy by selecting a passage-reading option that best fits your students.

Passage Reading: Accuracy

(Select a passage-reading procedure that matches the size of your group and the competency of your students.

Option A

If you are teaching a small group of students who are having difficulty, use Option A:

Have students read one paragraph silently. Then, call on one student to orally read a paragraph or a portion of the paragraph to the class. Call on students in random order, varying the amount that each student reads.

Option B

If you are teaching a small group with students who are not having difficulty, use Option B:

Have students read the entire article silently, rereading it if they finish before their classmates. Then, call on one student to orally read a paragraph or a portion of a paragraph to the class. Call on students in random order, varying the amount that each student reads.

Option C

If you are teaching a large group with students who are having difficulty, use Option C:

Have students read one paragraph silently. Then, have students read the paragraph to a partner. Alternate partner-reading turns.

Option D

If you are teaching a large group with students who are not having difficulty, use Option D:

Have students read the entire article silently, rereading it if they finish before their classmates. Then, have students read the passage with their partners, alternating on each paragraph.)

APPLICATION LESSON

3

ACTIVITY D *Passage Reading and Comprehension*

Pirates and Piracy

What Are Pirates?

3	Pirates are familiar characters. Books and movies like *Peter Pan* or *Treasure*
15	*Island* have romanticized them. But real pirates are criminals, known especially
26	for attacking ships and stealing their cargo while on the high seas. Piracy is
40	different from other types of robbery because it occurs outside the jurisdiction
52	of any one government. Although pirates existed in Roman times and still do
65	today, the ones who inspired the famous images in the movies lived in the 17th
80	and 18th centuries. This era is known as the "Golden Age of Piracy." (#1)
93	Several different kinds of pirates sailed the seas, stealing goods from other
105	ships. Because they came from various countries and differed in their intentions,
117	they were called pirates, privateers, buccaneers, or marooners. (#2)

Pirates

125	
126	The term *pirates* refers to a general classification of sailors who used their
139	skills to attack other ships. The pirates attacked any ship that seemed to have
153	something worth stealing, whether it was gold, precious cargo, or the ship itself.
166	Unlike other types of pirates, these sailors plundered ships from all nations
178	strictly for their private gain. Bartholomew Roberts, known more commonly as
189	Black Bart, was probably the most successful pirate ever. He captured more
201	than 400 ships in less than four years, traveling the coasts of South America,
215	North America, the Caribbean, and the Bahamas. (#3)

Privateers

222	
223	A privateer traveled on a ship that carried official papers from a government
236	or company. These papers were called a *Letter of Marque*. The Letter of
249	Marque gave the ship permission to act on behalf of a specific government or
263	company. For example, if England was at war with Spain, the English
275	government sponsored privateers to attack and plunder Spanish ships.
284	Theoretically, the Letter of Marque protected the privateers from punishment.
294	But frequently they were tried and punished by the nations they were
306	"permitted" to attack. Sir Francis Drake, famous for being the first Englishman
318	to circumnavigate the globe, was a privateer for England. His ship attacked and
331	looted Spanish ships as he traveled in the name of Queen Elizabeth. (#4)

32 *REWARDS Plus: Reading Strategies Applied to Social Studies Passages*

Passage Reading: Comprehension Questions

(You may wish to ask the following questions as the passage is being read. Numbers corresponding to the questions are indicated at the point at which they could be asked.)

#1 How did piracy differ from other types of robbery?
Piracy took place on the high seas, out of the jurisdiction of a government.

#2 What are the names of different kinds of pirates?
Pirates, privateers, buccaneers, and marooners.

#3 What was the primary goal of pirates?
To steal things of value for personal gain.

#4 How did a privateer differ from a pirate?
A privateer was given a set of official papers from a government that gave permission to attack ships from other countries.

343	**Buccaneers**
344	Buccaneers were French, English, and Dutch pirates who specifically
353	targeted Spanish commerce ships in the Spanish Main (the coastal areas from
365	northern Florida through the Caribbean and along South America). These
375	pirates differed from privateers because they did not have any state sponsorship.
387	They manned smaller ships than did other pirates, focusing on inlets, bays, and
400	other shallow waters. (#5)
403	**Life on a Ship**
407	In the movies, the life of a pirate seems adventurous and exciting. In reality,
421	however, it was difficult and dangerous. The pirates did not eat well because
434	fresh food rotted quickly. They ate mostly hard tack (a dry, plain biscuit) and
448	dried meat, which didn't give them much nutrition. Water often went bad,
460	forcing the pirates to drink beer and rum instead. Many pirates got food
473	poisoning or seasickness. The ships had no toilets and smelled terribly. (#6)
484	Even though the captain was in charge, the ships were often run democratically.
497	The whole crew voted on an issue. Members of the crew obeyed rules, known as
512	*articles.* The articles included rules of conduct for the ship, punishments for crimes
525	committed, and rules of engagement with other ships. (#7)
533	**Pirates Today**
535	Piracy still occurs today in several different forms. People who steal
546	computer software are known as pirates. In the Caribbean and the South China
559	seas, armed men still board ships to take over the crew and cargo. Instead of
574	large sailing ships, they use small motorboats. Although criminals still sail on the
587	high seas, international law, trade regulations, and naval patrols ensure that
598	piracy will never again return to the intensity of its golden years. (#8)
610	

ACTIVITY E *Fluency Building*

Cold Timing [ ]   Practice 1 [ ]

Practice 2 [ ]   Hot Timing [ ]

Student Book: Application Lesson 3   **33**

#5 Why might buccaneers have attacked Spanish ships in the Caribbean?

Spanish ships were likely to be carrying valuable objects, including gold, back to Spain from the New World.

#6 What were some of the hardships faced by pirates on ships?

Ideas: Pirates had very poor quality food, water, and sanitation; the ships smelled bad; the sailors became ill.

#7 Why do you think democratic rule worked on pirate ships?

Ideas: All men participated in making the rules; the men worked better together; cooperation was necessary to carry out criminal acts and to survive hardships.

#8 How does piracy continue today?

Ideas: People steal computer software; in certain parts of the world, people still steal things from ships at sea.

ACTIVITY E
Fluency Building

ACTIVITY PROCEDURE

(See the *Student Book*, page 33.)

In this activity, students will be using a repeated reading procedure of the Activity D article to increase their reading fluency. First, have students do a Cold Timing, in which they whisper-read for one minute as you time them. Have them record in their books the number of correct words they read. Then, have students repeat with one or two practice readings to attempt to beat their Cold Timing. Finally, students exchange books in preparation for a Hot Timing. Have students listen to a partner read for one minute, underlining any word errors, and have them determine the number of correct words their partner read. When both students have completed their Hot Timing, they return each other's books and complete their own Fluency Graphs by indicating the number of words they read correctly in the one-minute Cold Timing and the one-minute Hot Timing.

Note E-1: When assigning partners for this activity, have the stronger reader read first. As a result, the other reader will have one additional practice opportunity.

1. Now, it's time for fluency building.
2. Find the beginning of the passage again. (Pause.)
3. Whisper-read. See how many words you can read in one minute. Begin._ (Time students for one minute.) Stop._ Circle the last word that you read._ Count the number of words you read in one minute. (Assist students in determining the number of words by counting from the number at the beginning of the line to the circled word.)_ Record the number of words you read after **Cold Timing** in **Activity E** at the bottom of page 33._
4. Let's practice again. Return to the beginning of the article. Remember to whisper-read. See if you can beat your Cold Timing. Begin._ (Time students for one minute.) Stop._ Put a box around the last word that you read._ Count the number of words you read in one minute._ Find **Practice 1**._ Record the number of words you read._
5. **Optional** Let's practice one more time before the Hot Timing. Return to the beginning of the article. Remember to whisper-read. See if you can beat your Cold Timing. Begin._ (Time students for one minute.) Stop._ Put a box around the last word that you read._ Count the number of words you read in

one minute._ Find **Practice 2.**_ Record the number of words you read._

6. Please exchange books with your partner._ Partner 1, you are going to read first. Partner 2, you are going to listen carefully to your partner as he or she reads. If your partner makes a mistake or leaves out a word, underline that word. Ones, get ready to read quietly to your partner. Begin._ (Time students for one minute.) Stop._ Twos, cross out the last word that your partner read._ Twos, determine the number of words your partner read in one minute._ Record the number in your partner's book after **Hot Timing.**_

7. Partner 2, you are going to read next. Partner 1, you are going to listen carefully to your partner as he or she reads. If your partner makes a mistake or leaves out a word, underline that word. Twos, get ready to read quietly to your partner. Begin._ (Time students for one minute.) Stop._ Ones, cross out the last word that your partner read._ Ones, determine the number of words your partner read in one minute._ Record the number in your partner's book after **Hot Timing.**_

8. Exchange books._ Turn to the Fluency Graph on the last page of your book, and indicate on the graph the number of Cold Timing and Hot Timing words you read correctly._

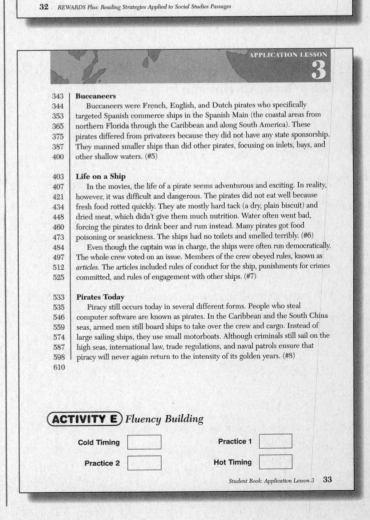

APPLICATION LESSON
3

ACTIVITY D *Passage Reading and Comprehension*

Pirates and Piracy

What Are Pirates?

3   Pirates are familiar characters. Books and movies like *Peter Pan* or *Treasure*
15   *Island* have romanticized them. But real pirates are criminals, known especially
26   for attacking ships and stealing their cargo while on the high seas. Piracy is
40   different from other types of robbery because it occurs outside the jurisdiction
52   of any one government. Although pirates existed in Roman times and still do
65   today, the ones who inspired the famous images in the movies lived in the 17th
80   and 18th centuries. This era is known as the "Golden Age of Piracy." (#1)
93   Several different kinds of pirates sailed the seas, stealing goods from other
105 ships. Because they came from various countries and differed in their intentions,
117 they were called pirates, privateers, buccaneers, or marooners. (#2)

125 **Pirates**
126   The term *pirates* refers to a general classification of sailors who used their
139 skills to attack other ships. The pirates attacked any ship that seemed to have
153 something worth stealing, whether it was gold, precious cargo, or the ship itself.
166 Unlike other types of pirates, these sailors plundered ships from all nations
178 strictly for their private gain. Bartholomew Roberts, known more commonly as
189 Black Bart, was probably the most successful pirate ever. He captured more
201 than 400 ships in less than four years, traveling the coasts of South America,
215 North America, the Caribbean, and the Bahamas. (#3)

222 **Privateers**
223   A privateer traveled on a ship that carried official papers from a government
236 or company. These papers were called a *Letter of Marque.* The Letter of
249 Marque gave the ship permission to act on behalf of a specific government or
263 company. For example, if England was at war with Spain, the English
275 government sponsored privateers to attack and plunder Spanish ships.
284 Theoretically, the Letter of Marque protected the privateers from punishment.
294 But frequently they were tried and punished by the nations they were
306 "permitted" to attack. Sir Francis Drake, famous for being the first Englishman
318 to circumnavigate the globe, was a privateer for England. His ship attacked and
331 looted Spanish ships as he traveled in the name of Queen Elizabeth. (#4)

32   *REWARDS Plus: Reading Strategies Applied to Social Studies Passages*

APPLICATION LESSON
3

343 **Buccaneers**
344   Buccaneers were French, English, and Dutch pirates who specifically
353 targeted Spanish commerce ships in the Spanish Main (the coastal areas from
365 northern Florida through the Caribbean and along South America). These
375 pirates differed from privateers because they did not have any state sponsorship.
387 They manned smaller ships than did other pirates, focusing on inlets, bays, and
400 other shallow waters. (#5)

403 **Life on a Ship**
407   In the movies, the life of a pirate seems adventurous and exciting. In reality,
421 however, it was difficult and dangerous. The pirates did not eat well because
434 fresh food rotted quickly. They ate mostly hard tack (a dry, plain biscuit) and
448 dried meat, which didn't give them much nutrition. Water often went bad,
460 forcing the pirates to drink beer and rum instead. Many pirates got food
473 poisoning or seasickness. The ships had no toilets and smelled terribly. (#6)
484   Even though the captain was in charge, the ships were often run democratically.
497 The whole crew voted on an issue. Members of the crew obeyed rules, known as
512 *articles.* The articles included rules of conduct for the ship, punishments for crimes
525 committed, and rules of engagement with other ships. (#7)

533 **Pirates Today**
535   Piracy still occurs today in several different forms. People who steal
546 computer software are known as pirates. In the Caribbean and the South China
559 seas, armed men still board ships to take over the crew and cargo. Instead of
574 large sailing ships, they use small motorboats. Although criminals still sail on the
587 high seas, international law, trade regulations, and naval patrols ensure that
598 piracy will never again return to the intensity of its golden years. (#8)
610

ACTIVITY E *Fluency Building*

| Cold Timing | | Practice 1 | |
| Practice 2 | | Hot Timing | |

Student Book: Application Lesson 3 **33**

ACTIVITY F

Comprehension Questions— Multiple Choice

ACTIVITY PROCEDURE

(See the *Student Book,* page 34.)

Have students complete item #1. Then, have students share the rationale for their answers. Encourage thoughtful discussion. Proceed item-by-item, emphasizing the rationale for the *best* answer. Have students record points for each correct item.

Note F-1: The correct Multiple Choice answers are circled.

Multiple Choice Comprehension

1. Turn to page 34. Find **Activity F**. Finish item #1. Be ready to explain why you selected your answer. (Wait while students complete the item. Call on individual students. Ask them why they chose their answer and why they eliminated the other choices. Encourage discussion.)

2. (Repeat Step 1 with items #2, #3, and #4.)

3. Count the number of items you got correct, and record that number as points in the blank half of the Multiple Choice Comprehension box._

ACTIVITY F *Comprehension Questions—Multiple Choice*

Comprehension Strategy—Multiple Choice

Step 1: Read the item.
Step 2: Read all of the choices.
Step 3: Think about why each choice might be correct or incorrect. Check the article as needed.
Step 4: From the possible correct choices, select the best answer.

1. (Vocabulary) **Read this sentence from the passage: "Piracy is different from other types of robbery because it occurs outside the *jurisdiction* of any one government." What does the word *jurisdiction* mean in that sentence?**
   a. The intention of a government.   c. Walled cities found within a country.
   b. The territory governed by   d. The jury system of a country.
      one country.

2. (Compare and Contrast) **What was the major difference between *pirates* and *privateers*?**
   a. Pirates were primarily from Spain, while privateers were from England.
   b. Pirates would attack any ship to steal items of value, but privateers focused their attacks on ships of enemy countries.
   c. The goal of the pirates was to steal items of value. However, the goal of privateers was to destroy other ships.
   d. Pirates were sailors by profession, while privateers were military commanders.

3. (Main Idea) **Which sentence gives the best summary of the article?**
   a. During the Golden Age of Piracy, there were a number of types of pirates, including pirates, privateers, and buccaneers.
   b. Pirates attacked ships to take gold.
   c. Life was very difficult for pirates because of the poor quality of their food and water.
   d. While the life of pirates has often been made very glamorous in movies, it was actually very difficult and dangerous.

4. (Cause and Effect) **Why were privateers often tried and punished by the nations they were "permitted" to attack?**
   a. The privateers did not always have the correct papers.
   b. The privateers attacked ships from countries not listed in their papers.
   c. The privateers were punished for attacking and plundering ships of enemy countries.
   d. The privateers did not have the necessary signatures on their papers.

MULTIPLE CHOICE COMPREHENSION 4

34   *REWARDS Plus: Reading Strategies Applied to Social Studies Passages*   *Points*

ACTIVITY G

Expository Writing—Summary

ACTIVITY PROCEDURE

(See the *Student Book*, pages 35–36.)

Have students read the prompt and record the topic of the summary. Next, have them **LIST** details in the Planning Box by referring back to the article. Encourage students to record notes rather than form complete sentences. When they are done with their lists, have them compare their lists of critical details with those of other classmates and the Example Summary Plan.

1. Turn to page 35._ Today, we are going to use the Summary Writing Strategy.
2. Read the prompt._ Write the topic "**Pirates and Piracy**" in the Planning Box.
3. Read **Step 1** of the Summary Writing Strategy._ Now, reread the article and write **important** details in your plan on page 35. You may wish to write one important idea from each paragraph._ (Monitor carefully as students record details.)
4. Compare your details to your partner's list._

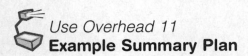

Use Overhead 11
Example Summary Plan

5. Let's read the list of details on the overhead. Your list should have some of the same ideas, but it does not need to be exactly the same._ If you want to fix up your list, do that now._

ACTIVITY PROCEDURE

Next, have students complete the additional steps in the Summary Writing Strategy. Have them reread their lists and **CROSS OUT** any weak or unimportant details. Then, have students **CONNECT** details that could go together in one sentence, **NUMBER** their ideas in a logical order, and **WRITE** their summaries on a separate piece of paper. When they are done, have them **EDIT** their paragraphs, revising for clarity and proofreading for errors in spelling, capitalization, and punctuation.

Have students read their summaries to their partners. Then, read the Example Summary.

Have students read each of the attributes on the rubric, examine their partners' summaries, and circle either "Yes" or "Fix up." Give students time to make changes in their summaries.

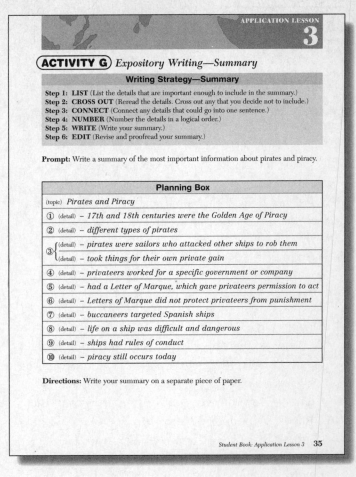

ACTIVITY G *Expository Writing—Summary*

APPLICATION LESSON

3

Writing Strategy—Summary

Step 1: **LIST** (List the details that are important enough to include in the summary.)
Step 2: **CROSS OUT** (Reread the details. Cross out any that you decide not to include.)
Step 3: **CONNECT** (Connect any details that could go into one sentence.)
Step 4: **NUMBER** (Number the details in a logical order.)
Step 5: **WRITE** (Write your summary.)
Step 6: **EDIT** (Revise and proofread your summary.)

Prompt: Write a summary of the most important information about pirates and piracy.

Planning Box
(topic) *Pirates and Piracy*
① (detail) – *17th and 18th centuries were the Golden Age of Piracy*
② (detail) – *different types of pirates*
③ (detail) – *pirates were sailors who attacked other ships to rob them* / (detail) – *took things for their own private gain*
④ (detail) – *privateers worked for a specific government or company*
⑤ (detail) – *had a Letter of Marque, which gave privateers permission to act*
⑥ (detail) – *Letters of Marque did not protect privateers from punishment*
⑦ (detail) – *buccaneers targeted Spanish ships*
⑧ (detail) – *life on a ship was difficult and dangerous*
⑨ (detail) – *ships had rules of conduct*
⑩ (detail) – *piracy still occurs today*

Directions: Write your summary on a separate piece of paper.

Student Book: Application Lesson 3   **35**

Optional: During or after the class session, fill in the third column of the rubric chart and assign points to the student summaries.

6. Read **Step 2**._ If you have any less-important or unimportant details, cross them out now._ What details did you eliminate and why? (Call on individual students.)
7. Read **Step 3**._ Please draw brackets on your list to connect ideas._ (Monitor carefully.)
8. Read **Step 4**._ Now, number the ideas in a logical order. If you have two or more connected ideas, give them only one number._ (Monitor.)
9. Read **Step 5**._ Write your summary._ (Monitor.)
10. Read **Step 6**._ Reread your summary. Check to be sure your summary is easy to understand. Fix any errors you find in spelling, capitalization, and punctuation._ (Monitor.)
11. Read your summary to your partner._

Use Overhead 12
Example Summary

12. Look at the overhead. Let's read this Example Summary. Yours doesn't need to be exactly the same, but it should be similar.

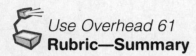

Use Overhead 61
Rubric—Summary

13. Turn to page 36. Today, you will be evaluating your partner's summary. You will use the questions in this rubric to determine what your partner needs to edit.

14. Please exchange summaries and books with your partner. Read the question for attribute 1._ Reread your partner's first sentence, and look for the topic and main idea. Circle "Yes" if your partner has it, or circle "Fix up" if your partner needs to revise it._ If you circled "Fix up," your partner will work on it later.

15. Read the question for attribute 2._ Reread the rest of your partner's sentences, and determine if your partner included important details. Circle "Yes" or "Fix up."_ If you circled "Fix up," your partner will work on it later.

16. Complete the ratings for the remaining questions. Remember to read each question, and then look at your partner's summary to make sure the criteria have been met.

17. (When the evaluation is complete, have students return the summaries and books to their partners. Give students time to make any necessary changes to their summaries. Have students enter their points in the blank half of the Writing box below the rubric.)

18. (Distribute Appendix A Reproducible 4: Writing Strategy—Summary. Have students place this in a notebook or a folder for future reference.)

APPLICATION LESSON
3

Rubric—Summary	Student or Partner Rating	Teacher Rating
1. Did the author state the topic and the main idea in the first sentence?	Yes Fix up	Yes No
2. Did the author focus on important details?	Yes Fix up	Yes No
3. Did the author combine details in some of the sentences?	Yes Fix up	Yes No
4. Is the summary easy to understand?	Yes Fix up	Yes No
5. Did the author correctly spell words, particularly the words found in the article?	Yes Fix up	Yes No
6. Did the author use correct capitalization, capitalizing the first word in the sentence and proper names of people, places, and things?	Yes Fix up	Yes No
7. Did the author use correct punctuation, including a period at the end of each sentence?	Yes Fix up	Yes No

WRITING 7
Points

Application Lesson 4

Materials Needed:

- *Student Book:* Application Lesson 4
- Application Overhead Transparencies 13–16
- Appendix B Optional Vocabulary Activities: Application Lesson 4
- Paper or cardboard to use when covering the overhead transparency
- Paper or cardboard for each student to use during spelling dictation
- Washable overhead transparency pen

Text Treatment Notes:

- Black text signifies teacher script (exact wording to say to students).
- Green text in parentheses signifies directions or prompts for the teacher.
- Green text signifies answers or examples of answers.
- Green graphics treatment signifies reproduction of Overhead information.
- Green text and green graphics treatment do not appear in the *Student Book.*

ACTIVITY A
Vocabulary

ACTIVITY PROCEDURE, List 1

(See the *Student Book*, page 37.)

Tell students each word in the list. Then, have students repeat the word and read the definition aloud. For each definition, provide any additional information that may be necessary. Then, have students practice reading the words themselves.

Note A.1-1: See Appendix E, Pronunciation Guide for Unique Words, for correct pronunciations of uncommon vocabulary words.

Note A.1-2: If you wish to emphasize the part of speech, have students say the part of speech before reading the definition.

Use Overhead 13: Activity A
List 1: Tell

1. (Show the top half of Overhead 13.) Before we read the passage, let's read the difficult words. (Point to **Britain**.) The first word is **Britain**. What word?_ Now, read the definition._
2. (Point to **empire**.) The next word is **empire**. What word?_ Now, read the definition._
3. (Pronounce each word in List 1, and then have students repeat each word and read the definition.)
4. Open your *Student Book* to **Application Lesson 4**, page 37._
5. Find **Activity A**, **List 1**, in your book._ Let's read the words again. First word._ Next word._ (Continue for all words in List 1.)

ACTIVITY PROCEDURE, List 2

(See the *Student Book*, page 37.)

Have students circle prefixes and suffixes, then underline the vowels. Using the overhead transparency, assist students in checking their work. Next, have students figure out each word to themselves, then say it aloud. Have them read the definition aloud.

Note A.2-1: Provide additional information for any definitions as needed.

Note A.2-2: If you wish to emphasize the part of speech, have students say the part of speech before reading the definition.

Note A.2-3: If you are teaching older students for whom "thumbs-up" is inappropriate, have students look at you when they can read the word.

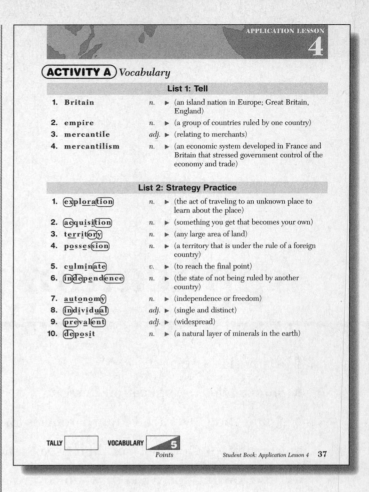

ACTIVITY A *Vocabulary*

List 1: Tell

1.	Britain	n. ▶	(an island nation in Europe; Great Britain, England)
2.	empire	n. ▶	(a group of countries ruled by one country)
3.	mercantile	adj. ▶	(relating to merchants)
4.	mercantilism	n. ▶	(an economic system developed in France and Britain that stressed government control of the economy and trade)

List 2: Strategy Practice

1.	exploration	n. ▶	(the act of traveling to an unknown place to learn about the place)
2.	acquisition	n. ▶	(something you get that becomes your own)
3.	territory	n. ▶	(any large area of land)
4.	possession	n. ▶	(a territory that is under the rule of a foreign country)
5.	culminate	v. ▶	(to reach the final point)
6.	independence	n. ▶	(the state of not being ruled by another country)
7.	autonomy	n. ▶	(independence or freedom)
8.	individual	adj. ▶	(single and distinct)
9.	prevalent	adj. ▶	(widespread)
10.	deposit	n. ▶	(a natural layer of minerals in the earth)

TALLY [ ] VOCABULARY 5 Points

Student Book: Application Lesson 4 **37**

Use Overhead 13: Activity A
List 2: Strategy Practice

1. Find **List 2**. Circle the prefixes and suffixes, and underline the vowels. Look up when you are done._
2. (Show the bottom half of Overhead 13.) Now, check and fix any mistakes._
3. Go back to the first word._ Sound out the word to yourself. Put your thumb up when you can read the word. Be sure that it is a real word._ What word?_ Now, read the definition._
4. (Continue Step 3 with all remaining words in List 2.)

Note A.2-4: You may wish to provide additional practice by having students read words to a partner.

ACTIVITY PROCEDURE, List 1 and 2

(See the *Student Book*, page 37.)

Tell students to look in List 1 or List 2 for a word you are thinking about. Have them circle the number of the word and tell you the word. Explain to students to make a tally mark for each correct word in the Tally box, and then enter the number of tally marks as points in the blank half of the Vocabulary box.

1. Remember, the words I'm thinking about will be in either List 1 or List 2. For every word you correctly identify, make a tally mark in the Tally box at the bottom of page 37. If you don't identify the correct word, don't do anything.
2. Circle the number of the appropriate word.
   - Something that is very widespread is said to be this. (Wait.) What word? **prevalent**
   - England is the largest part of this island nation in Europe. (Wait.) What word? **Britain**
   - When you get something that you keep as your own, you have one of these. (Wait.) What word? **acquisition**
   - As opposed to a group right or responsibility, this is a single and distinct right or responsibility. (Wait.) What word? **individual**
   - When discussions reach an agreement or a final point, they are said to do this. (Wait.) What word? **culminate**
3. Count all the tally marks, and enter that number as points in the blank half of the Vocabulary box.

ACTIVITY PROCEDURE, List 3

(See the *Student Book*, page 38.)

The words in the third list are related. Have students use the *REWARDS* Strategies to figure out the first word in each family. Have them read the definition and then read the other two words in the family.

Note A.3-1: Provide additional information for any definitions as needed.

Note A.3-2: If you wish to emphasize the part of speech, have students say the part of speech before reading the definition.

Note A.3-3: If you are teaching older students for whom "thumbs-up" is inappropriate, have students look at you when they can read the word.

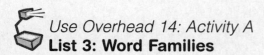
Use Overhead 14: Activity A
List 3: Word Families

1. Turn to page 38. Find **Family 1** in **List 3**. Figure out the first word. Use your pencil if you wish. Put

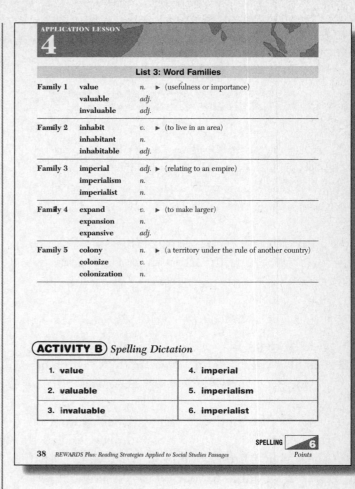

APPLICATION LESSON
4

List 3: Word Families			
Family 1	value	n. ▶	(usefulness or importance)
	valuable	adj.	
	invaluable	adj.	
Family 2	inhabit	v. ▶	(to live in an area)
	inhabitant	n.	
	inhabitable	adj.	
Family 3	imperial	adj. ▶	(relating to an empire)
	imperialism	n.	
	imperialist	n.	
Family 4	expand	v. ▶	(to make larger)
	expansion	n.	
	expansive	adj.	
Family 5	colony	n. ▶	(a territory under the rule of another country)
	colonize	v.	
	colonization	n.	

ACTIVITY B *Spelling Dictation*

1. value		4. imperial	
2. valuable		5. imperialism	
3. invaluable		6. imperialist	

SPELLING **6**

your thumb up when you know the word._ What word?_ Read the definition._

2. Look at the next word in Family 1. Figure out the word._ What word?_
3. Next word. Figure out the word._ What word?_
4. (Repeat Steps 1–3 for all word families in List 3.)

Note A.3-4: You may wish to provide additional practice by having students read a word family to the group or to a partner.

Note A.3-5: Additional vocabulary practice activities are provided in Appendix B of the Teacher's Guide. These activities are optional and can be assigned during class, for homework, or as small group, in-class activities.

ACTIVITY B
Spelling Dictation

ACTIVITY PROCEDURE

(See the *Student Book*, page 38.)

For each word, tell students the word, then have students say the parts of the word to themselves while they write the word. Then, have students enter the number of correctly spelled words as points in the blank half of the Spelling box.

Note B-1: Distribute a piece of light cardboard to students so they can cover their page during spelling dictation. Students can also use the cardboard as a bookmark to quickly locate pages at the beginning of lessons.

 Use Overhead 14: Activity B

1. Find **Activity B**.
2. The first word is **value**. What word?_ Say the parts in **value** to yourself as you write the word. (Pause and monitor.)
3. (Show **value** on the overhead.) Check **value**. If you misspelled it, cross it out and write it correctly.
4. The second word is **valuable**. What word?_ Say the parts in **valuable** to yourself as you write the word. (Pause and monitor.)
5. (Show **valuable** on the overhead.) Check **valuable**. If you misspelled it, cross it out and write it correctly.
6. (Repeat the procedures for the words **invaluable**, **imperial**, **imperialism**, and **imperialist**.)
7. Count the number of words you spelled correctly, and record that number as points in the blank half of the Spelling box at the bottom of the page.

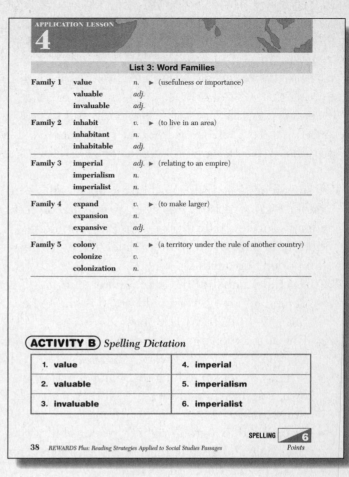

APPLICATION LESSON

4

List 3: Word Families

Family 1	value	n.	▶ (usefulness or importance)
	valuable	adj.	
	invaluable	adj.	
Family 2	inhabit	v.	▶ (to live in an area)
	inhabitant	n.	
	inhabitable	adj.	
Family 3	imperial	adj.	▶ (relating to an empire)
	imperialism	n.	
	imperialist	n.	
Family 4	expand	v.	▶ (to make larger)
	expansion	n.	
	expansive	adj.	
Family 5	colony	n.	▶ (a territory under the rule of another country)
	colonize	v.	
	colonization	n.	

ACTIVITY B *Spelling Dictation*

1. value	4. imperial
2. valuable	5. imperialism
3. invaluable	6. imperialist

SPELLING [6]
Points

38 REWARDS Plus: Reading Strategies Applied to Social Studies Passages

ACTIVITY C

Background Knowledge

ACTIVITY PROCEDURE

(See the *Student Book,* page 39.)

Read the Background Knowledge paragraph using one of three methods: read it to students, have students read it together, or call on individual students to read. Examine the timeline and the related graphic together. Then, preview the passage together by examining the title and the headings. Have students tell partners two things the passage will tell about.

1. Turn to page 39. Let's read the paragraph. (Read or ask students to read. Then examine the timeline and graphic together.)
2. Now, let's turn the page and preview the passage. Read the title.＿ What is the whole passage going to tell about?＿
3. Now, let's read the headings. Read the first heading.＿ Read the next heading.＿ (Continue until students have read all headings.)
4. Turn to your partner. Without looking, tell two things this passage will tell about.＿

ACTIVITY C *Background Knowledge*

A.D. 1600 — 1760 Britain gains Canada — A.D. 1800 — 1841 Britain acquires Hong Kong — A.D. 2000

1788 Britain settles Australia — 1922 British Empire begins to break apart

Like many European countries, Great Britain sought to expand its power and wealth by acquiring territories overseas. In this map, you can see the extent of Britain's territories (in black) as of 1914. Some of its largest possessions included Canada in North America, Australia, and India, on the continent of Asia. By examining the map, you will also notice some major possessions in Africa: Nigeria, Kenya, and South Africa. While these countries later became independent, they were all influenced by British culture.

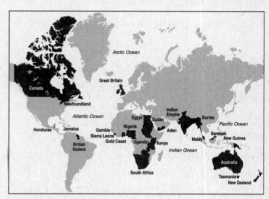

Map of the British Empire, Early 1900s

Student Book: Application Lesson 4 **39**

ACTIVITY D

Passage Reading and Comprehension

ACTIVITY PROCEDURE

(See the *Student Book*, pages 40–41.)

Have students work on reading accuracy by selecting a passage-reading option that best fits your students.

Passage Reading: Accuracy

(Select a passage-reading procedure that matches the size of your group and the competency of your students.

Option A

If you are teaching a small group of students who are having difficulty, use Option A:

Have students read one paragraph silently. Then, call on one student to orally read a paragraph or a portion of the paragraph to the class. Call on students in random order, varying the amount that each student reads.

Option B

If you are teaching a small group with students who are not having difficulty, use Option B:

Have students read the entire article silently, rereading it if they finish before their classmates. Then, call on one student to orally read a paragraph or a portion of a paragraph to the class. Call on students in random order, varying the amount that each student reads.

Option C

If you are teaching a large group with students who are having difficulty, use Option C:

Have students read one paragraph silently. Then, have students read the paragraph to a partner. Alternate partner-reading turns.

Option D

If you are teaching a large group with students who are not having difficulty, use Option D:

Have students read the entire article silently, rereading it if they finish before their classmates. Then, have students read the passage with their partners, alternating on each paragraph.)

APPLICATION LESSON
4

ACTIVITY D *Passage Reading and Comprehension*

The British Empire

12   Britain, like many European nations, rushed to explore and expand during the
23   15th and 16th centuries. Explorers from England, France, Spain, and Portugal
37   sailed the seas, discovering new lands and people. Of all the countries that sought
51   new trade routes and new worlds, Britain alone turned its discoveries into a vast
64   empire that would continue well into the 1900s. The growth of the British
     Empire had far-reaching effects on world politics and trade. (#1)

74   **A Mercantile Empire**
77   Initially, the expansion of the British Empire was based on *mercantilism*, or
89   trade. Britain realized that its own land had inadequate resources. It needed to
102   look to other lands for goods. The empire began with the exploration and
115   acquisition of the eastern coast of North America and with the West Indies, a
129   chain of islands stretching from the coast of Florida to South America. The
142   British traded goods for slaves in the West Indies and on the western coast of
157   Africa, where they also had settlements. These slaves were taken to southern
169   colonies, such as Virginia, Georgia, and South Carolina. The slaves supported
180   the growing of cotton and tobacco, goods that were then shipped back to
193   Britain, along with rum and sugar from the West Indies. (#2)
203   Meanwhile, the East India Company, a British company, had established a
214   stronghold in India. The company set up valuable trading posts for spices and
227   other goods. Eventually, the East India Company would come to rule India.
239   That rule would eventually be turned over to the British government. (#3)

250   **Expansion Continues**
252   The British Empire continued to expand for trade reasons. But there were
264   other reasons involved as well. Some of Britain's possessions in eastern Asia
276   were acquired as a result of several wars fought in that region in the 19th
291   century. Other countries were added for more unique reasons. Australia was
302   colonized as a penal colony (a place to send criminals for punishment). But 30
316   years after the first convicts came to Australia, Britain opened it to free citizens
330   and eventually stopped sending criminals there. South Africa, originally
339   colonized by the Dutch, was taken over by the British to try to keep the French
355   away. Once Britain had the land, they felt it was their duty to bring "civilized"
370   British culture to the land's inhabitants. British culture was prevalent throughout

40   REWARDS Plus: Reading Strategies Applied to Social Studies Passages

Passage Reading: Comprehension Questions

(You may wish to ask the following questions as the passage is being read. Numbers corresponding to the questions are indicated at the point at which they could be asked.)

#1 What are some possible reasons that a small nation such as Great Britain might want to expand its territories?
Ideas: To obtain valuable natural resources; to have places to sell its goods; to increase its power through acquisitions; to establish distant military posts to protect it; to increase its population.

#2 Britain's empire was based on trade, or mercantilism. What were some of the trade goods?
Ideas: Cotton, tobacco, rum, and sugar.

381 the world. By 1909, 20% of the land and 23% of the population of the world
397 belonged to the British Empire. (#4)

402 **Wealth Brings Power**
405 The British maintained and expanded their empire through trade and other
416 wealth-building. Many of their territories turned out to be rich in valuable
429 natural resources, adding to the wealth Britain would gain from colonies. West
441 Africa, for example, had rich deposits of gold and plenty of ivory. South Africa
455 had vast diamond mines, which are still the principal source of diamonds today.
468 The American colonies had furs, lumber, cotton, and tobacco. Britain was both
480 rich and powerful. (#5)

483 **The Decline of the Empire**
488 This vast, wealthy empire covered much of the earth. People said that the
501 sun never set on the British Empire. Why then does it no longer exist? The
516 primary reason is that the individual territories got tired of being under British
529 rule. Many of them wanted self-government. In some cases—as in Canada and
543 Australia—the British government granted that autonomy. But in other cases,
554 the colonists fought for independence, as they did in America and India.
566 Gradually, Britain's possessions dwindled. This decline of a great empire
576 culminated with the return of Hong Kong to China in 1997. Today, Britain
589 retains only a few small territories, which are too tiny to govern themselves. (#6)
602

ACTIVITY E *Fluency Building*

Cold Timing		Practice 1	
Practice 2		Hot Timing	

Student Book: Application Lesson 4 **41**

#3 Why might the British government have wanted to take over rule of India?

Ideas: To increase its power; to have access to the goods produced in India, such as spices; to have a place to sell its own goods; to have a foothold in Asia.

#4 Why was Australia originally colonized?

To establish a penal colony where prisoners could be sent.

#5 Why did Great Britain become a wealthy nation?

Its territories had valuable resources, such as gold, diamonds, lumber, tobacco, and ivory.

#6 Why did the British Empire decline?

Its territories sought independence.

ACTIVITY E
Fluency Building

ACTIVITY PROCEDURE

(See the *Student Book,* page 41.)

In this activity, students will be using a repeated reading procedure of the Activity D article to increase their reading fluency. First, have students do a Cold Timing, in which they whisper-read for one minute as you time them. Have them record in their books the number of correct words they read. Then, have students repeat with one or two practice readings to attempt to beat their Cold Timing. Finally, students exchange books in preparation for a Hot Timing. Have students listen to a partner read for one minute, underlining any word errors, and have them determine the number of correct words their partner read. When both students have completed their Hot Timing, they return each other's books and complete their own Fluency Graphs by indicating the number of words they read correctly in the one-minute Cold Timing and the one-minute Hot Timing.

Note E-1: When assigning partners for this activity, have the stronger reader read first. As a result, the other reader will have one additional practice opportunity.

1. Now, it's time for fluency building.
2. Find the beginning of the passage again. (Pause.)
3. Whisper-read. See how many words you can read in one minute. Begin._ (Time students for one minute.) Stop._ Circle the last word that you read._ Count the number of words you read in one minute. (Assist students in determining the number of words by counting from the number at the beginning of the line to the circled word._) Record the number of words you read after **Cold Timing** in **Activity E** at the bottom of page 41._
4. Let's practice again. Return to the beginning of the article. Remember to whisper-read. See if you can beat your Cold Timing. Begin._ (Time students for one minute.) Stop._ Put a box around the last word that you read._ Count the number of words you read in one minute._ Find **Practice 1**._ Record the number of words you read._
5. **Optional** Let's practice one more time before the Hot Timing. Return to the beginning of the article. Remember to whisper-read. See if you can beat your Cold Timing. Begin._ (Time students for one minute.) Stop._ Put a box around the last word that you read._ Count the number of words you read in

one minute._ Find **Practice 2**._ Record the number of words you read._

6. Please exchange books with your partner._ Partner 1, you are going to read first. Partner 2, you are going to listen carefully to your partner as he or she reads. If your partner makes a mistake or leaves out a word, underline that word. Ones, get ready to read quietly to your partner. Begin._ (Time students for one minute.) Stop._ Twos, cross out the last word that your partner read._ Twos, determine the number of words your partner read in one minute._ Record the number in your partner's book after **Hot Timing**._

7. Partner 2, you are going to read next. Partner 1, you are going to listen carefully to your partner as he or she reads. If your partner makes a mistake or leaves out a word, underline that word. Twos, get ready to read quietly to your partner. Begin._ (Time students for one minute.) Stop._ Ones, cross out the last word that your partner read._ Ones, determine the number of words your partner read in one minute._ Record the number in your partner's book after **Hot Timing**._

8. Exchange books._ Turn to the Fluency Graph on the last page of your book, and indicate on the graph the number of Cold Timing and Hot Timing words you read correctly._

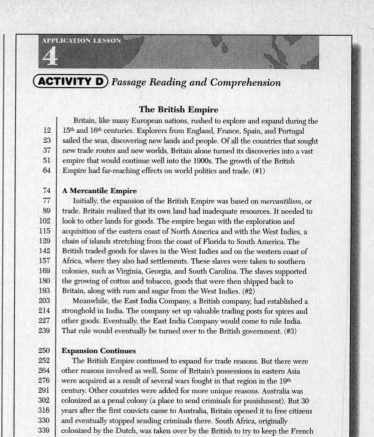

ACTIVITY D *Passage Reading and Comprehension*

The British Empire

12	Britain, like many European nations, rushed to explore and expand during the
23	15th and 16th centuries. Explorers from England, France, Spain, and Portugal
37	sailed the seas, discovering new lands and people. Of all the countries that sought
51	new trade routes and new worlds, Britain alone turned its discoveries into a vast
64	empire that would continue well into the 1900s. The growth of the British
	Empire had far-reaching effects on world politics and trade. (#1)
74	**A Mercantile Empire**
77	Initially, the expansion of the British Empire was based on *mercantilism*, or
89	trade. Britain realized that its own land had inadequate resources. It needed to
102	look to other lands for goods. The empire began with the exploration and
115	acquisition of the eastern coast of North America and with the West Indies, a
129	chain of islands stretching from the coast of Florida to South America. The
142	British traded goods for slaves in the West Indies and on the western coast of
157	Africa, where they also had settlements. These slaves were taken to southern
169	colonies, such as Virginia, Georgia, and South Carolina. The slaves supported
180	the growing of cotton and tobacco, goods that were then shipped back to
193	Britain, along with rum and sugar from the West Indies. (#2)
203	Meanwhile, the East India Company, a British company, had established a
214	stronghold in India. The company set up valuable trading posts for spices and
227	other goods. Eventually, the East India Company would come to rule India.
239	That rule would eventually be turned over to the British government. (#3)
250	**Expansion Continues**
252	The British Empire continued to expand for trade reasons. But there were
264	other reasons involved as well. Some of Britain's possessions in eastern Asia
276	were acquired as a result of several wars fought in that region in the 19th
291	century. Other countries were added for more unique reasons. Australia was
302	colonized as a penal colony (a place to send criminals for punishment). But 30
316	years after the first convicts came to Australia, Britain opened it to free citizens
330	and eventually stopped sending criminals there. South Africa, originally
339	colonized by the Dutch, was taken over by the British to try to keep the French
355	away. Once Britain had the land, they felt it was their duty to bring "civilized"
370	British culture to the land's inhabitants. British culture was prevalent throughout

40 *REWARDS Plus: Reading Strategies Applied to Social Studies Passages*

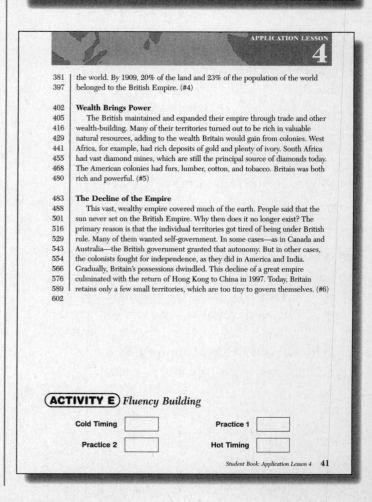

381	the world. By 1909, 20% of the land and 23% of the population of the world
397	belonged to the British Empire. (#4)
402	**Wealth Brings Power**
405	The British maintained and expanded their empire through trade and other
416	wealth-building. Many of their territories turned out to be rich in valuable
429	natural resources, adding to the wealth Britain would gain from colonies. West
441	Africa, for example, had rich deposits of gold and plenty of ivory. South Africa
455	had vast diamond mines, which are still the principal source of diamonds today.
468	The American colonies had furs, lumber, cotton, and tobacco. Britain was both
480	rich and powerful. (#5)
483	**The Decline of the Empire**
488	This vast, wealthy empire covered much of the earth. People said that the
501	sun never set on the British Empire. Why then does it no longer exist? The
516	primary reason is that the individual territories got tired of being under British
529	rule. Many of them wanted self-government. In some cases—as in Canada and
543	Australia—the British government granted that autonomy. But in other cases,
554	the colonists fought for independence, as they did in America and India.
566	Gradually, Britain's possessions dwindled. This decline of a great empire
576	culminated with the return of Hong Kong to China in 1997. Today, Britain
589	retains only a few small territories, which are too tiny to govern themselves. (#6)
602	

ACTIVITY E *Fluency Building*

Cold Timing		Practice 1	
Practice 2		Hot Timing	

Student Book: Application Lesson 4 **41**

ACTIVITY F

Comprehension Questions— Multiple Choice and Short Answer

ACTIVITY PROCEDURE

(See the *Student Book*, page 42.)

Have students complete item #1. Then, have students share the rationale for their answers. Encourage thoughtful discussion. Proceed item-by-item, emphasizing the rationale for the *best* answer. Have students record points for each correct item.

Note F-1: The correct Multiple Choice answers are circled.

Multiple Choice Comprehension

1. Turn to page 42. Find **Activity F**. Finish item #1. Be ready to explain why you selected your answer. (Wait while students complete the item. Call on individual students. Ask them why they chose their answer and why they eliminated the other choices. Encourage discussion.)
2. (Repeat Step 1 with items #2, #3, and #4.)
3. Count the number of items you got correct, and record that number as points in the blank half of the Multiple Choice Comprehension box.⌐

ACTIVITY PROCEDURE

(See the *Student Book*, page 43.)

Have students read each step in the Short Answer Strategy. Stress the importance of changing the question into part of the answer. Have students read question #1 and Jonathan's answer. Have students circle words in Jonathan's answer that come from the question. Repeat the same procedure for question #2. Explain that two points will be awarded for each question's answer: one point for changing the question into part of the answer, and one point for correctness of the answer (total of 4 points possible for two complete answers).

Short Answer Comprehension

1. Turn to page 43. Often, you have to complete short-answer items on tests and assignments. Today, we are going to learn a strategy for completing these items.
2. Let's read the steps in the Short Answer Strategy at the top of the page. Read **Step 1**.⌐

APPLICATION LESSON

4

ACTIVITY F *Comprehension Questions— Multiple Choice and Short Answer*

Comprehension Strategy—Multiple Choice

Step 1: Read the item.
Step 2: Read all of the choices.
Step 3: Think about why each choice might be correct or incorrect. Check the article as needed.
Step 4: From the possible correct choices, select the best answer.

1. (Main Idea) **In the article, the statement "the sun never set on the British Empire" means that:**
   a. the British Empire never experienced the darkness of night.
   b. the glory of the British Empire was as bright as the sun.
   c. the British Empire was so wonderful that nothing could dim its greatness.
   ⓓ the British Empire was large and worldwide.

2. (Cause and Effect) **What was the *major* reason Great Britain acquired territories overseas?**
   a. Great Britain wanted to obtain slaves who could work in the colonies.
   b. Great Britain wanted to bring its culture to other parts of the world.
   ⓒ Great Britain wanted to expand its wealth and power.
   d. Great Britain wanted to trade in Asia.

3. (Main Idea) **If this article were given a new title, which would be best?**
   a. *British Rule in India, South Africa, and Australia*
   ⓑ *The Rise and Fall of the British Empire*
   c. *Sunrise Over the British Empire*
   d. *The Growth of Trade*

4. (Cause and Effect) **Why did many of the territories of the British Empire want freedom from British rule?**
   ⓐ They wanted to govern themselves.
   b. They wanted lower taxes.
   c. They wanted to select their own language and country name.
   d. They wanted to trade with countries other than Great Britain.

MULTIPLE CHOICE COMPREHENSION | 4
Points

42   REWARDS Plus: Reading Strategies Applied to Social Studies Passages

---

APPLICATION LESSON

4

Comprehension Strategy—Short Answer

Step 1: Read the item.
Step 2: Turn the question into part of the answer and write it down.
Step 3: Think of the answer or locate the answer in the article.
Step 4: Complete your answer.

1. **Why was expansion of the British Empire initially based on trade?**
   The British Empire was initially based on trade because Britain wanted the power, wealth, and resources that could come from possessions overseas.

2. **What are some of the resources Britain found in its territories that helped to make it a wealthy country?**
   Some of the resources Britain found in its territories that helped to make it a wealthy country included gold, ivory, diamonds, furs, and lumber.

SHORT ANSWER COMPREHENSION | 4 | 4
Points

ACTIVITY G *Expository Writing—Summary*

Writing Strategy—Summary

Step 1: LIST (List the details that are important enough to include in the summary.)
Step 2: CROSS OUT (Reread the details. Cross out any that you decide not to include.)
Step 3: CONNECT (Connect any details that could go into one sentence.)
Step 4: NUMBER (Number the details in a logical order.)
Step 5: WRITE (Write your summary.)
Step 6: EDIT (Revise and proofread your summary.)

Prompt: Write a summary of the information on the British Empire.

Student Book: Application Lesson 4   **43**

Teacher's Guide: Application Lesson 4 ▪ 103

3. Read **Step 2.** This is the most important step. If you turn the question into part of the answer, you are more likely to have an accurate answer that is a complete sentence.

4. Read **Step 3.** When the article or material is available, it is useful to look back at it to locate the answer. However, in some cases, you will have to remember or create the answer.

5. Read **Step 4.**

6. Today, we are going to look at Jonathan's answers. Read question #1. Now, read Jonathan's answer. Jonathan turned the question into part of the answer before completely answering it. Please circle the words in his answer that are from the question. (When students are done, give them feedback.)

7. Read question #2. Now, read Jonathan's answer. Please circle the words in his answer that are from the question. (When students are done, give them feedback.)

8. You can see that with both answers complete and correct, the score in the Short Answer Comprehension box is 4 out of a possible 4 points. Jonathan's answers were correct, and he used words from the question in his answer. In the next lesson, you will be using this strategy to answer questions.

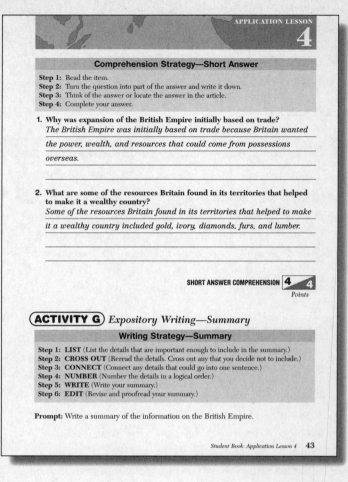

APPLICATION LESSON 4

Comprehension Strategy—Short Answer

Step 1: Read the item.
Step 2: Turn the question into part of the answer and write it down.
Step 3: Think of the answer or locate the answer in the article.
Step 4: Complete your answer.

1. Why was expansion of the British Empire initially based on trade?
The British Empire was initially based on trade because Britain wanted the power, wealth, and resources that could come from possessions overseas.

2. What are some of the resources Britain found in its territories that helped to make it a wealthy country?
Some of the resources Britain found in its territories that helped to make it a wealthy country included gold, ivory, diamonds, furs, and lumber.

SHORT ANSWER COMPREHENSION **4** / **4** Points

ACTIVITY G *Expository Writing—Summary*

Writing Strategy—Summary

Step 1: **LIST** (List the details that are important enough to include in the summary.)
Step 2: **CROSS OUT** (Reread the details. Cross out any that you decide not to include.)
Step 3: **CONNECT** (Connect any details that could go into one sentence.)
Step 4: **NUMBER** (Number the details in a logical order.)
Step 5: **WRITE** (Write your summary.)
Step 6: **EDIT** (Revise and proofread your summary.)

Prompt: Write a summary of the information on the British Empire.

Student Book: Application Lesson 4 **43**

ACTIVITY G
Expository Writing—Summary

ACTIVITY PROCEDURE

(See the *Student Book,* pages 43–44.)

Have students read the prompt and record the topic of the summary. Next, have them **LIST** details in the Planning Box by referring back to the article. Encourage students to record notes rather than form complete sentences. When they are done with their lists, have them compare their lists of critical details with those of other classmates and the Example Summary Plan.

1. Today, you will use the steps of the Summary Writing Strategy at the bottom of page 43 to plan and write a summary. First, read the prompt, and then write your topic name in the Planning Box at the top of page 44. Then, **LIST** your details. When you are finished, compare your list to your partner's list.—

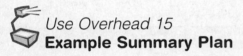
Use Overhead 15
Example Summary Plan

2. Now, compare your list to the list on the overhead.—

ACTIVITY PROCEDURE

Next, have students complete the additional steps in the Summary Writing Strategy. Have them reread their lists and **CROSS OUT** any weak or unimportant details. Then, have students **CONNECT** details that could go together in one sentence, **NUMBER** their ideas in a logical order, and **WRITE** their summaries on a separate piece of paper. When they are done, have them **EDIT** their paragraphs, revising for clarity and proofreading for errors in spelling, capitalization, and punctuation.

Have students read their summaries to their partners. Then, read the Example Summary.

Have students read each of the attributes on the rubric, examine their partners' summaries, and circle either "Yes" or "Fix up." Give students time to make changes in their summaries.

Optional: During or after the class session, fill in the third column of the rubric chart and assign points to the student summaries.

APPLICATION LESSON 4

Comprehension Strategy—Short Answer

Step 1: Read the item.
Step 2: Turn the question into part of the answer and write it down.
Step 3: Think of the answer or locate the answer in the article.
Step 4: Complete your answer.

1. **Why was expansion of the British Empire initially based on trade?**
The British Empire was initially based on trade because Britain wanted the power, wealth, and resources that could come from possessions overseas.

2. **What are some of the resources Britain found in its territories that helped to make it a wealthy country?**
Some of the resources Britain found in its territories that helped to make it a wealthy country included gold, ivory, diamonds, furs, and lumber.

SHORT ANSWER COMPREHENSION **4** **4** *Points*

ACTIVITY G *Expository Writing—Summary*

Writing Strategy—Summary

Step 1: **LIST** (List the details that are important enough to include in the summary.)
Step 2: **CROSS OUT** (Reread the details. Cross out any that you decide not to include.)
Step 3: **CONNECT** (Connect any details that could go into one sentence.)
Step 4: **NUMBER** (Number the details in a logical order.)
Step 5: **WRITE** (Write your summary.)
Step 6: **EDIT** (Revise and proofread your summary.)

Prompt: Write a summary of the information on the British Empire.

Student Book: Application Lesson 4 **43**

APPLICATION LESSON 4

Planning Box

(topic) *The British Empire*
① { (detail) – *empire began with trade* / (detail) – *looked for resources in other lands*
② (detail) – *established colonies where the resources were*
③ (detail) – *acquired land through wars*
④ (detail) – *established British culture in the acquired lands*
⑤ (detail) – *resources made Britain wealthy*
⑥ (detail) – *empire declined*
⑦ (detail) – *colonies wanted independence*
⑧ (detail) – *some countries fought for it*
⑨ (detail) – *Britain granted independence to some countries*

Directions: Write your summary on a separate piece of paper.

Rubric—Summary	Student or Partner Rating	Teacher Rating
1. Did the author state the topic and the main idea in the first sentence?	Yes Fix up	Yes No
2. Did the author focus on important details?	Yes Fix up	Yes No
3. Did the author combine details in some of the sentences?	Yes Fix up	Yes No
4. Is the summary easy to understand?	Yes Fix up	Yes No
5. Did the author correctly spell words, particularly the words found in the article?	Yes Fix up	Yes No
6. Did the author use correct capitalization, capitalizing the first word in the sentence and proper names of people, places, and things?	Yes Fix up	Yes No
7. Did the author use correct punctuation, including a period at the end of each sentence?	Yes Fix up	Yes No

WRITING **7** *Points*

44 *REWARDS Plus: Reading Strategies Applied to Social Studies Passages*

Teacher's Guide: Application Lesson 4 ▪ **105**

Optional: Have students date their writing and place the sample in a folder. Thus, students will be able to look back at their summaries and extended responses and literally see their writing improvement.

3. Now, **CROSS OUT**, **CONNECT**, **NUMBER**, and **WRITE**._

4. Reread your summary and **EDIT**. Check to be sure that your summary is easy to understand. Fix any errors you find in spelling, capitalization, and punctuation._ (Monitor.)

5. Read your summary to your partner._

Use Overhead 16
Example Summary

6. Look at the overhead. Let's read this Example Summary. Yours doesn't need to be exactly the same, but it should be similar.

7. Turn to page 44. Today, you will be evaluating your partner's summary. Use the questions in this rubric to determine what your partner needs to edit.

8. Please exchange summaries and books with your partner. Read the questions, read your partner's summary, and circle "Yes" or "Fix up."_

9. (When the evaluation is complete, have students return the summaries and books to their partners. Give students adequate time to make any necessary changes to their summaries. Have students enter their points in the blank half of the Writing box below the rubric.)

APPLICATION LESSON
4

Planning Box
(topic) *The British Empire*
① { (detail) – *empire began with trade* / (detail) – *looked for resources in other lands*
② (detail) – *established colonies where the resources were*
③ (detail) – *acquired land through wars*
④ (detail) – *established British culture in the acquired lands*
⑤ (detail) – *resources made Britain wealthy*
⑥ (detail) – *empire declined*
⑦ (detail) – *colonies wanted independence*
⑧ (detail) – *some countries fought for it*
⑨ (detail) – *Britain granted independence to some countries*

Directions: Write your summary on a separate piece of paper.

Rubric— Summary	Student or Partner Rating		Teacher Rating	
1. Did the author state the topic and the main idea in the first sentence?	Yes	Fix up	Yes	No
2. Did the author focus on important details?	Yes	Fix up	Yes	No
3. Did the author combine details in some of the sentences?	Yes	Fix up	Yes	No
4. Is the summary easy to understand?	Yes	Fix up	Yes	No
5. Did the author correctly spell words, particularly the words found in the article?	Yes	Fix up	Yes	No
6. Did the author use correct capitalization, capitalizing the first word in the sentence and proper names of people, places, and things?	Yes	Fix up	Yes	No
7. Did the author use correct punctuation, including a period at the end of each sentence?	Yes	Fix up	Yes	No

WRITING [7]

44   REWARDS Plus: Reading Strategies Applied to Social Studies Passages   Points

---

Application Lesson 5

Materials Needed:

- *Student Book:* Application Lesson 5

- Application Overhead Transparencies 17–20

- Application Overhead Transparency 62

- Appendix A Reproducible 5: Comprehension Strategy—Short Answer

- Appendix B Optional Vocabulary Activities: Application Lesson 5

- Paper or cardboard to use when covering the overhead transparency

- Paper or cardboard for each student to use during spelling dictation

- Washable overhead transparency pen

Text Treatment Notes:

- Black text signifies teacher script (exact wording to say to students).

- Green text in parentheses signifies directions or prompts for the teacher.

- Green text signifies answers or examples of answers.

- Green graphics treatment signifies reproduction of Overhead information.

- Green text and green graphics treatment do not appear in the *Student Book.*

ACTIVITY A
Vocabulary

ACTIVITY PROCEDURE, List 1

(See the *Student Book*, page 45.)

Tell students each word in the list. Then have students repeat the word and read the definition aloud. For each definition, provide any additional information that may be necessary. Then, have students practice reading the words themselves.

Note A.1-1: See Appendix E, Pronunciation Guide for Unique Words, for correct pronunciations of uncommon vocabulary words.

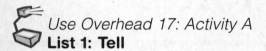

Use Overhead 17: Activity A
List 1: Tell

1. (Show the top half of Overhead 17.) Before we read the passage, let's read the difficult words. (Point to **Mohandas Gandhi**.) These words are **Mohandas Gandhi**. What words?_ Now, read the definition._
2. (Point to **Mahatma**.) The next word is **Mahatma**. What word?_ Now, read the definition._
3. (Point to **campaign**.) The last word is **campaign**. What word?_ Now, read the definition._
4. Open your *Student Book* to **Application Lesson 5**, page 45._
5. Find **Activity A**, **List 1**, in your book._ Let's read the words again. First word._ Next word._ Next word._

ACTIVITY PROCEDURE, List 2

(See the *Student Book*, page 45.)

Have students circle prefixes and suffixes, then underline the vowels. Using the overhead transparency, assist students in checking their work. Next, have students figure out each word to themselves, then say it aloud. Have them read the definition aloud.

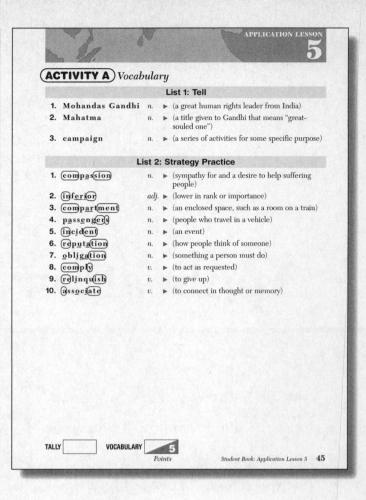

APPLICATION LESSON
5

ACTIVITY A *Vocabulary*

List 1: Tell

1.	Mohandas Gandhi	n. ▶	(a great human rights leader from India)
2.	Mahatma	n. ▶	(a title given to Gandhi that means "great-souled one")
3.	campaign	n. ▶	(a series of activities for some specific purpose)

List 2: Strategy Practice

1.	compassion	n. ▶	(sympathy for and a desire to help suffering people)
2.	inferior	adj. ▶	(lower in rank or importance)
3.	compartment	n. ▶	(an enclosed space, such as a room on a train)
4.	passengers	n. ▶	(people who travel in a vehicle)
5.	incident	n. ▶	(an event)
6.	reputation	n. ▶	(how people think of someone)
7.	obligation	n. ▶	(something a person must do)
8.	comply	v. ▶	(to act as requested)
9.	relinquish	v. ▶	(to give up)
10.	associate	v. ▶	(to connect in thought or memory)

TALLY [ ] VOCABULARY [5] Points

Student Book: Application Lesson 5 **45**

Use Overhead 17: Activity A
List 2: Strategy Practice

1. Find **List 2**. Circle the prefixes and suffixes, and underline the vowels. Look up when you are done._
2. (Show the bottom half of Overhead 17.) Before you check your work on List 2, look at item #10. (Point to the third example and the **as** that is circled.) From now on, you can also circle **as**. The prefix is /as/. Say it._ Now, go back to item #1. Check and fix any mistakes._
3. Go back to the first word again._ Sound out the word to yourself. Put your thumb up when you can read the word. Be sure that it is a real word._ What word?_ Now, read the definition._
4. (Continue Step 3 with all remaining words in List 2.)

Note A.2-1: You may wish to provide additional practice by having students read words to a partner.

ACTIVITY PROCEDURE, List 1 and 2

(See the *Student Book*, page 45.)

Tell students to look in List 1 or List 2 for a word you are thinking about. Have them circle the number of the word and tell you the word. Explain to students to make a tally mark for each correct word in the Tally box, and then enter the number of tally marks as points in the blank half of the Vocabulary box.

1. Remember, the words I'm thinking about will be in either List 1 or List 2. For every word you correctly identify, make a tally mark in the Tally box at the bottom of page 45. If you don't identify the correct word, don't do anything.
2. Circle the number of the appropriate word.
   - People who work with those who are less fortunate and who suffer are said to have a lot of this. (Wait.) What word? **compassion**
   - If you must do something, you have this. (Wait.) What word? **obligation**
   - When someone acts as they were requested to, they do this. (Wait.) What word? **comply**
   - People who give up their right to do something are said to do this with that right. (Wait.) What word ? **relinquish**
   - Armies often undertake this series of activities. (Wait.) What word? **campaign**
3. Count all of the tally marks, and enter that number as points in the blank half of the Vocabulary box.

ACTIVITY PROCEDURE, List 3

(See the *Student Book*, page 46.)

The words in the third list are related. Have students use the *REWARDS* Strategies to figure out the first word in each family. Have them read the definition and then read the other two words in the family.

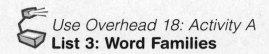

Use Overhead 18: Activity A
List 3: Word Families

1. Turn to page 46. Find **Family 1** in **List 3**. Figure out the first word. Use your pencil if you wish. Put your thumb up when you know the word._ What word?_ Read the definition._
2. Look at the next word in Family 1. Figure out the word._ What word?_

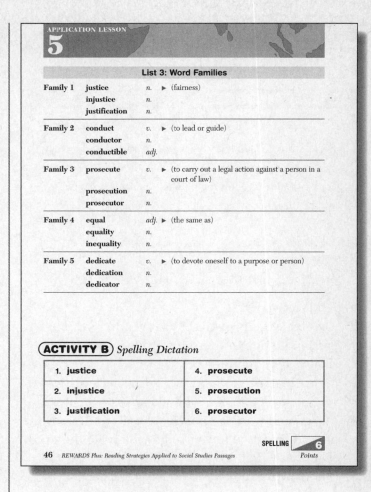

List 3: Word Families

Family 1	justice	n.	▶ (fairness)
	injustice	n.	
	justification	n.	
Family 2	conduct	v.	▶ (to lead or guide)
	conductor	n.	
	conductible	adj.	
Family 3	prosecute	v.	▶ (to carry out a legal action against a person in a court of law)
	prosecution	n.	
	prosecutor	n.	
Family 4	equal	adj.	▶ (the same as)
	equality	n.	
	inequality	n.	
Family 5	dedicate	v.	▶ (to devote oneself to a purpose or person)
	dedication	n.	
	dedicator	n.	

ACTIVITY B *Spelling Dictation*

1. justice	4. prosecute
2. injustice	5. prosecution
3. justification	6. prosecutor

SPELLING 6

3. Next word. Figure out the word._ What word?_
4. (Repeat Steps 1–3 for all word families in List 3.)

Note A.3-1: You may wish to provide additional practice by having students read a word family to the group or to a partner.

Note A.3-2: Additional vocabulary practice activities are provided in Appendix B of the Teacher's Guide. These activities are optional and can be assigned during class, for homework, or as small group, in-class activities.

ACTIVITY B

Spelling Dictation

ACTIVITY PROCEDURE

(See the *Student Book*, page 46.)

For each word, tell students the word, then have students say the parts of the word to themselves while they write the word. Then, have students enter the number of correctly spelled words as points in the blank half of the Spelling box.

Note B-1: Distribute a piece of light cardboard to each of the students.

 Use Overhead 18: Activity B

1. Find **Activity B**.
2. The first word is **justice**. What word?_ Say the parts in **justice** to yourself as you write the word. (Pause and monitor.)
3. (Show **justice** on the overhead.) Check **justice**. If you misspelled it, cross it out and write it correctly.
4. The second word is **injustice**. What word?_ Say the parts in **injustice** to yourself as you write the word. (Pause and monitor.)
5. (Show **injustice** on the overhead.) Check **injustice**. If you misspelled it, cross it out and write it correctly.
6. (Repeat the procedures for the words **justification**, **prosecute**, **prosecution**, and **prosecutor**.)
7. Count the number of words you spelled correctly, and record that number as points in the blank half of the Spelling box at the bottom of the page.

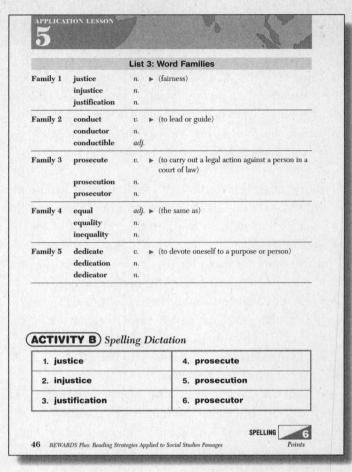

List 3: Word Families

Family 1	justice	*n.* ▶	(fairness)
	injustice	*n.*	
	justification	*n.*	
Family 2	conduct	*v.* ▶	(to lead or guide)
	conductor	*n.*	
	conductible	*adj.*	
Family 3	prosecute	*v.* ▶	(to carry out a legal action against a person in a court of law)
	prosecution	*n.*	
	prosecutor	*n.*	
Family 4	equal	*adj.* ▶	(the same as)
	equality	*n.*	
	inequality	*n.*	
Family 5	dedicate	*v.* ▶	(to devote oneself to a purpose or person)
	dedication	*n.*	
	dedicator	*n.*	

ACTIVITY B *Spelling Dictation*

1. justice	4. prosecute
2. injustice	5. prosecution
3. justification	6. prosecutor

SPELLING **6** Points

ACTIVITY C
Background Knowledge

ACTIVITY PROCEDURE

(See the *Student Book,* page 47.)

Read the Background Knowledge paragraphs using one of three methods: read them to students, have students read them together, or call on individual students to read. Examine the timeline and the related graphic together. Then, preview the passage together by examining the title and the headings. Have students tell partners two things the passage will tell about.

1. Turn to page 47. Let's read the two paragraphs. (Read or ask students to read. Then examine the timeline and graphic together.)
2. Now, let's turn the page and preview the passage. Read the title._ What is the whole passage going to tell about?_
3. Now, let's read the headings. Read the first heading._ Read the next heading._ (Continue until students have read all headings.)
4. Turn to your partner. Without looking, tell two things this passage will tell about._

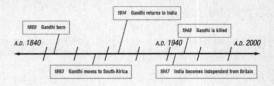

ACTIVITY C *Background Knowledge*

	1914 Gandhi returns to India	
1869 Gandhi born		1948 Gandhi is killed
A.D. 1840	A.D. 1940	A.D. 2000
1893 Gandhi moves to South Africa	1947 India becomes independent from Britain	

In the last article, we read about the expansion of the British Empire. Mahatma Gandhi was certainly a product of the British Empire. He was born in *India* in 1869, went to law school in *Great Britain,* lived in *South Africa* for more than 20 years, and returned to *India,* where he led a struggle for home rule and human rights until he was assassinated in 1948. Gandhi believed that nonviolent procedures should be used to gain human rights. These nonviolent procedures included non-cooperation by the people in forms of boycotting courts, resigning from government positions, and not attending school. These actions helped to propel India into independence from Great Britain.

However, Gandhi's career as a human rights leader did not start in India. Instead, it began during his years in South Africa. This is the period of his life discussed in this article.

Mohandas ("Mahatma") Gandhi

ACTIVITY D

Passage Reading and Comprehension

ACTIVITY PROCEDURE

(See the *Student Book*, pages 48–49.)

Have students work on reading accuracy by selecting a passage-reading option that best fits your students.

Passage Reading: Accuracy

(Select a passage-reading procedure that matches the size of your group and the competency of your students.

Option A

If you are teaching a small group of students who are having difficulty, use Option A:

Have students read one paragraph silently. Then, call on one student to orally read a paragraph or a portion of the paragraph to the class. Call on students in random order, varying the amount that each student reads.

Option B

If you are teaching a small group with students who are not having difficulty, use Option B:

Have students read the entire article silently, rereading it if they finish before their classmates. Then, call on one student to orally read a paragraph or a portion of a paragraph to the class. Call on students in random order, varying the amount that each student reads.

Option C

If you are teaching a large group with students who are having difficulty, use Option C:

Have students read one paragraph silently. Then, have students read the paragraph to a partner. Alternate partner-reading turns.

Option D

If you are teaching a large group with students who are not having difficulty, use Option D:

Have students read the entire article silently, rereading it if they finish before their classmates. Then, have students read the passage with their partners, alternating on each paragraph.)

ACTIVITY D *Passage Reading and Comprehension*

Gandhi

10	Mohandas Gandhi is known throughout the world for his compassion,
23	dedication to peace, and commitment to nonviolence. He enacted a great deal of
38	change in his lifetime and made life better for many people of India. His success
50	inspired other leaders, such as Martin Luther King Jr., to adopt nonviolent
62	resistance techniques in their own struggles against injustice. But Gandhi was not
	born a leader. Specific events early in his life led him to that path. (#1)

	Becoming a Lawyer
76	
79	Gandhi attended University College in London, England, where he studied
89	successfully to become a lawyer. This training in law would provide an important
102	base of knowledge for Gandhi throughout his lifetime. When he completed
113	school, he returned to India and attempted to start a law practice in Bombay.
127	He was not very successful. Few clients approached him; he was not making
140	enough money to live. So when an offer came to work as a legal advisor in South
157	Africa, he gladly accepted it. (#2)

	South Africa
162	
164	Like India, South Africa was still under British rule when Gandhi moved
176	there in 1893. In South Africa, Gandhi realized that the large numbers of
189	Indians (people from India) who were settled there were looked down upon as
202	racial outcasts. South African whites considered the Indians inferior just because
213	they were Indian. One day, Gandhi boarded a train with a first-class ticket in his
229	hand. But when he sat down in the compartment, a white passenger complained
242	about the presence of a dark-skinned man in first class. The conductor ordered
256	him to move back to third class. When Gandhi refused, because he had
269	purchased a first-class ticket, the conductor threw him and his luggage off the
283	train. He sat through a cold winter night in a waiting room, trying to decide
298	whether he should stay and fulfill his obligations to his law client or return to
313	India. He decided to stay. (#3)

	Passive Resistance
318	
320	Later, on the same journey, Gandhi had to travel by stagecoach. The
332	conductor made Gandhi sit outside of the stagecoach box while he sat inside with
346	the white passengers. Afraid of being thrown off and getting stranded, Gandhi

Passage Reading: Comprehension Questions

(You may wish to ask the following questions as the passage is being read. Numbers corresponding to the questions are indicated at the point at which they could be asked.)

#1 What is Gandhi remembered for?
Ideas: Being a human rights leader; using nonviolent procedures to promote change; being dedicated to peace.

#2 Though Gandhi was not a successful lawyer in India, why might his legal knowledge have been important as a leader of a human rights movement?
Ideas: He was able to understand legal actions; could read legal documents; knew how to interact with government officials.

358	complied. But when the same conductor ordered Gandhi to move out of his seat
372	and sit on the dirty footboard, Gandhi refused. The conductor was very angry
385	and hit Gandhi repeatedly, trying to force him off the stagecoach. Gandhi was not
399	willing to fight back, and he was not willing to concede. Finally, some of the
414	other passengers made the conductor stop. Gandhi remained in his seat. (#4)

Becoming a Leader

425	
428	These incidents awoke Gandhi's awareness to the terrible racial injustices
438	being done in South Africa. He began to try to organize his fellow Indians and
453	others who disagreed with the government's actions. He made speeches and
464	wrote petitions and pamphlets. People in Britain and India began to become
476	aware of what was happening in South Africa. (#5)

Nonviolent Resistance

484	
486	As Gandhi's campaign wore on, people who did not approve of the changes
499	he was trying to enact often confronted him. On one occasion, he was attacked
513	by an angry mob of people and nearly killed. But he refused to prosecute his
528	attackers, saying that they would find their own way to the truth. He began to be
544	known as much for his love and compassion for his enemies as for his political
559	successes. (#6)

The Mahatma

560	
562	As his reputation for compassion grew, Gandhi became known as the
573	*Mahatma*, or "great-souled one." He relinquished the lifestyle of a lawyer and
586	began to live the simple, sparse life that we associate with Gandhi today. Out of
601	these experiences in South Africa, he developed his practice of *satyagraha*, or
613	nonviolent resistance to injustice. His experiences with hatred, injustice, and
623	prejudice led him to become a great leader for peace and equality in India, his
638	homeland, and around the world. (#7)
643	

ACTIVITY E *Fluency Building*

| Cold Timing | ☐ | Practice 1 | ☐ |
| Practice 2 | ☐ | Hot Timing | ☐ |

Student Book: Application Lesson 5 **49**

#3 How did Gandhi experience racial discrimination in South Africa?
He was treated as an inferior and a racial outcast. He was not allowed to travel first class on a train with white passengers.

#4 What nonviolent actions did Gandhi take to protest his treatment?
He refused to get out of his seat. He did not fight back when he was hit.

#5 What actions did Gandhi take when he experienced and witnessed the treatment given to Indians living in South Africa?
Ideas: He organized people; wrote and distributed pamphlets; gave speeches.

#6 What action showed that Gandhi had compassion for his enemies?
He refused to prosecute them.

#7 What does the practice of *satyagraha* refer to?
Nonviolence.

ACTIVITY E
Fluency Building

ACTIVITY PROCEDURE

(See the *Student Book*, page 49.)

Have students complete a Cold Timing, one or two practices, and a Hot Timing of the Activity D article. For each timing, have students record the number of correct words read. Finally, have students complete their Fluency Graphs.

Note E-1: When assigning partners for this activity, have the stronger reader read first. As a result, the other reader will have one additional practice opportunity.

1. Now, it's time for fluency building.
2. Find the beginning of the passage again. (Pause.)
3. Whisper-read. See how many words you can read in one minute. Begin.＿ (Time students for one minute.) Stop.＿ Circle the last word that you read.＿ Record the number of words you read after **Cold Timing** in **Activity E** at the bottom of page 49.＿
4. Let's practice again. Begin.＿ (Time students for one minute.) Stop.＿ Put a box around the last word that you read.＿ Record the number of words you read after **Practice 1**.＿
5. **Optional** Let's practice one more time before the Hot Timing. Begin.＿ (Time students for one minute.) Stop.＿ Put a box around the last word that you read.＿ Record the number of words you read after **Practice 2**.＿
6. Please exchange books with your partner.＿ Partner 1, you are going to read first. Partner 2, listen carefully and underline any mistakes or words left out. Ones, begin.＿ (Time students for one minute.) Stop.＿ Twos, cross out the last word that your partner read.＿ Twos, record the number of words in your partner's book after **Hot Timing**.＿
7. Partner 2, you are going to read next. Partner 1, listen carefully and underline any mistakes or words left out. Twos, begin. (Time students for one minute.) Stop.＿ Ones, cross out the last word that your partner read.＿ Ones, record the number of words in your partner's book after **Hot Timing**.＿
8. Exchange books.＿ Turn to the Fluency Graph on the last page of your book, and indicate on the graph the number of Cold Timing and Hot Timing words you read correctly.＿

ACTIVITY F

Comprehension Questions— Multiple Choice and Short Answer

ACTIVITY PROCEDURE

(See the *Student Book*, page 50.)

Have students complete item #1. Then, have students share the rationale for their answers. Encourage thoughtful discussion. Proceed item-by-item, emphasizing the rationale for the *best* answer. Have students record points for each correct item.

Note F-1: The correct Multiple Choice answers are circled.

Multiple Choice Comprehension

1. Turn to page 50. Find **Activity F**. Finish item #1. Be ready to explain why you selected your answer._ (Wait while students complete the item. Call on individual students. Ask them why they chose their answer and why they eliminated the other choices. Encourage discussion.)
2. (Repeat Step 1 with items #2, #3, and #4.)
3. Count the number of items you got correct, and record that number as points in the blank half of the Multiple Choice Comprehension box._

ACTIVITY F *Comprehension Questions— Multiple Choice and Short Answer*

Comprehension Strategy—Multiple Choice

Step 1: Read the item.
Step 2: Read all of the choices.
Step 3: Think about why each choice might be correct or incorrect. Check the article as needed.
Step 4: From the possible correct choices, select the best answer.

1. (Vocabulary) **What did the author mean with this statement: "Mahatma Gandhi was certainly a *product* of the British Empire."**
   a. Gandhi's ideas were the same as the leaders of countries in the British Empire.
   b. The British Empire made Gandhi a political leader because he earned a law degree in Great Britain.
   c. Gandhi learned from his experiences in three countries of the British Empire: India, Great Britain, and South Africa.
   d. Gandhi's goals were the same as those who wrote the laws of the British Empire.

2. (Cause and Effect) **Why did the conductor try to force Gandhi off the stagecoach?**
   a. There was great prejudice against people of color in South Africa.
   b. Gandhi had failed to pay the same fare as the other passengers.
   c. The conductor did not realize that Gandhi was a lawyer and deserved respect.
   d. Gandhi was not a British citizen.

3. (Vocabulary) **What do you think the heading *Passive Resistance* means?**
   a. Resistance that is "in passing" (only temporary).
   b. Resistance that does not involve passing over other people.
   c. Resistance that does not involve action, such as fighting.
   d. Resistance that involves getting other people to protect you.

4. (Main Idea) **If Gandhi were given an award, which of these titles would be best?**
   a. *Nonviolent Peace Seeker*
   b. *Leader of the British Empire*
   c. *Beloved Leader of Bombay*
   d. *Recognized Lawyer*

MULTIPLE CHOICE COMPREHENSION
Points

Comprehension Strategy—Short Answer

Step 1: Read the item.
Step 2: Turn the question into part of the answer and write it down.
Step 3: Think of the answer or locate the answer in the article.
Step 4: Complete your answer.

1. **Why was life difficult for the Indians who lived in South Africa?**
   Example answer: Life was difficult for the Indians who lived in South Africa because they were treated as inferior and racial outcasts. For example, they were not allowed to ride in train compartments with whites.

2. **What kinds of nonviolent actions did Gandhi support?**
   Example answer: Gandhi supported many kinds of nonviolent actions. For example, Gandhi encouraged people to not hit back when they were attacked and to not cooperate with government officials.

SHORT ANSWER COMPREHENSION
Points

ACTIVITY G *Expository Writing—Extended Response*

Writing Strategy—Extended Response

Step 1: LIST (List the reasons for your position. For each reason, explain with details.)
Step 2: CROSS OUT (Reread your reasons and details. Cross out any that you decide not to include.)
Step 3: CONNECT (Connect any details that could go into one sentence.)
Step 4: NUMBER (Number the reasons in a logical order.)
Step 5: WRITE (Write your response.)
Step 6: EDIT (Revise and proofread your response.)

Prompt: Describe some of the parts of Gandhi's life that led him to be a great leader for peace.

ACTIVITY PROCEDURE

(See the *Student Book*, page 51.)

Have students read each step in the Short Answer Strategy. Stress the importance of changing the question into part of the answer. Have students read question #1. Prompt students to suggest wording from the question that could be incorporated into the answer. Have students record that wording, locate the answers in the article, and complete the answer. Have students use the Short Answer Strategy steps on the remaining question. Have students record points for each question's answer: one point for using the wording of the question in the answer, and one point for accuracy of the answer (total of 4 points possible for two complete answers).

Short Answer Comprehension

1. Turn to page 51._ Today, we are going to use the Short Answer Strategy for completing these items.

2. Let's read the steps in the strategy at the top of the page. Read **Step 1.**_

3. Read **Step 2.**_ This is the most important step. If you turn the question into part of the answer, you are more likely to have an accurate answer that is a complete sentence.

4. Read **Step 3.**_

5. Read **Step 4.**_

6. Read question #1._ What wording might you use from the question in your answer?_ (**Example answer:** Life was difficult for the Indians who lived in South Africa because...) Complete your answer._ Read your answer to your partner._ (When students are done, give them feedback.)

7. Read question #2._ What wording might you use from the question in your answer?_ (**Example answer:** Gandhi supported many kinds of nonviolent actions. For example,...) Complete your answer._ Read your answer to your partner._ (When students are done, give them feedback.)

8. For each question's answer, award yourself points: one point for using words from the question in your answer, and one point for correctness of your answer. Count your number of points (a maximum of 4 points for the two answers), and add that number in the blank half of the Short Answer Comprehension box.

9. (Distribute Appendix A Reproducible 5: Comprehension Strategy—Short Answer. Have each student place this in a notebook or a folder for future reference.)

Comprehension Strategy—Short Answer

Step 1: Read the item.
Step 2: Turn the question into part of the answer and write it down.
Step 3: Think of the answer or locate the answer in the article.
Step 4: Complete your answer.

1. **Why was life difficult for the Indians who lived in South Africa?**
   Example answer: Life was difficult for the Indians who lived in South Africa because they were treated as inferior and racial outcasts. For example, they were not allowed to ride in train compartments with whites.

2. **What kinds of nonviolent actions did Gandhi support?**
   Example answer: Gandhi supported many kinds of nonviolent actions. For example, Gandhi encouraged people to not hit back when they were attacked and to not cooperate with government officials.

SHORT ANSWER COMPREHENSION **4** *Points*

ACTIVITY G *Expository Writing—Extended Response*

Writing Strategy—Extended Response

Step 1: LIST (List the reasons for your position. For each reason, explain with details.)
Step 2: CROSS OUT (Reread your reasons and details. Cross out any that you decide not to include.)
Step 3: CONNECT (Connect any details that could go into one sentence.)
Step 4: NUMBER (Number the reasons in a logical order.)
Step 5: WRITE (Write your response.)
Step 6: EDIT (Revise and proofread your response.)

Prompt: Describe some of the parts of Gandhi's life that led him to be a great leader for peace.

Student Book: Application Lesson 5 **51**

ACTIVITY G
Expository Writing—Extended Response

ACTIVITY PROCEDURE

(See the *Student Book*, pages 51–53.)

Have students read the prompt. Point out the position that Jessica wrote in her plan, and have students record the position. Explain how Jessica reread the article and made a **LIST** of strong reasons. For each reason, she supported it with an explanation. Have students read Jessica's reasons and explanations. Explain that less-important reasons or explanations should be **CROSSED OUT**, and have them cross out the same reason as Jessica. Next, explain how ideas can be **CONNECTED** into one sentence, and have students connect ideas as Jessica did in her plan. Have students **NUMBER** their reasons in the same manner as Jessica. Finally, have students read Jessica's extended response.

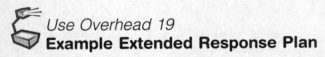

Use Overhead 19
Example Extended Response Plan

1. Find **Activity G** at the bottom of page 51._ Oftentimes, you are asked to write an answer in which you take a position and support it. We can use the same writing steps that we used when writing summaries. Today, we will examine Jessica's extended response. In the next lesson, you will be writing a similar response.
2. Read the prompt._ Next, Jessica wrote her position in her plan. Read her position in the Planning Box on page 52._ Then, she followed the steps in the Extended Response Writing Strategy on page 51 to write her response.
3. Read **Step 1**._ In the Example Plan, Jessica wrote reasons that supported her position. To make the response stronger, she added an explanation for each reason. Let's read her **list** on page 52._

Comprehension Strategy—Short Answer

Step 1: Read the item.
Step 2: Turn the question into part of the answer and write it down.
Step 3: Think of the answer or locate the answer in the article.
Step 4: Complete your answer.

1. **Why was life difficult for the Indians who lived in South Africa?**
   Example answer: Life was difficult for the Indians who lived in South
   Africa because they were treated as inferior and racial outcasts. For
   example, they were not allowed to ride in train compartments with whites.

2. **What kinds of nonviolent actions did Gandhi support?**
   Example answer: Gandhi supported many kinds of nonviolent actions.
   For example, Gandhi encouraged people to not hit back when they were
   attacked and to not cooperate with government officials.

SHORT ANSWER COMPREHENSION **4**
Points

ACTIVITY G *Expository Writing—Extended Response*

Writing Strategy—Extended Response

Step 1: LIST (List the reasons for your position. For each reason, explain with details.)
Step 2: CROSS OUT (Reread your reasons and details. Cross out any that you decide not to include.)
Step 3: CONNECT (Connect any details that could go into one sentence.)
Step 4: NUMBER (Number the reasons in a logical order.)
Step 5: WRITE (Write your response.)
Step 6: EDIT (Revise and proofread your response.)

Prompt: Describe some of the parts of Gandhi's life that led him to be a great leader for peace.

Example Extended Response Plan

Planning Box
(position) *Many factors in Gandhi's life led him to be a great leader for peace.*
(reason) — ~~lived throughout the British Empire~~
(explain) — ~~born in India~~
— ~~also lived in South Africa and Great Britain~~
① (reason) – *knew what it was like to be a racial outcast*
(explain) – *conductor told him to sit with other dark-skinned people in third-class section on the train*
– *thrown off the train when he refused*
② (reason) – *responded to violence with nonviolence*
(explain) – *hit repeatedly on the stagecoach*
– *refused to fight back*
③ (reason) – *organized people who disagreed with the government*
(explain) – *wrote pamphlets and petitions*
– *made speeches*
– *people became more aware of what was happening*

Directions: Write your extended response on a separate piece of paper.

ACTIVITY PROCEDURE

Next, have students complete the additional steps in the Extended Response Writing Strategy. Have them reread their lists and **CROSS OUT** any weak or unimportant reasons or explanations. Then, have students **CONNECT** explanations that could go together in one sentence, **NUMBER** their reasons in a logical order, and **WRITE** their extended responses on a separate piece of paper. When they are done, have them **EDIT** their paragraphs, revising for clarity and proofreading for errors in spelling, capitalization, and punctuation.

Have students read their extended responses to their partners. Then, read the Example Extended Response.

Have students read each of the attributes on the rubric, examine their extended responses, and circle either "Yes" or "Fix up." Give students time to make necessary changes.

Optional: During or after the class session, fill in the third column of the rubric chart and assign points to the extended responses.

Optional: Have students date their writing and place the sample in a folder. Thus, students will be able to look back at their summaries and extended responses and literally see their writing improvement.

4. Turn back to page 51. Read **Step 2**._ Next, Jessica reread her list and **crossed out** any reasons and explanations that were not logical or strong. What did she cross out?_ Why do you think this reason and these explanations were eliminated?_ Cross out the same reason and explanations on your paper on page 52._
5. Turn back to page 51. Read **Step 3**._ Please draw brackets on your paper to **connect** the ideas that Jessica connected._
6. Turn back to page 51. Read **Step 4**._ Jessica then **numbered** the reasons in the order they would appear in her response. Number your paper as Jessica did._
7. Turn back to page 51. Read **Step 5**._ Jessica then **wrote** her response. The first sentence states her position. The remaining sentences give her reasons and explanations.

Example Extended Response

Many factors in Gandhi's life led him to become a great leader for peace. First, he knew what it was like to be a racial outcast. On one trip, he was told to sit with other dark-skinned people in third class, even though he had a first-class ticket. When he refused, he was thrown off the train. Another factor is that he responded to violence with nonviolence. He was once hit repeatedly for refusing to move onto the footboard of a stagecoach, but he would not fight back. Finally, Gandhi organized people who disagreed with the government. He wrote pamphlets and petitions, and he made speeches. He made people more aware of what was happening in regard to the government and civil rights.

Rubric— Extended Response	Student or Partner Rating	Teacher Rating
1. Did the author tell his/her position in the first sentence?	Yes Fix up	Yes No
2. Did the author include at least three **strong, logical** reasons for his/her position?	Yes Fix up	Yes No
3. Did the author provide a **strong, logical** explanation for each of his/her reasons?	Yes Fix up	Yes No
4. Is the response easy to understand?	Yes Fix up	Yes No
5. Did the author correctly spell words, particularly the words found in the article?	Yes Fix up	Yes No
6. Did the author use correct capitalization, capitalizing the first word in the sentence and proper names of people, places, and things?	Yes Fix up	Yes No
7. Did the author use correct punctuation, including a period at the end of each sentence?	Yes Fix up	Yes No

WRITING **7** Points

Student Book: Application Lesson 5 **53**

 Use Overhead 20
Example Extended Response

8. Turn back to page 51. Read **Step 6**._ Jessica reread and **edited** her response. Turn to page 53. Let's read her extended response._

 Use Overhead 62
Rubric—Extended Response

9. The questions in this rubric define attributes of well-written responses. We'll use these questions to evaluate Jessica's paragraph and to determine what she needs to edit.
10. Read question #1._ Now, reread Jessica's first sentence and determine if she told her position. Circle "Yes" if she did. Circle "Fix up" if she didn't._ What did you circle?_
11. Read question #2._ Reexamine Jessica's extended response to determine if she included at least three strong, logical reasons for her position. Then, circle "Yes" or "Fix up."_ What did you circle?_
12. Complete the ratings for the remaining questions. Remember to read each question, and then look at

the Example Extended Response to make sure the criteria have been met.

13. Let's compare your ratings with my ratings of this extended response. (Compare your ratings with students' ratings. Tell them that Jessica should work on improving any items circled "Fix up." Direct students to add the number of questions that were answered "Yes" by both you and them, and then enter that number as points in the blank half of the Writing box below the rubric.)

Example Extended Response

 Many factors in Gandhi's life led him to become a great leader for peace. First, he knew what it was like to be a racial outcast. On one trip, he was told to sit with other dark-skinned people in third class, even though he had a first-class ticket. When he refused, he was thrown off the train. Another factor is that he responded to violence with nonviolence. He was once hit repeatedly for refusing to move onto the footboard of a stagecoach, but he would not fight back. Finally, Gandhi organized people who disagreed with the government. He wrote pamphlets and petitions, and he made speeches. He made people more aware of what was happening in regard to the government and civil rights.

Rubric— Extended Response	Student or Partner Rating	Teacher Rating
1. Did the author tell his/her position in the first sentence?	Yes Fix up	Yes No
2. Did the author include at least three **strong, logical** reasons for his/her position?	Yes Fix up	Yes No
3. Did the author provide a **strong, logical** explanation for each of his/her reasons?	Yes Fix up	Yes No
4. Is the response easy to understand?	Yes Fix up	Yes No
5. Did the author correctly spell words, particularly the words found in the article?	Yes Fix up	Yes No
6. Did the author use correct capitalization, capitalizing the first word in the sentence and proper names of people, places, and things?	Yes Fix up	Yes No
7. Did the author use correct punctuation, including a period at the end of each sentence?	Yes Fix up	Yes No

WRITING 7

Points

Student Book: Application Lesson 5   **53**

Application Lesson 6

Materials Needed:

- *Student Book:* Application Lesson 6
- Application Overhead Transparencies 21–24
- Application Overhead Transparency 62
- Appendix B Optional Vocabulary Activities: Application Lesson 6
- Paper or cardboard to use when covering the overhead transparency
- Paper or cardboard for each student to use during spelling dictation
- Washable overhead transparency pen

Text Treatment Notes:

- Black text signifies teacher script (exact wording to say to students).
- Green text in parentheses signifies directions or prompts for the teacher.
- Green text signifies answers or examples of answers.
- Green graphics treatment signifies reproduction of Overhead information.
- Green text and green graphics treatment do not appear in the *Student Book*.

ACTIVITY A
Vocabulary

ACTIVITY PROCEDURE, List 1

(See the Student Book, page 55.)

Tell students each word in the list. Then, have students repeat the word and read the definition aloud. For each definition, provide any additional information that may be necessary. Then, have students practice reading the words themselves.

Note A.1-1: See Appendix E, Pronunciation Guide for Unique Words, for correct pronunciations of uncommon vocabulary words.

Use Overhead 21: Activity A
List 1: Tell

1. (Show the top half of Overhead 21.) Before we read the passage, let's read the names of some of the people in the passage. (Point to **Sybil Ludington**.) The first name is **Sybil Ludington**. What name?_ Now, read the definition._
2. (Point to **Susanna Boiling**.) The next name is **Susanna Boiling**. What name?_ Now, read the definition._
3. (Pronounce each name in List 1, and then have students repeat each name and read the definition.)
4. Open your *Student Book* to **Application Lesson 6**, page 55._
5. Find **Activity A**, **List 1**, in your book._ Let's read the names again. First name._ Next name._ (Continue for all names in List 1.)

ACTIVITY PROCEDURE, List 2

(See the Student Book, page 55.)

Have students circle prefixes and suffixes, then underline the vowels. Using the overhead transparency, assist students in checking their work. Next, have students figure out each word to themselves, then say it aloud. Have them read the definition aloud.

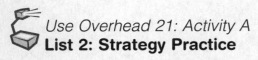

Use Overhead 21: Activity A
List 2: Strategy Practice

1. Find **List 2**. Circle the prefixes and suffixes, and underline the vowels. Look up when you are done._

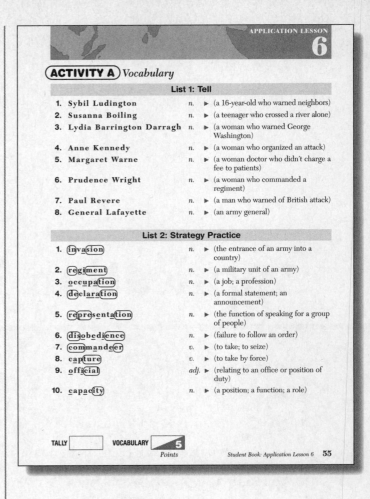

ACTIVITY A *Vocabulary*

List 1: Tell

1.	Sybil Ludington	n. ▶	(a 16-year-old who warned neighbors)
2.	Susanna Boiling	n. ▶	(a teenager who crossed a river alone)
3.	Lydia Barrington Darragh	n. ▶	(a woman who warned George Washington)
4.	Anne Kennedy	n. ▶	(a woman who organized an attack)
5.	Margaret Warne	n. ▶	(a woman doctor who didn't charge a fee to patients)
6.	Prudence Wright	n. ▶	(a woman who commanded a regiment)
7.	Paul Revere	n. ▶	(a man who warned of British attack)
8.	General Lafayette	n. ▶	(an army general)

List 2: Strategy Practice

1.	invasion	n. ▶	(the entrance of an army into a country)
2.	regiment	n. ▶	(a military unit of an army)
3.	occupation	n. ▶	(a job; a profession)
4.	declaration	n. ▶	(a formal statement; an announcement)
5.	representation	n. ▶	(the function of speaking for a group of people)
6.	disobedience	n. ▶	(failure to follow an order)
7.	commandeer	v. ▶	(to take; to seize)
8.	capture	v. ▶	(to take by force)
9.	official	adj. ▶	(relating to an office or position of duty)
10.	capacity	n. ▶	(a position; a function; a role)

TALLY [　]　VOCABULARY ▸ 5
Points　　Student Book: Application Lesson 6　**55**

2. (Show the bottom half of Overhead 21.) Now, check and fix any mistakes._
3. Go back to the first word._ Sound out the word to yourself. Put your thumb up when you can read the word. Be sure that it is a real word._ What word?_ Now, read the definition._
4. (Continue Step 3 with all remaining words in List 2.)

Note A.2-1: You may wish to provide additional practice by having students read words to a partner.

ACTIVITY PROCEDURE, List 1 and 2

(See the *Student Book*, page 55.)

Tell students to look in List 1 or List 2 for a word you are thinking about. Have them circle the number of the word and tell you the word. Explain to students to make a tally mark for each correct word in the Tally box, and then enter the number of tally marks as points in the blank half of the Vocabulary box.

1. Remember, the words I'm thinking about will be in either List 1 or List 2. For every word you correctly identify, make a tally mark in the Tally box at the bottom of page 55. If you don't identify the correct word, don't do anything.
2. Circle the number of the appropriate word.
   - Your job or profession is also called this. (Wait.) What word? **occupation**
   - If you fail to follow an order from a superior, you will probably be punished for this. (Wait.) What word? **disobedience**
   - When speaking to reporters, the politician made a formal statement, which is sometimes known as this. (Wait.). What word? **declaration**
   - What do we call a military group? (Wait.) What word? **regiment**
   - A letter or document issued by a government representative or agency is referred to as being this. (Wait.) What word? **official**
3. Count all the tally marks, and enter that number as points in the blank half of the Vocabulary box.

ACTIVITY PROCEDURE, List 3

(See the *Student Book*, page 56.)

The words in the third list are related. Have students use the *REWARDS* Strategies to figure out the first word in each family. Have them read the definition and then read the other two words in the family.

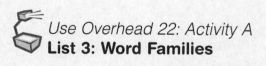

Use Overhead 22: Activity A
List 3: Word Families

1. Turn to page 56. Find **Family 1** in **List 3**. Figure out the first word. Use your pencil if you wish. Put your thumb up when you know the word._ What word?_ Read the definition._
2. Look at the next word in Family 1. Figure out the word._ What word?_
3. Next word. Figure out the word._ What word?_

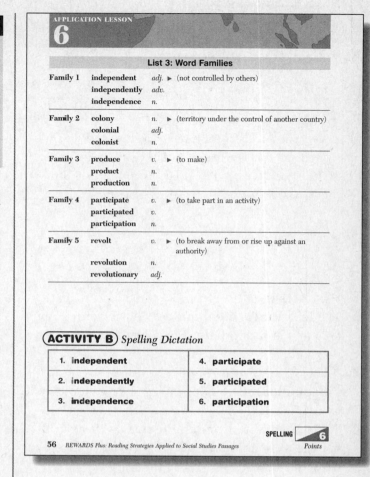

List 3: Word Families

Family 1	independent	*adj.* ►	(not controlled by others)
	independently	*adv.*	
	independence	*n.*	
Family 2	colony	*n.* ►	(territory under the control of another country)
	colonial	*adj.*	
	colonist	*n.*	
Family 3	produce	*v.* ►	(to make)
	product	*n.*	
	production	*n.*	
Family 4	participate	*v.* ►	(to take part in an activity)
	participated	*v.*	
	participation	*n.*	
Family 5	revolt	*v.* ►	(to break away from or rise up against an authority)
	revolution	*n.*	
	revolutionary	*adj.*	

(ACTIVITY B) *Spelling Dictation*

1. **independent**	4. **participate**
2. **independently**	5. **participated**
3. **independence**	6. **participation**

SPELLING ⬟ 6
Points

4. (Repeat Steps 1–3 for all word families in List 3.)

Note A.3-1: You may wish to provide additional practice by having students read a word family to the group or to a partner.

Note A.3-2: Additional vocabulary practice activities are provided in Appendix B of the Teacher's Guide. These activities are optional and can be assigned during class, for homework, or as small group, in-class activities.

ACTIVITY B

Spelling Dictation

ACTIVITY PROCEDURE

(See the *Student Book*, page 56.)

For each word, tell students the word, then have students say the parts of the word to themselves while they write the word. Then, have students enter the number of correctly spelled words as points in the blank half of the Spelling box.

Note B-1: Distribute a piece of light cardboard to each of the students.

 Use Overhead 22: Activity B

1. Find **Activity B**.
2. The first word is **independent**. What word?_ Say the parts in **independent** to yourself as you write the word. (Pause and monitor.)
3. (Show **independent** on the overhead.) Check **independent**. If you misspelled it, cross it out and write it correctly.
4. The second word is **independently**. What word?_ Say the parts in **independently** to yourself as you write the word. (Pause and monitor.)
5. (Show **independently** on the overhead.) Check **independently**. If you misspelled it, cross it out and write it correctly.
6. (Repeat the procedures for the words **independence**, **participate**, **participated**, and **participation**.)
7. Count the number of words you spelled correctly, and record that number as points in the blank half of the Spelling box at the bottom of the page.

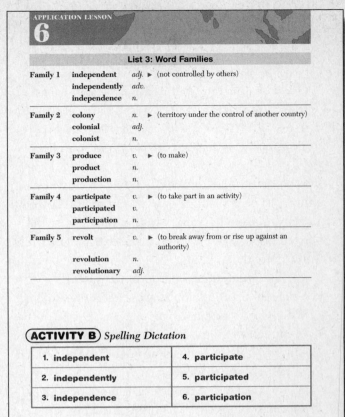

APPLICATION LESSON
6

List 3: Word Families

Family 1	independent	adj.	▶ (not controlled by others)
	independently	adv.	
	independence	n.	
Family 2	colony	n.	▶ (territory under the control of another country)
	colonial	adj.	
	colonist	n.	
Family 3	produce	v.	▶ (to make)
	product	n.	
	production	n.	
Family 4	participate	v.	▶ (to take part in an activity)
	participated	v.	
	participation	n.	
Family 5	revolt	v.	▶ (to break away from or rise up against an authority)
	revolution	n.	
	revolutionary	adj.	

ACTIVITY B *Spelling Dictation*

1. independent	4. participate
2. independently	5. participated
3. independence	6. participation

SPELLING 6
Points

56   *REWARDS Plus: Reading Strategies Applied to Social Studies Passages*

ACTIVITY C

Background Knowledge

ACTIVITY PROCEDURE

(See the *Student Book,* page 57.)

Read the Background Knowledge paragraph using one of three methods: read it to students, have students read it together, or call on individual students to read. Examine the timeline and the related graphic together. Then, preview the passage together by examining the title and the headings. Have students tell partners two things the passage will tell about.

1. Turn to page 57. Let's read the paragraph. (Read or ask students to read. Then examine the timeline and graphic together.)
2. Now, let's turn the page and preview the passage. Read the title._ What is the whole passage going to tell about?_
3. Now, let's read the headings. Read the first heading._ Read the next heading._ (Continue until students have read all headings.)
4. Turn to your partner. Without looking, tell two things this passage will tell about._

ACTIVITY C *Background Knowledge*

A.D. 1600   A.D. 1800   A.D. 2000

1775–1783   Revolutionary War

In this article, you will read about the role of women in the Revolutionary War, which was fought from 1775 to 1783. You probably wonder why Americans decided to fight this war. In the years leading up to the war, the British ruled the people in the American colonies without representation. The British expected the colonists to pay a lot of taxes and to follow laws they didn't believe in. The colonists made a declaration of independence and fought the British to become independent. Many American women helped defeat the British.

The Original 13 American Colonies, 1775

ACTIVITY D
Passage Reading and Comprehension

ACTIVITY PROCEDURE

(See the *Student Book,* pages 58–59.)

Have students work on reading accuracy by selecting a passage-reading option that best fits your students.

Passage Reading: Accuracy

(Select a passage-reading procedure that matches the size of your group and the competency of your students.

Option A

If you are teaching a small group of students who are having difficulty, use Option A:

Have students read one paragraph silently. Then, call on one student to orally read a paragraph or a portion of the paragraph to the class. Call on students in random order, varying the amount that each student reads.

Option B

If you are teaching a small group with students who are not having difficulty, use Option B:

Have students read the entire article silently, rereading it if they finish before their classmates. Then, call on one student to orally read a paragraph or a portion of a paragraph to the class. Call on students in random order, varying the amount that each student reads.

Option C

If you are teaching a large group with students who are having difficulty, use Option C:

Have students read one paragraph silently. Then, have students read the paragraph to a partner. Alternate partner-reading turns.

Option D

If you are teaching a large group with students who are not having difficulty, use Option D:

Have students read the entire article silently, rereading it if they finish before their classmates. Then, have students read the passage with their partners, alternating on each paragraph.)

(**ACTIVITY D**) *Passage Reading and Comprehension*

Women in the American Revolution

12	The Revolutionary War brings many images to mind. You might think of colonial men fighting against the British men in their red coats. Or, you might
26	think of George Washington and other founding fathers. But did you know that
39	there were many women who played a role in the American Revolution as well?
53	They were soldiers, spies, and nurses, and they worked hard to fight for
66	independence from the British. (#1)
70	**Warnings**
71	Most Americans know the story of Paul Revere's ride through the town,
83	warning of British invasion. But few people have heard of 16-year-old Sybil
97	Ludington. On a dark night in 1777, she rode through her Connecticut town to
111	rouse, or awaken, her neighbors. She had witnessed the British attack of a
124	nearby supply house. Because of her warning, the colonists were able to save
137	their supply depot. (#2)
140	There were other young American women who braved danger to warn of
152	impending British attacks. Susanna Boiling, a teenager, crossed a river alone one
164	night to inform General Lafayette of an attack the British were planning. Lydia
177	Barrington Darragh, a 48-year-old woman who had nine children, spied on a
191	meeting of British commanders. She traveled across enemy lines to notify
202	George Washington of the British plan to attack his soldiers. (#3)
212	**Supply Lines**
214	Some of the Revolutionary women focused their attention on supporting war
225	efforts. Women provided passing colonial troops with food, shelter, candles, and
236	soap. Some women formed patriotic societies. Some of these societies raised
247	money to purchase boots and gunpowder for their soldiers. Some sewed and
259	sent shirts, socks, quilts, and bandages for troops. Some women even took over
272	the businesses that their husbands ran. They became butchers, bakers, millers,
283	fishmongers, and blacksmiths during the war so that production needs would
294	continue to be met. (#4)
298	**Disobedience**
299	During the war, British soldiers would often commandeer (take) farms, crop
310	supplies, or homes in order to supply their armies. A number of women refused

Passage Reading: Comprehension Questions

(You may wish to ask the following questions as the passage is being read. Numbers corresponding to the questions are indicated at the point at which they could be asked.)

#1 What roles did women play in fighting the Revolutionary War?
Soldiers, spies, and nurses.

#2 How did a 16-year-old woman assist in the war effort?
She roused her neighbors in order to save a supply depot.

#3 What kinds of risks did women take to help win the war?
Ideas: Crossing a river alone at night; traveling across enemy lines.

324 to cooperate with the British. Some women burned their crops, preventing the
336 British from taking them. Others defended their own homes against British
347 occupation. Anne Kennedy, a woman from South Carolina, organized an attack
358 against British forces that were attempting to take her home and her crops. She
372 was wounded in the battle, but the British fled. (#5)

381 **Nurses and Soldiers**
384   The colonial armies required nurses to help tend the sick and the wounded.
397 Congress granted them one nurse for every ten patients. The nurses were paid
410 monthly and given one food ration per day. Other women participated in a less
424 official capacity. Margaret Warne was a physician from New Jersey. During the war,
437 she would ride through the country and aid soldiers and their families at no charge.
452   Some women fought on the battlefields. They fought alongside their
462 husbands, helping them to clean and load cannons or carry water. Many women
475 who fought as soldiers disguised themselves as men in order to enlist in the
489 army. Prudence Wright, from Massachusetts, actually commanded a regiment
498 entirely made up of women dressed as men. They defended their town and
511 captured a British messenger and his plans. (#6)

518 **Founding Fathers . . . and Women, Too**
523   Women provided a great deal of support during the Revolutionary War, both
535 on the battlefield and back at home. Although their stories are not as well
549 known as their male counterparts' stories, women played important roles in the
561 war effort. Together, colonial men and women defeated the British and helped
573 to shape America. (#7)
576

ACTIVITY E *Fluency Building*

Cold Timing		Practice 1	
Practice 2		Hot Timing	

Student Book: Application Lesson 6   **59**

#4 What would have happened if women had not raised money, sewed, and taken over husbands' businesses?
Production needs would not have been met.

#5 What did women do in order to keep the British from taking their homes and crops?
Ideas: Burned crops, defended homes, attacked British forces.

#6 How did woman get away with fighting as soldiers?
They dressed in men's uniforms.

#7 Why do you think that women's stories of war aid and bravery are not as well known as men's stories?
Ideas: Most historians are male; typically, women weren't soldiers in the 1700s; history focused on the actions of men.

ACTIVITY E
Fluency Building

ACTIVITY PROCEDURE

(See the *Student Book*, page 59.)

Have students complete a Cold Timing, one or two practices, and a Hot Timing of the Activity D article. For each timing, have students record the number of correct words read. Finally, have students complete their Fluency Graphs.

Note E-1: When assigning partners for this activity, have the stronger reader read first. As a result, the other reader will have one additional practice opportunity.

1. Now, it's time for fluency building.
2. Find the beginning of the passage again. (Pause.)
3. Whisper-read. See how many words you can read in one minute. Begin._ (Time students for one minute.) Stop._ Circle the last word that you read._ Record the number of words you read after **Cold Timing** in **Activity E** at the bottom of page 59._
4. Let's practice again. Begin._ (Time students for one minute.) Stop._ Put a box around the last word that you read._ Record the number of words you read after **Practice 1**._
5. **Optional** Let's practice one more time before the Hot Timing. Begin._ (Time students for one minute.) Stop._ Put a box around the last word that you read._ Record the number of words you read after **Practice 2**._
6. Please exchange books with your partner._ Partner 1, you are going to read first. Partner 2, listen carefully and underline any mistakes or words left out. Ones, begin._ (Time students for one minute.) Stop._ Twos, cross out the last word that your partner read._ Twos, record the number of words in your partner's book after **Hot Timing**._
7. Partner 2, you are going to read next. Partner 1, listen carefully and underline any mistakes or words left out. Twos, begin. (Time students for one minute.) Stop._ Ones, cross out the last word that your partner read._ Ones, record the number of words in your partner's book after **Hot Timing**._
8. Exchange books._ Turn to the Fluency Graph on the last page of your book, and indicate on the graph the number of Cold Timing and Hot Timing words you read correctly._

ACTIVITY F

Comprehension Questions—Multiple Choice and Short Answer

ACTIVITY PROCEDURE

(See the *Student Book,* page 60.)

Have students complete all the Multiple Choice items. Then, have students share their answers and rationales. Encourage thoughtful discussion. Have students record points for each correct item.

Note F-1: The correct Multiple Choice answers are circled.

Multiple Choice Comprehension

1. Turn to page 60. Find **Activity F**. Answer all the items on your own. But, be ready to explain why you selected your answers._
2. (Wait while students complete all the items. Call on individual students. For each item, ask why they chose their answer and why they eliminated the other choices. Encourage discussion.)
3. Count the number of items you got correct, and record that number as points in the blank half of the Multiple Choice Comprehension box._

ACTIVITY PROCEDURE

(See the *Student Book,* page 61.)

Have students complete the Short Answer questions on the passage. Give feedback to students on their answers. Have students record points for each question's answer: one point for using the wording of the question in the answer, and one point for accuracy of the answer (total of 4 points possible for two complete answers).

Short Answer Comprehension

1. Turn to page 61._ Use the Short Answer Strategy on your own.
2. (When students are done, give them feedback.)
3. Count your number of points (a maximum of 4 points for the two answers), and add that number in the blank half of the Short Answer Comprehension box.

 ACTIVITY F *Comprehension Questions—*
Multiple Choice and Short Answer

Comprehension Strategy—Multiple Choice

Step 1: Read the item.
Step 2: Read all of the choices.
Step 3: Think about why each choice might be correct or incorrect. Check the article as needed.
Step 4: From the possible correct choices, select the best answer.

1. (Vocabulary) **What two words from the article are synonyms?**
   a. arouse and awaken
   b. warning and attack
   c. ration and capacity
   d. witness and notify

2. (Main Idea) **What is the main idea of this article?**
   a. During the Revolutionary War, women served as nurses and soldiers.
   b. Women, as well as men, played important roles in the Revolutionary War.
   c. The colonists defeated the British in the Revolutionary War.
   d. Some women, disguised as men, actually fought as soldiers in the Revolutionary War.

3. (Vocabulary) **Read this sentence from the passage: "There were other young American women who braved danger to warn of *impending* British attacks." What does the word *impending* mean?**
   a. dangerous
   b. about to end
   c. about to happen
   d. deadly

4. (Cause and Effect) **Why did the women who fought as soldiers disguise themselves?**
   a. They wanted to go behind the British lines.
   b. Male soldiers were less likely to be killed in battle.
   c. Only men were allowed to enlist in the army.
   d. The soldiers' uniforms were more comfortable than the nurses' clothing.

MULTIPLE CHOICE COMPREHENSION **4**
Points

60   *REWARDS Plus: Reading Strategies Applied to Social Studies Passages*

Comprehension Strategy—Short Answer

Step 1: Read the item.
Step 2: Turn the question into part of the answer and write it down.
Step 3: Think of the answer or locate the answer in the article.
Step 4: Complete your answer.

1. **What conclusions about the Revolutionary War does the author of this article want you to reach?**
   Example answer: The author of this article wants you to conclude that women helped America during the Revolutionary War. The author wants you to remember that women did things that were just as important as the men to help win the war.

2. **What were three of the most dangerous things women did during the Revolutionary War?**
   Example answer: Three of the most dangerous things women did during the Revolutionary War were enlisting as soldiers, spying on the British soldiers, and warning others about British activity.

SHORT ANSWER COMPREHENSION **4**
Points

Student Book: Application Lesson 6 **61**

ACTIVITY G

Expository Writing—Extended Response

ACTIVITY PROCEDURE

(See the *Student Book,* pages 62–63.)

Have students read the prompt and record their position. Next, have them **LIST** reasons and explanations in the Planning Box by referring back to the article. Encourage them to record notes rather than write complete sentences. When students are done with their lists, have them compare their reasons and explanations with those of their classmates and the Example Plan.

1. Turn to page 62.⎵ Today, we are going to use the Extended Response Writing Strategy.
2. Read the prompt.⎵ Write your position in the Planning Box.
3. Read **Step 1**.⎵ Now, write reasons to support your position. Make the response stronger by writing an explanation for each reason.⎵ (Monitor carefully as students record reasons and explanations.)
4. Compare your list to your partner's list.⎵

Use Overhead 23
Example Extended Response Plan

5. Let's read the reasons and explanations on the overhead. Your list should have some of the same ideas, but it does not need to be exactly the same.⎵ If you want to fix up your list, do that now.⎵

ACTIVITY PROCEDURE

Next, have students complete the additional steps in the Extended Response Writing Strategy. Have them reread their lists and **CROSS OUT** any weak or unimportant reasons or explanations. Then, have students **CONNECT** explanations that could go together in one sentence, **NUMBER** their reasons in a logical order, and **WRITE** their extended responses on a separate piece of paper. When they are done, have them **EDIT** their paragraphs, revising for clarity and proofreading for errors in spelling, capitalization, and punctuation.

Have students read their extended responses to their partners. Then, read the Example Extended Response.

Have students read each of the attributes on the rubric, examine their extended responses, and circle either "Yes" or "Fix up." Give students time to make necessary changes.

ACTIVITY G *Expository Writing—Extended Response*

Writing Strategy—Extended Response

Step 1: LIST (List the reasons for your position. For each reason, explain with details.)
Step 2: CROSS OUT (Reread your reasons and details. Cross out any that you decide not to include.)
Step 3: CONNECT (Connect any details that could go into one sentence.)
Step 4: NUMBER (Number the reasons in a logical order.)
Step 5: WRITE (Write your response.)
Step 6: EDIT (Revise and proofread your response.)

Prompt: Explain why women's roles were as important as men's roles in defeating the British during the Revolutionary War.

Planning Box
(position) *Women's roles were as important as men's roles in defeating the British.*
① (reason) – *women saw things and warned other people*
(explain) – *Sybil Ludington witnessed attack on supply house and warned neighbors*
– *Susanna Boiling, teenager, crossed river and warned General Lafayette*
② (reason) – *women supported war efforts with supplies for colonial troops*
(explain) – *provided food, candles, soap, shelter*
– *raised money to purchase boots, gunpowder*
③ (reason) – *women protected crops and homes*
(explain) – *burned crops, Anne Kennedy attacked British on her land*
(reason) – ~~*women were nurses and soldiers*~~
(explain) – ~~*one nurse for every ten patients*~~
~~*fought alongside husbands, dressed like men*~~

Directions: Write your extended response on a separate piece of paper.

62 *REWARDS Plus: Reading Strategies Applied to Social Studies Passages*

Rubric— Extended Response	Student or Partner Rating		Teacher Rating	
1. Did the author tell his/her position in the first sentence?	Yes	Fix up	Yes	No
2. Did the author include at least three **strong, logical** reasons for his/her position?	Yes	Fix up	Yes	No
3. Did the author provide a **strong, logical** explanation for each of his/her reasons?	Yes	Fix up	Yes	No
4. Is the response easy to understand?	Yes	Fix up	Yes	No
5. Did the author correctly spell words, particularly the words found in the article?	Yes	Fix up	Yes	No
6. Did the author use correct capitalization, capitalizing the first word in the sentence and proper names of people, places, and things?	Yes	Fix up	Yes	No
7. Did the author use correct punctuation, including a period at the end of each sentence?	Yes	Fix up	Yes	No

WRITING **7** *Points*

Optional: During or after the class session, fill in the third column of the rubric chart and assign points to the extended responses.

Optional: Have students date their writing and place the sample in a folder. Thus, students will be able to look back at their summaries and extended responses and literally see their writing improvement.

6. Read **Step 2**._ If you have any reasons that are not logical or strong, cross them out now._ What reasons did you eliminate, and why? (**Call on individual students._**)

7. Read **Step 3**._ Look at your list. What ideas might you combine into one sentence? (**Call on individual students._**) Please draw brackets on your list to connect ideas._ (**Monitor carefully.**)

8. Read **Step 4**._ Now, number the ideas in a logical order. If your have two connected ideas, give them only one number._ (**Monitor.**)

9. Read **Step 5**. Write your extended response on a separate piece of paper. Be sure that your first sentence tells your position. The rest of your sentences should include reasons and explanations._ (**Monitor.**)

10. Read **Step 6**. Reread your extended response. Check to be sure your response is easy to understand. Fix any errors you find in spelling, capitalization, and punctuation._ (**Monitor.**)

11. Reread your response to your partner._

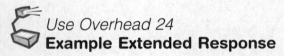
Use Overhead 24
Example Extended Response

12. Look at the overhead. Let's read this Example Extended Response. Yours doesn't need to be exactly the same, but it should be similar.

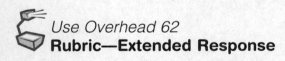
Use Overhead 62
Rubric—Extended Response

13. Turn to page 63._ Today, you will be evaluating your own response. You will use the questions in this rubric to determine what you need to edit.

14. Read the question for attribute 1._ Reread your first sentence, and look for your position. Circle "Yes" if you have it, or circle "Fix up" if you need to revise it._ If you need to improve your first sentence, you will work on it later.

APPLICATION LESSON
6

(ACTIVITY G) *Expository Writing—Extended Response*

Writing Strategy—Extended Response

Step 1: LIST (List the reasons for your position. For each reason, explain with details.)
Step 2: CROSS OUT (Reread your reasons and details. Cross out any that you decide not to include.)
Step 3: CONNECT (Connect any details that could go into one sentence.)
Step 4: NUMBER (Number the reasons in a logical order.)
Step 5: WRITE (Write your response.)
Step 6: EDIT (Revise and proofread your response.)

Prompt: Explain why women's roles were as important as men's roles in defeating the British during the Revolutionary War.

Planning Box

(position) *Women's roles were as important as men's roles in defeating the British.*

① (reason) – *women saw things and warned other people*

{ (explain) – *Sybil Ludington witnessed attack on supply house and warned neighbors*
– *Susanna Boiling, teenager, crossed river and warned General Lafayette*

② (reason) – *women supported war efforts with supplies for colonial troops*

(explain) – *provided food, candles, soap, shelter*
– *raised money to purchase boots, gunpowder*

③ (reason) – *women protected crops and homes*

(explain) – *burned crops, Anne Kennedy attacked British on her land*

(reason) – ~~*women were nurses and soldiers*~~

(explain) – ~~*one nurse for every ten patients*~~
– ~~*fought alongside husbands, dressed like men*~~

Directions: Write your extended response on a separate piece of paper.

Rubric— Extended Response	Student or Partner Rating		Teacher Rating	
1. Did the author tell his/her position in the first sentence?	Yes	Fix up	Yes	No
2. Did the author include at least three **strong, logical** reasons for his/her position?	Yes	Fix up	Yes	No
3. Did the author provide a **strong, logical** explanation for each of his/her reasons?	Yes	Fix up	Yes	No
4. Is the response easy to understand?	Yes	Fix up	Yes	No
5. Did the author correctly spell words, particularly the words found in the article?	Yes	Fix up	Yes	No
6. Did the author use correct capitalization, capitalizing the first word in the sentence and proper names of people, places, and things?	Yes	Fix up	Yes	No
7. Did the author use correct punctuation, including a period at the end of each sentence?	Yes	Fix up	Yes	No

WRITING **7**
Points

15. Read the question for attribute 2._ Reread the rest of your sentences, and determine if you included reasons and explanations. Circle "Yes" or "Fix up."_ If you circle "Fix up," work on it later.

16. Complete the ratings for the remaining questions. Remember to read each question, and then look at your response to make sure the criteria have been met.

17. (When the evaluation is complete, give students adequate time to make any necessary changes. Have students enter their points in the blank half of the Writing box below the rubric.)

Application Lesson 7

Materials Needed:

- *Student Book:* Application Lesson 7

- Application Overhead Transparencies 25–28

- Appendix A Reproducible 6: Writing Strategy—Extended Response

- Appendix B Optional Vocabulary Activities: Application Lesson 7

- Paper or cardboard to use when covering the overhead transparency

- Paper or cardboard for each student to use during spelling dictation

- Washable overhead transparency pen

Text Treatment Notes:

- Black text signifies teacher script (exact wording to say to students).

- Green text in parentheses signifies directions or prompts for the teacher.

- Green text signifies answers or examples of answers.

- Green graphics treatment signifies reproduction of Overhead information.

- Green text and green graphics treatment do not appear in the *Student Book.*

ACTIVITY A
Vocabulary

ACTIVITY PROCEDURE, List 1

(See the *Student Book,* page 65.)

Tell students each word in the list. Then, have students repeat the word and read the definition aloud. For each definition, provide any additional information that may be necessary. Then, have students practice reading the words themselves.

Note A.1-1: See Appendix E, Pronunciation Guide for Unique Words, for correct pronunciations of uncommon vocabulary words.

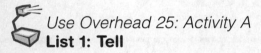

Use Overhead 25: Activity A
List 1: Tell

1. (Show the top half of Overhead 25.) Before we read the passage, let's read the difficult words. (Point to **the Senate**.) The first words are **the Senate**. What words?_ Now, read the definition._
2. (Point to **senators**.) The next word is **senators**. What word?_ Now, read the definition._
3. (Pronounce each word in List 1, and then have students repeat each word and read the definition.)
4. Open your *Student Book* to **Application Lesson 7**, page 65._
5. Find **Activity A**, **List 1**, in your book._ Let's read the words again. First word._ Next word._ (Continue for all words in List 1.)

ACTIVITY PROCEDURE, List 2

(See the *Student Book,* page 65.)

Have students circle prefixes and suffixes, then underline the vowels. Using the overhead transparency, assist students in checking their work. Next, have students figure out each word to themselves, then say it aloud. Have them read the definition aloud.

Use Overhead 25: Activity A
List 2: Strategy Practice

1. Find **List 2**. Circle the prefixes and suffixes, and underline the vowels. Look up when you are done._
2. (Show the bottom half of Overhead 25.) Now, check and fix any mistakes._

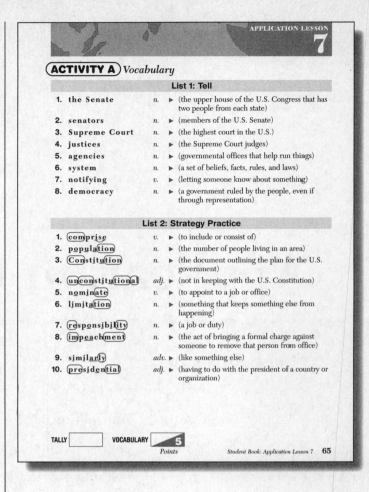

ACTIVITY A *Vocabulary*

List 1: Tell

1.	the Senate	n.	► (the upper house of the U.S. Congress that has two people from each state)
2.	senators	n.	► (members of the U.S. Senate)
3.	Supreme Court	n.	► (the highest court in the U.S.)
4.	justices	n.	► (the Supreme Court judges)
5.	agencies	n.	► (governmental offices that help run things)
6.	system	n.	► (a set of beliefs, facts, rules, and laws)
7.	notifying	v.	► (letting someone know about something)
8.	democracy	n.	► (a government ruled by the people, even if through representation)

List 2: Strategy Practice

1.	comprise	v.	► (to include or consist of)
2.	population	n.	► (the number of people living in an area)
3.	Constitution	n.	► (the document outlining the plan for the U.S. government)
4.	unconstitutional	adj.	► (not in keeping with the U.S. Constitution)
5.	nominate	v.	► (to appoint to a job or office)
6.	limitation	n.	► (something that keeps something else from happening)
7.	responsibility	n.	► (a job or duty)
8.	impeachment	n.	► (the act of bringing a formal charge against someone to remove that person from office)
9.	similarly	adv.	► (like something else)
10.	presidential	adj.	► (having to do with the president of a country or organization)

TALLY [ ] VOCABULARY [5] Points

Student Book: Application Lesson 7 **65**

3. Go back to the first word._ Sound out the word to yourself. Put your thumb up when you can read the word. Be sure that it is a real word._ What word?_ Now, read the definition._
4. (Continue Step 3 with all remaining words in List 2.)

Note A.2-1: You may wish to provide additional practice by having students read words to a partner.

ACTIVITY PROCEDURE, List 1 and 2

(See the *Student Book*, page 65.)

Tell students to look in List 1 or List 2 for a word you are thinking about. Have them circle the number of the word and tell you the word. Explain to students to make a tally mark for each correct word in the Tally box, and then enter the number of tally marks as points in the blank half of the Vocabulary box.

1. Remember, the words I'm thinking about will be in either List 1 or List 2. For every word you correctly identify, make a tally mark in the Tally box at the bottom of page 65. If you don't identify the correct word, don't do anything.
2. Circle the number of the appropriate word.
   - What do we call the total number of people in a city, town, state, or country? (Wait.) What word? **population**
   - The plan for the U.S. government is called this. (Wait.) What word? **Constitution**
   - Formal charges brought against a person to remove that person from office are called an act of this. (Wait.) What word? **impeachment**
   - When we want to appoint someone to a job or to an office, we do this to that person. (Wait.) What word? **nominate**
   - If you let someone know about something that is about to happen or may happen, you are doing this. (Wait.) What word? **notifying**
3. Count all the tally marks, and enter that number as points in the blank half of the Vocabulary box.

ACTIVITY PROCEDURE, List 3

(See the *Student Book*, page 66.)

The words in the third list are related. Have students use the *REWARDS* Strategies to figure out the first word in each family. Have them read the definition and then read the other two words in the family.

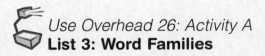
Use Overhead 26: Activity A
List 3: Word Families

1. Turn to page 66. Find **Family 1** in **List 3**. Figure out the first word. Use your pencil if you wish. Put your thumb up when you know the word._ What word?_ Read the definition._
2. Look at the next word in Family 1. Figure out the word._ What word?_

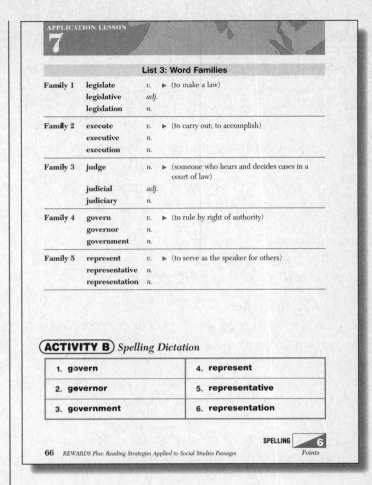

APPLICATION LESSON
7

List 3: Word Families

Family 1	legislate	v.	▶	(to make a law)
	legislative	adj.		
	legislation	n.		
Family 2	execute	v.	▶	(to carry out; to accomplish)
	executive	n.		
	execution	n.		
Family 3	judge	n.	▶	(someone who hears and decides cases in a court of law)
	judicial	adj.		
	judiciary	n.		
Family 4	govern	v.	▶	(to rule by right of authority)
	governor	n.		
	government	n.		
Family 5	represent	v.	▶	(to serve as the speaker for others)
	representative	n.		
	representation	n.		

ACTIVITY B *Spelling Dictation*

1. **govern**	4. **represent**
2. **governor**	5. **representative**
3. **government**	6. **representation**

SPELLING **6**
Points

66 REWARDS Plus: Reading Strategies Applied to Social Studies Passages

3. Next word. Figure out the word._ What word?_
4. (Repeat Steps 1–3 for all word families in List 3.)

Note A.3-1: You may wish to provide additional practice by having students read a word family to the group or to a partner.

Note A.3-2: Additional vocabulary practice activities are provided in Appendix B of the Teacher's Guide. These activities are optional and can be assigned during class, for homework, or as small group, in-class activities.

ACTIVITY B
Spelling Dictation

ACTIVITY PROCEDURE

(See the *Student Book,* page 66.)

For each word, tell students the word, then have students say the parts of the word to themselves while they write the word. Then, have students enter the number of correctly spelled words as points in the blank half of the Spelling box.

Note B-1: Distribute a piece of light cardboard to each of the students.

 Use Overhead 26: Activity B

1. Find **Activity B**.
2. The first word is **govern**. What word?_ Say the parts in **govern** to yourself as you write the word. (Pause and monitor.)
3. (Show **govern** on the overhead.) Check **govern**. If you misspelled it, cross it out and write it correctly.
4. The second word is **governor**. What word?_ Say the parts in **governor** to yourself as you write the word. (Pause and monitor.)
5. (Show **governor** on the overhead.) Check **governor**. If you misspelled it, cross it out and write it correctly.
6. (Repeat the procedures for the words **government**, **represent**, **representative,** and **representation**.)
7. Count the number of words you spelled correctly, and record that number as points in the blank half of the Spelling box at the bottom of the page.

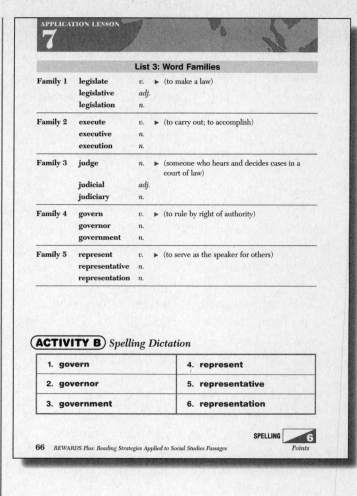

APPLICATION LESSON
7

List 3: Word Families

Family 1	legislate	v. ►	(to make a law)
	legislative	adj.	
	legislation	n.	
Family 2	execute	v. ►	(to carry out; to accomplish)
	executive	n.	
	execution	n.	
Family 3	judge	n. ►	(someone who hears and decides cases in a court of law)
	judicial	adj.	
	judiciary	n.	
Family 4	govern	v. ►	(to rule by right of authority)
	governor	n.	
	government	n.	
Family 5	represent	v. ►	(to serve as the speaker for others)
	representative	n.	
	representation	n.	

ACTIVITY B *Spelling Dictation*

1. govern	4. represent
2. governor	5. representative
3. government	6. representation

SPELLING ☐ 6
Points

66   *REWARDS Plus: Reading Strategies Applied to Social Studies Passages*

ACTIVITY C
Background Knowledge

ACTIVITY PROCEDURE

(See the *Student Book*, page 67.)

Read the Background Knowledge paragraph using one of three methods: read it to students, have students read it together, or call on individual students to read. Examine the timeline and the related graphic together. Then, preview the passage together by examining the title and the headings. Have students tell partners two things the passage will tell about.

1. Turn to page 67. Let's read the paragraph. (Read or ask students to read. Then examine the timeline and graphic together.)
2. Now, let's turn the page and preview the passage. Read the title._ What is the whole passage going to tell about?_
3. Now, let's read the headings. Read the first heading._ Read the next heading._ (Continue until students have read all headings.)
4. Turn to your partner. Without looking, tell two things this passage will tell about._

ACTIVITY C *Background Knowledge*

A.D. 1600   A.D. 1800   A.D. 2000

1787, 1788   U.S. Constitution drafted, approved

This article tells about the three branches of government described in the U.S. Constitution, which was drafted in 1787 and approved by the original 13 states in 1788. After the colonists defeated the British, they needed a way to rule themselves, so they created a document and called it the Constitution. The colonists wanted to create a government that was different from what they experienced under British rule. For example, they wanted to make sure that power belonged to the people. So, they wrote a Bill of Rights, which listed the rights of individuals that cannot be taken away by the government, and they created a system of representation. The colonists also made sure that the powers granted to any of the three branches of government were balanced against each other.

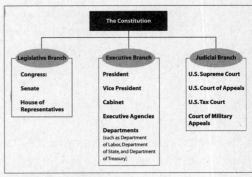

Diagram of U.S. Government Branches

Student Book: Application Lesson 7 **67**

ACTIVITY D

Passage Reading and Comprehension

ACTIVITY PROCEDURE

(See the *Student Book*, pages 68–69.)

Have students work on reading accuracy by selecting a passage-reading option that best fits your students.

Passage Reading: Accuracy

(Select a passage-reading procedure that matches the size of your group and the competency of your students.

Option A

If you are teaching a small group of students who are having difficulty, use Option A:

Have students read one paragraph silently. Then, call on one student to orally read a paragraph or a portion of the paragraph to the class. Call on students in random order, varying the amount that each student reads.

Option B

If you are teaching a small group with students who are not having difficulty, use Option B:

Have students read the entire article silently, rereading it if they finish before their classmates. Then, call on one student to orally read a paragraph or a portion of a paragraph to the class. Call on students in random order, varying the amount that each student reads.

Option C

If you are teaching a large group with students who are having difficulty, use Option C:

Have students read one paragraph silently. Then, have students read the paragraph to a partner. Alternate partner-reading turns.

Option D

If you are teaching a large group with students who are not having difficulty, use Option D:

Have students read the entire article silently, rereading it if they finish before their classmates. Then, have students read the passage with their partners, alternating on each paragraph.)

APPLICATION LESSON

7

ACTIVITY D *Passage Reading and Comprehension*

Branches of the United States Government

12	When the colonists drew up the Constitution, in which they constructed a
25	system of government, they wanted to be sure that the government was strong.
38	But, they also wanted to make sure that the power remained balanced. They
50	finally decided that they would create a government that has three branches:
	legislative, executive, and judicial. (#1)

54	**Legislative Branch**
56	Article 1 of the Constitution is concerned with the legislative branch of the
69	government, which is the system of representation the colonists created. The
80	primary function of the legislative branch, or Congress, is to enact legislation, or
93	make laws, for the country. Congress is comprised of two groups: the Senate and
107	the House of Representatives. Each state has two senators who are elected by
120	the people. One-third of the Senate seats come up for election every two years.
135	This way, the Senate is never totally new. The House of Representatives is much
149	larger, because each state elects a certain number of representatives based on its
162	population. The greater the number of people living in a state, the higher the
176	number of representatives. Elections for representatives are held every two
186	years. (#2)

187	**Executive Branch**
189	The president, vice president, Cabinet members, and executive agencies are
199	all part of the executive branch of government. The executive branch was
211	established in Article 2 of the Constitution. It is the duty of the executive branch
226	of government to make sure that the nation follows its laws. The president acts
240	as the commander-in-chief of the armed forces. The president is also
253	responsible for notifying Congress about the well-being of the country and can
266	request a special session of Congress, if necessary. In addition, the president has
279	the power to pardon federal criminals. The president is limited to two four-year
293	terms in office. (#3)

296	**Judicial Branch**
298	Established by Article 3 of the Constitution, the judicial branch is
309	responsible for deciding if the laws enacted by Congress and by the states are
323	constitutional, or in line with the Constitution. The primary arm of the judicial

68 *REWARDS Plus: Reading Strategies Applied to Social Studies Passages*

Passage Reading: Comprehension Questions

(You may wish to ask the following questions as the passage is being read. Numbers corresponding to the questions are indicated at the point at which they could be asked.)

#1 Why did the colonists establish three branches in the U.S. government?
To make sure power was balanced.

#2 What do senators and representatives primarily do?
Make laws; enact legislation.

#3 What does the executive branch primarily do?
Makes sure everyone follows the laws.

#4 What do the nine Justices of the Supreme Court primarily do?
Decide if laws are constitutional.

336 | branch of government is the Supreme Court. The Supreme Court was created
348 | according to the Constitution. Later, Congress also created several lower federal
359 | courts. The Supreme Court has nine members, called *justices*. These justices are
371 | nominated by the president, but must be approved by Congress. Justices do not
384 | have any term limitations; once they are appointed, they hold office for life or
398 | until they retire. (#4)

401 | **Checks and Balances**
404 | The government's responsibilities and powers were spread over three
413 | different branches to ensure that no one person or agency gains too much
426 | power. Therefore, within the system the United States currently has, a number
438 | of checks and balances are built in. *Veto power* is one example. This means that
453 | if Congress votes to pass a law, the president has the power to keep the law from
470 | happening by vetoing that law. Then, if Congress can muster a two-thirds vote in
485 | favor of the law, it can override the president's veto. (#5)
495 | Another example of checks and balances is *impeachment*. If the president
506 | abuses official power or breaks the law in some way, Congress and the Supreme
520 | Court have the power to remove the president from office. Both groups in
533 | Congress must vote in agreement for presidential impeachment to take place.
544 | Similarly, Supreme Court justices can be impeached if they abuse their position.
556 | The Supreme Court can also declare laws or presidential actions
566 | unconstitutional. (#6)
567 | The founding fathers remembered what they didn't like about being under
578 | British rule. By splitting the power of the United States government, they
590 | helped to ensure that the leadership of the country would be balanced. They
603 | created a system of checks and balances to make sure that no one part of the
619 | government could become too powerful. The founding fathers established rule
629 | by representation and listed individuals' rights on paper, thus forming the
640 | foundation of a democracy that has been operating for more than 200 years. (#7)
653 |

(ACTIVITY E) *Fluency Building*

Cold Timing		Practice 1	
Practice 2		Hot Timing	

Student Book: Application Lesson 7 **69**

#5 What is one example of the checks and balances built into the U.S. government?
Ideas: The president can veto a law; Congress can override a veto.

#6 What is another example of checks and balances?
Ideas: Congress and the Supreme Court can impeach the president; Supreme Court Justices can be impeached; laws and presidential acts can be declared unconstitutional.

#7 What are some of the characteristics of a democracy?
Ideas: Rule is by the people, either directly or through representation; no single branch of the government is all-powerful.

(ACTIVITY E)
Fluency Building

ACTIVITY PROCEDURE

(See the *Student Book*, page 69.)

Have students complete a Cold Timing, one or two practices, and a Hot Timing of the Activity D article. For each timing, have students record the number of correct words read. Finally, have students complete their Fluency Graphs.

Note E-1: When assigning partners for this activity, have the stronger reader read first. As a result, the other reader will have one additional practice opportunity.

1. Now, it's time for fluency building.
2. Find the beginning of the passage again. (Pause.)
3. Whisper-read. See how many words you can read in one minute. Begin.— (Time students for one minute.) Stop.— Circle the last word that you read.— Record the number of words you read after **Cold Timing** in **Activity E** at the bottom of page 69.—
4. Let's practice again. Begin.— (Time students for one minute.) Stop.— Put a box around the last word that you read.— Record the number of words you read after **Practice 1**.—
5. **Optional** Let's practice one more time before the Hot Timing. Begin.— (Time students for one minute.) Stop.— Put a box around the last word that you read.— Record the number of words you read after **Practice 2**.—
6. Please exchange books with your partner.— Partner 1, you are going to read first. Partner 2, listen carefully and underline any mistakes or words left out. Ones, begin.— (Time students for one minute.) Stop.— Twos, cross out the last word that your partner read.— Twos, record the number of words in your partner's book after **Hot Timing**.—
7. Partner 2, you are going to read next. Partner 1, listen carefully and underline any mistakes or words left out. Twos, begin. (Time students for one minute.) Stop.— Ones, cross out the last word that your partner read.— Ones, record the number of words in your partner's book after **Hot Timing**.—
8. Exchange books.— Turn to the Fluency Graph on the last page of your book, and indicate on the graph the number of Cold Timing and Hot Timing words you read correctly.—

ACTIVITY F

Comprehension Questions— Multiple Choice and Short Answer

ACTIVITY PROCEDURE

(See the *Student Book*, page 70.)

Have students complete all the Multiple Choice items. Then, have students share their answers and rationales. Encourage thoughtful discussion. Have students record points for each correct item.

Note F-1: The correct Multiple Choice answers are circled.

Multiple Choice Comprehension

1. Turn to page 70. Find **Activity F**. Answer all the items on your own. But, be ready to explain why you selected your answers._
2. (Wait while students complete all the items. Call on individual students. For each item, ask why they chose their answer and why they eliminated the other choices. Encourage discussion.)
3. Count the number of items you got correct, and record that number as points in the blank half of the Multiple Choice Comprehension box._

ACTIVITY PROCEDURE

(See the *Student Book*, page 71.)

Have students complete the Short Answer questions on the passage. Give feedback to students on their answers. Have students record points for each question's answer: one point for using the wording of the question in the answer, and one point for accuracy of the answer (total of 4 points possible for two complete answers).

Short Answer Comprehension

1. Turn to page 71._ Use the Short Answer Strategy on your own.
2. (When students are done, give them feedback.)
3. Count your number of points (a maximum of 4 points for the two answers), and add that number in the blank half of the Short Answer Comprehension box.

ACTIVITY F *Comprehension Questions— Multiple Choice and Short Answer*

Comprehension Strategy—Multiple Choice

Step 1: Read the item.
Step 2: Read all of the choices.
Step 3: Think about why each choice might be correct or incorrect. Check the article as needed.
Step 4: From the possible correct choices, select the best answer.

1. (Vocabulary) **What does the term "checks and balances" mean when referring to the U.S. government?**
   a. An accounting system in which each checkbook is balanced.
   b. A system in which the voters can check the actions of politicians.
   c. A system of government in which the president can override legislative actions.
   d. A system in which power is divided among three branches of government, and safeguards are built in to ensure that no branch has too much power.

2. (Cause and Effect) **Why did the Constitution form three branches of government rather than just one?**
   a. So that more people would have government jobs.
   b. So that the president could keep a law from happening by vetoing the law.
   c. So that no one person or branch would have too much power.
   d. So that the president could be impeached, if necessary.

3. (Compare and Contrast) **How are the Senate and the House of Representatives the same?**
   a. The length of time representatives and senators serve.
   b. The number of people in each group.
   c. The law-making function.
   d. How often seats come up for election.

4. (Main Idea) **Which of these similes best describes the government established by the U.S. Constitution?**
   a. The American government is like a tree with strong branches and a strong root system.
   b. The American government is like an umbrella that opens to protect its citizens.
   c. The American government is like a mansion with hidden rooms.
   d. The American government is like apple pie à la mode (with ice cream).

MULTIPLE CHOICE COMPREHENSION   **4**
Points

Comprehension Strategy—Short Answer

Step 1: Read the item.
Step 2: Turn the question into part of the answer and write it down.
Step 3: Think of the answer or locate the answer in the article.
Step 4: Complete your answer.

1. **How is the Senate different from the House of Representatives?**
   Example answer: The Senate is different from the House of Representatives because each state gets two senators, but the number of representatives each state gets is based on the state's population.

2. **How do Supreme Court justices get their jobs?**
   Example answer: Supreme Court justices get their jobs by being nominated by the president and approved by Congress.

SHORT ANSWER COMPREHENSION   **4**
Points

ACTIVITY G

Expository Writing—Extended Response

ACTIVITY PROCEDURE

(See the *Student Book,* pages 72–73.)

Have students read the prompt and record their position. Next, have them **LIST** reasons and explanations in the Planning Box by referring back to the article. Encourage them to record notes rather than write complete sentences. When students are done with their lists, have them compare their reasons and explanations with those of their classmates and the Example Plan.

1. Turn to page 72. Today, you will use the steps of the Extended Response Writing Strategy to plan and write a response. First, read the prompt and write your position. Then, **LIST** your reasons and explanations. When you are finished, compare your list to your partner's list.

Use Overhead 27
Example Extended Response Plan

2. Now, compare your list to the list on the overhead.

ACTIVITY PROCEDURE

Next, have students complete the additional steps in the Extended Response Writing Strategy. Have them reread their lists and **CROSS OUT** any weak or unimportant reasons or explanations. Then, have students **CONNECT** explanations that could go together in one sentence, **NUMBER** their reasons in a logical order, and **WRITE** their extended responses on a separate piece of paper. When they are done, have them **EDIT** their paragraphs, revising for clarity and proofreading for errors in spelling, capitalization, and punctuation.

Have students read their extended responses to their partners. Then, read the Example Extended Response.

Have students read each of the attributes on the rubric, examine their partners' extended responses, and circle either "Yes" or "Fix up." Give students time to make necessary changes.

Optional: During or after the class session, fill in the third column of the rubric chart and assign points to the extended responses.

ACTIVITY G *Expository Writing—Extended Response*

Writing Strategy—Extended Response

Step 1: LIST (List the reasons for your position. For each reason, explain with details.)
Step 2: CROSS OUT (Reread your reasons and details. Cross out any that you decide not to include.)
Step 3: CONNECT (Connect any details that could go into one sentence.)
Step 4: NUMBER (Number the reasons in a logical order.)
Step 5: WRITE (Write your response.)
Step 6: EDIT (Revise and proofread your response.)

Prompt: If you could choose a job in one branch of the U.S. government, tell which branch and why.

Planning Box
(position) *If I could choose a job, I would choose the legislative branch.*
① (reason) *– makes more difference than other branches*
(explain) *– makes laws that are enforced by executive branch and judged by judicial branch*
(reason) *– has lots of opportunities*
(explain) *– many representatives and senators*
② (reason) *– important to people in 50 states*
(explain) *– represent people of state*
– focus on state issues
③ (reason) *– many different issues would be considered*
(explain) *– environment, social issues, foreign affairs*

Directions: Write your extended response on a separate piece of paper.

Rubric— Extended Response	Student or Partner Rating	Teacher Rating
1. Did the author tell his/her position in the first sentence?	Yes Fix up	Yes No
2. Did the author include at least three **strong, logical** reasons for his/her position?	Yes Fix up	Yes No
3. Did the author provide a **strong, logical** explanation for each of his/her reasons?	Yes Fix up	Yes No
4. Is the response easy to understand?	Yes Fix up	Yes No
5. Did the author correctly spell words, particularly the words found in the article?	Yes Fix up	Yes No
6. Did the author use correct capitalization, capitalizing the first word in the sentence and proper names of people, places, and things?	Yes Fix up	Yes No
7. Did the author use correct punctuation, including a period at the end of each sentence?	Yes Fix up	Yes No

WRITING 7
Points

Optional: Have students date their writing and place the sample in a folder. Thus, students will be able to look back at their summaries and extended responses and literally see their writing improvement.

3. Now, **CROSS OUT**, **CONNECT**, **NUMBER**, and **WRITE**‿

4. Reread your response and **EDIT**. Check to be sure your response is easy to understand. Fix any errors you find in spelling, capitalization, and punctuation‿ (Monitor.)

5. Read your response to your partner‿

 Use Overhead 28
Example Extended Response

6. Look at the overhead. Let's read this Example Extended Response. Yours doesn't need to be exactly the same, but it should be similar.

7. Turn to page 73‿ Today, you will be evaluating your partner's response. Use the questions in this rubric to determine what your partner needs to edit.

8. Please exchange responses and books with your partner. Read the questions, read your partner's response, and circle "Yes" or "Fix up."‿

9. (When the evaluation is complete, have students return the responses and books to their partners. Give students adequate time to make any necessary changes to their extended responses. Have students enter their points in the blank half of the Writing box below the rubric.)

10. (Distribute Appendix A Reproducible 6: Writing Strategy—Extended Response. Have students place this in a notebook or a folder for future reference.)

(ACTIVITY G) *Expository Writing—Extended Response*

Writing Strategy—Extended Response

Step 1: **LIST** (List the reasons for your position. For each reason, explain with details.)
Step 2: **CROSS OUT** (Reread your reasons and details. Cross out any that you decide not to include.)
Step 3: **CONNECT** (Connect any details that could go into one sentence.)
Step 4: **NUMBER** (Number the reasons in a logical order.)
Step 5: **WRITE** (Write your response.)
Step 6: **EDIT** (Revise and proofread your response.)

Prompt: If you could choose a job in one branch of the U.S. government, tell which branch and why.

Planning Box
(position) *If I could choose a job, I would choose the legislative branch.*
① (reason) – *makes more difference than other branches*
(explain) – *makes laws that are enforced by executive branch and judged by judicial branch*
(reason) – *has lots of opportunities*
(explain) – *many representatives and senators*
② (reason) – *important to people in 50 states*
(explain) – *represent people of state* *– focus on state issues*
③ (reason) – *many different issues would be considered*
(explain) – *environment, social issues, foreign affairs*

Directions: Write your extended response on a separate piece of paper.

Rubric— Extended Response	Student or Partner Rating		Teacher Rating	
1. Did the author tell his/her position in the first sentence?	Yes	Fix up	Yes	No
2. Did the author include at least three **strong, logical** reasons for his/her position?	Yes	Fix up	Yes	No
3. Did the author provide a **strong, logical** explanation for each of his/her reasons?	Yes	Fix up	Yes	No
4. Is the response easy to understand?	Yes	Fix up	Yes	No
5. Did the author correctly spell words, particularly the words found in the article?	Yes	Fix up	Yes	No
6. Did the author use correct capitalization, capitalizing the first word in the sentence and proper names of people, places, and things?	Yes	Fix up	Yes	No
7. Did the author use correct punctuation, including a period at the end of each sentence?	Yes	Fix up	Yes	No

WRITING
Points

Application Lesson 8

Materials Needed:

- *Student Book:* Application Lesson 8
- Application Overhead Transparencies 29–32
- Appendix B Optional Vocabulary Activities: Application Lesson 8
- Paper or cardboard to use when covering the overhead transparency
- Paper or cardboard for each student to use during spelling dictation
- Washable overhead transparency pen

Text Treatment Notes:

- Black text signifies teacher script (exact wording to say to students).
- Green text in parentheses signifies directions or prompts for the teacher.
- Green text signifies answers or examples of answers.
- Green graphics treatment signifies reproduction of Overhead information.
- Green text and green graphics treatment do not appear in the *Student Book*.

ACTIVITY A
Vocabulary

ACTIVITY PROCEDURE, List 1

(See the *Student Book*, page 75.)

Tell students each word in the list. Then, have students repeat the word and read the definition aloud. For each definition, provide any additional information that may be necessary. Then, have students practice reading the words themselves.

Note A.1-1: See Appendix E, Pronunciation Guide for Unique Words, for correct pronunciations of uncommon vocabulary words.

Use Overhead 29: Activity A
List 1: Tell

1. (Show the top half of Overhead 29.) Before we read the passage, let's read the difficult words. (**Point to guarantee.**) The first word is **guarantee**. What word?_ Now, read the definition._
2. (Point to **aliens**.) The next word is **aliens**. What word?_ Now, read the definition._
3. (Pronounce each word in List 1, and then have students repeat each word and read the definition.)
4. Open your *Student Book* to **Application Lesson 8**, page 75._
5. Find **Activity A**, **List 1**, in your book._ Let's read the words again. First word._ Next word._ (Continue for all words in List 1.)

ACTIVITY PROCEDURE, List 2

(See the *Student Book*, page 75.)

Have students circle prefixes and suffixes, then underline the vowels. Using the overhead transparency, assist students in checking their work. Next, have students figure out each word to themselves, then say it aloud. Have them read the definition aloud.

Use Overhead 29: Activity A
List 2: Strategy Practice

1. Find **List 2**. Circle the prefixes and suffixes, and underline the vowels. Look up when you are done._
2. (Show the bottom half of Overhead 29.) Before you check your work, look at item #1. (Point to the

---

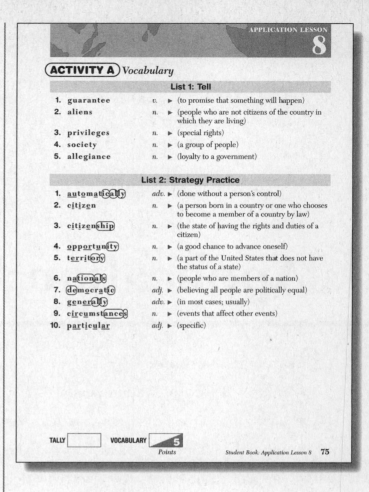

ACTIVITY A *Vocabulary*

List 1: Tell

1.	guarantee	v.	▶ (to promise that something will happen)
2.	aliens	n.	▶ (people who are not citizens of the country in which they are living)
3.	privileges	n.	▶ (special rights)
4.	society	n.	▶ (a group of people)
5.	allegiance	n.	▶ (loyalty to a government)

List 2: Strategy Practice

1.	automatically	adv.	▶ (done without a person's control)
2.	citizen	n.	▶ (a person born in a country or one who chooses to become a member of a country by law)
3.	citizenship	n.	▶ (the state of having the rights and duties of a citizen)
4.	opportunity	n.	▶ (a good chance to advance oneself)
5.	territory	n.	▶ (a part of the United States that does not have the status of a state)
6.	nationals	n.	▶ (people who are members of a nation)
7.	democratic	adj.	▶ (believing all people are politically equal)
8.	generally	adv.	▶ (in most cases; usually)
9.	circumstances	n.	▶ (events that affect other events)
10.	particular	adj.	▶ (specific)

TALLY [ ] VOCABULARY [5]
Points

Student Book: Application Lesson 8 **75**

---

second example and the **auto** that is circled.) From now on, you can also circle **auto**. The prefix is /auto/. Say it._ Look at item #3. (Point to the first example and the **ship** that is circled.) Remember, you can also circle **ship**. What suffix?_ Now, go back to item #1. Check and fix any mistakes._

3. Go back to the first word again._ Sound out the word to yourself. Put your thumb up when you can read the word. Be sure that it is a real word._ What word?_ Now, read the definition._
4. (Continue Step 3 with all remaining words in List 2.)

Note A.2-1: You may wish to provide additional practice by having students read words to a partner.

(See the *Student Book,* page 75.)

Tell students to look in List 1 or List 2 for a word you are thinking about. Have them circle the number of the word and tell you the word. Explain to students to make a tally mark for each correct word in the Tally box, and then enter the number of tally marks as points in the blank half of the Vocabulary box.

1. Remember, the words I'm thinking about will be in either List 1 or List 2. Make a tally mark in the Tally box at the bottom of page 75 for every correctly identified word.
2. Circle the number of the appropriate word.
   - This word applies to things that happen in most cases. (Wait.) What word? **generally**
   - If you have a good chance to advance yourself, you have this. (Wait.) What word? **opportunity**
   - These events can affect other events in unforeseen ways. (Wait.) What word? **circumstances**
   - Some people have these special rights. (Wait.) What word? **privileges**
   - If someone promises you that something will happen, they do this. (Wait.) What word? **guarantee**
3. Count all the tally marks, and enter that number as points in the blank half of the Vocabulary box.

(See the *Student Book,* page 76.)

The words in the third list are related. Have students use the *REWARDS* Strategies to figure out the first word in each family. Have them read the definition and then read the other two words in the family.

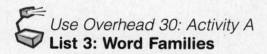

Use Overhead 30: Activity A
List 3: Word Families

1. Turn to page 76. Find **Family 1** in **List 3**. Figure out the first word. Use your pencil if you wish. Put your thumb up when you know the word._ What word?_ Read the definition._
2. Look at the next word in Family 1. Figure out the word._ What word?_
3. Next word. Figure out the word._ What word?_
4. (Repeat Steps 1–3 for all word families in List 3.)

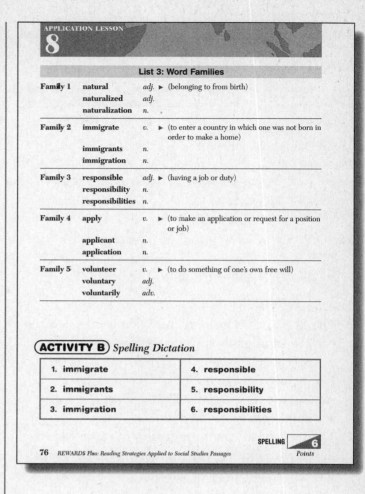

List 3: Word Families

Family 1	natural	adj.	(belonging to from birth)
	naturalized	adj.	
	naturalization	n.	
Family 2	immigrate	v.	▶ (to enter a country in which one was not born in order to make a home)
	immigrants	n.	
	immigration	n.	
Family 3	responsible	adj.	▶ (having a job or duty)
	responsibility	n.	
	responsibilities	n.	
Family 4	apply	v.	▶ (to make an application or request for a position or job)
	applicant	n.	
	application	n.	
Family 5	volunteer	v.	▶ (to do something of one's own free will)
	voluntary	adj.	
	voluntarily	adv.	

ACTIVITY B *Spelling Dictation*

1. immigrate	4. responsible
2. immigrants	5. responsibility
3. immigration	6. responsibilities

SPELLING 6

76 *REWARDS Plus: Reading Strategies Applied to Social Studies Passages* Points

Note A.3-1: You may wish to provide additional practice by having students read a word family to the group or to a partner.

Note A.3-2: Additional vocabulary practice activities are provided in Appendix B of the Teacher's Guide. These activities are optional and can be assigned during class, for homework, or as small group, in-class activities.

ACTIVITY B

Spelling Dictation

ACTIVITY PROCEDURE

(See the *Student Book,* page 76.)

For each word, tell students the word, then have students say the parts of the word to themselves while they write the word. Then, have students enter the number of correctly spelled words as points in the blank half of the Spelling box.

Note B-1: Distribute a piece of light cardboard to each of the students.

 Use Overhead 30: Activity B

1. Find **Activity B**.
2. The first word is **immigrate**. What word?_ Say the parts in **immigrate** to yourself as you write the word. (Pause and monitor.)
3. (Show **immigrate** on the overhead.) Check **immigrate**. If you misspelled it, cross it out and write it correctly.
4. The second word is **immigrants**. What word?_ Say the parts in **immigrants** to yourself as you write the word. (Pause and monitor.)
5. (Show **immigrants** on the overhead.) Check **immigrants**. If you misspelled it, cross it out and write it correctly.
6. (Repeat the procedures for the words **immigration**, **responsible**, **responsibility**, and **responsibilities**.)
7. Count the number of words you spelled correctly, and record that number as points in the blank half of the Spelling box at the bottom of the page.

APPLICATION LESSON

8

List 3: Word Families			
Family 1	natural	*adj.* ▶	(belonging to from birth)
	naturalized	*adj.*	
	naturalization	*n.*	
Family 2	immigrate	*v.* ▶	(to enter a country in which one was not born in order to make a home)
	immigrants	*n.*	
	immigration	*n.*	
Family 3	responsible	*adj.* ▶	(having a job or duty)
	responsibility	*n.*	
	responsibilities	*n.*	
Family 4	apply	*v.* ▶	(to make an application or request for a position or job)
	applicant	*n.*	
	application	*n.*	
Family 5	volunteer	*v.* ▶	(to do something of one's own free will)
	voluntary	*adj.*	
	voluntarily	*adv.*	

ACTIVITY B *Spelling Dictation*

1. **immigrate**		4. **responsible**	
2. **immigrants**		5. **responsibility**	
3. **immigration**		6. **responsibilities**	

 SPELLING 6 Points

76 *REWARDS Plus: Reading Strategies Applied to Social Studies Passages*

ACTIVITY C

Background Knowledge

ACTIVITY PROCEDURE

(See the *Student Book,* page 77.)

Read the Background Knowledge paragraph using one of three methods: read it to students, have students read it together, or call on individual students to read. Examine the timeline and the related graphic together. Then, preview the passage together by examining the title and the headings. Have students tell partners two things the passage will tell about.

1. Turn to page 77. Let's read the paragraph. (Read or ask students to read. Then examine the timeline and graphic together.)
2. Now, let's turn the page and preview the passage. Read the title._ What is the whole passage going to tell about?_
3. Now, let's read the headings. Read the first heading._ Read the next heading._ (Continue until students have read all headings.)
4. Turn to your partner. Without looking, tell two things this passage will tell about._

ACTIVITY C *Background Knowledge*

A.D. 1600   A.D. 1800   A.D. 2000

1788 Constitution approved: citizenship laws in place

When a person is born in a particular country, the person is considered a citizen of that country. However, some people choose to move to another country to join family members or to obtain work. When people go to a new country, they may wish to become citizens of that new country. This may be an easy or difficult process, depending on the country and the person's circumstances. In this article, you will learn about the citizenship process that has been used in the United States since 1788. In the United States, citizens have full legal and political rights. Full citizenship brings with it all of the protections and privileges guaranteed by the Constitution.

Immigrants in New York, Late 1800s

Student Book: Application Lesson 8 **77**

ACTIVITY D

Passage Reading and Comprehension

ACTIVITY PROCEDURE

(See the *Student Book*, pages 78–79.)

Have students work on reading accuracy by selecting a passage-reading option that best fits your students.

Passage Reading: Accuracy

(Select a passage-reading procedure that matches the size of your group and the competency of your students.

Option A

If you are teaching a small group of students who are having difficulty, use Option A:

Have students read one paragraph silently. Then, call on one student to orally read a paragraph or a portion of the paragraph to the class. Call on students in random order, varying the amount that each student reads.

Option B

If you are teaching a small group with students who are not having difficulty, use Option B:

Have students read the entire article silently, rereading it if they finish before their classmates. Then, call on one student to orally read a paragraph or a portion of a paragraph to the class. Call on students in random order, varying the amount that each student reads.

Option C

If you are teaching a large group with students who are having difficulty, use Option C:

Have students read one paragraph silently. Then, have students read the paragraph to a partner. Alternate partner-reading turns.

Option D

If you are teaching a large group with students who are not having difficulty, use Option D:

Have students read the entire article silently, rereading it if they finish before their classmates. Then, have students read the passage with their partners, alternating on each paragraph.)

APPLICATION LESSON

8

ACTIVITY D *Passage Reading and Comprehension*

United States Citizenship

15	People from all over the world come to the United States of America to live.
29	They come to find opportunity, to seek freedom, or to be with family. People
42	come to the United States because they know that U.S. citizens are guaranteed
57	certain rights, such as the right to believe and practice any religion they want or
70	the right to freedom of speech. But just because someone moves here from
84	another country doesn't mean he or she is automatically a citizen. If a person
101	was not born in the United States, or if you were born to a United States citizen
101	living in a foreign country, it is necessary to apply for citizenship. (#1)

Naturalization

113	
114	When people from a foreign country want to become citizens of the United
127	States, they must go through a process called *naturalization*. There are three
139	steps to this process. First, they must file an application with the government.
152	This application asks them for information about their background. They must
163	also provide photographs and legal documents. The government takes the
173	applicant's fingerprints. (#2)
175	Second, the applicants must take a test. This test asks questions about United
188	States history and government. Applicants can take classes to help them study
200	for the test. They also have to take an English test to make sure they know the
217	language well. (#3)
219	Lastly, the applicants must appear before a judge. The judge asks each of
232	them why they want to be a citizen and if they are willing to take an oath of
250	allegiance, or loyalty, to the United States. After the applicant answers, the
262	judge decides whether or not he or she may become a citizen. (#4)

Aliens' and Nationals' Rights

274	
278	People who have just moved to the United States from a foreign country are
292	known as *aliens*. This means they live here, but they are not full citizens of the
308	country. They have some of the rights of a citizen, but there are some rights—
323	such as voting and federal work—that they cannot have. However, once they go
337	through naturalization, naturalized citizens can have jobs with the government,
347	obtain a passport from the United States, and request that family members be
360	allowed to immigrate to the United States. (#5)

78 REWARDS *Plus: Reading Strategies Applied to Social Studies Passages*

Passage Reading: Comprehension Questions

(You may wish to ask the following questions as the passage is being read. Numbers corresponding to the questions are indicated at the point at which they could be asked.)

#1 What are some reasons that people move to the United States?

Ideas: To be with family; to seek freedom; to practice any religion; to have freedom of speech; to get a better job.

#2 What do we call the process when someone from another country becomes a U.S. citizen?

Naturalization.

#3 What tests do applicants have to take for citizenship?

A test on U.S. history and government and a test on the English language.

367	People who live in American territories (such as Puerto Rico, Guam, or the
380	Virgin Islands) are known as *nationals*. They share all of the legal rights of U.S.
395	citizens but have different political rights. For example, they are not represented
407	in Congress, and they cannot run for president. (#6)
415	**Citizens' Responsibilities**
417	Citizens have many rights, but they also have responsibilities. In the United
429	States, a citizen may be called to be on a jury. A jury helps decide the outcome
446	of a court case. If citizens are requested for jury duty, they have to be on the
463	jury for as long as the court case continues. (#7)
472	American citizens also have a responsibility to exercise their right to vote.
484	The democratic process by which this country is governed depends on
495	individual involvement. By voting, Americans can support or disagree with
505	policies or leaders. Participation in local government is also a good way to show
519	responsibility as a citizen. (#8)
523	Male citizens may be drafted into the military during times of war. If the
537	government deems it necessary, then citizens must help defend the country.
548	During peacetime, all citizens, male or female, may enlist voluntarily in the
560	military. (#9)
561	Finally, all citizens are responsible for upholding the laws of their
572	communities, states, and nation. This includes paying income tax and other taxes
584	to state and federal agencies and respecting the rights of other citizens. Each
597	citizen must do his or her part to help the society to continue to run smoothly.
613	Becoming a citizen of the United States is a great privilege, but it is also a great
630	responsibility. (#10)
631	

ACTIVITY E *Fluency Building*

Cold Timing [ ]   Practice 1 [ ]

Practice 2 [ ]   Hot Timing [ ]

Student Book: Application Lesson 8   **79**

#4 **What must an applicant be willing to do in order to become a U.S. citizen?**
Take an oath of allegiance to the United States.

#5 **What is the difference between an alien and a naturalized citizen?**
Aliens have fewer rights than naturalized citizens.

#6 **What is the difference between nationals and U.S. citizens?**
Nationals have the same legal rights as U.S. citizens, but they have different political rights.

#7 **What is jury duty?**
Idea: A citizen's duty to sit on a jury when requested.

#8 **Why is it important for citizens to vote?**
Ideas: Voting allows citizens to disagree with or support policies or leaders; voting shows citizen responsibility; voting gives citizens political representation.

#9 **What is the draft?**
The federal government deeming that male citizens of a certain age must enter the military during times of war.

#10 **Name some responsibilities of all U.S. citizens.**
Ideas: Upholding laws; paying taxes; respecting other people's rights; helping society run smoothly; voting; joining the military.

ACTIVITY E
Fluency Building

ACTIVITY PROCEDURE

(See the *Student Book,* page 79.)

Have students complete a Cold Timing, one or two practices, and a Hot Timing of the Activity D article. For each timing, have students record the number of correct words read. Finally, have students complete their Fluency Graphs.

Note E-1: When assigning partners for this activity, have the stronger reader read first. As a result, the other reader will have one additional practice opportunity.

1. Now, it's time for fluency building.
2. Find the beginning of the passage again. (Pause.)
3. Whisper-read. See how many words you can read in one minute. Begin._ (Time students for one minute.) Stop._ Circle the last word that you read._ Record the number of words you read after **Cold Timing** in **Activity E** at the bottom of page 79._
4. Let's practice again. Begin._ (Time students for one minute.) Stop._ Put a box around the last word that you read._ Record the number of words you read after **Practice 1**._
5. **Optional** Let's practice one more time before the Hot Timing. Begin._ (Time students for one minute.) Stop._ Put a box around the last word that you read._ Record the number of words you read after **Practice 2**._
6. Please exchange books with your partner._ Partner 1, you are going to read first. Partner 2, listen carefully and underline any mistakes or words left out. Ones, begin._ (Time students for one minute.) Stop._ Twos, cross out the last word that your partner read._ Twos, record the number of words in your partner's book after **Hot Timing**._
7. Partner 2, you are going to read next. Partner 1, listen carefully and underline any mistakes or words left out. Twos, begin. (Time students for one minute.) Stop._ Ones, cross out the last word that your partner read._ Ones, record the number of words in your partner's book after **Hot Timing**._
8. Exchange books._ Turn to the Fluency Graph on the last page of your book, and indicate on the graph the number of Cold Timing and Hot Timing words you read correctly._

ACTIVITY D *Passage Reading and Comprehension*

United States Citizenship

15	People from all over the world come to the United States of America to live.
29	They come to find opportunity, to seek freedom, or to be with family. People
42	come to the United States because they know that U.S. citizens are guaranteed
57	certain rights, such as the right to believe and practice any religion they want or
70	the right to freedom of speech. But just because someone moves here from
84	another country doesn't mean he or she is automatically a citizen. If a person
101	was not born in the United States, or if you were born to a United States citizen
	living in a foreign country, it is necessary to apply for citizenship. (#1)

113	**Naturalization**
114	When people from a foreign country want to become citizens of the United
127	States, they must go through a process called *naturalization.* There are three
139	steps to this process. First, they must file an application with the government.
152	This application asks them for information about their background. They must
163	also provide photographs and legal documents. The government takes the
173	applicant's fingerprints. (#2)
175	Second, the applicants must take a test. This test asks questions about United
188	States history and government. Applicants can take classes to help them study
200	for the test. They also have to take an English test to make sure they know the
217	language well. (#3)
219	Lastly, the applicants must appear before a judge. The judge asks each of
232	them why they want to be a citizen and if they are willing to take an oath of
250	allegiance, or loyalty, to the United States. After the applicant answers, the
262	judge decides whether or not he or she may become a citizen. (#4)

274	**Aliens' and Nationals' Rights**
278	People who have just moved to the United States from a foreign country are
292	known as *aliens.* This means they live here, but they are not full citizens of the
308	country. They have some of the rights of a citizen, but there are some rights—
323	such as voting and federal work—that they cannot have. However, once they go
337	through naturalization, naturalized citizens can have jobs with the government,
347	obtain a passport from the United States, and request that family members be
360	allowed to immigrate to the United States. (#5)

367	People who live in American territories (such as Puerto Rico, Guam, or the
380	Virgin Islands) are known as *nationals.* They share all of the legal rights of U.S.
395	citizens but have different political rights. For example, they are not represented
407	in Congress, and they cannot run for president. (#6)

415	**Citizens' Responsibilities**
417	Citizens have many rights, but they also have responsibilities. In the United
429	States, a citizen may be called to be on a jury. A jury helps decide the outcome
446	of a court case. If citizens are requested for jury duty, they have to be on the
463	jury for as long as the court case continues. (#7)
472	American citizens also have a responsibility to exercise their right to vote.
484	The democratic process by which this country is governed depends on
495	individual involvement. By voting, Americans can support or disagree with
505	policies or leaders. Participation in local government is also a good way to show
519	responsibility as a citizen. (#8)
523	Male citizens may be drafted into the military during times of war. If the
537	government deems it necessary, then citizens must help defend the country.
548	During peacetime, all citizens, male or female, may enlist voluntarily in the
560	military. (#9)
561	Finally, all citizens are responsible for upholding the laws of their
572	communities, states, and nation. This includes paying income tax and other taxes
584	to state and federal agencies and respecting the rights of other citizens. Each
597	citizen must do his or her part to help the society to continue to run smoothly.
613	Becoming a citizen of the United States is a great privilege, but it is also a great
630	responsibility. (#10)
631	

ACTIVITY E *Fluency Building*

Cold Timing	[ ]	Practice 1	[ ]
Practice 2	[ ]	Hot Timing	[ ]

ACTIVITY F

Comprehension Questions—Multiple Choice and Short Answer

ACTIVITY PROCEDURE

(See the *Student Book*, page 80.)

Have students complete all the Multiple Choice items. Then, have students share their answers and rationales. Encourage thoughtful discussion. Have students record points for each correct item.

Note F-1: The correct Multiple Choice answers are circled.

Multiple Choice Comprehension

1. Turn to page 80. Find **Activity F**. Answer all the items on your own. But, be ready to explain why you selected your answers._
2. (Wait while students complete all the items. Call on individual students. For each item, ask why they chose their answer and why they eliminated the other choices. Encourage discussion.)
3. Count the number of items you got correct, and record that number as points in the blank half of the Multiple Choice Comprehension box._

ACTIVITY PROCEDURE

(See the *Student Book*, page 81.)

Have students complete the Short Answer questions on the passage. Give feedback to students on their answers. Have students record points for each question's answer: one point for using the wording of the question in the answer, and one point for accuracy of the answer (total of 4 points possible for two complete answers).

Short Answer Comprehension

1. Turn to page 81._ Use the Short Answer Strategy on your own.
2. (When students are done, give them feedback.)
3. Count your number of points (a maximum of 4 points for the two answers), and add that number in the blank half of the Short Answer Comprehension box.

APPLICATION LESSON
8

ACTIVITY F *Comprehension Questions—Multiple Choice and Short Answer*

Comprehension Strategy—Multiple Choice

Step 1: Read the item.
Step 2: Read all of the choices.
Step 3: Think about why each choice might be correct or incorrect. Check the article as needed.
Step 4: From the possible correct choices, select the best answer.

1. (Vocabulary) **What two words from the article are synonyms?**
   a. application and document
   b. guarantee and automatic
   c. privileges and rights
   d. rights and responsibilities

2. (Compare and Contrast) **What right does a U.S. citizen have that an alien does *not* have?**
   a. The right to practice their religion.
   b. The right to vote.
   c. The right to speak freely about political issues.
   d. The right to purchase things they need.

3. (Main Idea) **Which statement gives the best summary of this article?**
   a. Aliens do not have the same rights as citizens. They cannot vote, run for office, or hold a U.S. passport.
   b. People may immigrate to the U.S. to be with their family, to seek freedom, or to search for economic opportunities.
   c. To become a naturalized citizen, you must apply, take a test, and appear in front of a judge.
   d. When you become an American citizen, you gain certain rights (such as the right to vote and have a U.S. passport), but you also gain responsibilities (such as serving on a jury).

4. (Vocabulary) **Which sentence *best* expresses the relationship between the words *application* and *applicant*?**
   a. An applicant fills out an application.
   b. An applicant receives people's applications.
   c. An application informs an applicant.
   d. An application lists an applicant.

MULTIPLE CHOICE COMPREHENSION   4
80   *REWARDS Plus: Reading Strategies Applied to Social Studies Passages*   *Points*

APPLICATION LESSON
8

Comprehension Strategy—Short Answer

Step 1: Read the item.
Step 2: Turn the question into part of the answer and write it down.
Step 3: Think of the answer or locate the answer in the article.
Step 4: Complete your answer.

1. **What three steps are necessary to become a naturalized citizen of the United States?**
   Example answer: The three steps necessary to become a naturalized citizen of the United States are to file an application with the government, to take tests, and to take an oath of citizenship before a judge.

2. **How do the rights of aliens differ from the rights of U.S. citizens?**
   Example answer: The rights of aliens differ from the rights of U.S. citizens in that aliens cannot vote or hold federal jobs.

SHORT ANSWER COMPREHENSION   4
Points

ACTIVITY G *Expository Writing—Extended Response*

Writing Strategy—Extended Response

Step 1: **LIST** (List the reasons for your position. For each reason, explain with details.)
Step 2: **CROSS OUT** (Reread your reasons and details. Cross out any that you decide not to include.)
Step 3: **CONNECT** (Connect any details that could go into one sentence.)
Step 4: **NUMBER** (Number the reasons in a logical order.)
Step 5: **WRITE** (Write your response.)
Step 6: **EDIT** (Revise and proofread your response.)

Prompt: Pretend that you are trying to convince an alien to become an American citizen. What reasons would you use to support that position?

Student Book: Application Lesson 8   **81**

ACTIVITY G

Expository Writing—Extended Response

ACTIVITY PROCEDURE

(See the *Student Book*, pages 81–83.)

Have students read the prompt and record their position. Next, have them **LIST** reasons and explanations in the Planning Box by referring back to the article. Encourage them to record notes rather than write complete sentences. When students are done with their lists, have them compare their reasons and explanations with those of their classmates and the Example Plan.

1. Time to write. First, read the prompt at the bottom of page 81. Then, use the Planning Box on page 82 to start thinking about your first sentence. Then, write your **LIST**. When you are finished, compare your list to your partner's list.

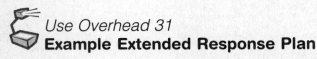

Use Overhead 31
Example Extended Response Plan

2. Now, compare your list to the list on the overhead.

ACTIVITY PROCEDURE

Next, have students complete the additional steps in the Extended Response Writing Strategy. Have them reread their lists and **CROSS OUT** any weak or unimportant reasons or explanations. Then, have students **CONNECT** explanations that could go together in one sentence, **NUMBER** their reasons in a logical order, and **WRITE** their extended responses on a separate piece of paper. When they are done, have them **EDIT** their paragraphs, revising for clarity and proofreading for errors in spelling, capitalization, and punctuation. Have students read their extended responses to their partners. Then, read the Example Extended Response.

Have students read each of the attributes on the rubric, examine their extended responses, and circle either "Yes" or "Fix up." Give students time to make necessary changes.

Optional: During or after the class session, fill in the third column of the rubric chart and assign points to the extended responses.

Optional: Have students date their writing and place the sample in a folder. Thus, students will be able to look back at their

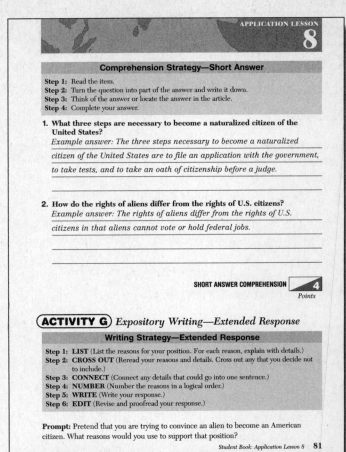

Comprehension Strategy—Short Answer

Step 1: Read the item.
Step 2: Turn the question into part of the answer and write it down.
Step 3: Think of the answer or locate the answer in the article.
Step 4: Complete your answer.

1. What three steps are necessary to become a naturalized citizen of the United States?
Example answer: The three steps necessary to become a naturalized citizen of the United States are to file an application with the government, to take tests, and to take an oath of citizenship before a judge.

2. How do the rights of aliens differ from the rights of U.S. citizens?
Example answer: The rights of aliens differ from the rights of U.S. citizens in that aliens cannot vote or hold federal jobs.

SHORT ANSWER COMPREHENSION

4 Points

ACTIVITY G *Expository Writing—Extended Response*

Writing Strategy—Extended Response

Step 1: **LIST** (List the reasons for your position. For each reason, explain with details.)
Step 2: **CROSS OUT** (Reread your reasons and details. Cross out any that you decide not to include.)
Step 3: **CONNECT** (Connect any details that could go into one sentence.)
Step 4: **NUMBER** (Number the reasons in a logical order.)
Step 5: **WRITE** (Write your response.)
Step 6: **EDIT** (Revise and proofread your response.)

Prompt: Pretend that you are trying to convince an alien to become an American citizen. What reasons would you use to support that position?

Student Book: Application Lesson 8 **81**

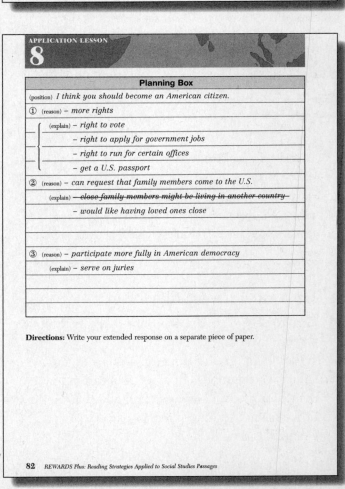

Planning Box

(position) *I think you should become an American citizen.*

① (reason) – *more rights*
  (explain) – *right to vote*
    – *right to apply for government jobs*
    – *right to run for certain offices*
    – *get a U.S. passport*

② (reason) – *can request that family members come to the U.S.*
  (explain) – ~~*close family members might be living in another country*~~
    – *would like having loved ones close*

③ (reason) – *participate more fully in American democracy*
  (explain) – *serve on juries*

Directions: Write your extended response on a separate piece of paper.

82 *REWARDS Plus: Reading Strategies Applied to Social Studies Passages*

summaries and extended responses and literally see their writing improvement.

3. Now, **CROSS OUT**, **CONNECT**, **NUMBER**, and **WRITE**._

4. Reread your response and **EDIT**. Check to be sure your response is easy to understand. Fix any errors you find in spelling, capitalization, and punctuation._ (Monitor.)

5. Read what you've written to your partner._

Use Overhead 32
Example Extended Response

6. Look at the overhead. Let's read this Example Extended Response. Yours doesn't need to be exactly the same, but it should be similar.

7. (Have students turn to the rubric on page 83. Ask students to evaluate their own or their partner's writing to determine what to edit. When they have finished the evaluation, give students adequate time to make changes. Have students enter their points in the blank half of the Writing box below the rubric.)

Rubric— Extended Response	Student or Partner Rating		Teacher Rating	
1. Did the author tell his/her position in the first sentence?	Yes	Fix up	Yes	No
2. Did the author include at least three **strong, logical** reasons for his/her position?	Yes	Fix up	Yes	No
3. Did the author provide a **strong, logical** explanation for each of his/her reasons?	Yes	Fix up	Yes	No
4. Is the response easy to understand?	Yes	Fix up	Yes	No
5. Did the author correctly spell words, particularly the words found in the article?	Yes	Fix up	Yes	No
6. Did the author use correct capitalization, capitalizing the first word in the sentence and proper names of people, places, and things?	Yes	Fix up	Yes	No
7. Did the author use correct punctuation, including a period at the end of each sentence?	Yes	Fix up	Yes	No

WRITING
Points

Student Book: Application Lesson 8 **83**

Application Lesson 9

Materials Needed:

- *Student Book:* Application Lesson 9

- Application Overhead Transparencies 33–36

- Appendix B Optional Vocabulary Activities: Application Lesson 9

- Paper or cardboard to use when covering the overhead transparency

- Paper or cardboard for each student to use during spelling dictation

- Washable overhead transparency pen

Text Treatment Notes:

- Black text signifies teacher script (exact wording to say to students).

- Green text in parentheses signifies directions or prompts for the teacher.

- Green text signifies answers or examples of answers.

- Green graphics treatment signifies reproduction of Overhead information.

- Green text and green graphics treatment do not appear in the *Student Book*.

ACTIVITY A
Vocabulary

ACTIVITY PROCEDURE, List 1

(See the *Student Book*, page 85.)

Tell students each word in the list. Then, have students repeat the word and read the definition aloud. For each definition, provide any additional information that may be necessary. Then, have students practice reading the words themselves.

Note A.1-1: See Appendix E, Pronunciation Guide for Unique Words, for correct pronunciations of uncommon vocabulary words.

Use Overhead 33: Activity A
List 1: **Tell**

1. (Show the top half of Overhead 33.) Before we read the passage, let's read the difficult words. (Point to **ratify**.) The first word is **ratify**. What word?_ Now, read the definition._
2. (Point to **relieve**.) The next word is **relieve**. What word?_ Now, read the definition._
3. (Pronounce each word in List 1, and then have students repeat each word and read the definition.)
4. Open your *Student Book* to **Application Lesson 9**, page 85._
5. Find **Activity A**, **List 1**, in your book_. Let's read the words again. First word._ Next word._ (Continue for all words in List 1.)

ACTIVITY PROCEDURE, List 2

(See the *Student Book*, page 85.)

Have students circle prefixes and suffixes, then underline the vowels. Using the overhead transparency, assist students in checking their work. Next, have students figure out each word to themselves, then say it aloud. Have them read the definition aloud.

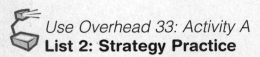

Use Overhead 33: Activity A
List 2: **Strategy Practice**

1. Find **List 2**. Circle the prefixes and suffixes, and underline the vowels. Look up when you are done._

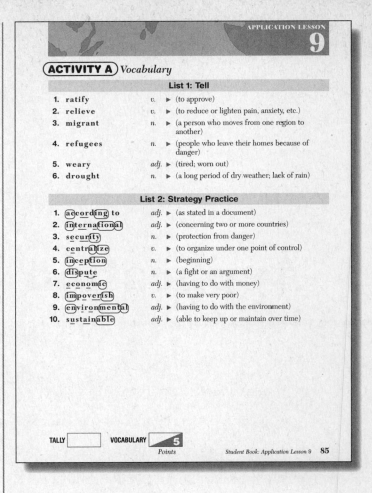

ACTIVITY A *Vocabulary*

List 1: Tell

1.	ratify	v.	▶	(to approve)
2.	relieve	v.	▶	(to reduce or lighten pain, anxiety, etc.)
3.	migrant	n.	▶	(a person who moves from one region to another)
4.	refugees	n.	▶	(people who leave their homes because of danger)
5.	weary	adj.	▶	(tired; worn out)
6.	drought	n.	▶	(a long period of dry weather; lack of rain)

List 2: Strategy Practice

1.	according to	adj.	▶	(as stated in a document)
2.	international	adj.	▶	(concerning two or more countries)
3.	security	n.	▶	(protection from danger)
4.	centralize	v.	▶	(to organize under one point of control)
5.	inception	n.	▶	(beginning)
6.	dispute	n.	▶	(a fight or an argument)
7.	economic	adj.	▶	(having to do with money)
8.	impoverish	v.	▶	(to make very poor)
9.	environmental	adj.	▶	(having to do with the environment)
10.	sustainable	adj.	▶	(able to keep up or maintain over time)

TALLY [   ] VOCABULARY [5   ] Points

Student Book: Application Lesson 9 **85**

2. (Show the bottom half of Overhead 33.) Before you check your work, look at item #4. (Point to the first example and the **ize** that is circled.) Remember, you can also circle **ize**. What suffix?_ Now, go back to item #1. Check and fix any mistakes._
3. Go back to the first word again._ Sound out the word to yourself. Put your thumb up when you can read the word. Be sure that it is a real word._ What word?_ Now, read the definition._
4. (Continue Step 3 with all remaining words in List 2.)

Note A.2-1: You may wish to provide additional practice by having students read words to a partner.

ACTIVITY PROCEDURE, List 1 and 2

(See the *Student Book,* page 85.)

Tell students to look in List 1 or List 2 for a word you are think-ing about. Have them circle the number of the word and tell you the word. Explain to students to make a tally mark for each correct word in the Tally box, and then enter the number of tally marks as points in the blank half of the Vocabulary box.

1. Remember, the words I'm thinking about will be in either List 1 or List 2. Make a tally mark in the Tally box at the bottom of page 85 for every correctly identified word.
2. Circle the number of the appropriate word.
   - These people leave their homes and, at times, even their countries, because of danger or hardship. (Wait.) What word? **refugees**
   - If we organized the government so there was only one point of control, we would do this. (Wait.) What word? **centralize**
   - A long period of time without rain is known as this. (Wait.) What word? **drought**
   - This word usually refers to something to do with money. (Wait.) What word? **economic**
   - What would we ask for to protect ourselves from danger? (Wait.) What word? **security**
3. Count all the tally marks, and enter that number as points in the blank half of the Vocabulary box.

ACTIVITY PROCEDURE, List 3

(See the *Student Book,* page 86.)

The words in the third list are related. Have students use the *REWARDS* Strategies to figure out the first word in each family. Have them read the definition and then read the other two words in the family.

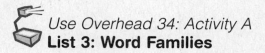

Use Overhead 34: Activity A
List 3: Word Families

1. Turn to page 86. Find **Family 1** in **List 3**. Figure out the first word. Use your pencil if you wish. Put your thumb up when you know the word._ What word?_ Read the definition._
2. Look at the next word in Family 1. Figure out the word._ What word?_
3. Next word. Figure out the word._ What word?_
4. (Repeat Steps 1–3 for all word families in List 3.)

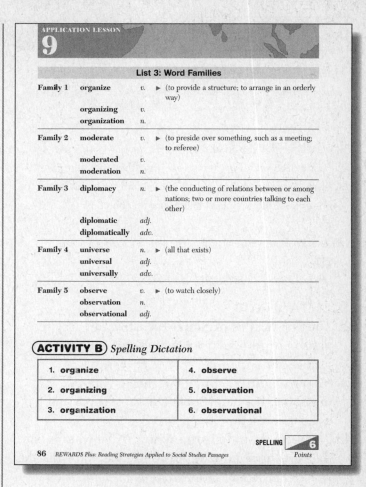

APPLICATION LESSON
9

List 3: Word Families

Family 1	organize	v.	▶ (to provide a structure; to arrange in an orderly way)
	organizing	v.	
	organization	n.	
Family 2	moderate	v.	▶ (to preside over something, such as a meeting; to referee)
	moderated	v.	
	moderation	n.	
Family 3	diplomacy	n.	▶ (the conducting of relations between or among nations; two or more countries talking to each other)
	diplomatic	adj.	
	diplomatically	adv.	
Family 4	universe	n.	▶ (all that exists)
	universal	adj.	
	universally	adv.	
Family 5	observe	v.	▶ (to watch closely)
	observation	n.	
	observational	adj.	

ACTIVITY B *Spelling Dictation*

1. organize	4. observe
2. organizing	5. observation
3. organization	6. observational

SPELLING 6 Points

86 *REWARDS Plus: Reading Strategies Applied to Social Studies Passages*

Note A.3-1: You may wish to provide additional practice by having students read a word family to the group or to a partner.

Note A.3-2: Additional vocabulary practice activities are provided in Appendix B of the Teacher's Guide. These activities are optional and can be assigned during class, for homework, or as small group, in-class activities.

ACTIVITY B
Spelling Dictation

ACTIVITY PROCEDURE

(See the *Student Book,* page 86.)

For each word, tell students the word, then have students say the parts of the word to themselves while they write the word. Then, have students enter the number of correctly spelled words as points in the blank half of the Spelling box.

Note B-1: Distribute a piece of light cardboard to each of the students.

 Use Overhead 34: Activity B

1. Find **Activity B**.
2. The first word is **organize**. What word?_ Say the parts in **organize** to yourself as you write the word. (Pause and monitor.)
3. (Show **organize** on the overhead.) Check **organize**. If you misspelled it, cross it out and write it correctly.
4. The second word is **organizing**. What word?_ Say the parts in **organizing** to yourself as you write the word. (Pause and monitor.)
5. (Show **organizing** on the overhead.) Check **organizing**. If you misspelled it, cross it out and write it correctly.
6. (Repeat the procedures for the words **organization**, **observe**, **observation**, and **observational**.)
7. Count the number of words you spelled correctly, and record that number as points in the blank half of the Spelling box at the bottom of the page.

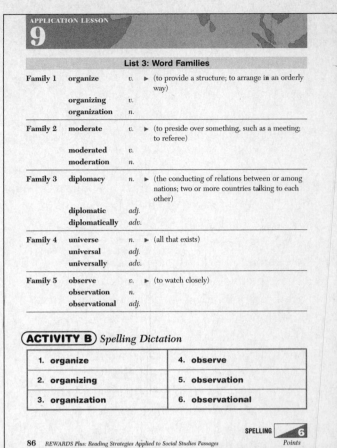

APPLICATION LESSON
9

List 3: Word Families

Family 1	organize	v.	▶ (to provide a structure; to arrange in an orderly way)
	organizing	v.	
	organization	n.	
Family 2	moderate	v.	▶ (to preside over something, such as a meeting; to referee)
	moderated	v.	
	moderation	n.	
Family 3	diplomacy	n.	▶ (the conducting of relations between or among nations; two or more countries talking to each other)
	diplomatic	adj.	
	diplomatically	adv.	
Family 4	universe	n.	▶ (all that exists)
	universal	adj.	
	universally	adv.	
Family 5	observe	v.	▶ (to watch closely)
	observation	n.	
	observational	adj.	

ACTIVITY B *Spelling Dictation*

1. organize	4. observe
2. organizing	5. observation
3. organization	6. observational

SPELLING 6 Points

86 *REWARDS Plus: Reading Strategies Applied to Social Studies Passages*

ACTIVITY C

Background Knowledge

ACTIVITY PROCEDURE

(See the *Student Book,* page 87.)

Read the Background Knowledge paragraph using one of three methods: read it to students, have students read it together, or call on individual students to read. Examine the timeline and the related graphic together. Then, preview the passage together by examining the title and the headings. Have students tell partners two things the passage will tell about.

1. Turn to page 87. Let's read the paragraph. (Read or ask students to read. Then examine the timeline and graphic together.)
2. Now, let's turn the page and preview the passage. Read the title._ What is the whole passage going to tell about?_
3. Now, let's read the headings. Read the first heading._ Read the next heading._ (Continue until students have read all headings.)
4. Turn to your partner. Without looking, tell two things this passage will tell about._

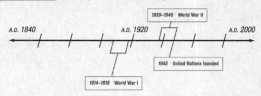

ACTIVITY C *Background Knowledge*

A.D. 1840   A.D. 1920   A.D. 2000

1939–1945 World War II

1945 United Nations founded

1914–1918 World War I

This article will describe why several nations came together in 1945 to create the United Nations. World War I (1914–1918) left much devastation in its wake, and many countries were horrified. Sixty-three countries (but not the United States) decided to become members of the League of Nations in order to work for peace. However, the League of Nations was unwilling to oppose the actions of Germany, Italy, and Japan in the 1930s and ultimately failed to prevent another world war. So, after World War II (1939–1945), the United States hosted a meeting for delegates from 50 countries, who created and agreed to a common set of rules to promote world peace and encourage cooperation.

The Flag of the United Nations

Student Book: Application Lesson 9 **87**

ACTIVITY D
Passage Reading and Comprehension

ACTIVITY PROCEDURE

(See the *Student Book*, pages 88–89.)

Have students work on reading accuracy by selecting a passage-reading option that best fits your students.

Passage Reading: Accuracy

(Select a passage-reading procedure that matches the size of your group and the competency of your students.

Option A

If you are teaching a small group of students who are having difficulty, use Option A:

Have students read one paragraph silently. Then, call on one student to orally read a paragraph or a portion of the paragraph to the class. Call on students in random order, varying the amount that each student reads.

Option B

If you are teaching a small group with students who are not having difficulty, use Option B:

Have students read the entire article silently, rereading it if they finish before their classmates. Then, call on one student to orally read a paragraph or a portion of a paragraph to the class. Call on students in random order, varying the amount that each student reads.

Option C

If you are teaching a large group with students who are having difficulty, use Option C:

Have students read one paragraph silently. Then, have students read the paragraph to a partner. Alternate partner-reading turns.

Option D

If you are teaching a large group with students who are not having difficulty, use Option D:

Have students read the entire article silently, rereading it if they finish before their classmates. Then, have students read the passage with their partners, alternating on each paragraph.)

ACTIVITY D *Passage Reading and Comprehension*

The United Nations

16	By 1945, the world was weary of war. The world had fought World War I and
	World War II, and many of the world's nations were intent on creating lasting
30	peace. On October 24, 1945, the United Nations was established to do that. (#1)
43	**The Charter**
45	The governing document of the U.N. is its charter. The charter has been
58	ratified, or approved, by all member nations. It describes the roles each member
71	must fulfill. According to the charter, the United Nations has many purposes.
83	One goal is to maintain international peace and security. It also tries to create
97	good relationships among nations and helps them to work with one another to
110	solve international problems. In addition, the U.N. strives to support and
121	improve human rights and basic freedoms. It acts as a centralizing organization
133	for nations that are working toward these goals. (#2)
141	**International Peace and Security**
145	Since its inception, the United Nations has played a major role in trying to
159	create and maintain peace throughout the world. The U.N. can moderate, or
171	referee, disputes among nations. It encourages the nations to resolve conflict
182	through diplomacy rather than war. The U.N. also moderates civil disputes, or
194	disagreements, among groups within one country. It helps a country to resolve
206	problems among its different groups in order to avoid civil war. When armed
219	conflict does occur, the U.N. can send in peacekeeping forces to help decrease
232	tensions. The U.N. can also help rebuild peaceful social, economic, and
243	government systems after a war is over. The United Nations even has a group
257	devoted to trying to make sure that outer space remains peaceful. (#3)
268	**Economic and Social Development**
272	There is a lot of news about the U.N.'s efforts at peacemaking and security,
286	but most of the work the United Nations does is in economic and social
300	development. It works in many parts of the world to relieve poverty.
312	Impoverished countries receive loans, food aid, medical help, and other forms of
324	assistance. The United Nations also addresses global issues that have economic
335	and social impact, such as drug trafficking, AIDS, and environmental problems.
346	It provides protection and help for refugees of countries engaged in armed

88 *REWARDS Plus: Reading Strategies Applied to Social Studies Passages*

Passage Reading: Comprehension Questions

(You may wish to ask the following questions as the passage is being read. Numbers corresponding to the questions are indicated at the point at which they could be asked.)

#1 Why was the U.N. established?
To create lasting peace in the world.

#2 What describes the purposes and roles of the U.N.?
Its charter.

#3 What can the U.N. do to help nations that are engaged in armed conflict?
The U.N. can send in peacekeeping forces to decrease tensions.

#4 What kinds of help does the U.N. give to countries?
Ideas: Loans; food; medicine; disaster relief; disaster preparation plans.

358	conflict. The U.N. also provides disaster relief for victims of major natural
370	disasters, such as earthquakes, floods, droughts, and storms. In developing
380	countries, the U.N. also helps disaster-prone areas—those areas consistently
391	affected by such things as hurricanes, earthquakes, and volcanic eruptions—
401	design preparation plans. These plans lessen the impact of a natural disaster. (#4)
413	**Human Rights**
415	In 1948, the United Nations adopted a Universal Declaration of Human
426	Rights. This document created an international standard for human rights for all
438	countries to uphold. Since then, the declaration has expanded. It now includes
450	more specific rights for women, minorities, children, migrant workers, and the
461	disabled. All of these human rights are protected by international law. When a
474	country is accused of not upholding these rights, the U.N. sends in an
487	observational team to find out what is happening. (#5)
495	**International Law**
497	The United Nations works very hard to develop treaties and agreements that
509	promote peace, security, and sustainable development. When a country signs a
520	United Nations agreement, it becomes part of their law. There are international
532	laws about how to use international waters and air. The U.N. has also created
546	laws to reduce environmental problems, to promote human rights, and to deal
558	with international crime, such as terrorism. These international standards
567	provide a basis for cooperation among many different nations. (#6)
576	**Building Peace**
578	Although not all nations cooperate with the United Nations, it is becoming
590	an increasingly powerful voice for peace in the world. The U.N. helps people
603	with basic needs, such as food, medicine, and human rights. But it also helps
617	countries resolve disputes, create agreements, and become friendlier with one
627	another. The United Nations stands apart from the world, trying to make sure its
641	citizens work together in the best ways possible. (#7)
649	

ACTIVITY E *Fluency Building*

Cold Timing	☐	Practice 1	☐
Practice 2	☐	Hot Timing	☐

Student Book: Application Lesson 9 **89**

#5 What is the purpose of the Universal Declaration of Human Rights?
To create a standard for human rights for all countries to honor.

#6 What are some of the things the U.N. has created international laws about?
Ideas: The use of international waters and air; environmental problems; human rights; international crime.

#7 Other than basic needs, such as food and medicine, how does the U.N. help countries?
It moderates disputes between countries, helps them create agreements, and helps them be friendlier with each other.

ACTIVITY E
Fluency Building

ACTIVITY PROCEDURE

(See the *Student Book*, page 89.)

Have students complete a Cold Timing, one or two practices, and a Hot Timing of the Activity D article. For each timing, have students record the number of correct words read. Finally, have students complete their Fluency Graphs.

Note E-1: When assigning partners for this activity, have the stronger reader read first. As a result, the other reader will have one additional practice opportunity.

1. Now, it's time for fluency building.
2. Find the beginning of the passage again. (Pause.)
3. Whisper-read. See how many words you can read in one minute. Begin._ (Time students for one minute.) Stop._ Circle the last word that you read._ Record the number of words you read after **Cold Timing** in **Activity E** at the bottom of page 89._
4. Let's practice again. Begin._ (Time students for one minute.) Stop._ Put a box around the last word that you read._ Record the number of words you read after **Practice 1**._
5. **Optional** Let's practice one more time before the Hot Timing. Begin._ (Time students for one minute.) Stop._ Put a box around the last word that you read._ Record the number of words you read after **Practice 2**._
6. Please exchange books with your partner._ Partner 1, you are going to read first. Partner 2, listen carefully and underline any mistakes or words left out. Ones, begin._ (Time students for one minute.) Stop._ Twos, cross out the last word that your partner read._ Twos, record the number of words in your partner's book after **Hot Timing**._
7. Partner 2, you are going to read next. Partner 1, listen carefully and underline any mistakes or words left out. Twos, begin. (Time students for one minute.) Stop._ Ones, cross out the last word that your partner read._ Ones, record the number of words in your partner's book after **Hot Timing**._
8. Exchange books._ Turn to the Fluency Graph on the last page of your book, and indicate on the graph the number of Cold Timing and Hot Timing words you read correctly._

ACTIVITY F

Comprehension Questions— Multiple Choice and Short Answer

ACTIVITY PROCEDURE

(See the *Student Book*, pages 90–91.)

Have students complete the Multiple Choice and Short Answer questions on the passage. Give feedback to students on their answers. Lead students in a discussion of their Multiple Choice answers and rationales. Have students record points for each correct item. For each Short Answer response, give one point for using the wording of the question in the answer, and one point for accuracy of the answer (total of 4 points possible for two complete answers).

Note F-1: The correct Multiple Choice answers are circled.

ACTIVITY F *Comprehension Questions— Multiple Choice and Short Answer*

Comprehension Strategy—Multiple Choice

Step 1: Read the item.
Step 2: Read all of the choices.
Step 3: Think about why each choice might be correct or incorrect. Check the article as needed.
Step 4: From the possible correct choices, select the best answer.

1. (Vocabulary) **Read these sentences from the article: "By 1945, the world was *weary* of war. The world had fought World War I and World War II, and many of the world's nations were intent on creating lasting peace." Based on how those sentences read, what does the word *weary* mean?**
   a. desirous
   b. extremely tired *(circled)*
   c. resentful
   d. afraid

2. (Compare and Contrast) **How were the League of Nations and the United Nations the same?**
   a. The same countries were members.
   b. Their main purpose was the same: promoting world peace. *(circled)*
   c. They had the same founders.
   d. Their ideas for preventing another world war were the same.

3. (Main Idea) **If the article needed a new title, which would be best?**
   a. *The League of Nations and the United Nations*
   b. *International Support of the United Nations*
   c. *The U.N. as a Peacekeeper*
   d. *The Many Purposes of the United Nations* *(circled)*

4. (Vocabulary) **In the term *United Nations*, *United* means:**
   a. joined together to form one government.
   b. joined together to protect the rights of poor countries.
   c. joined together for a common purpose. *(circled)*
   d. joined together to protect against enemies.

MULTIPLE CHOICE COMPREHENSION
Points

Comprehension Strategy—Short Answer

Step 1: Read the item.
Step 2: Turn the question into part of the answer and write it down.
Step 3: Think of the answer or locate the answer in the article.
Step 4: Complete your answer.

1. **Name three issues the United Nations addressed through the creation of international laws.**
   Example answer: Three issues the United Nations addressed through the creation of international laws include the environment, human rights, and international crime.

2. **How might the U.N. be able to help a very poor country?**
   Example answer: The U.N. might be able to help a very poor country by providing food and medicine. They might also be able to help by giving loans.

SHORT ANSWER COMPREHENSION
Points

ACTIVITY G *Expository Writing—Summary*

Writing Strategy—Summary

Step 1: LIST (List the details that are important enough to include in the summary.)
Step 2: CROSS OUT (Reread the details. Cross out any that you decide not to include.)
Step 3: CONNECT (Connect any details that could go into one sentence.)
Step 4: NUMBER (Number the details in a logical order.)
Step 5: WRITE (Write your summary.)
Step 6: EDIT (Revise and proofread your summary.)

Prompt: Write a summary of the information contained in *The United Nations* article.

ACTIVITY G
Expository Writing—Summary

ACTIVITY PROCEDURE

(See the *Student Book*, pages 91–92.)

Have students read the prompt and record the topic of the summary. Next, have them **LIST** details in the Planning Box by referring back to the article. Encourage students to record notes rather than form complete sentences. When they are done with their lists, have them compare their lists of critical details with those of other classmates and the Example Summary Plan.

1. Time to write. First, read the prompt at the bottom of page 91. Then, use the Planning Box on page 92 to start thinking about your first sentence. Then, write your **LIST**. When you are finished, compare your list to your partner's list._

Use Overhead 35
Example Summary Plan

2. Now, compare your list to the list on the overhead._

ACTIVITY PROCEDURE

Next, have students complete the additional steps in the Summary Writing Strategy. Have them reread their lists and **CROSS OUT** any weak or unimportant details. Then, have students **CONNECT** details that could go together in one sentence, **NUMBER** their ideas in a logical order, and **WRITE** their summaries on a separate piece of paper. When they are done, have them **EDIT** their paragraphs, revising for clarity and proofreading for errors in spelling, capitalization, and punctuation.

Have students read their summaries to their partners. Then, read the Example Summary.

Have students read each of the attributes on the rubric, examine their summaries, and circle either "Yes" or "Fix up." Give students time to make changes in their summaries.

Optional: During or after the class session, fill in the third column of the rubric chart and assign points to the student summaries.

Optional: Have students date their writing and place the sample in a folder. Thus, students will be able to look back at their

---

Comprehension Strategy—Short Answer

Step 1: Read the item.
Step 2: Turn the question into part of the answer and write it down.
Step 3: Think of the answer or locate the answer in the article.
Step 4: Complete your answer.

1. **Name three issues the United Nations addressed through the creation of international laws.**
   Example answer: Three issues the United Nations addressed through the creation of international laws include the environment, human rights, and international crime.

2. **How might the U.N. be able to help a very poor country?**
   Example answer: The U.N. might be able to help a very poor country by providing food and medicine. They might also be able to help by giving loans.

SHORT ANSWER COMPREHENSION | **4** *Points*

ACTIVITY G *Expository Writing—Summary*

Writing Strategy—Summary

Step 1: **LIST** (List the details that are important enough to include in the summary.)
Step 2: **CROSS OUT** (Reread the details. Cross out any that you decide not to include.)
Step 3: **CONNECT** (Connect any details that could go into one sentence.)
Step 4: **NUMBER** (Number the details in a logical order.)
Step 5: **WRITE** (Write your summary.)
Step 6: **EDIT** (Revise and proofread your summary.)

Prompt: Write a summary of the information contained in *The United Nations* article.

Planning Box

(topic) *The United Nations*	
① (detail)	– *United Nations established in 1945*
② (detail)	– *U.N. charter describes its purposes*
③ (detail)	– *U.N. acts as a central organization for many nations*
④ (detail)	– *tries to create and maintain international peace*
⑤ (detail)	– *works to relieve poverty in poor nations*
(detail)	– *addresses other economic and social issues*
⑥ (detail)	– *provides disaster relief*
⑦ (detail)	– *created a Universal Declaration of Human Rights*
(detail)	– *makes sure countries uphold human rights*
⑧ (detail)	– *creates international laws*
(detail)	– *laws provide a way for many nations to cooperate*

Directions: Write your summary on a separate piece of paper.

Rubric— Summary	Student or Partner Rating		Teacher Rating	
1. Did the author state the topic and the main idea in the first sentence?	Yes	Fix up	Yes	No
2. Did the author focus on important details?	Yes	Fix up	Yes	No
3. Did the author combine details in some of the sentences?	Yes	Fix up	Yes	No
4. Is the summary easy to understand?	Yes	Fix up	Yes	No
5. Did the author correctly spell words, particularly the words found in the article?	Yes	Fix up	Yes	No
6. Did the author use correct capitalization, capitalizing the first word in the sentence and proper names of people, places, and things?	Yes	Fix up	Yes	No
7. Did the author use correct punctuation, including a period at the end of each sentence?	Yes	Fix up	Yes	No

WRITING | **7** *Points*

---

summaries and extended responses and literally see their writing improvement.

3. Now, **CROSS OUT**, **CONNECT**, **NUMBER**, and **WRITE**._

4. Reread your response and **EDIT**. Check to be sure your response is easy to understand. Fix any errors you find in spelling, capitalization, and punctuation._ (Monitor.)

5. Read what you've written to your partner._

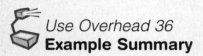
Use Overhead 36
Example Summary

6. Look at the overhead. Let's read this Example Summary. Yours doesn't need to be exactly the same, but it should be similar.

7. (Have students look at the rubric on page 92. Ask students to evaluate their own or their partner's writing to determine what to edit. When they have finished the evaluation, give students adequate time to make changes. Have students enter their points in the blank half of the Writing box below the rubric.)

Comprehension Strategy—Short Answer

Step 1: Read the item.
Step 2: Turn the question into part of the answer and write it down.
Step 3: Think of the answer or locate the answer in the article.
Step 4: Complete your answer.

1. **Name three issues the United Nations addressed through the creation of international laws.**
   Example answer: Three issues the United Nations addressed through the creation of international laws include the environment, human rights, and international crime.

2. **How might the U.N. be able to help a very poor country?**
   Example answer: The U.N. might be able to help a very poor country by providing food and medicine. They might also be able to help by giving loans.

SHORT ANSWER COMPREHENSION **4** *Points*

(ACTIVITY G) *Expository Writing—Summary*

Writing Strategy—Summary

Step 1: **LIST** (List the details that are important enough to include in the summary.)
Step 2: **CROSS OUT** (Reread the details. Cross out any that you decide not to include.)
Step 3: **CONNECT** (Connect any details that could go into one sentence.)
Step 4: **NUMBER** (Number the details in a logical order.)
Step 5: **WRITE** (Write your summary.)
Step 6: **EDIT** (Revise and proofread your summary.)

Prompt: Write a summary of the information contained in *The United Nations* article.

Planning Box

(topic) *The United Nations*

① (detail) – *United Nations established in 1945*
② (detail) – *U.N. charter describes its purposes*
③ (detail) – *U.N. acts as a central organization for many nations*
④ (detail) – *tries to create and maintain international peace*
⑤ { (detail) – *works to relieve poverty in poor nations*
   (detail) – *addresses other economic and social issues*
⑥ (detail) – *provides disaster relief*
⑦ { (detail) – *created a Universal Declaration of Human Rights*
   (detail) – *makes sure countries uphold human rights*
⑧ { (detail) – *creates international laws*
   (detail) – *laws provide a way for many nations to cooperate*

Directions: Write your summary on a separate piece of paper.

Rubric—Summary	Student or Partner Rating		Teacher Rating	
1. Did the author state the topic and the main idea in the first sentence?	Yes	Fix up	Yes	No
2. Did the author focus on important details?	Yes	Fix up	Yes	No
3. Did the author combine details in some of the sentences?	Yes	Fix up	Yes	No
4. Is the summary easy to understand?	Yes	Fix up	Yes	No
5. Did the author correctly spell words, particularly the words found in the article?	Yes	Fix up	Yes	No
6. Did the author use correct capitalization, capitalizing the first word in the sentence and proper names of people, places, and things?	Yes	Fix up	Yes	No
7. Did the author use correct punctuation, including a period at the end of each sentence?	Yes	Fix up	Yes	No

WRITING **7** *Points*

Application Lesson 10

Materials Needed:

- *Student Book:* Application Lesson 10

- Application Overhead Transparencies 37–40

- Appendix B Optional Vocabulary Activities: Application Lesson 10

- Paper or cardboard to use when covering the overhead transparency

- Paper or cardboard for each student to use during spelling dictation

- Washable overhead transparency pen

Text Treatment Notes:

- Black text signifies teacher script (exact wording to say to students).

- Green text in parentheses signifies directions or prompts for the teacher.

- Green text signifies answers or examples of answers.

- Green graphics treatment signifies reproduction of Overhead information.

- Green text and green graphics treatment do not appear in the *Student Book*.

ACTIVITY A
Vocabulary

ACTIVITY PROCEDURE, List 1

(See the *Student Book*, page 93.)

Tell students each word in the list. Then, have students repeat the word and read the definition aloud. For each definition, provide any additional information that may be necessary. Then, have students practice reading the words themselves.

Note A.1-1: See Appendix E, Pronunciation Guide for Unique Words, for correct pronunciations of uncommon vocabulary words.

Use Overhead 37: Activity A
List 1: Tell

1. (Show the top half of Overhead 37.) Before we read the passage, let's read the difficult words. (Point to **barrier**.) The first word is **barrier**. What word?＿ Now, read the definition.＿
2. (Point to **elite**.) The next word is **elite**. What word?＿ Now, read the definition.＿
3. (Pronounce each word in List 1, and then have students repeat each word and read the definition.)
4. Open your *Student Book* to **Application Lesson 10**, page 93.＿
5. Find **Activity A**, **List 1**, in your book.＿ Let's read the words again. First word.＿ Next word.＿ (Continue for all words in List 1.)

ACTIVITY PROCEDURE, List 2

(See the *Student Book*, page 93.)

Have students circle prefixes and suffixes, then underline the vowels. Using the overhead transparency, assist students in checking their work. Next, have students figure out each word to themselves, then say it aloud. Have them read the definition aloud.

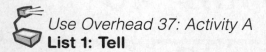

Use Overhead 37: Activity A
List 2: Strategy Practice

1. Find **List 2**. Circle the prefixes and suffixes, and underline the vowels. Look up when you are done.＿
2. (Show the bottom half of Overhead 37.) Before you check your work, look at item #5. (Point to the

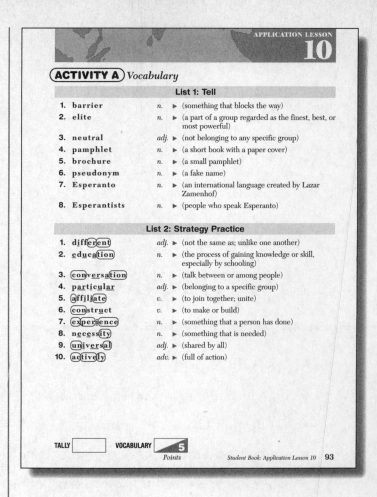

ACTIVITY A *Vocabulary*

List 1: Tell

1.	barrier	n.	▶ (something that blocks the way)
2.	elite	n.	▶ (a part of a group regarded as the finest, best, or most powerful)
3.	neutral	adj.	▶ (not belonging to any specific group)
4.	pamphlet	n.	▶ (a short book with a paper cover)
5.	brochure	n.	▶ (a small pamphlet)
6.	pseudonym	n.	▶ (a fake name)
7.	Esperanto	n.	▶ (an international language created by Lazar Zamenhof)
8.	Esperantists	n.	▶ (people who speak Esperanto)

List 2: Strategy Practice

1.	different	adj.	▶ (not the same as; unlike one another)
2.	education	n.	▶ (the process of gaining knowledge or skill, especially by schooling)
3.	conversation	n.	▶ (talk between or among people)
4.	particular	adj.	▶ (belonging to a specific group)
5.	affiliate	v.	▶ (to join together; unite)
6.	construct	v.	▶ (to make or build)
7.	experience	n.	▶ (something that a person has done)
8.	necessity	n.	▶ (something that is needed)
9.	universal	adj.	▶ (shared by all)
10.	actively	adv.	▶ (full of action)

TALLY ☐ VOCABULARY ◣ 5 Points

Student Book: Application Lesson 10 **93**

third example and to the **af** that is circled.) From now on, you can also circle **af**. The prefix is /af/. Say it.＿ Now, go back to item #1. Check and fix any mistakes.＿
3. Go back to the first word again.＿ Sound out the word to yourself. Put your thumb up when you can read the word. Be sure that it is a real word.＿ What word?＿ Now, read the definition.＿
4. (Continue Step 3 with all remaining words in List 2.)

Note A.2-1: You may wish to provide additional practice by having students read words to a partner.

ACTIVITY PROCEDURE, List 1 and 2

(See the _Student Book_, page 93.)

Tell students to look in List 1 or List 2 for a word you are think-ing about. Have them circle the number of the word and tell you the word. Explain to students to make a tally mark for each correct word in the Tally box, and then enter the number of tally marks as points in the blank half of the Vocabulary box.

1. Remember, the words I'm thinking about will be in either List 1 or List 2. Make a tally mark in the Tally box at the bottom of page 93 for every correctly identified word.
2. Circle the number of the appropriate word.
   - People who want to hide who they are often use this. (Wait.) What word? **pseudonym**
   - What do we call people who are the finest or most powerful members of a group? (Wait.) What word? **elite**
   - Values and customs that are shared by all people are described as this. (Wait.) What word? **universal**
   - When you become a member of a group, you do this with the group. (Wait.) What word? **affiliate**
   - Something that you really want can be a goal, but something that you really need is this. (Wait.) What word? **necessity**
3. Count all the tally marks, and enter that number as points in the blank half of the Vocabulary box.

ACTIVITY PROCEDURE, List 3

(See the _Student Book_, page 94.)

The words in the third list are related. Have students use the _REWARDS_ Strategies to figure out the first word in each family. Have them read the definition and then read the other two words in the family.

Use Overhead 38: Activity A
List 3: Word Families

1. Turn to page 94. Find **Family 1** in **List 3**. Figure out the first word. Use your pencil if you wish. Put your thumb up when you know the word._ What word?_ Read the definition._
2. Look at the next word in Family 1. Figure out the word._ What word?_
3. Next word. Figure out the word._ What word?_

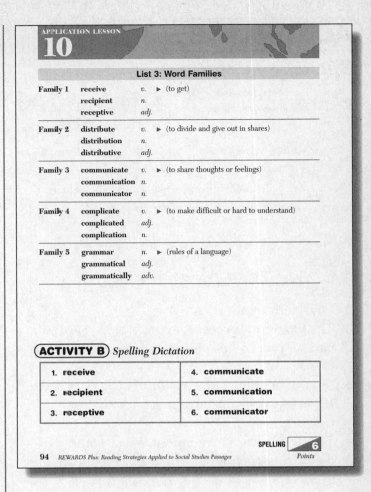

List 3: Word Families

Family 1	receive	v.	▶ (to get)
	recipient	n.	
	receptive	adj.	
Family 2	distribute	v.	▶ (to divide and give out in shares)
	distribution	n.	
	distributive	adj.	
Family 3	communicate	v.	▶ (to share thoughts or feelings)
	communication	n.	
	communicator	n.	
Family 4	complicate	v.	▶ (to make difficult or hard to understand)
	complicated	adj.	
	complication	n.	
Family 5	grammar	n.	▶ (rules of a language)
	grammatical	adj.	
	grammatically	adv.	

ACTIVITY B _Spelling Dictation_

1. receive	4. communicate
2. recipient	5. communication
3. receptive	6. communicator

SPELLING 6 Points

94 _REWARDS Plus: Reading Strategies Applied to Social Studies Passages_

4. (Repeat Steps 1–3 for all word families in List 3.)

Note A.3-1: You may wish to provide additional practice by having students read a word family to the group or to a partner.

Note A.3-2: Additional vocabulary practice activities are provided in Appendix B of the Teacher's Guide. These activities are optional and can be assigned during class, for homework, or as small group, in-class activities.

ACTIVITY B

Spelling Dictation

ACTIVITY PROCEDURE

(See the *Student Book,* page 94.)

For each word, tell students the word, then have students say the parts of the word to themselves while they write the word. Then, have students enter the number of correctly spelled words as points in the blank half of the Spelling box.

Note B-1: Distribute a piece of light cardboard to each of the students.

 Use Overhead 38: Activity B

1. Find **Activity B**.
2. The first word is **receive**. What word?_ Say the parts in **receive** to yourself as you write the word. (Pause and monitor.)
3. (Show **receive** on the overhead.) Check **receive**. If you misspelled it, cross it out and write it correctly.
4. The second word is **recipient**. What word?_ Say the parts in **recipient** to yourself as you write the word. (Pause and monitor.)
5. (Show **recipient** on the overhead.) Check **recipient**. If you misspelled it, cross it out and write it correctly.
6. (Repeat the procedures for the words **receptive**, **communicate**, **communication**, and **communicator**.)
7. Count the number of words you spelled correctly, and record that number as points in the blank half of the Spelling box at the bottom of the page.

APPLICATION LESSON 10

List 3: Word Families

Family 1	receive	v.	▶ (to get)
	recipient	n.	
	receptive	adj.	
Family 2	distribute	v.	▶ (to divide and give out in shares)
	distribution	n.	
	distributive	adj.	
Family 3	communicate	v.	▶ (to share thoughts or feelings)
	communication	n.	
	communicator	n.	
Family 4	complicate	v.	▶ (to make difficult or hard to understand)
	complicated	adj.	
	complication	n.	
Family 5	grammar	n.	▶ (rules of a language)
	grammatical	adj.	
	grammatically	adv.	

ACTIVITY B *Spelling Dictation*

1. receive	4. communicate
2. recipient	5. communication
3. receptive	6. communicator

SPELLING ___ / 6 Points

ACTIVITY C

Background Knowledge

ACTIVITY PROCEDURE

(See the *Student Book*, page 95.)

Read the Background Knowledge paragraph using one of three methods: read it to students, have students read it together, or call on individual students to read. Examine the timeline and the English-Esperanto translation together. Then, preview the passage together by examining the title and the headings. Have students tell partners two things the passage will tell about.

1. Turn to page 95. Let's read the paragraph. (Read or ask students to read. Then examine the timeline and the English-Esperanto translation together.)
2. Now, let's turn the page and preview the passage. Read the title.__ What is the whole passage going to tell about?__
3. Now, let's read the headings. Read the first heading.__ Read the next heading.__ (Continue until students have read all headings.)
4. Turn to your partner. Without looking, tell two things this passage will tell about.__

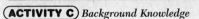
ACTIVITY C *Background Knowledge*

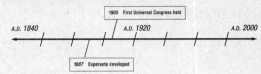

In this article, you will read about Esperanto, which was first proposed in 1887. Esperanto is a constructed language, which is a language that has been invented by a person, rather than evolving over time. Languages such as English, French, and Japanese developed over thousands of years of use. But Esperanto and other constructed languages have been deliberately created. Here is an example of a sentence from the *Wizard of Oz*, written first in English and then in Esperanto, so you can see what it looks like.

Dorothy lived in the midst of the great Kansas prairies, with Uncle Henry, who was a farmer, and Aunt Em, who was the farmer's wife.

Doroteo logxis en la mezo de la granda kamparo de Kansas, kun Onklo Henriko, kiu estis kultivisto, kaj Onklino Em, kiu estis la edzino de la kultivisto.

Student Book: Application Lesson 10 **95**

ACTIVITY D

Passage Reading and Comprehension

ACTIVITY PROCEDURE

(See the *Student Book*, pages 96–97.)

Have students work on reading accuracy by selecting a passage-reading option that best fits your students.

Passage Reading: Accuracy

(Select a passage-reading procedure that matches the size of your group and the competency of your students.

Option A

If you are teaching a small group of students who are having difficulty, use Option A:

Have students read one paragraph silently. Then, call on one student to orally read a paragraph or a portion of the paragraph to the class. Call on students in random order, varying the amount that each student reads.

Option B

If you are teaching a small group with students who are not having difficulty, use Option B:

Have students read the entire article silently, rereading it if they finish before their classmates. Then, call on one student to orally read a paragraph or a portion of a paragraph to the class. Call on students in random order, varying the amount that each student reads.

Option C

If you are teaching a large group with students who are having difficulty, use Option C:

Have students read one paragraph silently. Then, have students read the paragraph to a partner. Alternate partner-reading turns.

Option D

If you are teaching a large group with students who are not having difficulty, use Option D:

Have students read the entire article silently, rereading it if they finish before their classmates. Then, have students read the passage with their partners, alternating on each paragraph.)

An International Language

13 In today's world, it is easier than ever to experience different cultures. People
26 can fly on airplanes to distant countries. They can exchange e-mail with people
40 all over the world. Communication happens at the speed of light. But one barrier
54 still remains to this idea of a global village—the language barrier. Someone who
66 speaks Russian is unable to communicate with someone who speaks Italian. A
77 traveler from Brazil cannot carry on a simple conversation in India. (#1)

88 Although English is often considered an international language, it really is
101 not. English is a complicated, difficult language to learn. It requires many years
117 of study for, say, a Chinese person to grasp the basics of English. Only the elite,
127 well-educated members of society would have enough education to
 communicate effectively in English if it is not their first language. (#2)

A Dream of Understanding

138
142 In the 1860s and 1870s, a boy named Lazar Zamenhof was growing up in the
157 Russian Empire. All around him, he saw people who could not communicate
169 with each other. People in the Russian Empire spoke Russian, German,
180 Hebrew, and Polish. Their language differences kept them separated. (#3)

189 Lazar dreamed that if one language could be created that all people could
202 easily learn and understand, then it would help the world become more
214 peaceful. It would be a neutral language—one that did not belong to any group
229 in particular, but to all of mankind. Lazar was very talented at languages and
243 learned Greek, Latin, German, Russian, French, and English. When he was 15,
255 he decided to begin work on his dream language. (#4)

The Birth of Esperanto

264
268 In 1887, Lazar published a pamphlet under the pseudonym Dr. Esperanto.
279 The pamphlet, or brochure, described the necessity of an international
289 language. It explained the simple grammatical rules and provided about 900
300 vocabulary words. It also showed several written examples of the language.
311 People called it "Dr. Esperanto's International Language." Later, they shortened
321 it to just "Esperanto." (#5)

325 People began to distribute the brochure to others. Recipients of the
336 brochure wrote letters to Zamenhof, expressing interest and support for the new
348 language. Some of the letters were even written in the new language! By 1905,

Passage Reading: Comprehension Questions

(You may wish to ask the following questions as the passage is being read. Numbers corresponding to the questions are indicated at the point at which they could be asked.)

#1 What is a big difficulty in trying to communicate with people from other countries?
The language barrier.

#2 Why isn't English the best choice for an international language?
Ideas: Difficult to learn; requires many years of study.

#3 Where did Lazar Zamenhof witness people who couldn't communicate with each other?
In the Russian Empire.

362	the support for Esperanto was so great that a Universal Congress was held.
375	People came from 20 different countries to explore this new idea. (#6)
386	**Why Does It Work?**
390	Esperanto is an effective international language for several reasons. First of
401	all, it is easy to learn. An average person can master the language in a year or so.
419	Second, it is a neutral language. It is not affiliated with any political or social
434	group. It is everyone's language. (#7)
439	**Esperanto Is Growing**
442	Esperanto has not yet become as widespread as Zamenhof hoped. But there
454	are still groups of people who actively promote its use. Around the world, the
468	number of people who use it continues to grow. It is especially popular in central
483	and eastern Europe, eastern Asia (especially mainland China), and some areas of
495	South America. People publish original works of literature and Web pages in
507	Esperanto. Some of the world's radio stations broadcast in Esperanto. Each year,
519	the Universal Congress is held in a different country for Esperantists. Even the
532	United Nations has recognized Esperanto's usefulness and potential. Although
541	Zamenhof's dream was not realized as quickly as he thought it might be, there
555	are many people dedicated to making sure that Esperanto continues to grow. (#8)
567	

ACTIVITY E *Fluency Building*

Cold Timing	☐	**Practice 1**	☐
Practice 2	☐	**Hot Timing**	☐

Student Book: Application Lesson 10 **97**

#4 Why did Lazar wish to create a neutral language?

Ideas: So that people could communicate; to help promote peace; so that the language didn't belong to any one country.

#5 What did Lazar's pamphlet contain?

Rules of grammar, 900 vocabulary words, and written examples of Esperanto.

#6 Why did the Esperantists hold the first Universal Congress?

So that people could get together to explore the idea of Esperanto.

#7 How long does it take an average person to learn Esperanto?

About one year.

#8 In what ways do people use Esperanto?

They write books and Web pages, and broadcast radio programs.

ACTIVITY E
Fluency Building

ACTIVITY PROCEDURE

(See the *Student Book*, page 97.)

Have students complete a Cold Timing, one or two practices, and a Hot Timing of the Activity D article. For each timing, have students record the number of correct words read. Finally, have students complete their Fluency Graphs.

Note E-1: When assigning partners for this activity, have the stronger reader read first. As a result, the other reader will have one additional practice opportunity.

1. Now, it's time for fluency building.
2. Find the beginning of the passage again. (Pause.)
3. Whisper-read. See how many words you can read in one minute. Begin.— (Time students for one minute.) Stop.— Circle the last word that you read.— Record the number of words you read after **Cold Timing** in **Activity E** at the bottom of page 97.—
4. Let's practice again. Begin.— (Time students for one minute.) Stop.— Put a box around the last word that you read.— Record the number of words you read after **Practice 1**.—
5. **Optional** Let's practice one more time before the Hot Timing. Begin.— (Time students for one minute.) Stop.— Put a box around the last word that you read.— Record the number of words you read after **Practice 2**.—
6. Please exchange books with your partner.— Partner 1, you are going to read first. Partner 2, listen carefully and underline any mistakes or words left out. Ones, begin.— (Time students for one minute.) Stop.— Twos, cross out the last word that your partner read.— Twos, record the number of words in your partner's book after **Hot Timing**.—
7. Partner 2, you are going to read next. Partner 1, listen carefully and underline any mistakes or words left out. Twos, begin. (Time students for one minute.) Stop.— Ones, cross out the last word that your partner read.— Ones, record the number of words in your partner's book after **Hot Timing**.—
8. Exchange books.— Turn to the Fluency Graph on the last page of your book, and indicate on the graph the number of Cold Timing and Hot Timing words you read correctly.—

ACTIVITY F

Comprehension Questions—Multiple Choice and Short Answer

ACTIVITY PROCEDURE

(See the *Student Book*, pages 98–99.)

Have students complete the Multiple Choice and Short Answer questions on the passage. Give feedback to students on their answers. Lead students in a discussion of their Multiple Choice answers and rationales. Have students record points for each correct item. For each Short Answer response, give one point for using the wording of the question in the answer, and one point for accuracy of the answer (total of 4 points possible for two complete answers).

Note F-1: The correct Multiple Choice answers are circled.

ACTIVITY F *Comprehension Questions—Multiple Choice and Short Answer*

Comprehension Strategy—Multiple Choice

Step 1: Read the item.
Step 2: Read all of the choices.
Step 3: Think about why each choice might be correct or incorrect. Check the article as needed.
Step 4: From the possible correct choices, select the best answer.

1. (Vocabulary) Read this sentence from the article: "Only the elite, well-educated members of society would have enough education to communicate *effectively* in English if it is not their first language." What does the word *effectively* mean in that sentence?
   a. loudly
   b. universally
   c. quickly
   d. well

2. (Main Idea) **The main reason that Lazar Zamenhof created Esperanto was:**
   a. because English is a complicated, difficult language to learn.
   b. to allow people of different cultures to communicate with each other.
   c. to bring together Russian, German, Hebrew, and Polish people.
   d. to allow international radio broadcasts.

3. (Cause and Effect) **Why was a *neutral* language created?**
   a. So that it did not belong to one specific group.
   b. So that it would be new.
   c. So that it would be accepted by English, Russian, and Spanish broadcasters.
   d. So that it would be easy to learn.

4. (Compare and Contrast) **Which of these statements about Esperanto and English is *not* true?**
   a. Both are used in many countries.
   b. Both are official languages of many countries.
   c. Both are used for oral and written communication.
   d. Both can be heard on the radio.

MULTIPLE CHOICE COMPREHENSION 4 *Points*

Comprehension Strategy—Short Answer

Step 1: Read the item.
Step 2: Turn the question into part of the answer and write it down.
Step 3: Think of the answer or locate the answer in the article.
Step 4: Complete your answer.

1. **Why is Esperanto considered a *constructed* language?**
   Example answer: Esperanto is considered a constructed language because it is not a natural language. It was constructed, or built, by Zamenhof according to selected grammatical structures and vocabulary words.

2. **Why did Lazar Zamenhof want to develop a new language?**
   Example answer: Lazar Zamenhof wanted to develop a new language because he thought that if people could communicate more easily, the world would be more peaceful.

SHORT ANSWER COMPREHENSION 4 *Points*

ACTIVITY G *Expository Writing—Extended Response*

Writing Strategy—Extended Response

Step 1: LIST (List the reasons for your position. For each reason, explain with details.)
Step 2: CROSS OUT (Reread your reasons and details. Cross out any that you decide not to include.)
Step 3: CONNECT (Connect any details that could go into one sentence.)
Step 4: NUMBER (Number the reasons in a logical order.)
Step 5: WRITE (Write your response.)
Step 6: EDIT (Revise and proofread your response.)

Prompt: Tell why Esperanto would make a good international language.

ACTIVITY G
Expository Writing—Extended Response

ACTIVITY PROCEDURE

(See the *Student Book*, pages 99–101.)

Have students read the prompt and record their position. Next, have them **LIST** reasons and explanations in the Planning Box by referring back to the article. Encourage them to record notes rather than write complete sentences. When students are done with their lists, have them compare their reasons and explanations with those of their classmates and the Example Plan.

1. Time to write. First, read the prompt at the bottom of page 99. Then, use the Planning Box on page 100 to start thinking about your first sentence. Then, write your **LIST**. When you are finished, compare your list to your partner's list.—

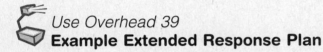

Use Overhead 39
Example Extended Response Plan

2. Now, compare your list to the list on the overhead.—

ACTIVITY PROCEDURE

Next, have students complete the additional steps in the Extended Response Writing Strategy. Have them reread their lists and **CROSS OUT** any weak or unimportant reasons or explanations. Then, have students **CONNECT** explanations that could go together in one sentence, **NUMBER** their reasons in a logical order, and **WRITE** their extended responses on a separate piece of paper. When they are done, have them **EDIT** their paragraphs, revising for clarity and proofreading for errors in spelling, capitalization, and punctuation.

Have students read their extended responses to their partners. Then, read the Example Extended Response.

Have students read each of the attributes on the rubric, examine their extended responses, and circle either "Yes" or "Fix up." Give students time to make necessary changes.

Optional: During or after the class session, fill in the third column of the rubric chart and assign points to the extended responses.

Comprehension Strategy—Short Answer

Step 1: Read the item.
Step 2: Turn the question into part of the answer and write it down.
Step 3: Think of the answer or locate the answer in the article.
Step 4: Complete your answer.

1. **Why is Esperanto considered a *constructed* language?**
   Example answer: Esperanto is considered a constructed language because it is not a natural language. It was constructed, or built, by Zamenhof according to selected grammatical structures and vocabulary words.

2. **Why did Lazar Zamenhof want to develop a new language?**
   Example answer: Lazar Zamenhof wanted to develop a new language because he thought that if people could communicate more easily, the world would be more peaceful.

SHORT ANSWER COMPREHENSION **4**
Points

ACTIVITY G *Expository Writing—Extended Response*

Writing Strategy—Extended Response

Step 1: **LIST** (List the reasons for your position. For each reason, explain with details.)
Step 2: **CROSS OUT** (Reread your reasons and details. Cross out any that you decide not to include.)
Step 3: **CONNECT** (Connect any details that could go into one sentence.)
Step 4: **NUMBER** (Number the reasons in a logical order.)
Step 5: **WRITE** (Write your response.)
Step 6: **EDIT** (Revise and proofread your response.)

Prompt: Tell why Esperanto would make a good international language.

Student Book: Application Lesson 10 **99**

Planning Box
(position) *Esperanto would make a good international language.*
① (reason) – *easy to learn*
{ (explain) – *simple grammatical rules*
– *can master in a year*
② (reason) – *a neutral language*
{ (explain) – *does not belong to one group of people*
– *not part of any political group*
③ (reason) – *used to communicate*
(explain) – *original books and Web pages in Esperanto*
– *some radio stations broadcast in Esperanto*
④ (reason) – *a community of people support Esperanto*
(explain) – *a Universal Congress is held each year*
~~*United Nations recognizes Esperanto*~~
– *popular in central and eastern Europe, eastern Asia, and parts of South America*

Directions: Write your extended response on a separate piece of paper.

Optional: Have students date their writing and place the sample in a folder. Thus, students will be able to look back at their summaries and extended responses and literally see their writing improvement.

3. Now, **CROSS OUT**, **CONNECT**, **NUMBER**, and **WRITE**.

4. Reread your response and **EDIT**. Check to be sure your response is easy to understand. Fix any errors you find in spelling, capitalization, and punctuation. (Monitor.)

5. Read what you've written to your partner.

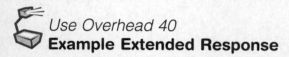
Use Overhead 40
Example Extended Response

6. Look at the overhead. Let's read this Example Extended Response. Yours doesn't need to be exactly the same, but it should be similar.

7. (Have students turn to the rubric on page 101. Ask students to evaluate their own or their partner's writing to determine what to edit. When they have finished the evaluation, give students adequate time to make changes. Have students enter their points in the blank half of the Writing box below the rubric.)

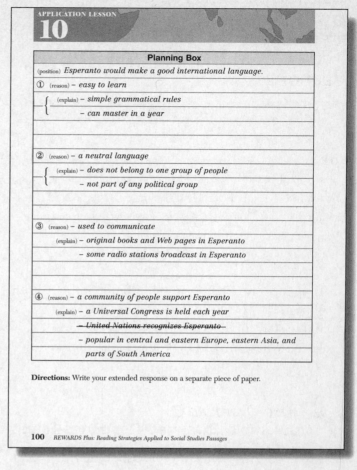

Planning Box

(position) *Esperanto would make a good international language.*

① (reason) – *easy to learn*
  { (explain) – *simple grammatical rules*
    – *can master in a year*

② (reason) – *a neutral language*
  { (explain) – *does not belong to one group of people*
    – *not part of any political group*

③ (reason) – *used to communicate*
  (explain) – *original books and Web pages in Esperanto*
    – *some radio stations broadcast in Esperanto*

④ (reason) – *a community of people support Esperanto*
  (explain) – *a Universal Congress is held each year*
    – ~~*United Nations recognizes Esperanto*~~
    – *popular in central and eastern Europe, eastern Asia, and parts of South America*

Directions: Write your extended response on a separate piece of paper.

Rubric— Extended Response	Student or Partner Rating		Teacher Rating	
1. Did the author tell his/her position in the first sentence?	Yes	Fix up	Yes	No
2. Did the author include at least three **strong, logical** reasons for his/her position?	Yes	Fix up	Yes	No
3. Did the author provide a **strong, logical** explanation for each of his/her reasons?	Yes	Fix up	Yes	No
4. Is the response easy to understand?	Yes	Fix up	Yes	No
5. Did the author correctly spell words, particularly the words found in the article?	Yes	Fix up	Yes	No
6. Did the author use correct capitalization, capitalizing the first word in the sentence and proper names of people, places, and things?	Yes	Fix up	Yes	No
7. Did the author use correct punctuation, including a period at the end of each sentence?	Yes	Fix up	Yes	No

WRITING **7**
Points

Application Lesson 11

Materials Needed:

- *Student Book:* Application Lesson 11
- Application Overhead Transparencies 41–44
- Appendix B Optional Vocabulary Activities: Application Lesson 11
- Paper or cardboard to use when covering the overhead transparency
- Paper or cardboard for each student to use during spelling dictation
- Washable overhead transparency pen

Text Treatment Notes:

- Black text signifies teacher script (exact wording to say to students).
- Green text in parentheses signifies directions or prompts for the teacher.
- Green text signifies answers or examples of answers.
- Green graphics treatment signifies reproduction of Overhead information.
- Green text and green graphics treatment do not appear in the *Student Book*.

ACTIVITY A
Vocabulary

ACTIVITY PROCEDURE, List 1

(See the *Student Book*, page 103.)

Tell students each word in the list. Then, have students repeat the word and read the definition aloud. For each definition, provide any additional information that may be necessary. Then, have students practice reading the words themselves.

Note A.1-1: See Appendix E, Pronunciation Guide for Unique Words, for correct pronunciations of uncommon vocabulary words.

 Use Overhead 41: Activity A
List 1: Tell

1. (Show the top half of Overhead 41.) Before we read the passage, let's read the difficult words. (Point to **kanji**.) The first word is **kanji**. What word?_ Now, read the definition._
2. (Point to **Korea**.) The next word is **Korea**. What word?_ Now, read the definition._
3. (Pronounce each word in List 1, and then have students repeat each word and read the definition.)
4. Open your *Student Book* to **Application Lesson 11**, page 103._
5. Find **Activity A**, **List 1**, in your book._ Let's read the words again. First word._ Next word._ (Continue for all words in List 1.)

ACTIVITY PROCEDURE, List 2

(See the *Student Book*, page 103.)

Have students circle prefixes and suffixes, then underline the vowels. Using the overhead transparency, assist students in checking their work. Next, have students figure out each word to themselves, then say it aloud. Have them read the definition aloud.

 *Use Overhead 41: Activity A*
List 2: Strategy Practice

1. Find **List 2**. Circle the prefixes and suffixes, and underline the vowels. Look up when you are done._
2. (Show the bottom half of Overhead 41.) Now, check and fix any mistakes._

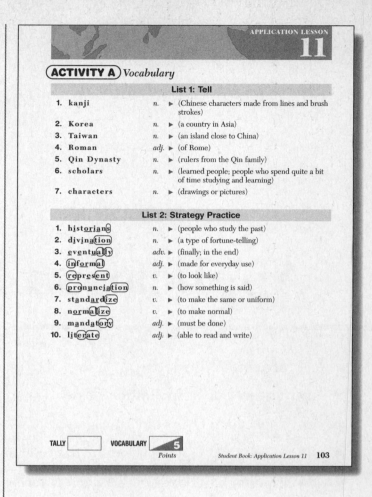

ACTIVITY A *Vocabulary*

List 1: Tell

1.	kanji	n. ▶	(Chinese characters made from lines and brush strokes)
2.	Korea	n. ▶	(a country in Asia)
3.	Taiwan	n. ▶	(an island close to China)
4.	Roman	adj. ▶	(of Rome)
5.	Qin Dynasty	n. ▶	(rulers from the Qin family)
6.	scholars	n. ▶	(learned people; people who spend quite a bit of time studying and learning)
7.	characters	n. ▶	(drawings or pictures)

List 2: Strategy Practice

1.	historians	n. ▶	(people who study the past)
2.	divination	n. ▶	(a type of fortune-telling)
3.	eventually	adv. ▶	(finally; in the end)
4.	informal	adj. ▶	(made for everyday use)
5.	represent	v. ▶	(to look like)
6.	pronunciation	n. ▶	(how something is said)
7.	standardize	v. ▶	(to make the same or uniform)
8.	normalize	v. ▶	(to make normal)
9.	mandatory	adj. ▶	(must be done)
10.	literate	adj. ▶	(able to read and write)

TALLY [　　] VOCABULARY [5] Points

Student Book: Application Lesson 11 **103**

3. Go back to the first word._ Sound out the word to yourself. Put your thumb up when you can read the word. Be sure that it is a real word._ What word?_ Now, read the definition._
4. (Continue Step 3 with all remaining words in List 2.)

Note A.2-1: You may wish to provide additional practice by having students read words to a partner.

ACTIVITY PROCEDURE, List 1 and 2

(See the *Student Book*, page 103.)

Tell students to look in List 1 or List 2 for a word you are thinking about. Have them circle the number of the word and tell you the word. Explain to students to make a tally mark for each correct word in the Tally box, and then enter the number of tally marks as points in the blank half of the Vocabulary box.

1. Remember, the words I'm thinking about will be in either List 1 or List 2. Make a tally mark in the Tally box at the bottom of page 103 for every correctly identified word.
2. Circle the number of the appropriate word.
   - If we make something the same for everyone, we do this to it. (Wait.) What word? **standardize**
   - People who are very learned are these. (Wait.) What word? **scholars**
   - If a particular task must be done, it is this type of task. (Wait.) What word? **mandatory**
   - This type of society has a large percentage of its population able to read and write. (Wait.) What word? **literate**
   - If clothing is made for everyday use, it can be described as this. (Wait.) What word? **informal**
3. Count all the tally marks, and enter that number as points in the blank half of the Vocabulary box.

ACTIVITY PROCEDURE, List 3

(See the *Student Book*, page 104.)

The words in the third list are related. Have students use the *REWARDS* Strategies to figure out the first word in each family. Have them read the definition and then read the other two words in the family.

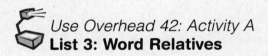

Use Overhead 42: Activity A
List 3: Word Relatives

1. Turn to page 104. Find **Family 1** in **List 3**. Figure out the first word. Use your pencil if you wish. Put your thumb up when you know the word._ What word?_ Read the definition._
2. Look at the next word in Family 1. Figure out the word._ What word?_
3. Next word. Figure out the word._ What word?_
4. (Repeat Steps 1–3 for all word families in List 3.)

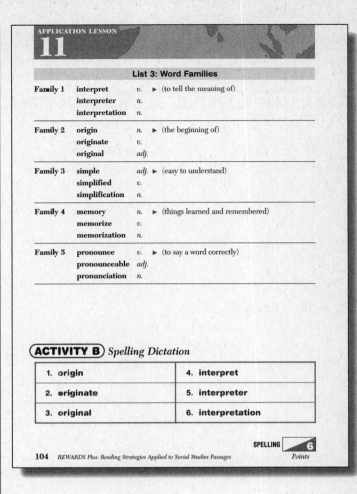

APPLICATION LESSON

11

List 3: Word Families

Family 1	interpret	v.	▶ (to tell the meaning of)
	interpreter	n.	
	interpretation	n.	
Family 2	origin	n.	▶ (the beginning of)
	originate	v.	
	original	adj.	
Family 3	simple	adj.	▶ (easy to understand)
	simplified	v.	
	simplification	n.	
Family 4	memory	n.	▶ (things learned and remembered)
	memorize	v.	
	memorization	n.	
Family 5	pronounce	v.	▶ (to say a word correctly)
	pronounceable	adj.	
	pronunciation	n.	

(ACTIVITY B) *Spelling Dictation*

1. origin	4. interpret
2. originate	5. interpreter
3. original	6. interpretation

SPELLING ▶ **6** *Points*

104   *REWARDS Plus: Reading Strategies Applied to Social Studies Passages*

Note A.3-1: You may wish to provide additional practice by having students read a word family to the group or to a partner.

Note A.3-2: Additional vocabulary practice activities are provided in Appendix B of the Teacher's Guide. These activities are optional and can be assigned during class, for homework, or as small group, in-class activities.

ACTIVITY B

Spelling Dictation

ACTIVITY PROCEDURE

(See the *Student Book*, page 104.)

For each word, tell students the word, then have students say the parts of the word to themselves while they write the word. Then, have students enter the number of correctly spelled words as points in the blank half of the Spelling box.

Note B-1: Distribute a piece of light cardboard to each of the students.

 Use Overhead 42: Activity B

1. Find **Activity B**.
2. The first word is **origin**. What word?_ Say the parts in **origin** to yourself as you write the word. (Pause and monitor.)
3. (Show **origin** on the overhead.) Check **origin**. If you misspelled it, cross it out and write it correctly.
4. The second word is **originate**. What word?_ Say the parts in **originate** to yourself as you write the word. (Pause and monitor.)
5. (Show **originate** on the overhead.) Check **originate**. If you misspelled it, cross it out and write it correctly.
6. (Repeat the procedures for the words **original**, **interpret**, **interpreter**, and **interpretation**.)
7. Count the number of words you spelled correctly, and record that number as points in the blank half of the Spelling box at the bottom of the page.

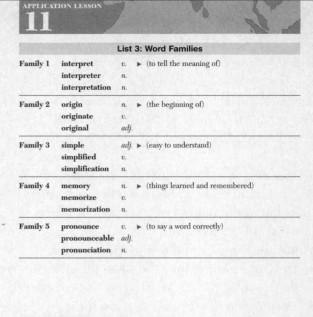

APPLICATION LESSON

11

List 3: Word Families

Family 1	interpret	v.	▶ (to tell the meaning of)
	interpreter	n.	
	interpretation	n.	
Family 2	origin	n.	▶ (the beginning of)
	originate	v.	
	original	adj.	
Family 3	simple	adj.	▶ (easy to understand)
	simplified	v.	
	simplification	n.	
Family 4	memory	n.	▶ (things learned and remembered)
	memorize	v.	
	memorization	n.	
Family 5	pronounce	v.	▶ (to say a word correctly)
	pronounceable	adj.	
	pronunciation	n.	

ACTIVITY B *Spelling Dictation*

1. origin	4. interpret
2. originate	5. interpreter
3. original	6. interpretation

SPELLING 6

Points

ACTIVITY C
Background Knowledge

ACTIVITY PROCEDURE

(See the *Student Book,* page 105.)

Read the Background Knowledge paragraph using one of three methods: read it to students, have students read it together, or call on individual students to read. Examine the timeline and the related graphic together. Then, preview the passage together by examining the title and the headings. Have students tell partners two things the passage will tell about.

1. Turn to page 105. Let's read the paragraph. (Read or ask students to read. Then examine the timeline and graphic together.)
2. Now, let's turn the page and preview the passage. Read the title._ What is the whole passage going to tell about?_
3. Now, let's read the headings. Read the first heading._ Read the next heading._ (Continue until students have read all headings.)
4. Turn to your partner. Without looking, tell two things this passage will tell about._

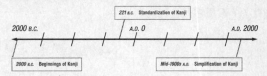

ACTIVITY C *Background Knowledge*

2000 B.C.   A.D. 0   A.D. 2000

221 B.C. Standardization of Kanji

2000 B.C. Beginnings of Kanji   Mid-1900s A.D. Simplification of Kanji

In this article, you will read about the beginnings, or the origins, of the Chinese written language around the year 2000 B.C., approximately 4000 years ago. People in different parts of the world developed different ways of representing their languages. Most alphabets use individual letters or groups of letters to represent sounds. In the Roman alphabet, which is the alphabet used to write English, Spanish, German, Italian, and French, the letters represent sounds and are grouped together to form individual words. In Chinese and Japanese writing, a series of brush strokes form a picture or character that represents a word or concept. Here are some kanji forms and their meanings.

山茶花

| shan | cha | hua |
| mountain | tea | flower(s) |

Some Examples of Modern Chinese Kanji

ACTIVITY D

Passage Reading and Comprehension

ACTIVITY PROCEDURE

(See the *Student Book*, pages 106–107.)

Have students work on reading accuracy by selecting a passage-reading option that best fits your students.

Passage Reading: Accuracy

(Select a passage-reading procedure that matches the size of your group and the competency of your students.

Option A

If you are teaching a small group of students who are having difficulty, use Option A:

Have students read one paragraph silently. Then, call on one student to orally read a paragraph or a portion of the paragraph to the class. Call on students in random order, varying the amount that each student reads.

Option B

If you are teaching a small group with students who are not having difficulty, use Option B:

Have students read the entire article silently, rereading it if they finish before their classmates. Then, call on one student to orally read a paragraph or a portion of a paragraph to the class. Call on students in random order, varying the amount that each student reads.

Option C

If you are teaching a large group with students who are having difficulty, use Option C:

Have students read one paragraph silently. Then, have students read the paragraph to a partner. Alternate partner-reading turns.

Option D

If you are teaching a large group with students who are not having difficulty, use Option D:

Have students read the entire article silently, rereading it if they finish before their classmates. Then, have students read the passage with their partners, alternating on each paragraph.)

ACTIVITY D *Passage Reading and Comprehension*

Kanji

13	Have you ever seen Chinese or Japanese writing? Its brush strokes and lines
27	look very different from the Roman alphabet (which uses letters like A, B, C,
41	etc.). This system of writing, used in Japan, Korea, Taiwan, and China, is known
	as *kanji*. (#1)

The Origin of Kanji

43	
47	Historians believe that kanji originated in China around 2000 B.C. At that
59	time, kings and other leaders would use *divination* in order to answer difficult
72	questions. Divination is like fortune-telling. These leaders interpreted the cracks
83	in bones and turtle shells to mean certain things. Generally, the meaning that
96	was given to a certain set of cracks was determined by the way the cracks
111	looked. In other words, if the cracks sort of looked like a bird, then they would
127	be interpreted to mean "bird." A scribe, an official writer, recorded these
139	interpretations for the king. He made a drawing of the crack and then a drawing
154	of the object it represented. (#2)
159	Eventually, some of these drawings began to be very familiar, as they appeared
172	over and over again. As they appeared more frequently, they were given an
185	informal definition and pronunciation, and the drawing became a character. It is
197	believed that there were about 3000 characters during this early period. Only half
210	of those characters can be understood today. With time, more and more scholars
223	came to view these characters as a sort of writing system. They used this writing
238	system as a way to interpret language through pictures and symbols. But it wasn't
252	until about 221 B.C. that the system began to be standardized. (#3)

The Standardization of Kanji

263	
267	The rulers of the Qin Dynasty decided that most things in China should be
281	normalized. They made roads all the same width and standardized weight and
293	distance measurements. They also created a set of official written characters.
304	The official index contained about 3300 characters, which were mandatory for
315	scholars to learn. (#4)

Kanji Expands

318	
320	Shortly after its standardization, kanji was introduced to Japan. The Japanese
331	adopted kanji as the written expression of their language. Before this, their

106 *REWARDS Plus: Reading Strategies Applied to Social Studies Passages*

Passage Reading: Comprehension Questions

(You may wish to ask the following questions as the passage is being read. Numbers corresponding to the questions are indicated at the point at which they could be asked.)

#1 What is kanji?

A system of writing, consisting of brush strokes and lines, that is used in Japan, Korea, Taiwan, and China.

#2 What was the scribe's job?

To record the leaders' interpretations of cracks by making a drawing of the cracks and then drawing the object the cracks represented.

#3 What happened to the drawings as they began to be familiar?

They were given definitions and pronunciations; they became standardized characters.

343   language was only spoken. During the next thousand years, kanji rapidly
354   expanded and changed. China was developing new technologies, ideas, and
364   concepts. Therefore, new words and characters were invented to express these
375   ideas. The number of characters the Chinese were using increased to about
387   30,000. (#5)

388   **Modern Kanji**
390   During the 20th century, both China and Japan simplified their kanji. Before
402   World War II, a person had to know more than 12,000 characters to be able to
418   read the newspaper. That is a lot of characters to memorize! Because kanji was
432   so difficult to learn, less than half the population of each country was able to
447   read. The governments of the two countries decided to simplify the characters.
459   However, they simplified the same characters in different ways. As a result, the
472   two written languages appear very different now. (#6)
479   Each country also determined a set of basic kanji for everyday life. There are
493   about 100,000 kanji in existence, but many of them are no longer used. Even the
508   most highly educated students may know only between 7,000 and 12,000
519   characters. In Japan, recognition of about 2,000 kanji is necessary to read
531   newspapers; in China, recognition of 4,000–8,000 kanji is necessary. Because of
543   the simplification of kanji, many more people are now literate in China and
556   Japan. Although it is still difficult to learn, kanji continues to be an important
570   part of Chinese and Japanese cultures. (#7)
576

ACTIVITY E *Fluency Building*

| Cold Timing | [ ] | Practice 1 | [ ] |
| Practice 2 | [ ] | Hot Timing | [ ] |

Student Book: Application Lesson 11   **107**

#4 **Why did the rulers of the Qin Dynasty create an official index of characters?**
So that the sets of characters would be normalized for everyone.

#5 **Why was there a need for kanji to expand?**
China needed new words and characters because new technologies, ideas, and concepts were being developed.

#6 **Why do the Chinese and Japanese languages look different today?**
Both countries simplified their kanji because the number of characters made the languages very hard to learn.

#7 **What was a direct result of the simplification of kanji in China and Japan?**
Many more people are literate now.

ACTIVITY E
Fluency Building

ACTIVITY PROCEDURE

(See the *Student Book*, page 107.)

Have students complete a Cold Timing, one or two practices, and a Hot Timing of the Activity D article. For each timing, have students record the number of correct words read. Finally, have students complete their Fluency Graphs.

Note E-1: When assigning partners for this activity, have the stronger reader read first. As a result, the other reader will have one additional practice opportunity.

1. Now, it's time for fluency building.
2. Find the beginning of the passage again. (Pause.)
3. Whisper-read. See how many words you can read in one minute. Begin._ (Time students for one minute.) Stop._ Circle the last word that you read._ Record the number of words you read after **Cold Timing** in **Activity E** at the bottom of page 107._
4. Let's practice again. Begin._ (Time students for one minute.) Stop._ Put a box around the last word that you read._ Record the number of words you read after **Practice 1**._
5. **Optional** Let's practice one more time before the Hot Timing. Begin._ (Time students for one minute.) Stop._ Put a box around the last word that you read._ Record the number of words you read after **Practice 2**._
6. Please exchange books with your partner._ Partner 1, you are going to read first. Partner 2, listen carefully and underline any mistakes or words left out. Ones, begin._ (Time students for one minute.) Stop._ Twos, cross out the last word that your partner read._ Twos, record the number of words in your partner's book after **Hot Timing**._
7. Partner 2, you are going to read next. Partner 1, listen carefully and underline any mistakes or words left out. Twos, begin. (Time students for one minute.) Stop._ Ones, cross out the last word that your partner read._ Ones, record the number of words in your partner's book after **Hot Timing**._
8. Exchange books._ Turn to the Fluency Graph on the last page of your book, and indicate on the graph the number of Cold Timing and Hot Timing words you read correctly._

ACTIVITY F

Comprehension Questions— Multiple Choice and Short Answer

ACTIVITY PROCEDURE

(See the *Student Book,* pages 108–109.)

Have students complete the Multiple Choice and Short Answer questions on the passage. Give feedback to students on their answers. Lead students in a discussion of their Multiple Choice answers and rationales. Have students record points for each correct item. For each Short Answer response, give one point for using the wording of the question in the answer, and one point for accuracy of the answer (total of 4 points possible for two complete answers).

Note F-1: The correct Multiple Choice answers are circled.

 Comprehension Questions— Multiple Choice and Short Answer

Comprehension Strategy—Multiple Choice

Step 1: Read the item.
Step 2: Read all of the choices.
Step 3: Think about why each choice might be correct or incorrect. Check the article as needed.
Step 4: From the possible correct choices, select the best answer.

1. (Vocabulary) **What does the heading "The *Standardization* of Kanji" mean?**
  a. The characters were made the same size.
  b. A set of official characters was selected in each country.
  c. The same characters were used in Japan, China, and Korea.
  d. The same number of characters was chosen in each country of Asia.

2. (Compare and Contrast) **What is the *major* difference between the Roman alphabet and kanji?**
  a. The Roman alphabet was developed in Europe, while kanji was developed in Asia.
  b. Kanji has been standardized recently, while the Roman alphabet was standardized many centuries ago.
  c. The Roman alphabet is used in many European countries, such as Spain and France, while kanji is used in China and Japan.
  d. The Roman alphabet letters represent sounds, while kanji characters represent words or concepts.

3. (Cause and Effect) **China and Japan simplified their kanji:**
  a. so that the two languages would look different.
  b. to make the drawings more attractive.
  c. to allow more people to become literate.
  d. to save time and paper.

4. (Main Idea) **Which sentence gives the best summary of this article?**
  a. Kanji characters look very different than the letters of the Roman alphabet used to represent English.
  b. Kanji, a system of writing that represents words with characters, was developed in Asia and has changed over time.
  c. Standardization of kanji led to an official set of characters that students could learn.
  d. To make kanji available to more people, it was simplified in China and Japan.

 MULTIPLE CHOICE COMPREHENSION **4** *Points*

108 *REWARDS Plus: Reading Strategies Applied to Social Studies Passages*

Comprehension Strategy—Short Answer

Step 1: Read the item.
Step 2: Turn the question into part of the answer and write it down.
Step 3: Think of the answer or locate the answer in the article.
Step 4: Complete your answer.

1. **How is kanji different from the Roman alphabet (e.g., A, B, C)?**
Example answer: Kanji is different from the Roman alphabet in that the characters are based on pictures and symbols. Also, there are many more characters in kanji than there are letters in the Roman alphabet.

2. **Why is kanji difficult to learn?**
Example answer: Kanji is difficult to learn because there are a lot of different characters you need to memorize in order to do everyday things, like read a newspaper.

 SHORT ANSWER COMPREHENSION **4** *Points*

ACTIVITY G *Expository Writing—Summary*

Writing Strategy—Summary

Step 1: LIST (List the details that are important enough to include in the summary.)
Step 2: CROSS OUT (Reread the details. Cross out any that you decide not to include.)
Step 3: CONNECT (Connect any details that could go into one sentence.)
Step 4: NUMBER (Number the details in a logical order.)
Step 5: WRITE (Write your summary.)
Step 6: EDIT (Revise and proofread your summary.)

Prompt: Write a summary of the information on kanji presented in this article.

Student Book: Application Lesson 11 **109**

ACTIVITY G
Expository Writing—Summary

ACTIVITY PROCEDURE

(See the *Student Book,* pages 109–110.)

Have students read the prompt and record the topic of the summary. Next, have them **LIST** details in the Planning Box by referring back to the article. Encourage students to record notes rather than form complete sentences. When they are done with their lists, have them compare their lists of critical details with those of other classmates and the Example Summary Plan.

1. Time to write. First, read the prompt at the bottom of page 109. Then, use the Planning Box on page 110 to start thinking about your first sentence. Then, write your **LIST**. When you are finished, compare your list to your partner's list._

Use Overhead 43
Example Summary Plan

2. Now, compare your list to the list on the overhead._

ACTIVITY PROCEDURE

(See the *Student Book,* page 109.)

Next, have students complete the additional steps in the Summary Writing Strategy. Have them reread their lists and **CROSS OUT** any weak or unimportant details. Then, have students **CONNECT** details that could go together in one sentence, **NUMBER** their ideas in a logical order, and **WRITE** their summaries on a separate piece of paper. When they are done, have them **EDIT** their paragraphs, revising for clarity and proofreading for errors in spelling, capitalization, and punctuation.

Have students read their summaries to their partners. Then, read the Example Summary.

Have students read each of the attributes on the rubric, examine their summaries, and circle either "Yes" or "Fix up." Give students time to make changes in their summaries.

Optional: During or after the class session, fill in the third column of the rubric chart and assign points to the student summaries.

Comprehension Strategy—Short Answer

Step 1: Read the item.
Step 2: Turn the question into part of the answer and write it down.
Step 3: Think of the answer or locate the answer in the article.
Step 4: Complete your answer.

1. **How is kanji different from the Roman alphabet (e.g., A, B, C)?**
Example answer: Kanji is different from the Roman alphabet in that the characters are based on pictures and symbols. Also, there are many more characters in kanji than there are letters in the Roman alphabet.

2. **Why is kanji difficult to learn?**
Example answer: Kanji is difficult to learn because there are a lot of different characters you need to memorize in order to do everyday things, like read a newspaper.

SHORT ANSWER COMPREHENSION **4**
Points

(**ACTIVITY G**) *Expository Writing—Summary*

Writing Strategy—Summary

Step 1: LIST (List the details that are important enough to include in the summary.)
Step 2: CROSS OUT (Reread the details. Cross out any that you decide not to include.)
Step 3: CONNECT (Connect any details that could go into one sentence.)
Step 4: NUMBER (Number the details in a logical order.)
Step 5: WRITE (Write your summary.)
Step 6: EDIT (Revise and proofread your summary.)

Prompt: Write a summary of the information on kanji presented in this article.

Student Book: Application Lesson 11 **109**

Planning Box	
(topic) *Kanji*	
① (detail) – *a system of writing*	
(detail) – *originated in China around 2000 B.C.*	
(detail) – *recorded interpretations of cracks in bones and turtle shells*	
② (detail) – *drawings given informal definition and pronunciation*	
③ (detail) – *standardized around 221 B.C., then introduced in Japan*	
④ (detail) – *grew to about 30,000 characters—too many to memorize*	
⑤ (detail) – *during 20th century, both countries simplified kanji*	
(detail) – *now, basic set of kanji for daily life*	

Directions: Write your summary on a separate piece of paper.

Rubric— Summary	Student or Partner Rating	Teacher Rating
1. Did the author state the topic and the main idea in the first sentence?	Yes Fix up	Yes No
2. Did the author focus on important details?	Yes Fix up	Yes No
3. Did the author combine details in some of the sentences?	Yes Fix up	Yes No
4. Is the summary easy to understand?	Yes Fix up	Yes No
5. Did the author correctly spell words, particularly the words found in the article?	Yes Fix up	Yes No
6. Did the author use correct capitalization, capitalizing the first word in the sentence and proper names of people, places, and things?	Yes Fix up	Yes No
7. Did the author use correct punctuation, including a period at the end of each sentence?	Yes Fix up	Yes No

WRITING **7**
Points

110 *REWARDS Plus: Reading Strategies Applied to Social Studies Passages*

Teacher's Guide: Application Lesson 11 ▪ 181

Optional: Have students date their writing and place the sample in a folder. Thus, students will be able to look back at their summaries and extended responses and literally see their writing improvement.

3. Now, **CROSS OUT**, **CONNECT**, **NUMBER**, and **WRITE**.

4. Reread your response and **EDIT**. Check to be sure your response is easy to understand. Fix any errors you find in spelling, capitalization, and punctuation. (Monitor.)

5. Read what you've written to your partner.

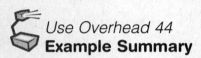

Use Overhead 44
Example Summary

6. Look at the overhead. Let's read this Example Summary. Yours doesn't need to be exactly the same, but it should be similar.

7. (Have students look at the rubric on page 110. Ask students to evaluate their own or their partner's writing to determine what to edit. When they have finished the evaluation, give students adequate time to make changes. Have students enter their points in the blank half of the Writing box below the rubric.)

Comprehension Strategy—Short Answer

Step 1: Read the item.
Step 2: Turn the question into part of the answer and write it down.
Step 3: Think of the answer or locate the answer in the article.
Step 4: Complete your answer.

1. **How is kanji different from the Roman alphabet (e.g., A, B, C)?**
Example answer: Kanji is different from the Roman alphabet in that the characters are based on pictures and symbols. Also, there are many more characters in kanji than there are letters in the Roman alphabet.

2. **Why is kanji difficult to learn?**
Example answer: Kanji is difficult to learn because there are a lot of different characters you need to memorize in order to do everyday things, like read a newspaper.

SHORT ANSWER COMPREHENSION — **4** Points

(**ACTIVITY G**) *Expository Writing—Summary*

Writing Strategy—Summary

Step 1: **LIST** (List the details that are important enough to include in the summary.)
Step 2: **CROSS OUT** (Reread the details. Cross out any that you decide not to include.)
Step 3: **CONNECT** (Connect any details that could go into one sentence.)
Step 4: **NUMBER** (Number the details in a logical order.)
Step 5: **WRITE** (Write your summary.)
Step 6: **EDIT** (Revise and proofread your summary.)

Prompt: Write a summary of the information on kanji presented in this article.

Planning Box

(topic) *Kanji*

① { (detail) – *a system of writing*
(detail) – *originated in China around 2000* B.C.
(detail) – *recorded interpretations of cracks in bones and turtle shells* }

② (detail) – *drawings given informal definition and pronunciation*

③ (detail) – *standardized around 221* B.C.*, then introduced in Japan*

④ (detail) – *grew to about 30,000 characters—too many to memorize*

⑤ { (detail) – *during 20th century, both countries simplified kanji*
(detail) – *now, basic set of kanji for daily life* }

Directions: Write your summary on a separate piece of paper.

Rubric— Summary	Student or Partner Rating		Teacher Rating	
1. Did the author state the topic and the main idea in the first sentence?	Yes	Fix up	Yes	No
2. Did the author focus on important details?	Yes	Fix up	Yes	No
3. Did the author combine details in some of the sentences?	Yes	Fix up	Yes	No
4. Is the summary easy to understand?	Yes	Fix up	Yes	No
5. Did the author correctly spell words, particularly the words found in the article?	Yes	Fix up	Yes	No
6. Did the author use correct capitalization, capitalizing the first word in the sentence and proper names of people, places, and things?	Yes	Fix up	Yes	No
7. Did the author use correct punctuation, including a period at the end of each sentence?	Yes	Fix up	Yes	No

WRITING — **7** Points

Application Lesson 12

Materials Needed:

- *Student Book:* Application Lesson 12
- Application Overhead Transparencies 45–48
- Appendix B Optional Vocabulary Activities: Application Lesson 12
- Paper or cardboard to use when covering the overhead transparency
- Paper or cardboard for each student to use during spelling dictation
- Washable overhead transparency pen

Text Treatment Notes:

- Black text signifies teacher script (exact wording to say to students).
- Green text in parentheses signifies directions or prompts for the teacher.
- Green text signifies answers or examples of answers.
- Green graphics treatment signifies reproduction of Overhead information.
- Green text and green graphics treatment do not appear in the *Student Book*.

ACTIVITY A
Vocabulary

ACTIVITY PROCEDURE, List 1

(See the *Student Book,* page 111.)

Tell students each word in the list. Then, have students repeat the word and read the definition aloud. For each definition, provide any additional information that may be necessary. Then, have students practice reading the words themselves.

Note A.1-1: See Appendix E, Pronunciation Guide for Unique Words, for correct pronunciations of uncommon vocabulary words.

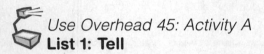
Use Overhead 45: Activity A
List 1: Tell

1. (Show the top half of Overhead 45.) Before we read the passage, let's read the difficult words. (Point to **Mozambique**.) The first word is **Mozambique**. What word?_ Now, read the definition._
2. (Point to **continent**.) The next word is **continent**. What word?_ Now, read the definition._
3. (Pronounce each word in List 1, and then have students repeat each word and read the definition.)
4. Open your *Student Book* to **Application Lesson 12**, page 111._
5. Find **Activity A**, **List 1**, in your book._ Let's read the words again. First word._ Next word._ (Continue for all words in List 1.)

ACTIVITY PROCEDURE, List 2

(See the *Student Book,* page 111.)

Have students circle prefixes and suffixes, then underline the vowels. Using the overhead transparency, assist students in checking their work. Next, have students figure out each word to themselves, then say it aloud. Have them read the definition aloud.

Use Overhead 45: Activity A
List 2: Strategy Practice

1. Find **List 2**. Circle the prefixes and suffixes, and underline the vowels. Look up when you are done._

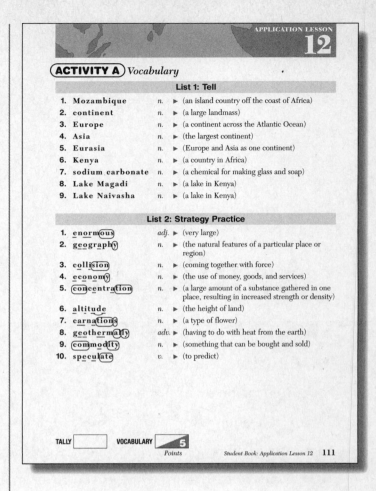

ACTIVITY A *Vocabulary*

List 1: Tell

1.	Mozambique	n. ▸	(an island country off the coast of Africa)
2.	continent	n. ▸	(a large landmass)
3.	Europe	n. ▸	(a continent across the Atlantic Ocean)
4.	Asia	n. ▸	(the largest continent)
5.	Eurasia	n. ▸	(Europe and Asia as one continent)
6.	Kenya	n. ▸	(a country in Africa)
7.	sodium carbonate	n. ▸	(a chemical for making glass and soap)
8.	Lake Magadi	n. ▸	(a lake in Kenya)
9.	Lake Naivasha	n. ▸	(a lake in Kenya)

List 2: Strategy Practice

1.	enormous	adj. ▸	(very large)
2.	geography	n. ▸	(the natural features of a particular place or region)
3.	collision	n. ▸	(coming together with force)
4.	economy	n. ▸	(the use of money, goods, and services)
5.	concentration	n. ▸	(a large amount of a substance gathered in one place, resulting in increased strength or density)
6.	altitude	n. ▸	(the height of land)
7.	carnations	n. ▸	(a type of flower)
8.	geothermally	adv. ▸	(having to do with heat from the earth)
9.	commodity	n. ▸	(something that can be bought and sold)
10.	speculate	v. ▸	(to predict)

TALLY [   ]   **VOCABULARY** [5]
Points

Student Book: Application Lesson 12 **111**

2. (Show the bottom half of Overhead 45.) Now, check and fix any mistakes._
3. Go back to the first word._ Sound out the word to yourself. Put your thumb up when you can read the word. Be sure that it is a real word._ What word?_ Now, read the definition._
4. (Continue Step 3 with all remaining words in List 2.)

Note A.2-1: You may wish to provide additional practice by having students read words to a partner.

ACTIVITY PROCEDURE, List 1 and 2

(See the *Student Book,* page 111.)

Tell students to look in List 1 or List 2 for a word you are thinking about. Have them circle the number of the word and tell you the word. Explain to students to make a tally mark for each correct word in the Tally box, and then enter the number of tally marks as points in the blank half of the Vocabulary box.

1. Remember, the words I'm thinking about will be in either List 1 or List 2. Make a tally mark in the Tally box at the bottom of page 111 for every correctly identified word.
2. Circle the number of the appropriate word.
   - When you talk about the height of land, you talk about this. (Wait.) What word? **altitude**
   - When you predict a certain outcome, you do this. (Wait.) What word? **speculate**
   - This is the largest of the seven continents. (Wait.) What word? **Asia**
   - What do we call the study of the natural features of a particular place or region? (Wait.) What word? **geography**
   - This was the name given to two continents that were once thought to be joined. (Wait.) What word? **Eurasia**
3. Count all the tally marks, and enter that number as points in the blank half of the Vocabulary box.

ACTIVITY PROCEDURE, List 3

(See the *Student Book,* page 112.)

The words in the third list are related. Have students use the *REWARDS* Strategies to figure out the first word in each family. Have them read the definition and then read the other two words in the family.

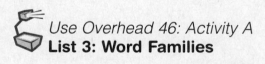

Use Overhead 46: Activity A
List 3: Word Families

1. Turn to page 112. Find **Family 1** in **List 3**. Figure out the first word. Use your pencil if you wish. Put your thumb up when you know the word._ What word?_ Read the definition._
2. Look at the next word in Family 1. Figure out the word._ What word?_
3. Next word. Figure out the word._ What word?_
4. (Repeat Steps 1–3 for all word families in List 3.)

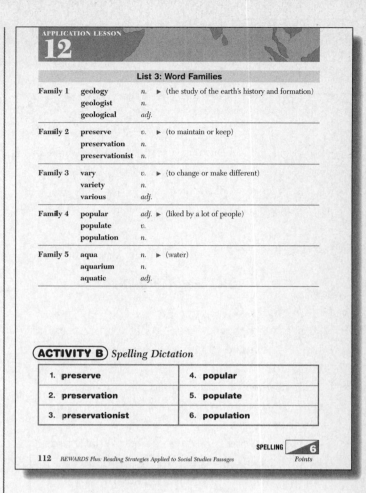

APPLICATION LESSON
12

List 3: Word Families

Family 1	geology	n.	▶ (the study of the earth's history and formation)
	geologist	n.	
	geological	adj.	
Family 2	preserve	v.	▶ (to maintain or keep)
	preservation	n.	
	preservationist	n.	
Family 3	vary	v.	▶ (to change or make different)
	variety	n.	
	various	adj.	
Family 4	popular	adj.	▶ (liked by a lot of people)
	populate	v.	
	population	n.	
Family 5	aqua	n.	▶ (water)
	aquarium	n.	
	aquatic	adj.	

ACTIVITY B *Spelling Dictation*

1. **preserve**	4. **popular**
2. **preservation**	5. **populate**
3. **preservationist**	6. **population**

SPELLING

6

112   *REWARDS Plus: Reading Strategies Applied to Social Studies Passages*   *Points*

Note A.3-1: You may wish to provide additional practice by having students read a word family to the group or to a partner.

Note A.3-2: Additional vocabulary practice activities are provided in Appendix B of the Teacher's Guide. These activities are optional and can be assigned during class, for homework, or as small group, in-class activities.

ACTIVITY B

Spelling Dictation

ACTIVITY PROCEDURE

(See the *Student Book,* page 112.)

For each word, tell students the word, then have students say the parts of the word to themselves while they write the word. Then, have students enter the number of correctly spelled words as points in the blank half of the Spelling box.

Note B-1: Distribute a piece of light cardboard to each of the students.

 Use Overhead 46: Activity B

1. Find **Activity B**.
2. The first word is **preserve**. What word?_ Say the parts in **preserve** to yourself as you write the word. (Pause and monitor.)
3. (Show **preserve** on the overhead.) Check **preserve**. If you misspelled it, cross it out and write it correctly.
4. The second word is **preservation**. What word?_ Say the parts in **preservation** to yourself as you write the word. (Pause and monitor.)
5. (Show **preservation** on the overhead.) Check **preservation**. If you misspelled it, cross it out and write it correctly.
6. (Repeat the procedures for the words **preservationist**, **popular**, **populate**, and **population**.)
7. Count the number of words you spelled correctly, and record that number as points in the blank half of the Spelling box at the bottom of the page.

List 3: Word Families

Family 1	geology	n.	▶ (the study of the earth's history and formation)
	geologist	n.	
	geological	adj.	
Family 2	preserve	v.	▶ (to maintain or keep)
	preservation	n.	
	preservationist	n.	
Family 3	vary	v.	▶ (to change or make different)
	variety	n.	
	various	adj.	
Family 4	popular	adj.	▶ (liked by a lot of people)
	populate	v.	
	population	n.	
Family 5	aqua	n.	▶ (water)
	aquarium	n.	
	aquatic	adj.	

ACTIVITY B *Spelling Dictation*

1. preserve	4. popular
2. preservation	5. populate
3. preservationist	6. population

SPELLING 6

ACTIVITY C
Background Knowledge

ACTIVITY PROCEDURE

(See the *Student Book,* page 113.)

Read the Background Knowledge paragraph using one of three methods: read it to students, have students read it together, or call on individual students to read. Examine the timeline and the related graphic together. Then, preview the passage together by examining the title and the headings. Have students tell partners two things the passage will tell about.

1. Turn to page 113. Let's read the paragraph. (Read or ask students to read. Then examine the timeline and graphic together.)
2. Now, let's turn the page and preview the passage. Read the title._ What is the whole passage going to tell about?_
3. Now, let's read the headings. Read the first heading._ Read the next heading._ (Continue until students have read all headings.)
4. Turn to your partner. Without looking, tell two things this passage will tell about._

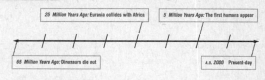

ACTIVITY C Background Knowledge

25 Million Years Ago: Eurasia collides with Africa   5 Million Years Ago: The first humans appear

65 Million Years Ago: Dinosaurs die out   A.D. 2000   Present-day

The article you will read today describes Africa's Great Rift Valley. A rift is an opening made by splitting. There are many rifts, or splits, in the earth's surface. The Great Rift Valley is a visible part of the longest rift in the world. You will learn where this very deep valley is located, how it was formed, and its importance to the people of the region.

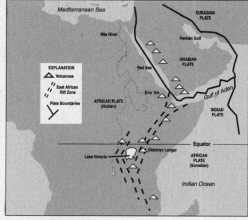

Map of the Great Rift Valley in Africa

ACTIVITY D

Passage Reading and Comprehension

ACTIVITY PROCEDURE

(See the *Student Book*, pages 114–115.)

Have students work on reading accuracy by selecting a passage-reading option that best fits your students.

Passage Reading: Accuracy

(Select a passage-reading procedure that matches the size of your group and the competency of your students.

Option A

If you are teaching a small group of students who are having difficulty, use Option A:

Have students read one paragraph silently. Then, call on one student to orally read a paragraph or a portion of the paragraph to the class. Call on students in random order, varying the amount that each student reads.

Option B

If you are teaching a small group with students who are not having difficulty, use Option B:

Have students read the entire article silently, rereading it if they finish before their classmates. Then, call on one student to orally read a paragraph or a portion of a paragraph to the class. Call on students in random order, varying the amount that each student reads.

Option C

If you are teaching a large group with students who are having difficulty, use Option C:

Have students read one paragraph silently. Then, have students read the paragraph to a partner. Alternate partner-reading turns.

Option D

If you are teaching a large group with students who are not having difficulty, use Option D:

Have students read the entire article silently, rereading it if they finish before their classmates. Then, have students read the passage with their partners, alternating on each paragraph.)

APPLICATION LESSON
12

ACTIVITY D *Passage Reading and Comprehension*

Africa's Great Rift Valley

14   In eastern Africa, a deep valley runs from north to south, framed on either
28 side by grassy plains and enormous mountains. This valley is home to many of
44 the world's deepest lakes. The valley is the visible part of a deep rift in the
54 earth's crust. This area, stretching from northeastern Africa down into
    Mozambique, is known as the Great Rift Valley. (#1)

62 **How It Was Formed**
66   The continents on the earth did not always look the way they do today. Many
81 millions of years ago, Europe and Asia were one continent. Geologists call that
94 continent Eurasia. Continents drift very slowly, moving around the earth's
104 surface. Perhaps 25 million years ago, Eurasia collided with Africa. This collision
116 created enough force to crack the earth's crust in eastern Africa in two places.
130 As these cracks pulled away from each other, the land dropped, and a valley
144 formed between them. The two cracks are known as the Western Rift and the
158 Eastern Rift. (#2)

160 **Geography of the Valley**
164   Because of the deep cracks in the earth's crust, the Rift Valley has a number
179 of active and inactive volcanoes. These volcanoes give the landscape its
190 mountainous appearance. In addition to the volcanoes, there are many lakes in
202 the Rift Valley. The Western Rift has some of the deepest lakes in the world.
217 Because the lakes are isolated, and the water does not flow anywhere, they can
231 be home to fish and aquatic life that cannot be found anywhere else in the
246 world. Many of the Rift Valley's lakes have high concentrations of minerals. In
259 some places, the lakes are rich in soda, which can be mined and sold as a raw
276 material. (#3)

277 **Climate**
278   There is a variety of climates in the Great Rift Valley. They vary greatly
292 because the altitude changes throughout the region. Generally, as the altitude
303 grows higher, the temperatures drop. Lower lands tend to be hotter and drier.
316 Around the shores of some of the lakes as well as on the coast, however, it is hot
334 and humid, with a high rainfall. (#4)

Passage Reading: Comprehension Questions

(You may wish to ask the following questions as the passage is being read. Numbers corresponding to the questions are indicated at the point at which they could be asked.)

#1 Where is the Great Rift Valley?

In eastern Africa; it stretches from northeastern Africa down into Mozambique.

#2 How was the Great Rift Valley formed?

By a collision between the continents of Eurasia and Africa. The collision cracked the earth's crust in eastern Africa in two places.

#3 Describe the lakes in the Great Rift Valley.

Ideas: Deep; isolated; home to many fish and aquatic life that cannot be found elsewhere; rich in soda [sodium carbonate].

340 | **Plant and Animal Life**
344 | Because there is such a variety of climates in the Great Rift Valley, it
358 | supports a staggering variety of plant and animal life. In the valley itself, you
372 | might find lions, elephants, leopards, zebras, and large birds of prey. Many of
385 | the lakes contain rare and unusual varieties of fish and aquatic plants, most of
399 | which do not exist anywhere else. Flamingos, pelicans, storks, and other fish-
411 | eating birds populate the shorelines. In some areas of the Great Rift Valley,
424 | national parks have been created to protect and preserve the numerous
435 | creatures and plants that are native to this amazing region. (#5)

445 | **Resources**
446 | The people who live in the various regions of the Great Rift Valley have
460 | discovered a number of resources that help drive their economies. In Kenya,
472 | they export the sodium carbonate from Lake Magadi. This is used as a raw
486 | material in making things such as soap and glass. The climate and rich soil near
501 | Lake Naivasha allow farmers to grow a popular flower, the carnation, which is
514 | then shipped to Europe for sale. The steam and heat that rise from the volcanic
529 | regions are harnessed geothermally, resulting in electricity. In addition,
538 | geologists predict that there may be sizeable quantities of oil in the Great Rift
552 | Valley. Fish from the various lakes provide food for local people as well as a
567 | commodity that can be sold. Finally, the vegetation, climate, and wildlife of such
580 | places as Kenya and Tanzania have created an increasingly popular tourist
591 | industry. (#6)

592 | **The Rift Continues**
595 | Amazingly, the valley is slowly widening as the rifts grow larger. Some
607 | geologists speculate that in millions of years, the eastern part of Africa may
620 | detach, forming a separate landmass. Although the changes happen slowly, the
631 | volcanoes, shifting rock, and human impact will continue to shape this unique
643 | and interesting region of the world. (#7)
649 |

ACTIVITY E *Fluency Building*

| Cold Timing | ☐ | Practice 1 | ☐ |
| Practice 2 | ☐ | Hot Timing | ☐ |

Student Book: Application Lesson 12 **115**

#4 Why does the climate vary greatly?
Because the altitude varies greatly; higher altitudes have lower temperatures, and lower altitudes are hotter and have more rainfall.

#5 Name some of the animals you would see in the Great Rift Valley.
Ideas: Elephants, leopards, lions, zebras, large birds of prey, unusual fish, flamingos, storks, pelicans.

#6 What resources can be found in the Great Rift Valley?
Ideas: Sodium carbonate, geothermal electricity, oil, fish.

#7 Why do some geologists think that eastern Africa may become a separate landmass?
Because the rift is growing larger, and the valley is slowly widening.

ACTIVITY E
Fluency Building

ACTIVITY PROCEDURE

(See the *Student Book*, page 115.)

Have students complete a Cold Timing, one or two practices, and a Hot Timing of the Activity D article. For each timing, have students record the number of correct words read. Finally, have students complete their Fluency Graphs.

Note E-1: When assigning partners for this activity, have the stronger reader read first. As a result, the other reader will have one additional practice opportunity.

1. Now, it's time for fluency building.
2. Find the beginning of the passage again. (Pause.)
3. Whisper-read. See how many words you can read in one minute. Begin._ (Time students for one minute.) Stop._ Circle the last word that you read._ Record the number of words you read after **Cold Timing** in **Activity E** at the bottom of page 115._
4. Let's practice again. Begin._ (Time students for one minute.) Stop._ Put a box around the last word that you read._ Record the number of words you read after **Practice 1**._
5. **Optional** Let's practice one more time before the Hot Timing. Begin._ (Time students for one minute.) Stop._ Put a box around the last word that you read._ Record the number of words you read after **Practice 2**._
6. Please exchange books with your partner._ Partner 1, you are going to read first. Partner 2, listen carefully and underline any mistakes or words left out. Ones, begin._ (Time students for one minute.) Stop._ Twos, cross out the last word that your partner read._ Twos, record the number of words in your partner's book after **Hot Timing**._
7. Partner 2, you are going to read next. Partner 1, listen carefully and underline any mistakes or words left out. Twos, begin. (Time students for one minute.) Stop._ Ones, cross out the last word that your partner read._ Ones, record the number of words in your partner's book after **Hot Timing**._
8. Exchange books._ Turn to the Fluency Graph on the last page of your book, and indicate on the graph the number of Cold Timing and Hot Timing words you read correctly._

ACTIVITY F

Comprehension Questions— Multiple Choice and Short Answer

ACTIVITY PROCEDURE

(See the *Student Book,* pages 116–117.)

Have students complete the Multiple Choice and Short Answer questions on the passage. Give feedback to students on their answers. Lead students in a discussion of their Multiple Choice answers and rationales. Have students record points for each correct item. For each Short Answer response, give one point for using the wording of the question in the answer, and one point for accuracy of the answer (total of 4 points possible for two complete answers).

Note F-1: The correct Multiple Choice answers are circled.

APPLICATION LESSON
12

ACTIVITY F *Comprehension Questions— Multiple Choice and Short Answer*

Comprehension Strategy—Multiple Choice

Step 1: Read the item.
Step 2: Read all of the choices.
Step 3: Think about why each choice might be correct or incorrect. Check the article as needed.
Step 4: From the possible correct choices, select the best answer.

1. (Vocabulary) **Read this sentence from the passage: "In eastern Africa, a deep valley runs from north to south, *framed* on either side by grassy plains and enormous mountains." What does *framed* mean in that sentence?**
   a. surrounded
   b. pictured
   c. visible
   d. mapped

2. (Cause and Effect) **The Great Rift Valley has a variety of altitudes (heights of land). As a *result*, the following is true:**
   a. Fish from the various lakes can be used as food.
   b. There is a variety of climates in the Great Rift Valley.
   c. Tourism has gradually expanded.
   d. The lakes contain high concentrations of minerals.

3. (Cause and Effect) **There is a huge variety of plants and animals in the Great Rift Valley because:**
   a. there are active and inactive volcanoes in the area.
   b. the plants and animals came from Eurasia and Africa when the continents collided.
   c. the minerals in the soil support the growth of plants and the animals that eat those plants.
   d. there is a variety of climates in the Great Rift Valley.

4. (Cause and Effect) **Many of the fish in the Great Rift Valley lakes are found only there because:**
   a. the fish can live only in the mineral-rich lakes of the Great Rift Valley.
   b. the fish live in lakes that don't flow into other rivers, lakes, or oceans.
   c. the fish can eat only the plants in the lakes.
   d. the fish cannot swim far enough to enter a different lake.

MULTIPLE CHOICE COMPREHENSION *Points*

116 *REWARDS Plus: Reading Strategies Applied to Social Studies Passages*

APPLICATION LESSON
12

Comprehension Strategy—Short Answer

Step 1: Read the item.
Step 2: Turn the question into part of the answer and write it down.
Step 3: Think of the answer or locate the answer in the article.
Step 4: Complete your answer.

1. **Name some of the resources of the Great Rift Valley.**
   Example answer: Some of the resources of the Great Rift Valley include sodium carbonate, carnations, geothermal electricity, fish, and tourism.

2. **What do some geologists think will happen in eastern Africa in a million years?**
   Example answer: Some geologists think that in a million years the eastern part of Africa may split from the rest of the continent, forming a separate landmass.

SHORT ANSWER COMPREHENSION *Points*

ACTIVITY G *Expository Writing—Summary*

Writing Strategy—Summary

Step 1: LIST (List the details that are important enough to include in the summary.)
Step 2: CROSS OUT (Reread the details. Cross out any that you decide not to include.)
Step 3: CONNECT (Connect any details that could go into one sentence.)
Step 4: NUMBER (Number the details in a logical order.)
Step 5: WRITE (Write your summary.)
Step 6: EDIT (Revise and proofread your summary.)

Prompt: Write a summary of the information about the Great Rift Valley.

Student Book: Application Lesson 12 117

ACTIVITY G
Expository Writing—Summary

ACTIVITY PROCEDURE

(See the *Student Book*, pages 117–118.)

Have students read the prompt and record the topic of the summary. Next, have them **LIST** details in the Planning Box by referring back to the article. Encourage students to record notes rather than form complete sentences. When they are done with their lists, have them compare their lists of critical details with those of other classmates and the Example Summary Plan.

1. Time to write. First, read the prompt at the bottom of page 117. Then, use the Planning Box on page 118 to start thinking about your first sentence. Then, write your **LIST**. When you are finished, compare your list to your partner's list._

Use Overhead 47
Example Summary Plan

2. Now, compare your list to the list on the overhead._

ACTIVITY PROCEDURE

Next, have students complete the additional steps in the Summary Writing Strategy. Have them reread their lists and **CROSS OUT** any weak or unimportant details. Then, have students **CONNECT** details that could go together in one sentence, **NUMBER** their ideas in a logical order, and **WRITE** their summaries on a separate piece of paper. When they are done, have them **EDIT** their paragraphs, revising for clarity and proofreading for errors in spelling, capitalization, and punctuation.

Have students read their summaries to their partners. Then, read the Example Summary.

Have students read each of the attributes on the rubric, examine their summaries, and circle either "Yes" or "Fix up." Give students time to make changes in their summaries.

Optional: During or after the class session, fill in the third column of the rubric chart and assign points to the student summaries.

Optional: Have students date their writing and place the sample in a folder. Thus, students will be able to look back at their summaries and extended responses and literally see their writing improvement.

Comprehension Strategy—Short Answer

Step 1: Read the item.
Step 2: Turn the question into part of the answer and write it down.
Step 3: Think of the answer or locate the answer in the article.
Step 4: Complete your answer.

1. Name some of the resources of the Great Rift Valley.
Example answer: Some of the resources of the Great Rift Valley include sodium carbonate, carnations, geothermal electricity, fish, and tourism.

2. What do some geologists think will happen in eastern Africa in a million years?
Example answer: Some geologists think that in a million years the eastern part of Africa may split from the rest of the continent, forming a separate landmass.

SHORT ANSWER COMPREHENSION **4**
Points

ACTIVITY G *Expository Writing—Summary*

Writing Strategy—Summary

Step 1: LIST (List the details that are important enough to include in the summary.)
Step 2: CROSS OUT (Reread the details. Cross out any that you decide not to include.)
Step 3: CONNECT (Connect any details that could go into one sentence.)
Step 4: NUMBER (Number the details in a logical order.)
Step 5: WRITE (Write your summary.)
Step 6: EDIT (Revise and proofread your summary.)

Prompt: Write a summary of the information about the Great Rift Valley.

Student Book: Application Lesson 12 **117**

Planning Box
(topic) *The Great Rift Valley*
① (detail) – *stretches from northeastern Africa to Mozambique*
(detail) – *crack in earth's crust created by collision of continents*
③ (detail) – *volcanoes give mountainous appearance*
(detail) – *deep lakes with unusual fish and aquatic life*
② ④ (detail) – *variety of climates*
(detail) – *variety of plant and animal life*
⑤ (detail) – *economy driven by natural resources, including sodium carbonate, rich soil, geothermal energy, oil, fish, wildlife*
(detail) – *continuing to widen*

Directions: Write your summary on a separate piece of paper.

Rubric— Summary	Student or Partner Rating		Teacher Rating	
1. Did the author state the topic and the main idea in the first sentence?	Yes	Fix up	Yes	No
2. Did the author focus on important details?	Yes	Fix up	Yes	No
3. Did the author combine details in some of the sentences?	Yes	Fix up	Yes	No
4. Is the summary easy to understand?	Yes	Fix up	Yes	No
5. Did the author correctly spell words, particularly the words found in the article?	Yes	Fix up	Yes	No
6. Did the author use correct capitalization, capitalizing the first word in the sentence and proper names of people, places, and things?	Yes	Fix up	Yes	No
7. Did the author use correct punctuation, including a period at the end of each sentence?	Yes	Fix up	Yes	No

WRITING **7**
Points

118 *REWARDS Plus: Reading Strategies Applied to Social Studies Passages*

Teacher's Guide: Application Lesson 12 ▪ 191

3. Now, **CROSS OUT**, **CONNECT**, **NUMBER**, and **WRITE.**_

4. Reread your response and **EDIT**. Check to be sure your response is easy to understand. Fix any errors you find in spelling, capitalization, and punctuation._ (Monitor.)

5. Read what you've written to your partner._

Use Overhead 48
Example Summary

6. Look at the overhead. Let's read this Example Summary. Yours doesn't need to be exactly the same, but it should be similar.

7. (Have students look at the rubric on page 118. Ask students to evaluate their own or their partner's writing to determine what to edit. When they have finished the evaluation, give students adequate time to make changes. Have students enter their points in the blank half of the Writing box below the rubric.)

Comprehension Strategy—Short Answer

Step 1: Read the item.
Step 2: Turn the question into part of the answer and write it down.
Step 3: Think of the answer or locate the answer in the article.
Step 4: Complete your answer.

1. **Name some of the resources of the Great Rift Valley.**
   Example answer: Some of the resources of the Great Rift Valley include sodium carbonate, carnations, geothermal electricity, fish, and tourism.

2. **What do some geologists think will happen in eastern Africa in a million years?**
   Example answer: Some geologists think that in a million years the eastern part of Africa may split from the rest of the continent, forming a separate landmass.

SHORT ANSWER COMPREHENSION ⟩ **4** *Points*

ACTIVITY G *Expository Writing—Summary*

Writing Strategy—Summary

Step 1: **LIST** (List the details that are important enough to include in the summary.)
Step 2: **CROSS OUT** (Reread the details. Cross out any that you decide not to include.)
Step 3: **CONNECT** (Connect any details that could go into one sentence.)
Step 4: **NUMBER** (Number the details in a logical order.)
Step 5: **WRITE** (Write your summary.)
Step 6: **EDIT** (Revise and proofread your summary.)

Prompt: Write a summary of the information about the Great Rift Valley.

Student Book: Application Lesson 12 **117**

APPLICATION LESSON **12**

Planning Box

(topic) *The Great Rift Valley*

① (detail) – *stretches from northeastern Africa to Mozambique*

(detail) – *crack in earth's crust created by collision of continents*

③ { (detail) – *volcanoes give mountainous appearance*
{ (detail) – *deep lakes with unusual fish and aquatic life*

② ④ { (detail) – *variety of climates*
{ (detail) – *variety of plant and animal life*

⑤ (detail) – *economy driven by natural resources, including sodium carbonate, rich soil, geothermal energy, oil, fish, wildlife*

(detail) – *continuing to widen*

Directions: Write your summary on a separate piece of paper.

Rubric—Summary	Student or Partner Rating		Teacher Rating	
1. Did the author state the topic and the main idea in the first sentence?	Yes	Fix up	Yes	No
2. Did the author focus on important details?	Yes	Fix up	Yes	No
3. Did the author combine details in some of the sentences?	Yes	Fix up	Yes	No
4. Is the summary easy to understand?	Yes	Fix up	Yes	No
5. Did the author correctly spell words, particularly the words found in the article?	Yes	Fix up	Yes	No
6. Did the author use correct capitalization, capitalizing the first word in the sentence and proper names of people, places, and things?	Yes	Fix up	Yes	No
7. Did the author use correct punctuation, including a period at the end of each sentence?	Yes	Fix up	Yes	No

WRITING ⟩ **7** *Points*

118 *REWARDS Plus: Reading Strategies Applied to Social Studies Passages*

Application Lesson 13

Materials Needed:

- *Student Book:* Application Lesson 13
- Application Overhead Transparencies 49–52
- Appendix B Optional Vocabulary Activities: Application Lesson 13
- Paper or cardboard to use when covering the overhead transparency
- Paper or cardboard for each student to use during spelling dictation
- Washable overhead transparency pen

Text Treatment Notes:

- Black text signifies teacher script (exact wording to say to students).
- Green text in parentheses signifies directions or prompts for the teacher.
- Green text signifies answers or examples of answers.
- Green graphics treatment signifies reproduction of Overhead information.
- Green text and green graphics treatment do not appear in the *Student Book.*

ACTIVITY A
Vocabulary

ACTIVITY PROCEDURE, List 1

(See the *Student Book*, page 119.)

Tell students each word in the list. Then, have students repeat the word and read the definition aloud. For each definition, provide any additional information that may be necessary. Then, have students practice reading the words themselves.

Note A.1-1: See Appendix E, Pronunciation Guide for Unique Words, for correct pronunciations of uncommon vocabulary words.

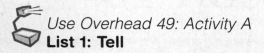

Use Overhead 49: Activity A
List 1: Tell

1. (Show the top half of Overhead 49.) Before we read the passage, let's read the difficult words. (Point to **Nepal**.) The first word is **Nepal**. What word?_ Now, read the definition._
2. (Point to **Mt. Everest**.) The next words are **Mt. Everest**. What words?_ Now, read the definition._
3. (Pronounce each word in List 1, and then have students repeat each word and read the definition.)
4. Open your *Student Book* to **Application Lesson 13**, page 119._
5. Find **Activity A**, **List 1**, in your book._ Let's read the words again. First word._ Next words._ (Continue for all words in List 1.)

ACTIVITY PROCEDURE, List 2

(See the *Student Book*, page 119.)

Have students circle prefixes and suffixes, then underline the vowels. Using the overhead transparency, assist students in checking their work. Next, have students figure out each word to themselves, then say it aloud. Have them read the definition aloud.

Use Overhead 49: Activity A
List 2: Strategy Practice

1. Find **List 2**. Circle the prefixes and suffixes, and underline the vowels. Look up when you are done._
2. (Show the bottom half of Overhead 49.) Before you check your work, look at item #7. (Point to the

---

ACTIVITY A *Vocabulary*

List 1: Tell

1.	Nepal	n. ▶	(a small country in eastern Asia)
2.	Mt. Everest	n. ▶	(the highest mountain in the world, located in Nepal)
3.	Sherpas	n. ▶	(people who live in the mountains of Nepal)
4.	Khumbu Valley	n. ▶	(south of Mt. Everest)
5.	Tibet	n. ▶	(a country next to Nepal)
6.	Nangpa La	n. ▶	(a mountain pass between Tibet and Nepal)
7.	Buddhism	n. ▶	(a religion based on the teachings of Buddha)
8.	Nyingmapa Buddhism	n. ▶	(a type of Buddhism)
9.	Tengboche Monastery	n. ▶	(a religious gathering place located on Mt. Everest)
10.	Chomolungma	n. ▶	(the Sherpa name for Mt. Everest)

List 2: Strategy Practice

1.	prowess	n. ▶	(great ability or skill)
2.	expedition	n. ▶	(a trip or journey for a definite purpose)
3.	fertilizer	n. ▶	(something added to the soil to help things grow)
4.	alienate	v. ▶	(to cause to be unfriendly)
5.	occupation	n. ▶	(the seizure and control of a country by military force)
6.	prosperity	n. ▶	(success, wealth)
7.	substantial	adj. ▶	(important)
8.	spirituality	n. ▶	(concern with things of the spirit or soul)
9.	deforestation	n. ▶	(the result of cutting down forests or trees)
10.	heritage	n. ▶	(something passed down through families)

TALLY ☐   VOCABULARY ◹5 Points

Student Book: Application Lesson 13 **119**

---

second example and the **sub** that is circled.) From now on, you can also circle **sub**. The prefix is /sub/. Say it._ Now, go back to item #1. Check and fix any mistakes._

3. Go back to the first word again._ Sound out the word to yourself. Put your thumb up when you can read the word. Be sure that it is a real word._ What word?_ Now, read the definition._
4. (Continue Step 3 with all remaining words in List 2.)

Note A.2-1: You may wish to provide additional practice by having students read words to a partner.

ACTIVITY PROCEDURE, List 1 and 2

(See the *Student Book,* page 119.)

Tell students to look in List 1 or List 2 for a word you are thinking about. Have them circle the number of the word and tell you the word. Explain to students to make a tally mark for each correct word in the Tally box, and then enter the number of tally marks as points in the blank half of the Vocabulary box.

1. Remember, the words I'm thinking about will be in either List 1 or List 2. Make a tally mark in the Tally box at the bottom of page 119 for every correctly identified word.
2. Circle the number of the appropriate word.
   - These people live in the mountains of Nepal. (Wait.) What word? **Sherpas**
   - If you cause someone to be unfriendly toward you, you do this to that person. (Wait.) What word? **alienate**
   - This is the highest mountain in the world and the climbing goal of many mountaineers. (Wait.) What words? **Mt. Everest**
   - People who have a lot of success or a lot of wealth are described as having this. (Wait.) What word? **prosperity**
   - This condition exists in many countries that cut down excessive amounts of trees and forests. It can cause major environmental changes. (Wait.) What word? **deforestation**
3. Count all the tally marks, and enter that number as points in the blank half of the Vocabulary box.

ACTIVITY PROCEDURE, List 3

(See the *Student Book,* page 120.)

The words in the third list are related. Have students use the *REWARDS* Strategies to figure out the first word in each family. Have them read the definition and then read the other two words in the family.

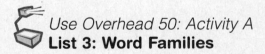
Use Overhead 50: Activity A
List 3: Word Families

1. Turn to page 120. Find **Family 1** in **List 3**. Figure out the first word. Use your pencil if you wish. Put your thumb up when you know the word._ What word?_ Read the definition._
2. Look at the next word in Family 1. Figure out the word._ What word?_

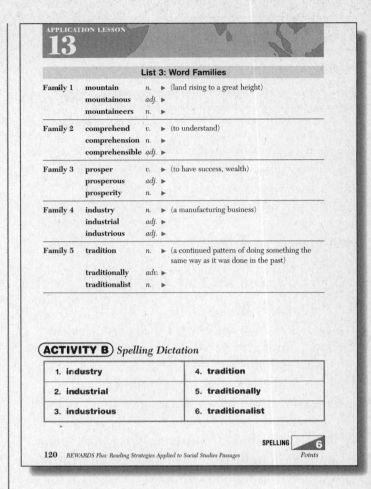

3. Next word. Figure out the word._ What word?_
4. (Repeat Steps 1–3 for all word families in List 3.)

Note A.3-1: You may wish to provide additional practice by having students read a word family to the group or to a partner.

Note A.3-2: Additional vocabulary practice activities are provided in Appendix B of the Teacher's Guide. These activities are optional and can be assigned during class, for homework, or as small group, in-class activities.

ACTIVITY B

Spelling Dictation

ACTIVITY PROCEDURE

(See the *Student Book*, page 120.)

For each word, tell students the word, then have students say the parts of the word to themselves while they write the word. Then, have students enter the number of correctly spelled words as points in the blank half of the Spelling box.

Note B-1: Distribute a piece of light cardboard to each of the students.

 Use Overhead 50: Activity B

1. Find **Activity B**.
2. The first word is **industry**. What word?_ Say the parts in **industry** to yourself as you write the word. (Pause and monitor.)
3. (Show **industry** on the overhead.) Check **industry**. If you misspelled it, cross it out and write it correctly.
4. The second word is **industrial**. What word?_ Say the parts in **industrial** to yourself as you write the word. (Pause and monitor.)
5. (Show **industrial** on the overhead.) Check **industrial**. If you misspelled it, cross it out and write it correctly.
6. (Repeat the procedures for the words **industrious**, **tradition**, **traditionally**, and **traditionalist**.)
7. Count the number of words you spelled correctly, and record that number as points in the blank half of the Spelling box at the bottom of the page.

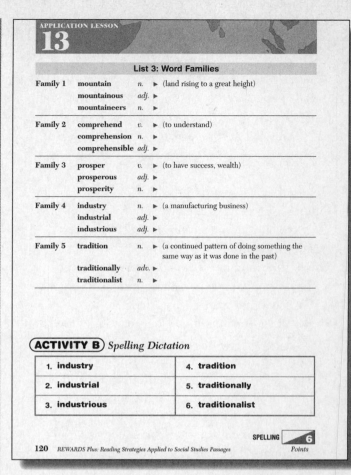

List 3: Word Families

Family 1	mountain	n.	► (land rising to a great height)
	mountainous	adj.	►
	mountaineers	n.	►
Family 2	comprehend	v.	► (to understand)
	comprehension	n.	►
	comprehensible	adj.	►
Family 3	prosper	v.	► (to have success, wealth)
	prosperous	adj.	►
	prosperity	n.	►
Family 4	industry	n.	► (a manufacturing business)
	industrial	adj.	►
	industrious	adj.	►
Family 5	tradition	n.	► (a continued pattern of doing something the same way as it was done in the past)
	traditionally	adv.	►
	traditionalist	n.	►

ACTIVITY B *Spelling Dictation*

1. industry	4. tradition
2. industrial	5. traditionally
3. industrious	6. traditionalist

SPELLING ◢ 6

ACTIVITY C
Background Knowledge

ACTIVITY PROCEDURE

(See the *Student Book*, page 121.)

Read the Background Knowledge paragraph using one of three methods: read it to students, have students read it together, or call on individual students to read. Examine the timeline and the related graphic together. Then, preview the passage together by examining the title and the headings. Have students tell partners two things the passage will tell about.

1. Turn to page 121. Let's read the paragraph. (Read or ask students to read. Then examine the timeline and graphic together.)
2. Now, let's turn the page and preview the passage. Read the title._ What is the whole passage going to tell about?_
3. Now, let's read the headings. Read the first heading._ Read the next heading._ (Continue until students have read all headings.)
4. Turn to your partner. Without looking, tell two things this passage will tell about._

ACTIVITY C *Background Knowledge*

A.D. 1920   A.D. 1960   A.D. 2000

1953   First successful Mt. Everest summit

1921   First Mt. Everest summit attempt

1993   First Sherpa woman summits Mt. Everest

The Sherpas are an ethnic group of people who live in the mountains of Nepal, the highest mountains in the world. Because they live and work in high, mountainous places, Sherpas have adapted to these altitudes, and thus often work as mountaineers for people who climb Mt. Everest. Since the first successful trip up Everest by Sir Edmund Hillary in 1953, Sherpa guides have been traveling with Everest expeditions.

Sherpa

ACTIVITY D

Passage Reading and Comprehension

ACTIVITY PROCEDURE

(See the *Student Book*, pages 122–123.)

Have students work on reading accuracy by selecting a passage-reading option that best fits your students.

Passage Reading: Accuracy

(Select a passage-reading procedure that matches the size of your group and the competency of your students.

Option A

If you are teaching a small group of students who are having difficulty, use Option A:

Have students read one paragraph silently. Then, call on one student to orally read a paragraph or a portion of the paragraph to the class. Call on students in random order, varying the amount that each student reads.

Option B

If you are teaching a small group with students who are not having difficulty, use Option B:

Have students read the entire article silently, rereading it if they finish before their classmates. Then, call on one student to orally read a paragraph or a portion of a paragraph to the class. Call on students in random order, varying the amount that each student reads.

Option C

If you are teaching a large group with students who are having difficulty, use Option C:

Have students read one paragraph silently. Then, have students read the paragraph to a partner. Alternate partner-reading turns.

Option D

If you are teaching a large group with students who are not having difficulty, use Option D:

Have students read the entire article silently, rereading it if they finish before their classmates. Then, have students read the passage with their partners, alternating on each paragraph.)

ACTIVITY D *Passage Reading and Comprehension*

Sherpas

14	High in the mountains of Nepal, the Sherpas live in the Khumbu Valley. This valley is considered the southern gateway to Mt. Everest. Sherpas are best
26	
37	known for their climbing prowess and excellent guidance to Everest climbing expeditions. But they have their own culture and customs apart from that as
50	mountain guides. (#1)

Food at 14,000 Feet

52	
56	Traditionally, Sherpas have made their living through trade and agriculture.
66	They herd yaks, a large shaggy mammal similar to a buffalo. The yak fur
80	provides wool for clothing, the hide provides leather for shoes, and the dung
93	(manure) provides fuel for cooking as well as fertilizer for agriculture. The
105	Sherpas drink the yak's milk. They also make it into butter and cheese. (#2)
118	The Sherpas used to trade with Tibet, across the Nangpa La Pass. They
131	would drive their yak herds across the 19,000-foot pass, carrying buffalo hides
144	and other items. They would return with salt and wool. But trade of goods
158	across the pass has almost completely stopped because of the Chinese
169	occupation of Tibet. (#3)
172	The Sherpas also grow food. Potatoes, which can still grow well at high
185	altitudes, are one of their staples, or basic foods. Potatoes are mixed with meats
199	and vegetables to form a stew. This stew, along with lentils and rice, is their
214	primary meal. Sherpas drink lots of tea, often sweetened with a great deal of
228	sugar and milk. (#4)

Religious Life

231	
233	The Sherpas practice a sect of Buddhism known as *Nyingmapa* Buddhism.
244	Because of their religious beliefs, the Sherpas have always honored the
255	mountains of their region as the homes of gods and goddesses. For example, the
269	Sherpas believe that Mt. Everest, known as *Chomolungma* in the Tibetan
280	language, is the home of the goddess of humans and prosperity. For centuries,
293	the Sherpas kept the mountains sacred by not climbing them. But the allure of
307	Westerners and their money tempted the Sherpas to accept climbing as part of
320	their culture. For modern religious ceremonies and festivals, the Sherpas often
331	gather at the famous Tengboche Monastery, located 16,000 feet up the north
343	side of Mt. Everest. (#5)

122 *REWARDS Plus: Reading Strategies Applied to Social Studies Passages*

Passage Reading: Comprehension Questions

(You may wish to ask the following questions as the passage is being read. Numbers corresponding to the questions are indicated at the point at which they could be asked.)

#1 What are Sherpas known for?
Their climbing ability and guidance on Mt. Everest climbing expeditions.

#2 Why are yaks important to the Sherpas' way of life?
Yaks provide wool for clothing, leather for shoes, and dung for fertilizer and fuel. Yaks also provide milk to drink, which Sherpas use to make into butter and cheese.

#3 Why has trade between the Sherpas and Tibet almost stopped?
The Chinese occupy Tibet with a military presence.

347 | **Language**
348 | The Sherpas speak a language that is related to modern Tibetan. But the two
362 | languages have grown to be more and more different from each other over the
376 | years. This makes communication between the two groups very difficult. Only
387 | parts of the language are mutually comprehensible. The languages grew apart for
399 | two reasons. First, the Sherpa language is not standardized, meaning that the rules
412 | of the language are not written down or formally recognized. Second, the Sherpa
425 | language does not have a written alphabet. Some people are trying to introduce a
439 | written script into the Sherpa language; however, the script would be based on the
453 | Tibetan alphabet. Many people feel that the Sherpas would not accept the script
466 | because it might not represent the language spoken by the Sherpas (#6)

477 | **Mountaineering**
478 | In 1921, some Englishmen made the first expedition to climb Mt. Everest.
490 | Sherpas were hired to help them. By the 1970s, mountaineering had become a
503 | substantial industry for the Sherpas. Many will travel from their villages to the cities,
517 | where the foreign climbing expeditions will hire local guides. The Western climbers
529 | have influenced the Sherpa culture. Many Sherpa men now wear Western-style
541 | clothing. The Sherpa culture and spirituality have influenced the climbers. But not
553 | all effects of mountaineering have been positive for the Sherpas. (#7)
563 | Western influences, such as deforestation and litter, have become major
573 | problems in the Sherpa region. Large numbers of trees have been cut down to
587 | make way for new settlements and more agriculture and to be used as fuel in
602 | the form of firewood. Everest base camp, the starting point for Everest
614 | expeditions, was littered with used oxygen bottles, garbage, and other evidence
625 | of the many climbers. However, recent efforts to clean up base camp and lower
639 | regions of Everest have succeeded. In 1976, the Khumbu region was declared a
652 | national park. The national park staff and other Sherpa groups have also begun
665 | to manage the forests and other natural resources. These efforts will help ensure
678 | that the Sherpas can continue to maintain their culture and heritage and to
691 | preserve their traditions and region. (#8)
696 |

ACTIVITY E *Fluency Building*

| Cold Timing | ____ | Practice 1 | ____ |
| Practice 2 | ____ | Hot Timing | ____ |

#4 What does the Sherpas' diet consist of?
Potatoes, meats, vegetables, lentils, rice, and sweet tea.

#5 Why is Mt. Everest important to the Sherpas' religious beliefs?
They believe that Mt. Everest is the home of the goddess of humans and prosperity.

#6 What does "the Sherpa language is not standardized" mean?
The language has not been written down or formally recognized as a language.

#7 How have Western people and Sherpas influenced each other?
Sherpas are now wearing Western-style clothing, while Westerners have been influenced by the Sherpas' spirituality.

#8 What types of Western influences have been introduced to the Sherpas' way of life?
Cutting down forests to provide firewood for burning; littering, especially on Mt. Everest.

ACTIVITY E
Fluency Building

ACTIVITY PROCEDURE

(See the *Student Book*, page 123.)

Have students complete a Cold Timing, one or two practices, and a Hot Timing of the Activity D article. For each timing, have students record the number of correct words read. Finally, have students complete their Fluency Graphs.

Note E-1: When assigning partners for this activity, have the stronger reader read first. As a result, the other reader will have one additional practice opportunity.

1. Now, it's time for fluency building.
2. Find the beginning of the passage again. (Pause.)
3. Whisper-read. See how many words you can read in one minute. Begin._ (Time students for one minute.) Stop._ Circle the last word that you read._ Record the number of words you read after **Cold Timing** in **Activity E** at the bottom of page 123._
4. Let's practice again. Begin._ (Time students for one minute.) Stop._ Put a box around the last word that you read._ Record the number of words you read after **Practice 1**._
5. **Optional** Let's practice one more time before the Hot Timing. Begin._ (Time students for one minute.) Stop._ Put a box around the last word that you read._ Record the number of words you read after **Practice 2**._
6. Please exchange books with your partner._ Partner 1, you are going to read first. Partner 2, listen carefully and underline any mistakes or words left out. Ones, begin._ (Time students for one minute.) Stop._ Twos, cross out the last word that your partner read._ Twos, record the number of words in your partner's book after **Hot Timing**._
7. Partner 2, you are going to read next. Partner 1, listen carefully and underline any mistakes or words left out. Twos, begin. (Time students for one minute.) Stop._ Ones, cross out the last word that your partner read._ Ones, record the number of words in your partner's book after **Hot Timing**._
8. Exchange books._ Turn to the Fluency Graph on the last page of your book, and indicate on the graph the number of Cold Timing and Hot Timing words you read correctly._

ACTIVITY F

Comprehension Questions— Multiple Choice and Short Answer

ACTIVITY PROCEDURE

(See the *Student Book*, pages 124–125.)

Have students complete the Multiple Choice and Short Answer questions on the passage. Give feedback to students on their answers. Lead students in a discussion of their Multiple Choice answers and rationales. Have students record points for each correct item. For each Short Answer response, give one point for using the wording of the question in the answer, and one point for accuracy of the answer (total of 4 points possible for two complete answers).

Note F-1: The correct Multiple Choice answers are circled.

ACTIVITY F *Comprehension Questions— Multiple Choice and Short Answer*

Comprehension Strategy—Multiple Choice

Step 1: Read the item.
Step 2: Read all of the choices.
Step 3: Think about why each choice might be correct or incorrect. Check the article as needed.
Step 4: From the possible correct choices, select the best answer.

1. (Vocabulary) **In the article, it states "…the *allure* of Westerners and their money led the Sherpas to accept climbing as part of their culture." What does that sentence mean?**
   a. The Sherpas had always climbed mountains, but now they did it for money.
   b. While the Sherpas had not always climbed the mountains, the promise of the Westerners' money made them change their ways.
   c. Up until the arrival of Westerners, climbing was a religious act.
   d. The Sherpas historically have followed Easterners, not Westerners.

2. (Main Idea) **Reread the second paragraph in the article. Which sentence below gives the main idea of the paragraph?**
   a. Yaks provide the Sherpas with food.
   b. Yaks are as important to the Sherpas as cattle are to us.
   c. Yaks meet many of the needs of the Sherpas.
   d. Yaks support agriculture by supplying fertilizer.

3. (Cause and Effect) **Which of the following is *not* a result of Western climbers' interactions with the Sherpas?**
   a. Many Sherpa men now wear Western-style clothing.
   b. Many Sherpa men work away from their villages.
   c. More Sherpa men work as guides for climbing expeditions.
   d. Sherpas no longer have the majority of their survival needs met by yaks.

4. (Main Idea) **If this article needed a new title, which would be best?**
   a. *East Meets West on Mount Everest*
   b. *The Culture of the Sherpas*
   c. *Mount Everest—Home of Gods and Goddesses*
   d. *The Climbers—Western Mountaineers and the Sherpas*

MULTIPLE CHOICE COMPREHENSION
4
Points

Comprehension Strategy—Short Answer

Step 1: Read the item.
Step 2: Turn the question into part of the answer and write it down.
Step 3: Think of the answer or locate the answer in the article.
Step 4: Complete your answer.

1. **What are some ways that yaks are useful to the Sherpas?**
   Example answer: Yaks are useful to the Sherpas because they provide Sherpas with meat, milk, and cheese. Also, yak hides are used for clothing and for leather.

2. **What are some of the foods eaten by the Sherpas?**
   Example answer: Some of the foods eaten by the Sherpas are rice, lentils, potatoes, and yak's milk, cheese, and meat. They also grow other vegetables. Sherpas drink a great deal of tea, sweetened with milk and sugar.

SHORT ANSWER COMPREHENSION
4
Points

ACTIVITY G *Expository Writing—Extended Response*

Writing Strategy—Extended Response

Step 1: **LIST** (List the reasons for your position. For each reason, explain with details.)
Step 2: **CROSS OUT** (Reread your reasons and details. Cross out any that you decide not to include.)
Step 3: **CONNECT** (Connect any details that could go into one sentence.)
Step 4: **NUMBER** (Number the reasons in a logical order.)
Step 5: **WRITE** (Write your response.)
Step 6: **EDIT** (Revise and proofread your response.)

Prompt: Describe how a Sherpa's life is different from your own.

ACTIVITY G

Expository Writing—Extended Response

ACTIVITY PROCEDURE

(See the *Student Book*, pages 125–127.)

Have students read the prompt and record their position. Next, have them **LIST** reasons and explanations in the Planning Box by referring back to the article. Encourage them to record notes rather than write complete sentences. When students are done with their lists, have them compare their reasons and explanations with those of their classmates and the Example Plan.

1. Time to write. First, read the prompt at the bottom of page 125. Then, use the Planning Box on page 126 to start thinking about your first sentence. Then, write your **LIST**. When you are finished, compare your list to your partner's list.

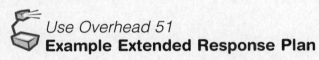

Use Overhead 51
Example Extended Response Plan

2. Now, compare your list to the list on the overhead.

ACTIVITY PROCEDURE

Next, have students complete the additional steps in the Extended Response Writing Strategy. Have them reread their lists and **CROSS OUT** any weak or unimportant reasons or explanations. Then, have students **CONNECT** explanations that could go together in one sentence, **NUMBER** their reasons in a logical order, and **WRITE** their extended responses on a separate piece of paper. When they are done, have them **EDIT** their paragraphs, revising for clarity and proofreading for errors in spelling, capitalization, and punctuation.

Have students read their extended responses to their partners. Then, read the Example Extended Response.

Have students read each of the attributes on the rubric, examine their extended responses, and circle either "Yes" or "Fix up." Give students time to make necessary changes.

Optional: During or after the class session, fill in the third column of the rubric chart and assign points to the extended responses.

Optional: Have students date their writing and place the sample in a folder. Thus, students will be able to look back at their

---

Comprehension Strategy—Short Answer

Step 1: Read the item.
Step 2: Turn the question into part of the answer and write it down.
Step 3: Think of the answer or locate the answer in the article.
Step 4: Complete your answer.

1. **What are some ways that yaks are useful to the Sherpas?**
Example answer: Yaks are useful to the Sherpas because they provide Sherpas with meat, milk, and cheese. Also, yak hides are used for clothing and for leather.

2. **What are some of the foods eaten by the Sherpas?**
Example answer: Some of the foods eaten by the Sherpas are rice, lentils, potatoes, and yak's milk, cheese, and meat. They also grow other vegetables. Sherpas drink a great deal of tea, sweetened with milk and sugar.

SHORT ANSWER COMPREHENSION **4** *Points*

ACTIVITY G *Expository Writing—Extended Response*

Writing Strategy—Extended Response

Step 1: **LIST** (List the reasons for your position. For each reason, explain with details.)
Step 2: **CROSS OUT** (Reread your reasons and details. Cross out any that you decide not to include.)
Step 3: **CONNECT** (Connect any details that could go into one sentence.)
Step 4: **NUMBER** (Number the reasons in a logical order.)
Step 5: **WRITE** (Write your response.)
Step 6: **EDIT** (Revise and proofread your response.)

Prompt: Describe how a Sherpa's life is different from your own.

Student Book: Application Lesson 13 **125**

Planning Box

(position) *A Sherpa's life is different from my life.*

① (reason) – *food is different*
   (explain) – *we purchase our food*
     – *they grow or raise their food*
     – *they eat yak meat, yak milk, yak cheese*
     – *we both eat a similar food: potatoes*

② (reason) – *yaks are important to their lives*
   (explain) – *we don't rely on yaks at all*
     – *yaks provide food, clothing, and shoe leather*

③ (reason) – *our religions may differ*
   (explain) – *they practice a form of Buddhism*
     – *they believe that mountains are homes of gods*

④ (reason) – *our languages differ*
   (explain) – *they speak a language similar to Tibetan*
     – *theirs is not a written language*

Directions: Write your extended response on a separate piece of paper.

126 *REWARDS Plus: Reading Strategies Applied to Social Studies Passages*

---

summaries and extended responses and literally see their writing improvement.

3. Now, **CROSS OUT**, **CONNECT**, **NUMBER**, and **WRITE**.

4. Reread your response and **EDIT**. Check to be sure your response is easy to understand. Fix any errors you find in spelling, capitalization, and punctuation. (Monitor.)

5. Read what you've written to your partner.

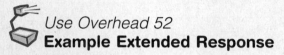
Use Overhead 52
Example Extended Response

6. Look at the overhead. Let's read this Example Extended Response. Yours doesn't need to be exactly the same, but it should be similar.

7. (Have students turn to the rubric on page 127. Ask students to evaluate their own or their partner's writing to determine what to edit. When they have finished the evaluation, give students adequate time to make changes. Have students enter their points in the blank half of the Writing box below the rubric.)

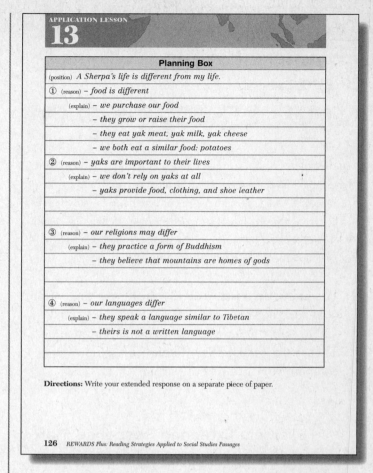

APPLICATION LESSON
13

Planning Box
(position) *A Sherpa's life is different from my life.*
① (reason) *– food is different*
(explain) *– we purchase our food*
– they grow or raise their food
– they eat yak meat, yak milk, yak cheese
– we both eat a similar food: potatoes
② (reason) *– yaks are important to their lives*
(explain) *– we don't rely on yaks at all*
– yaks provide food, clothing, and shoe leather
③ (reason) *– our religions may differ*
(explain) *– they practice a form of Buddhism*
– they believe that mountains are homes of gods
④ (reason) *– our languages differ*
(explain) *– they speak a language similar to Tibetan*
– theirs is not a written language

Directions: Write your extended response on a separate piece of paper.

126   *REWARDS Plus: Reading Strategies Applied to Social Studies Passages*

APPLICATION LESSON
13

Rubric— Extended Response	Student or Partner Rating	Teacher Rating
1. Did the author tell his/her position in the first sentence?	Yes Fix up	Yes No
2. Did the author include at least three **strong, logical** reasons for his/her position?	Yes Fix up	Yes No
3. Did the author provide a **strong, logical** explanation for each of his/her reasons?	Yes Fix up	Yes No
4. Is the response easy to understand?	Yes Fix up	Yes No
5. Did the author correctly spell words, particularly the words found in the article?	Yes Fix up	Yes No
6. Did the author use correct capitalization, capitalizing the first word in the sentence and proper names of people, places, and things?	Yes Fix up	Yes No
7. Did the author use correct punctuation, including a period at the end of each sentence?	Yes Fix up	Yes No

WRITING   **7**
Points

Student Book: Application Lesson 13   **127**

Application Lesson 14

Materials Needed:

- *Student Book:* Application Lesson 14
- Application Overhead Transparencies 53–56
- Appendix B Optional Vocabulary Activities: Application Lesson 14
- Paper or cardboard to use when covering the overhead transparency
- Paper or cardboard for each student to use during spelling dictation
- Washable overhead transparency pen

Text Treatment Notes:

- Black text signifies teacher script (exact wording to say to students).
- Green text in parentheses signifies directions or prompts for the teacher.
- Green text signifies answers or examples of answers.
- Green graphics treatment signifies reproduction of Overhead information.
- Green text and green graphics treatment do not appear in the *Student Book*.

ACTIVITY A
Vocabulary

ACTIVITY PROCEDURE, List 1

(See the *Student Book,* page 129.)

Tell students each word in the list. Then, have students repeat the word and read the definition aloud. For each definition, provide any additional information that may be necessary. Then, have students practice reading the words themselves.

Note A.1-1: See Appendix E, Pronunciation Guide for Unique Words, for correct pronunciations of uncommon vocabulary words.

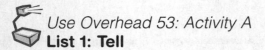

Use Overhead 53: Activity A
List 1: Tell

1. (Show the top half of Overhead 53.) Before we read the passage, let's read the difficult words. (Point to **Rapa Nui**.) The first words are **Rapa Nui**. What words?— Now, read the definition.—
2. (Point to **Chile**.) The next word is **Chile**. What word?— Now, read the definition.—
3. (Pronounce each word in List 1, and then have students repeat each word and read the definition.)
4. Open your *Student Book* to **Application Lesson 14**, page 129.—
5. Find **Activity A**, **List 1**, in your book.— Let's read the words again. First words.— Next word.— (Continue for all words in List 1.)

ACTIVITY PROCEDURE, List 2

(See the *Student Book,* page 129.)

Have students circle prefixes and suffixes, then underline the vowels. Using the overhead transparency, assist students in checking their work. Next, have students figure out each word to themselves, then say it aloud. Have them read the definition aloud.

Use Overhead 53: Activity A
List 2: Strategy Practice

1. Find **List 2**. Circle the prefixes and suffixes, and underline the vowels. Look up when you are done.—

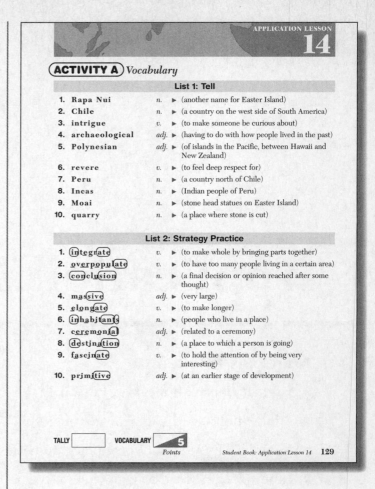

ACTIVITY A *Vocabulary*

List 1: Tell

1.	Rapa Nui	*n.*	▶ (another name for Easter Island)
2.	Chile	*n.*	▶ (a country on the west side of South America)
3.	intrigue	*v.*	▶ (to make someone be curious about)
4.	archaeological	*adj.*	▶ (having to do with how people lived in the past)
5.	Polynesian	*adj.*	▶ (of islands in the Pacific, between Hawaii and New Zealand)
6.	revere	*v.*	▶ (to feel deep respect for)
7.	Peru	*n.*	▶ (a country north of Chile)
8.	Incas	*n.*	▶ (Indian people of Peru)
9.	Moai	*n.*	▶ (stone head statues on Easter Island)
10.	quarry	*n.*	▶ (a place where stone is cut)

List 2: Strategy Practice

1.	integrate	*v.*	▶ (to make whole by bringing parts together)
2.	overpopulate	*v.*	▶ (to have too many people living in a certain area)
3.	conclusion	*n.*	▶ (a final decision or opinion reached after some thought)
4.	massive	*adj.*	▶ (very large)
5.	elongate	*v.*	▶ (to make longer)
6.	inhabitants	*n.*	▶ (people who live in a place)
7.	ceremonial	*adj.*	▶ (related to a ceremony)
8.	destination	*n.*	▶ (a place to which a person is going)
9.	fascinate	*v.*	▶ (to hold the attention of by being very interesting)
10.	primitive	*adj.*	▶ (at an earlier stage of development)

TALLY ☐ VOCABULARY ▱ 5 Points

Student Book: Application Lesson 14 **129**

2. (Show the bottom half of Overhead 53.) Before you check your work on List 2, look at item #2. (**Point to the second example and the over** that is circled.) From now on, you can also circle **over**. The prefix is /over/. Say it.— Now, go back to item #1. Check and fix any mistakes.—
3. Go back to the first word again.— Sound out the word to yourself. Put your thumb up when you can read the word. Be sure that it is a real word.— What word?— Now, read the definition.—
4. (Continue Step 3 with all remaining words in List 2.)

Note A.2-1: You may wish to provide additional practice by having students read words to a partner.

ACTIVITY PROCEDURE, List 1 and 2

(See the *Student Book*, page 129.)

Tell students to look in List 1 or List 2 for a word you are thinking about. Have them circle the number of the word and tell you the word. Explain to students to make a tally mark for each correct word in the Tally box, and then enter the number of tally marks as points in the blank half of the Vocabulary box.

1. Remember, the words I'm thinking about will be in either List 1 or List 2. Make a tally mark in the Tally box at the bottom of page 129 for every correctly identified word.
2. Circle the number of the appropriate word.
   - When too many people live in a certain area, they do this. (Wait.) What word? **overpopulate**
   - If something or someone holds your interest, it does this to you. (Wait.) What word? **fascinate**
   - What do we call those people who live in certain places? (Wait.) What word? **inhabitants**
   - Your final opinion about someone or something is this. (Wait.) What word? **conclusion**
   - These people were the original inhabitants of the country of Peru. (Wait.) What word? **Incas**
3. Count all the tally marks, and enter that number as points in the blank half of the Vocabulary box.

ACTIVITY PROCEDURE, List 3

(See the *Student Book*, page 130.)

The words in the third list are related. Have students use the *REWARDS* Strategies to figure out the first word in each family. Have them read the definition and then read the other two words in the family.

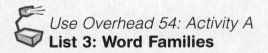
Use Overhead 54: Activity A
List 3: Word Families

1. Turn to page 130. Find **Family 1** in **List 3**. Figure out the first word. Use your pencil if you wish. Put your thumb up when you know the word._ What word?_ Read the definition._
2. Look at the next word in Family 1. Figure out the word._ What word?_
3. Next word. Figure out the word._ What word?_
4. (Repeat Steps 1–3 for all word families in List 3.)

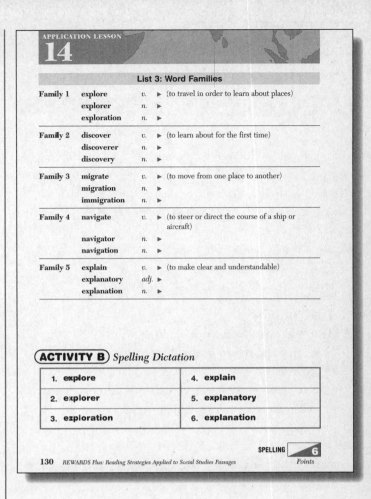

APPLICATION LESSON
14

List 3: Word Families

Family 1	explore	v.	▶	(to travel in order to learn about places)
	explorer	n.	▶	
	exploration	n.	▶	
Family 2	discover	v.	▶	(to learn about for the first time)
	discoverer	n.	▶	
	discovery	n.	▶	
Family 3	migrate	v.	▶	(to move from one place to another)
	migration	n.	▶	
	immigration	n.	▶	
Family 4	navigate	v.	▶	(to steer or direct the course of a ship or aircraft)
	navigator	n.	▶	
	navigation	n.	▶	
Family 5	explain	v.	▶	(to make clear and understandable)
	explanatory	adj.	▶	
	explanation	n.	▶	

ACTIVITY B *Spelling Dictation*

1. **explore**	4. **explain**
2. **explorer**	5. **explanatory**
3. **exploration**	6. **explanation**

SPELLING ⬛ 6

130   *REWARDS Plus: Reading Strategies Applied to Social Studies Passages*   Points

Note A.3-1: You may wish to provide additional practice by having students read a word family to the group or to a partner.

Note A.3-2: Additional vocabulary practice activities are provided in Appendix B of the Teacher's Guide. These activities are optional and can be assigned during class, for homework, or as small group, in-class activities.

ACTIVITY B
Spelling Dictation

ACTIVITY PROCEDURE

(See the *Student Book*, page 130.)

For each word, tell students the word, then have students say the parts of the word to themselves while they write the word. Then, have students enter the number of correctly spelled words as points in the blank half of the Spelling box.

Note B-1: Distribute a piece of light cardboard to each of the students.

 Use Overhead 54: Activity B

1. Find **Activity B**.
2. The first word is **explore**. What word?_ Say the parts in **explore** to yourself as you write the word. (Pause and monitor.)
3. (Show **explore** on the overhead.) Check **explore**. If you misspelled it, cross it out and write it correctly.
4. The second word is **explorer**. What word?_ Say the parts in **explorer** to yourself as you write the word. (Pause and monitor.)
5. (Show **explorer** on the overhead.) Check **explorer**. If you misspelled it, cross it out and write it correctly.
6. (Repeat the procedures for the words **exploration**, **explain**, **explanatory**, and **explanation**.)
7. Count the number of words you spelled correctly, and record that number as points in the blank half of the Spelling box at the bottom of the page.

APPLICATION LESSON
14

List 3: Word Families

Family 1	explore	v.	▶ (to travel in order to learn about places)
	explorer	n.	▶
	exploration	n.	▶
Family 2	discover	v.	▶ (to learn about for the first time)
	discoverer	n.	▶
	discovery	n.	▶
Family 3	migrate	v.	▶ (to move from one place to another)
	migration	n.	▶
	immigration	n.	▶
Family 4	navigate	v.	▶ (to steer or direct the course of a ship or aircraft)
	navigator	n.	▶
	navigation	n.	▶
Family 5	explain	v.	▶ (to make clear and understandable)
	explanatory	adj.	▶
	explanation	n.	▶

ACTIVITY B *Spelling Dictation*

1. explore	4. explain
2. explorer	5. explanatory
3. exploration	6. explanation

SPELLING 6 Points

ACTIVITY C

Background Knowledge

ACTIVITY PROCEDURE

(See the *Student Book,* page 131.)

Read the Background Knowledge paragraph using one of three methods: read it to students, have students read it together, or call on individual students to read. Examine the timeline and the related graphic together. Then, preview the passage together by examining the title and the headings. Have students tell partners two things the passage will tell about.

1. Turn to page 131. Let's read the paragraph. (Read or ask students to read. Then examine the timeline and graphic together.)
2. Now, let's turn the page and preview the passage. Read the title._ What is the whole passage going to tell about?_
3. Now, let's read the headings. Read the first heading._ Read the next heading._ (Continue until students have read all headings.)
4. Turn to your partner. Without looking, tell two things this passage will tell about._

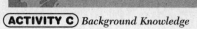

ACTIVITY C *Background Knowledge*

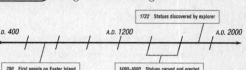

A.D. 400   A.D. 1200   A.D. 2000

1722 Statues discovered by explorer

700 First people on Easter Island

1400–1600 Statues carved and erected

Since ancient times, people have built and erected statues to honor their ancestors and the gods whom they worshipped. The article you will read today describes the discovery of massive stone heads located on a small, isolated island in the Pacific Ocean. These statues were erected about 400 to 600 years ago. They are quite remarkable for their shape, size, and positioning. Interestingly, scientists still cannot explain their significance or their presence on Easter Island.

Easter Island Statues

Student Book: Application Lesson 14 **131**

ACTIVITY D

Passage Reading and Comprehension

ACTIVITY PROCEDURE

(See the *Student Book*, pages 132–133.)

Have students work on reading accuracy by selecting a passage-reading option that best fits your students.

Passage Reading: Accuracy

(Select a passage-reading procedure that matches the size of your group and the competency of your students.

Option A

If you are teaching a small group of students who are having difficulty, use Option A:

Have students read one paragraph silently. Then, call on one student to orally read a paragraph or a portion of the paragraph to the class. Call on students in random order, varying the amount that each student reads.

Option B

If you are teaching a small group with students who are not having difficulty, use Option B:

Have students read the entire article silently, rereading it if they finish before their classmates. Then, call on one student to orally read a paragraph or a portion of a paragraph to the class. Call on students in random order, varying the amount that each student reads.

Option C

If you are teaching a large group with students who are having difficulty, use Option C:

Have students read one paragraph silently. Then, have students read the paragraph to a partner. Alternate partner-reading turns.

Option D

If you are teaching a large group with students who are not having difficulty, use Option D:

Have students read the entire article silently, rereading it if they finish before their classmates. Then, have students read the passage with their partners, alternating on each paragraph.)

ACTIVITY D *Passage Reading and Comprehension*

Easter Island

15	Easter Island, also known as Rapa Nui, is located west of Chile, in the South
27	Pacific Ocean. It is called Easter Island because the Dutch explorer who
39	discovered the island landed there on Easter Day, 1722. He discovered an
54	isolated island and a group of people who lived there. He also discovered a series
	of enormous statues. These statues continue to puzzle and intrigue scientists. (#1)

The Early Inhabitants

65	
68	Surrounded on all sides by thousands of miles of open ocean, Easter Island
81	has been home to people for more than a thousand years. Archaeological
93	evidence suggests that people have lived there since around A.D. 700. Easter
105	Island legend tells of a Polynesian chief who was the first to come to the island.
121	(The Polynesian people hail, or come, from islands in the Pacific between
133	Hawaii and New Zealand.) He brought his wife and extended family in a double
147	canoe from an unknown island and founded Easter Island culture. (#2)

Island Culture

157	
159	Pacific Islanders have always been deeply connected to the ocean. Unlike
170	Europeans, who feared the open seas, islanders revere and respect the water,
182	integrating it into their lives. They traveled from island to island in double
195	canoes. Double canoes were made of island woods and fibers and were used for
209	ocean travel. Early Polynesians were masters of navigation, finding their way
220	from place to place by stars and other natural signs. When small islands became
234	overpopulated, they would set out in their canoes to other islands. This concept
247	may be part of the legend Easter Islanders tell about their origins. (#3)
259	In spite of this legend, scientists have not come to any final conclusions
272	about the origins of the people of Easter Island. Some evidence suggests that
285	people did, in fact, migrate from other Polynesian Islands. But other evidence
297	suggests that the original Easter Island people were Incas who migrated from
309	Peru. Scientists continue to debate the origins of Easter Islanders. But this is
322	not the only puzzle that Easter Island has to offer. (#4)

The Moai

332	
334	Along Easter Island's coast stand massive stone heads. They are an average of
347	13 feet high and weigh 14 tons. The islanders call them *Moai*. There are nearly

Passage Reading: Comprehension Questions

(You may wish to ask the following questions as the passage is being read. Numbers corresponding to the questions are indicated at the point at which they could be asked.)

#1 On Easter Island, what puzzles and intrigues scientists, and why?
Ideas: The enormous statues; there is no explanation for the statues being there.

#2 How does legend explain the arrival of the first people to Easter Island?
Legend tells that a Polynesian chief brought his family to the island by double canoe and founded the culture.

#3 Why did early Polynesians search out new islands?
The small islands they lived on became overpopulated, and they needed new land.

362 | 900 of the statues on the island. Each statue stands with its back to the sea.
378 | Scientists speculate that they were all carved, moved, and raised between A.D.
390 | 1400 and 1600. They are all carved in the same style—gigantic heads with
404 | elongated ears and noses. Each statue is carved from a soft volcanic rock called
418 | *tuff*. The rock was mined from a crater on the island. Explorers found large
432 | unfinished statues still in the quarry. (#5)
438 | But there is no explanation of how or why they got where they are. How did
454 | the people transport and erect such enormous statues? Why did they carve them
467 | at all? Some speculate that the heads are likenesses of great leaders. Others
480 | suggest that the heads, because of their size, are of ceremonial importance,
492 | serving as a connection between the people and their gods. (#6)

502 | **Easter Island Today**
505 | Today, Easter Island is a popular travel destination. People are attracted to
517 | its mystery and its statues. The inhabitants of Easter Island, descendants of the
530 | primitive sculptors, run the tourism industry themselves. They celebrate their
540 | Polynesian and island heritage through festivals and tours. Archaeologists and
550 | other scientists continue to study the Moai, trying to learn the secrets of the
564 | giant heads. Fortunately, the entire island has been preserved as a Chilean
576 | national park, ensuring that its beauty and wonders will continue to fascinate
588 | people for years to come. (#7)
593 |

(ACTIVITY E) *Fluency Building*

Cold Timing [ ]	Practice 1 [ ]
Practice 2 [ ]	Hot Timing [ ]

Student Book: Application Lesson 14   **133**

#4 What other explanations have been offered to explain the origins of the Easter Islanders?
Some evidence suggests that the native people who inhabit the island are descendents of Incas from Peru.

#5 What is the greatest puzzle of Easter Island?
There are almost 900 massive stone heads carved from volcanic rock, standing with their backs to the sea.

#6 What are some of the puzzling aspects about these statues?
How they were moved; how they were stood upright; why they were carved; who they are likenesses of.

#7 Why is it important that Easter Island has been designated a national park?
Ideas: So that the statues are preserved for study; so that the island will continue to be beautiful and mysterious.

ACTIVITY E
Fluency Building

ACTIVITY PROCEDURE

(See the *Student Book*, page 133.)

Have students complete a Cold Timing, one or two practices, and a Hot Timing of the Activity D article. For each timing, have students record the number of correct words read. Finally, have students complete their Fluency Graphs.

Note E-1: When assigning partners for this activity, have the stronger reader read first. As a result, the other reader will have one additional practice opportunity.

1. Now, it's time for fluency building.
2. Find the beginning of the passage again. (Pause.)
3. Whisper-read. See how many words you can read in one minute. Begin.＿ (Time students for one minute.) Stop.＿ Circle the last word that you read.＿ Record the number of words you read after **Cold Timing** in **Activity E** at the bottom of page 133.＿
4. Let's practice again. Begin.＿ (Time students for one minute.) Stop.＿ Put a box around the last word that you read.＿ Record the number of words you read after **Practice 1**.＿
5. **Optional** Let's practice one more time before the Hot Timing. Begin.＿ (Time students for one minute.) Stop.＿ Put a box around the last word that you read.＿ Record the number of words you read after **Practice 2**.＿
6. Please exchange books with your partner.＿ Partner 1, you are going to read first. Partner 2, listen carefully and underline any mistakes or words left out. Ones, begin.＿ (Time students for one minute.) Stop.＿ Twos, cross out the last word that your partner read.＿ Twos, record the number of words in your partner's book after **Hot Timing**.＿
7. Partner 2, you are going to read next. Partner 1, listen carefully and underline any mistakes or words left out. Twos, begin. (Time students for one minute.) Stop.＿ Ones, cross out the last word that your partner read.＿ Ones, record the number of words in your partner's book after **Hot Timing**.＿
8. Exchange books.＿ Turn to the Fluency Graph on the last page of your book, and indicate on the graph the number of Cold Timing and Hot Timing words you read correctly.＿

ACTIVITY F

Comprehension Questions—Multiple Choice and Short Answer

ACTIVITY PROCEDURE

(See the *Student Book*, pages 134–135.)

Have students complete the Multiple Choice and Short Answer questions on the passage. Give feedback to students on their answers. Lead students in a discussion of their Multiple Choice answers and rationales. Have students record points for each correct item. For each Short Answer response, give one point for using the wording of the question in the answer, and one point for accuracy of the answer (total of 4 points possible for two complete answers).

Note F-1: The correct Multiple Choice answers are circled.

ACTIVITY F *Comprehension Questions—Multiple Choice and Short Answer*

Comprehension Strategy—Multiple Choice

Step 1: Read the item.
Step 2: Read all of the choices.
Step 3: Think about why each choice might be correct or incorrect. Check the article as needed.
Step 4: From the possible correct choices, select the best answer.

1. (Vocabulary) **Read this sentence from the article: "*Archaeologists* and other scientists continue to study the Moai, trying to learn the secrets of the giant heads." What does the word *archaeologists* mean in that sentence?**
   a. People who study past human life as revealed by relics (e.g., dishes, paintings, tools).
   b. Ancient people who lived before a written language was developed.
   c. People who study ancient people by interviewing them.
   d. People who sell art, including paintings and statues.

2. (Cause and Effect) **Scientists are intrigued by the statues on Easter Island because:**
   a. of the legend about the Polynesian chief who brought his family to Easter Island.
   b. the statues are huge and face away from the sea.
   c. the origins of the people on the island remain a mystery.
   d. how and why the statues were built remain a mystery.

3. (Cause and Effect) **What is the main reason that people might visit Easter Island today?**
   a. People love the warm climate and white-sand beaches.
   b. People are very curious about why and how people arrived on Easter Island.
   c. People are very curious about why and how the statues were constructed.
   d. People wish to celebrate Easter on Easter Island.

4. (Main Idea) **If the article needed a new title, which would be best?**
   a. *Easter Island—A New Home to Polynesians*
   b. *Easter Island—Land of Mystery*
   c. *Easter Island—A Holy Destination*
   d. *Easter Island—A Chilean National Park*

MULTIPLE CHOICE COMPREHENSION
Points

Comprehension Strategy—Short Answer

Step 1: Read the item.
Step 2: Turn the question into part of the answer and write it down.
Step 3: Think of the answer or locate the answer in the article.
Step 4: Complete your answer.

1. **What do archaeologists think the stone heads might represent?**
   Example answer: Archaeologists think that the stone heads might represent great past leaders of the Easter Island people. Others think that the stone heads represent a religious connection between the people and their gods.

2. **Why do you think people might like to travel to Easter Island on vacation?**
   Example answer: People might like to travel to Easter Island on vacation to see the mysterious stone heads. Vacationers also might like it because it is a beautiful island.

SHORT ANSWER COMPREHENSION
Points

ACTIVITY G
Expository Writing—Summary

ACTIVITY PROCEDURE

(See the *Student Book*, pages 136–137.)

Have students read the prompt and record the topic of the summary. Next, have them **LIST** details in the Planning Box by referring back to the article. Encourage students to record notes rather than form complete sentences. When they are done with their lists, have them compare their lists of critical details with those of other classmates and the Example Summary Plan.

1. Time to write. First, read the prompt on page 136. Then, use the Planning Box on page 136 to start thinking about your first sentence. Then, write your **LIST**. When you are finished, compare your list to your partner's list._

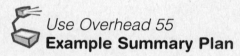

Use Overhead 55
Example Summary Plan

2. Now, compare your list to the list on the overhead._

ACTIVITY PROCEDURE

Next, have students complete the additional steps in the Summary Writing Strategy. Have them reread their lists and **CROSS OUT** any weak or unimportant details. Then, have students **CONNECT** details that could go together in one sentence, **NUMBER** their ideas in a logical order, and **WRITE** their summaries on a separate piece of paper. When they are done, have them **EDIT** their paragraphs, revising for clarity and proofreading for errors in spelling, capitalization, and punctuation.

Have students read their summaries to their partners. Then, read the Example Summary.

Have students read each of the attributes on the rubric, examine their summaries, and circle either "Yes" or "Fix up." Give students time to make changes in their summaries.

Optional: During or after the class session, fill in the third column of the rubric chart and assign points to the student summaries.

Optional: Have students date their writing and place the sample in a folder. Thus, students will be able to look back at their

---

ACTIVITY G *Expository Writing—Summary*

Writing Strategy—Summary

Step 1: LIST (List the details that are important enough to include in the summary.)
Step 2: CROSS OUT (Reread the details. Cross out any that you decide not to include.)
Step 3: CONNECT (Connect any details that could go into one sentence.)
Step 4: NUMBER (Number the details in a logical order.)
Step 5: WRITE (Write your summary.)
Step 6: EDIT (Revise and proofread your summary.)

Prompt: Write a summary of the information you read in the *Easter Island* article.

Planning Box
(topic) *Easter Island*
① (detail) – *Easter Island is located west of Chile, in the South Pacific Ocean*
② (detail) – *people have lived there since* A.D. *700*
③ (detail) – *they may have come from other Polynesian Islands*   (detail) – *islanders used a double canoe to navigate the ocean*
(detail) – ~~*scientists are unsure about the origins of Easter Islanders*~~
④ (detail) – *Easter Island has many large stone statues of heads called Moai*
⑤ (detail) – *the statues are all made of volcanic rock*
⑥ (detail) – *the statues are very large and heavy*   (detail) – *no one knows how the statues were moved*
(detail) – ~~*today, Easter Island is a national park of Chile*~~
⑦ (detail) – *people travel there to see the statues*
⑧ (detail) – *people want to know why the statues were carved*

Directions: Write your summary on a separate piece of paper.

Rubric—Summary	Student or Partner Rating		Teacher Rating	
1. Did the author state the topic and the main idea in the first sentence?	Yes	Fix up	Yes	No
2. Did the author focus on important details?	Yes	Fix up	Yes	No
3. Did the author combine details in some of the sentences?	Yes	Fix up	Yes	No
4. Is the summary easy to understand?	Yes	Fix up	Yes	No
5. Did the author correctly spell words, particularly the words found in the article?	Yes	Fix up	Yes	No
6. Did the author use correct capitalization, capitalizing the first word in the sentence and proper names of people, places, and things?	Yes	Fix up	Yes	No
7. Did the author use correct punctuation, including a period at the end of each sentence?	Yes	Fix up	Yes	No

WRITING
Points

summaries and extended responses and literally see their writing improvement.

3. Now, **CROSS OUT**, **CONNECT**, **NUMBER**, and **WRITE**._

4. Reread your response and **EDIT**. Check to be sure your response is easy to understand. Fix any errors you find in spelling, capitalization, and punctuation._ (Monitor.)

5. Read what you've written to your partner._

Use Overhead 56
Example Summary

6. Look at the overhead. Let's read this Example Summary. Yours doesn't need to be exactly the same, but it should be similar.

7. (Have students turn to the rubric on page 137. Ask students to evaluate their own or their partner's writing to determine what to edit. When they have finished the evaluation, give students adequate time to make changes. Have students enter their points in the blank half of the Writing box below the rubric.)

(**ACTIVITY G**) *Expository Writing—Summary*

Writing Strategy—Summary

Step 1: **LIST** (List the details that are important enough to include in the summary.)
Step 2: **CROSS OUT** (Reread the details. Cross out any that you decide not to include.)
Step 3: **CONNECT** (Connect any details that could go into one sentence.)
Step 4: **NUMBER** (Number the details in a logical order.)
Step 5: **WRITE** (Write your summary.)
Step 6: **EDIT** (Revise and proofread your summary.)

Prompt: Write a summary of the information you read in the *Easter Island* article.

Planning Box
(topic) *Easter Island*
① (detail) – *Easter Island is located west of Chile, in the South Pacific Ocean*
② (detail) – *people have lived there since A.D. 700*
③ { (detail) – *they may have come from other Polynesian Islands* / (detail) – *islanders used a double canoe to navigate the ocean*
(detail) – ~~*scientists are unsure about the origins of Easter Islanders*~~
④ (detail) – *Easter Island has many large stone statues of heads called Moai*
⑤ (detail) – *the statues are all made of volcanic rock*
⑥ { (detail) – *the statues are very large and heavy* / (detail) – *no one knows how the statues were moved*
(detail) – ~~*today, Easter Island is a national park of Chile*~~
⑦ (detail) – *people travel there to see the statues*
⑧ (detail) – *people want to know why the statues were carved*

Directions: Write your summary on a separate piece of paper.

Rubric—Summary	Student or Partner Rating		Teacher Rating	
1. Did the author state the topic and the main idea in the first sentence?	Yes	Fix up	Yes	No
2. Did the author focus on important details?	Yes	Fix up	Yes	No
3. Did the author combine details in some of the sentences?	Yes	Fix up	Yes	No
4. Is the summary easy to understand?	Yes	Fix up	Yes	No
5. Did the author correctly spell words, particularly the words found in the article?	Yes	Fix up	Yes	No
6. Did the author use correct capitalization, capitalizing the first word in the sentence and proper names of people, places, and things?	Yes	Fix up	Yes	No
7. Did the author use correct punctuation, including a period at the end of each sentence?	Yes	Fix up	Yes	No

WRITING **7**
Points

Application Lesson 15

Materials Needed:

- *Student Book:* Application Lesson 15

- Application Overhead Transparencies 57–60

- Appendix B Optional Vocabulary Activities: Application Lesson 15

- Paper or cardboard to use when covering the overhead transparency

- Paper or cardboard for each student to use during spelling dictation

- Washable overhead transparency pen

Text Treatment Notes:

- Black text signifies teacher script (exact wording to say to students).

- Green text in parentheses signifies directions or prompts for the teacher.

- Green text signifies answers or examples of answers.

- Green graphics treatment signifies reproduction of Overhead information.

- Green text and green graphics treatment do not appear in the *Student Book*.

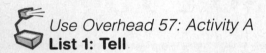

ACTIVITY A
Vocabulary

ACTIVITY PROCEDURE, List 1

(See the *Student Book,* page 139.)

Tell students each word in the list. Then, have students repeat the word and read the definition aloud. For each definition, provide any additional information that may be necessary. Then, have students practice reading the words themselves.

Note A.1-1: See Appendix E, Pronunciation Guide for Unique Words, for correct pronunciations of uncommon vocabulary words.

Use Overhead 57: Activity A
List 1: Tell

1. (Show the top half of Overhead 57.) Before we read the passage, let's read the difficult words. (Point to **Egypt**.) The first word is **Egypt**. What word?_ Now, read the definition._
2. (Point to **Cairo**.) The next word is **Cairo**. What word?_ Now, read the definition._
3. (Pronounce each word in List 1, and then have students repeat each word and read the definition.)
4. Open your *Student Book* to **Application Lesson 15**, page 139._
5. Find **Activity A**, **List 1**, in your book._ Let's read the words again. First word._ Next word._ (Continue for all words in List 1.)

ACTIVITY PROCEDURE, List 2

(See the *Student Book,* page 139.)

Have students circle prefixes and suffixes, then underline the vowels. Using the overhead transparency, assist students in checking their work. Next, have students figure out each word to themselves, then say it aloud. Have them read the definition aloud.

Use Overhead 57: Activity A
List 2: Strategy Practice

1. Find **List 2**. Circle the prefixes and suffixes, and underline the vowels. Look up when you are done._

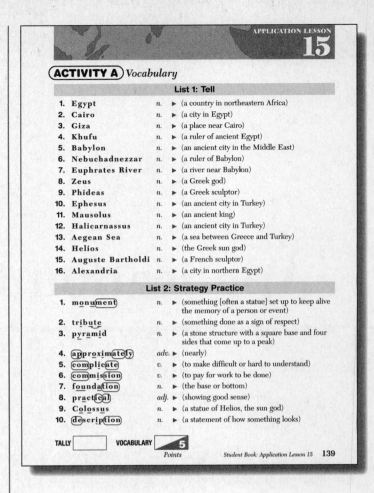

ACTIVITY A *Vocabulary*

List 1: Tell

1.	Egypt	n.	► (a country in northeastern Africa)
2.	Cairo	n.	► (a city in Egypt)
3.	Giza	n.	► (a place near Cairo)
4.	Khufu	n.	► (a ruler of ancient Egypt)
5.	Babylon	n.	► (an ancient city in the Middle East)
6.	Nebuchadnezzar	n.	► (a ruler of Babylon)
7.	Euphrates River	n.	► (a river near Babylon)
8.	Zeus	n.	► (a Greek god)
9.	Phideas	n.	► (a Greek sculptor)
10.	Ephesus	n.	► (an ancient city in Turkey)
11.	Mausolus	n.	► (an ancient king)
12.	Halicarnassus	n.	► (an ancient city in Turkey)
13.	Aegean Sea	n.	► (a sea between Greece and Turkey)
14.	Helios	n.	► (the Greek sun god)
15.	Auguste Bartholdi	n.	► (a French sculptor)
16.	Alexandria	n.	► (a city in northern Egypt)

List 2: Strategy Practice

1.	monument	n.	► (something [often a statue] set up to keep alive the memory of a person or event)
2.	tribute	n.	► (something done as a sign of respect)
3.	pyramid	n.	► (a stone structure with a square base and four sides that come up to a peak)
4.	approximately	adv.	► (nearly)
5.	complicate	v.	► (to make difficult or hard to understand)
6.	commission	v.	► (to pay for work to be done)
7.	foundation	n.	► (the base or bottom)
8.	practical	adj.	► (showing good sense)
9.	Colossus	n.	► (a statue of Helios, the sun god)
10.	description	n.	► (a statement of how something looks)

TALLY [ ]   VOCABULARY [5] Points

Student Book: Application Lesson 15 **139**

2. (Show the bottom half of Overhead 57.) Before you check your work on List 2, look at item #4. (Point to the first example and the **ap** that is circled.) Remember, you can also circle **ap**. What prefix?_ Now, go back to item #1. Check and fix any mistakes._
3. Go back to the first word again._ Sound out the word to yourself. Put your thumb up when you can read the word. Be sure that it is a real word._ What word?_ Now, read the definition._
4. (Continue Step 3 with all remaining words in List 2.)

Note A.2-1: You may wish to provide additional practice by having students read words to a partner.

ACTIVITY PROCEDURE, List 1 and 2

(See the *Student Book,* page 139.)

Tell students to look in List 1 or List 2 for a word you are thinking about. Have them circle the number of the word and tell you the word. Explain to students to make a tally mark for each correct word in the Tally box, and then enter the number of tally marks as points in the blank half of the Vocabulary box.

1. Remember, the words I'm thinking about will be in either List 1 or List 2. Make a tally mark in the Tally box at the bottom of page 139 for every correctly identified word.
2. Circle the number of the appropriate word.
   - This is set up to honor a person or an event. (Wait.) What word? **monument**
   - If someone will pay you for work to be done, they will do this. (Wait.) What word? **commission**
   - This country is in northeastern Africa. (Wait.) What word? **Egypt**
   - If the directions are difficult to understand, it can do this to a task. (Wait.) What word? **complicate**
   - What do we call something done as a sign of respect? (Wait.) What word? **tribute**
3. Count all the tally marks, and enter that number as points in the blank half of the Vocabulary box.

ACTIVITY PROCEDURE, List 3

(See the *Student Book,* page 140.)

The words in the third list are related. Have students use the *REWARDS* Strategies to figure out the first word in each family. Have them read the definition and then read the other two words in the family.

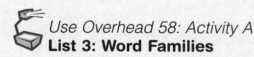

Use Overhead 58: Activity A
List 3: Word Families

1. Turn to page 140. Find **Family 1** in **List 3**. Figure out the first word. Use your pencil if you wish. Put your thumb up when you know the word._ What word?_ Read the definition._
2. Look at the next word in Family 1. Figure out the word._ What word?_
3. Next word. Figure out the word._ What word?_
4. (Repeat Steps 1–3 for all word families in List 3.)

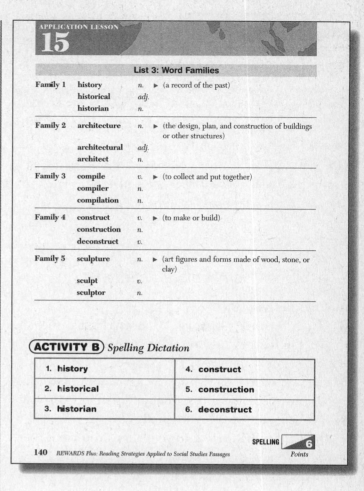

APPLICATION LESSON
15

List 3: Word Families

Family 1	history	n.	▶ (a record of the past)
	historical	adj.	
	historian	n.	
Family 2	architecture	n.	▶ (the design, plan, and construction of buildings or other structures)
	architectural	adj.	
	architect	n.	
Family 3	compile	v.	▶ (to collect and put together)
	compiler	n.	
	compilation	n.	
Family 4	construct	v.	▶ (to make or build)
	construction	n.	
	deconstruct	v.	
Family 5	sculpture	n.	▶ (art figures and forms made of wood, stone, or clay)
	sculpt	v.	
	sculptor	n.	

ACTIVITY B *Spelling Dictation*

1. history	4. construct
2. historical	5. construction
3. historian	6. deconstruct

SPELLING **6**
Points

140   *REWARDS Plus: Reading Strategies Applied to Social Studies Passages*

Note A.3-1: You may wish to provide additional practice by having students read a word family to the group or to a partner.

Note A.3-2: Additional vocabulary practice activities are provided in Appendix B of the Teacher's Guide. These activities are optional and can be assigned during class, for homework, or as small group, in-class activities.

ACTIVITY B
Spelling Dictation

ACTIVITY PROCEDURE

(See the *Student Book,* page 140.)

For each word, tell students the word, then have students say the parts of the word to themselves while they write the word. Then, have students enter the number of correctly spelled words as points in the blank half of the Spelling box.

Note B-1: Distribute a piece of light cardboard to each of the students.

 Use Overhead 58: Activity B

1. Find **Activity B**.
2. The first word is **history**. What word?_ Say the parts in **history** to yourself as you write the word. (Pause and monitor.)
3. (Show **history** on the overhead.) Check **history**. If you misspelled it, cross it out and write it correctly.
4. The second word is **historical**. What word?_ Say the parts in **historical** to yourself as you write the word. (Pause and monitor.)
5. (Show **historical** on the overhead.) Check **historical**. If you misspelled it, cross it out and write it correctly.
6. (Repeat the procedures for the words **historian**, **construct**, **construction**, and **deconstruct**.)
7. Count the number of words you spelled correctly, and record that number as points in the blank half of the Spelling box at the bottom of the page.

APPLICATION LESSON
15

List 3: Word Families

Family 1	history	n.	▶ (a record of the past)
	historical	adj.	
	historian	n.	
Family 2	architecture	n.	▶ (the design, plan, and construction of buildings or other structures)
	architectural	adj.	
	architect	n.	
Family 3	compile	v.	▶ (to collect and put together)
	compiler	n.	
	compilation	n.	
Family 4	construct	v.	▶ (to make or build)
	construction	n.	
	deconstruct	v.	
Family 5	sculpture	n.	▶ (art figures and forms made of wood, stone, or clay)
	sculpt	v.	
	sculptor	n.	

ACTIVITY B *Spelling Dictation*

1. history	4. construct
2. historical	5. construction
3. historian	6. deconstruct

SPELLING 6

140   *REWARDS Plus: Reading Strategies Applied to Social Studies Passages*   *Points*

ACTIVITY C
Background Knowledge

ACTIVITY PROCEDURE

(See the *Student Book,* page 141.)

Read the Background Knowledge paragraph using one of three methods: read it to students, have students read it together, or call on individual students to read. Examine the timeline and the related graphic together. Then, preview the passage together by examining the title and the headings. Have students tell partners two things the passage will tell about.

1. Turn to page 141. Let's read the paragraph. (Read or ask students to read. Then examine the timeline and graphic together.)
2. Now, let's turn the page and preview the passage. Read the title._ What is the whole passage going to tell about?_
3. Now, let's read the headings. Read the first heading._ Read the next heading._ (Continue until students have read all headings.)
4. Turn to your partner. Without looking, tell two things this passage will tell about._

ACTIVITY C *Background Knowledge*

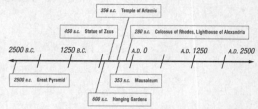

Everyone makes lists: lists of things to do, to buy, and to wish for. In this article, you will read about a famous list compiled by an ancient Greek writer around the second century B.C. You've probably heard of his list. It's called the Seven Wonders of the Ancient World. This list named the greatest sculptural and architectural monuments of ancient time and became one of the best-known lists of all time. The writer chose the number 7 because it was thought to be a magical number. Many other "Seven Wonders" lists have been written since then; however, the original list is the most widely accepted among historians and scholars throughout time.

The Locations of the Seven Wonders of the Ancient World

Student Book: Application Lesson 15 **141**

ACTIVITY D

Passage Reading and Comprehension

ACTIVITY PROCEDURE

(See the *Student Book*, pages 142–143.)

Have students work on reading accuracy by selecting a passage-reading option that best fits your students.

Passage Reading: Accuracy

(Select a passage-reading procedure that matches the size of your group and the competency of your students.

Option A

If you are teaching a small group of students who are having difficulty, use Option A:

Have students read one paragraph silently. Then, call on one student to orally read a paragraph or a portion of the paragraph to the class. Call on students in random order, varying the amount that each student reads.

Option B

If you are teaching a small group with students who are not having difficulty, use Option B:

Have students read the entire article silently, rereading it if they finish before their classmates. Then, call on one student to orally read a paragraph or a portion of a paragraph to the class. Call on students in random order, varying the amount that each student reads.

Option C

If you are teaching a large group with students who are having difficulty, use Option C:

Have students read one paragraph silently. Then, have students read the paragraph to a partner. Alternate partner-reading turns.

Option D

If you are teaching a large group with students who are not having difficulty, use Option D:

Have students read the entire article silently, rereading it if they finish before their classmates. Then, have students read the passage with their partners, alternating on each paragraph.)

APPLICATION LESSON

15

ACTIVITY D *Passage Reading and Comprehension*

The Seven Wonders of the Ancient World

As far back as the fifth century B.C., seven great monuments and structures
13 were recognized as the Seven Wonders of the Ancient World. In the second
26 century B.C., a Greek writer compiled the list. The buildings and monuments
38 were tributes to science, religion, art, and power. (#1)
46 Although only one of the Seven Wonders of the Ancient World remains
58 intact today, historical descriptions have provided information about the others.
68 Many of these great works inspired later architects and artists. Pieces of some of
82 the structures, or art that they contained, can be seen at museums all around the
97 world. (#2)

98 **The Great Pyramid**
101 The oldest of the Seven Wonders is also the only one that still stands today.
116 The Great Pyramid was built in Giza (near present-day Cairo) around 2500 B.C.
130 as a tomb for the Egyptian pharaoh Khufu. Approximately two million stones
142 were used to build the pyramid, each weighing about two tons. The structure is
156 so well built that you cannot even slip a card between the stones. (#3)

169 **The Hanging Gardens of Babylon**
174 King Nebuchadnezzar built an elaborate garden for his queen around 600
185 B.C. Many terraced steps were constructed and then filled with plants. A
197 complicated system of tunnels and pulleys brought water to the 300-foot-high
210 gardens from the nearby Euphrates River. (#4)

216 **The Statue of Zeus**
220 In Olympia, Greece, the birthplace of the ancient Olympic games, people
231 gathered to compete in sports and honor Zeus, an important Greek god. In the
245 fifth century B.C., a sculptor named Phideas carved an enormous gold and ivory
258 figure of the god. Historians believe the statue may have been 40 feet high. No
273 trace of the statue remains today, except for reproductions (copies) that the
285 Greeks put on their coins. (#5)

290 **The Temple of Artemis at Ephesus**
296 This beautiful work of architecture was built in present-day Turkey around
308 356 B.C. to honor the goddess Diana. It sported more than 100 columns that

142 REWARDS Plus: Reading Strategies Applied to Social Studies Passages

Passage Reading: Comprehension Questions

(You may wish to ask the following questions as the passage is being read. Numbers corresponding to the questions are indicated at the point at which they could be asked.)

#1 Why were the Seven Wonders compiled into a list?

They were tributes to science, religion, art, and power.

#2 How many of the Seven Wonders remain today?

Only one remains standing; you can see pieces of the others in museums. You can find historical descriptions of many.

#3 Why was the Great Pyramid built?

To be a tomb for the Egyptian pharaoh Khufu.

#4 What did the Hanging Gardens of Babylon look like?

They were terraced steps, filled with plants.

322 supported a massive roof. The temple was thought to be the first structure made
336 entirely of marble. The temple was destroyed in A.D. 262 by Goths who invaded
350 the country. (#6)

352 **The Mausoleum at Halicarnassus**
356   Built in 353 B.C., the Mausoleum of Halicarnassus was a huge tomb. King
369 Mausolus commissioned the work to be built in Bodrum, a city on the Aegean Sea
384 in southwest Turkey. The massive structure and its stunning sculpture and artwork
396 remained intact for 16 centuries until it was damaged in an earthquake. Later,
409 Crusade soldiers deconstructed, or took apart, the mausoleum and used its
420 polished stone in the construction of their castle. The castle remains standing
432 today, but nothing remains at the site of the mausoleum except its foundation. (#7)

445 **The Colossus of Rhodes**
449   The Colossus was a 30-meter-tall statue of the Greek sun god, Helios. The
464 statue, which was made of bronze, was erected to guard the entrance at the
478 harbor of Rhodes, an island in Greece. It took 12 years to build and was
493 destroyed by an earthquake a mere 56 years later. It completely disappeared after
506 the pieces were sold to a man from Syria. But the wonder of the statue inspired
522 the French sculptor Auguste Bartholdi to create the Statue of Liberty. (#8)

533 **The Lighthouse of Alexandria**
537   Of the Seven Wonders, only the Lighthouse of Alexandria had a practical
549 purpose. The lighthouse helped sailors gain safe entry to the Great Harbor,
561 which is where the Nile River flows into the Mediterranean Sea. It was the
575 tallest building in the world at the time of its construction, around 280 B.C. At
590 the top was a mirror, used to reflect light from the sun or from a fire out to the
609 sea to guide sailors. Scientists are fascinated by descriptions of this mirror, which
622 was said to reflect light as far away as 35 miles. The lighthouse was weakened
637 and later destroyed by several earthquakes. (#9)
643

(ACTIVITY E) *Fluency Building*

| Cold Timing | _____ | Practice 1 | _____ |
| Practice 2 | _____ | Hot Timing | _____ |

Student Book: Application Lesson 15 **143**

#5 What was the Statue of Zeus made from?
Gold and ivory.

#6 Why was the Temple of Artemis at Ephesus built?
To honor the goddess Diana.

#7 What was the cause of damage to the Mausoleum?
An earthquake.

#8 What did the Colossus of Rhodes inspire?
The French sculptor Auguste Bartholdi's creation of the Statue of Liberty.

#9 How did the Lighthouse of Alexandria work?
A mirror at the top reflected light from the sun or from a fire.

ACTIVITY E
Fluency Building

ACTIVITY PROCEDURE

(See the *Student Book*, page 143.)

Have students complete a Cold Timing, one or two practices, and a Hot Timing of the Activity D article. For each timing, have students record the number of correct words read. Finally, have students complete their Fluency Graphs.

Note E-1: When assigning partners for this activity, have the stronger reader read first. As a result, the other reader will have one additional practice opportunity.

1. Now, it's time for fluency building.
2. Find the beginning of the passage again. (Pause.)
3. Whisper-read. See how many words you can read in one minute. Begin._ (Time students for one minute.) Stop._ Circle the last word that you read._ Record the number of words you read after **Cold Timing** in **Activity E** at the bottom of page 143._
4. Let's practice again. Begin._ (Time students for one minute.) Stop._ Put a box around the last word that you read._ Record the number of words you read after **Practice 1**._
5. **Optional** Let's practice one more time before the Hot Timing. Begin._ (Time students for one minute.) Stop._ Put a box around the last word that you read._ Record the number of words you read after **Practice 2**._
6. Please exchange books with your partner._ Partner 1, you are going to read first. Partner 2, listen carefully and underline any mistakes or words left out. Ones, begin._ (Time students for one minute.) Stop._ Twos, cross out the last word that your partner read._ Twos, record the number of words in your partner's book after **Hot Timing**._
7. Partner 2, you are going to read next. Partner 1, listen carefully and underline any mistakes or words left out. Twos, begin. (Time students for one minute.) Stop._ Ones, cross out the last word that your partner read._ Ones, record the number of words in your partner's book after **Hot Timing**._
8. Exchange books._ Turn to the Fluency Graph on the last page of your book, and indicate on the graph the number of Cold Timing and Hot Timing words you read correctly._

ACTIVITY F

Comprehension Questions— Multiple Choice and Short Answer

ACTIVITY PROCEDURE

(See the *Student Book,* pages 144–145.)

Have students complete the Multiple Choice and Short Answer questions on the passage. Give feedback to students on their answers. Lead students in a discussion of their Multiple Choice answers and rationales. Have students record points for each correct item. For each Short Answer response, give one point for using the wording of the question in the answer, and one point for accuracy of the answer (total of 4 points possible for two complete answers).

Note F-1: The correct Multiple Choice answers are circled.

ACTIVITY F *Comprehension Questions— Multiple Choice and Short Answer*

Comprehension Strategy—Multiple Choice

Step 1: Read the item.
Step 2: Read all of the choices.
Step 3: Think about why each choice might be correct or incorrect. Check the article as needed.
Step 4: From the possible correct choices, select the best answer.

1. (Vocabulary) **Read this sentence from the passage: "In the second century B.C., a Greek writer *compiled* the list." What does the word *compiled* mean in that sentence?**
   a. Put together items for the list.
   b. Used the Greek language.
   c. Made a pile of items for the list.
   d. Stacked up cards with names of items written on them.

2. (Cause and Effect) **The writer's purpose in creating the list of the Seven Wonders of the Ancient World was to:**
   a. have each site named a historical place.
   b. direct people to great vacation destinations.
   c. recognize very important buildings and monuments of ancient times.
   d. establish the basis for a movie on ancient accomplishments.

3. (Compare and Contrast) **How is the Great Pyramid different from the other six Wonders of the Ancient World?**
   a. The Great Pyramid is the only Wonder of the Ancient World that is a structure rather than artwork.
   b. The Great Pyramid is the only Wonder of the Ancient World that is located in Egypt.
   c. The Great Pyramid is the only Wonder of the Ancient World made from stone.
   d. The Great Pyramid is the only Wonder of the Ancient World that still stands today.

4. (Main Idea) **Which sentence gives the best summary of the article?**
   a. The "Seven Wonders of the Ancient World" list names monuments that all educated people should visit.
   b. The "Seven Wonders of the Ancient World" list contains important buildings and monuments of ancient times.
   c. The Seven Wonders of the Ancient World were so important that no current structure or monument will ever be greater.
   d. The Greek writer compiled the list for his own use in planning vacations.

MULTIPLE CHOICE COMPREHENSION | 4 Points

Comprehension Strategy—Short Answer

Step 1: Read the item.
Step 2: Turn the question into part of the answer and write it down.
Step 3: Think of the answer or locate the answer in the article.
Step 4: Complete your answer.

1. **How did we learn about these ancient wonders?**
   Example answer: We learned about these ancient wonders through historical descriptions written down by scholars. Also, these wonders inspired many artists and architects who went on to create great art and buildings. Finally, pieces of some of the structures and the art from within can be found in museums throughout the world.

2. **Why do you think these seven things were chosen to be the Seven Wonders of the Ancient World?**
   Example answer: I think these seven things were chosen to be the Seven Wonders of the Ancient World because they were the "best" representations of art and architecture of that time period. People probably thought they would last forever as reminders of their cultures and civilizations.

SHORT ANSWER COMPREHENSION | 4 Points

ACTIVITY G

Expository Writing—Extended Response

ACTIVITY PROCEDURE

(See the *Student Book*, pages 146–147.)

Have students read the prompt and record their position. Next, have them **LIST** reasons and explanations in the Planning Box by referring back to the article. Encourage them to record notes rather than write complete sentences. When students are done with their lists, have them compare their reasons and explanations with those of their classmates and the Example Plan.

1. Time to write. First, read the prompt on page 146. Then, use the Planning Box on page 146 to start thinking about your first sentence. Then, write your **LIST**. When you are finished, compare your list to your partner's list.

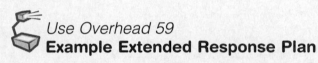

Use Overhead 59
Example Extended Response Plan

2. Now, compare your list to the list on the overhead.

ACTIVITY PROCEDURE

Next, have students complete the additional steps in the Extended Response Writing Strategy. Have them reread their lists and **CROSS OUT** any weak or unimportant reasons or explanations. Then, have students **CONNECT** explanations that could go together in one sentence, **NUMBER** their reasons in a logical order, and **WRITE** their extended responses on a separate piece of paper. When they are done, have them **EDIT** their paragraphs, revising for clarity and proofreading for errors in spelling, capitalization, and punctuation.

Have students read their extended responses to their partners. Then, read the Example Extended Response.

Have students read each of the attributes on the rubric, examine their extended responses, and circle either "Yes" or "Fix up." Give students time to make necessary changes.

Optional: During or after the class session, fill in the third column of the rubric chart and assign points to the extended responses.

Optional: Have students date their writing and place the sample in a folder. Thus, students will be able to look back at their

---

ACTIVITY G *Expository Writing—Extended Response*

Writing Strategy—Extended Response

Step 1: LIST (List the reasons for your position. For each reason, explain with details.)
Step 2: CROSS OUT (Reread your reasons and details. Cross out any that you decide not to include.)
Step 3: CONNECT (Connect any details that could go into one sentence.)
Step 4: NUMBER (Number the reasons in a logical order.)
Step 5: WRITE (Write your response.)
Step 6: EDIT (Revise and proofread your response.)

Prompt: What three modern inventions do you think have made the most difference in the world and why?

Planning Box
(position) *Three modern inventions have made the most difference in the world.*
① (reason) – *telephone improved communication*
(explain) – *letters take days or weeks*
– *people can communicate instantly*
– *hear voices of friends and family*
② (reason) – *refrigerator made food last longer*
(explain) – *possible to transport food or keep it in storage longer*
– *things spoil less easily*
③ (reason) – *computer made difficult tasks simpler*
(explain) – *math-based tasks, like bookkeeping, take less time*
– *people share information easily with disks and e-mail*

Directions: Write your extended response on a separate piece of paper.

Rubric— Extended Response	Student or Partner Rating		Teacher Rating	
1. Did the author tell his/her position in the first sentence?	Yes	Fix up	Yes	No
2. Did the author include at least three **strong, logical** reasons for his/her position?	Yes	Fix up	Yes	No
3. Did the author provide a **strong, logical** explanation for each of his/her reasons?	Yes	Fix up	Yes	No
4. Is the response easy to understand?	Yes	Fix up	Yes	No
5. Did the author correctly spell words, particularly the words found in the article?	Yes	Fix up	Yes	No
6. Did the author use correct capitalization, capitalizing the first word in the sentence and proper names of people, places, and things?	Yes	Fix up	Yes	No
7. Did the author use correct punctuation, including a period at the end of each sentence?	Yes	Fix up	Yes	No

WRITING **7**
Points

---

summaries and extended responses and literally see their writing improvement.

3. Now, **CROSS OUT**, **CONNECT**, **NUMBER**, and **WRITE**._

4. Reread your response and **EDIT**. Check to be sure your response is easy to understand. Fix any errors you find in spelling, capitalization, and punctuation._ (Monitor.)

5. Read what you've written to your partner._

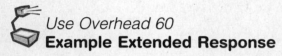

Use Overhead 60
Example Extended Response

6. Look at the overhead. Let's read this Example Extended Response. Yours doesn't need to be exactly the same, but it should be similar.

7. (Have students turn to the rubric on page 147. Ask students to evaluate their own or their partner's writing to determine what to edit. When they have finished the evaluation, give students adequate time to make changes. Have students enter their points in the blank half of the Writing Box below the rubric.)

ACTIVITY G *Expository Writing—Extended Response*

Writing Strategy—Extended Response

Step 1: **LIST** (List the reasons for your position. For each reason, explain with details.)
Step 2: **CROSS OUT** (Reread your reasons and details. Cross out any that you decide not to include.)
Step 3: **CONNECT** (Connect any details that could go into one sentence.)
Step 4: **NUMBER** (Number the reasons in a logical order.)
Step 5: **WRITE** (Write your response.)
Step 6: **EDIT** (Revise and proofread your response.)

Prompt: What three modern inventions do you think have made the most difference in the world and why?

Planning Box

(position)	*Three modern inventions have made the most difference in the world.*
① (reason)	*– telephone improved communication*
(explain)	*– letters take days or weeks*
	– people can communicate instantly
	– hear voices of friends and family
② (reason)	*– refrigerator made food last longer*
(explain)	*– possible to transport food or keep it in storage longer*
	– things spoil less easily
③ (reason)	*– computer made difficult tasks simpler*
(explain)	*– math-based tasks, like bookkeeping, take less time*
	– people share information easily with disks and e-mail

Directions: Write your extended response on a separate piece of paper.

Rubric— Extended Response	Student or Partner Rating	Teacher Rating
1. Did the author tell his/her position in the first sentence?	Yes Fix up	Yes No
2. Did the author include at least three **strong, logical** reasons for his/her position?	Yes Fix up	Yes No
3. Did the author provide a **strong, logical** explanation for each of his/her reasons?	Yes Fix up	Yes No
4. Is the response easy to understand?	Yes Fix up	Yes No
5. Did the author correctly spell words, particularly the words found in the article?	Yes Fix up	Yes No
6. Did the author use correct capitalization, capitalizing the first word in the sentence and proper names of people, places, and things?	Yes Fix up	Yes No
7. Did the author use correct punctuation, including a period at the end of each sentence?	Yes Fix up	Yes No

WRITING **7**
Points

Blackline Masters for Overhead Transparencies

Review Lessons

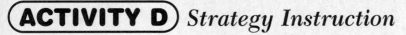

Overhead A

ACTIVITY D *Strategy Instruction*

1. abstract	insist	impact
2. distraught	misfit	admit

ACTIVITY E *Strategy Practice*

1. birthday	misplay	discard
2. maintain	disband	indistinct
3. modern	addict	imprint
4. absurd	insert	railway

Overhead B

ACTIVITY D *Strategy Instruction*

1. beside	readjust	prepay
2. combine	provide	defraud

ACTIVITY E *Strategy Practice*

1. backbone	reprint	costume
2. mistake	promote	prescribe
3. obsolete	propose	sunstroke
4. decode	holiday	subscribe

Overhead C

(ACTIVITY D) *Strategy Practice*

1. perturb   uncurl   confess
2. afraid   expert   engrave

(ACTIVITY E) *Independent Strategy Practice*

1. misinform   disagree   spellbound
2. sweepstake   reproduce   protect
3. turmoil   bemoan   discontent
4. imperfect   boycott   reconstruct

Overhead D

(ACTIVITY D) *Strategy Practice*

1. regardless   softness   unfortunate
2. programmer   slowest   historical
3. organism   inventor   personal

(ACTIVITY E) *Independent Strategy Practice*

1. abnormal   respectful   proposal
2. exaggerate   exhaust   untruthful
3. careless   unfaithful   astonish
4. alarmist   energetic   exclude

Overhead E

ACTIVITY D Strategy Practice

1. advertisement   delightful   disinfectant
2. intentionally   property   expressionless
3. personality   admittance   incoherence

ACTIVITY E Independent Strategy Practice

1. perfectionist   independently   dictionary
2. contaminate   precautionary   deductive
3. inconsistently   excitement   repulsive
4. opinion   hoodwink   imperfect

ACTIVITY D *Strategy Practice*

1. official	substantial	delicious
2. pretentious	impressionable	incombustible
3. conjecture	inconspicuous	disadvantage

ACTIVITY E *Independent Strategy Practice*

1. administrative	performance	threadbare
2. circumstantial	investigation	professionalism
3. precipitation	environmentally	communication
4. unconventional	consolidate	misconception

Blackline Masters for Overhead Transparencies

Application Lessons

ACTIVITY A *Vocabulary*

List 1: Tell

1.	Thrace	*n.* ▶	(a region of Greece)
2.	Thracians	*n.* ▶	(the people of Thrace)
3.	Dionysus	*n.* ▶	(a Greek god)
4.	Thespis	*n.* ▶	(a Greek actor)
5.	Pisistratus	*n.* ▶	(a ruler of ancient Greece)
6.	chorus	*n.* ▶	(a group of singers)
7.	dithyramb	*n.* ▶	(a chant)
8.	dialogue	*n.* ▶	(a conversation in a play)
9.	ceremony	*n.* ▶	(activities done on an important occasion)
10.	theatrical	*adj.* ▶	(relating to the theater)

List 2: Strategy Practice

1.	production	*n.* ▶	(a play, movie, or video)
2.	protagonist	*n.* ▶	(the main character in a play)
3.	audience	*n.* ▶	(a group of people gathered to see a production)
4.	commentary or commentary	*n.* ▶	(a series of comments or explanations)
5.	morality	*n.* ▶	(whether an act is right or wrong)
6.	tradition	*n.* ▶	(doing something the same way it was done in the past)
7.	visible	*adj.* ▶	(can be seen)
8.	accommodate or accommodate or accommodate	*v.* ▶	(to make room for)
9.	appreciate or appreciate or appreciate	*v.* ▶	(to like something)
10.	interact	*v.* ▶	(to talk with someone)

ACTIVITY A *Vocabulary*

List 3: Word Families

Family 1	**religion**	*n.* ▶	(a set of beliefs or moral principles)
	religious	*adj.*	
	religiously	*adv.*	
Family 2	**compete**	*v.* ▶	(to strive against others; to try to win)
	competition	*n.*	
	competitive	*adj.*	
Family 3	**politics**	*n.* ▶	(activities related to the government)
	political	*adj.*	
	politically	*adv.*	
Family 4	**tragedy**	*n.* ▶	(a play with a sad ending)
	tragic	*adj.*	
	tragically	*adv.*	
Family 5	**comedy**	*n.* ▶	(a play that is funny)
	comedic	*adj.*	
	comedian	*n.*	

ACTIVITY B *Spelling Dictation*

1. **politics**	4. **compete**
2. **political**	5. **competitive**
3. **politically**	6. **competition**

ACTIVITY G *Expository Writing—Summary*

Prompt: Write a summary of the information you read in the *Greek Theater* article.

Example Summary Plan

Planning Box
(topic) *Greek Theater*
① (detail) – *began as a religious ceremony*   (detail) – *honored the Greek god Dionysus*
(detail) – ~~*beliefs in Dionysus began to spread southward*~~
② (detail) – *choruses chanted lyrics*
③ (detail) – *actors joined the choruses*
④ (detail) – *the Dionysus festival in Athens became a drama competition*   (detail) – *amphitheaters were built*
⑤ (detail) – *performed tragedies that taught lessons*   (detail) – *performed comedies that made fun of life*
⑥ (detail) – *declined when playwrights died and the government changed*

ACTIVITY G *Expository Writing—Summary*

Example Summary

The roots of modern theater can be found in early Greek theater. Greek theater began as a religious ceremony that honored the Greek god Dionysus. At first, choruses chanted lyrics. When actors were added to interact with the chorus, theater was born. Later, the Dionysus festival in Athens became a drama competition, and amphitheaters were built to accommodate the event. Both tragedies, which taught lessons, and comedies, which made fun of life, were performed. Greek theater declined when the great playwrights died and the government changed.

Overhead 5

ACTIVITY A *Vocabulary*

List 1: Tell

1.	Marco Polo	*n.* ▶	(a 13th century traveler and storyteller)
2.	Italy	*n.* ▶	(a country in Europe)
3.	Venice	*n.* ▶	(a city in Italy)
4.	Venetian	*adj.* ▶	(pertaining to Venice or its people)
5.	Genoa	*n.* ▶	(a city in Italy)
6.	Genoese	*adj.* ▶	(pertaining to Genoa or its people)
7.	Mongolian	*adj.* ▶	(pertaining to Mongolia or its people)
8.	khan	*n.* ▶	(a ruler of ancient China)
9.	Rustichello	*n.* ▶	(a famous writer)
10.	porcelain	*n.* ▶	(a fine, white ceramic material)

List 2: Strategy Practice

1.	merchant	*n.* ▶	(a person whose job is buying and selling things)
2.	navigator	*n.* ▶	(a person who directs the course of a ship)
3.	voyage	*n.* ▶	(a trip, usually by ship)
4.	translate *or* translate	*v.* ▶	(to change into another language)
5.	accompany *or* accompany *or* accompany	*v.* ▶	(to go along with)
6.	encourage	*v.* ▶	(to inspire)
7.	skepticism	*n.* ▶	(doubt or unbelief)
8.	diplomatic	*adj.* ▶	(pertaining to relationships between nations)
9.	relatively	*adv.* ▶	(somewhat)
10.	extensively	*adv.* ▶	(large in amount)

Overhead 6

ACTIVITY A *Vocabulary*

List 3: Word Families

Family 1	establish	v.	▶ (to set up permanently)
	established	adj.	
	establishment	n.	

Family 2	converse	v.	▶ (to talk together)
	conversation	n.	
	conversational	adj.	

Family 3	describe	v.	▶ (to tell about)
	description	n.	
	descriptively	adv.	

Family 4	respect	v.	▶ (admiration of someone or something)
	respectful	adj.	
	respectfully	adv.	

Family 5	inform	v.	▶ (to tell)
	information	n.	
	informant	n.	

ACTIVITY B *Spelling Dictation*

1. converse	4. respect
2. conversation	5. respectful
3. conversational	6. respectfully

ACTIVITY G *Expository Writing—Summary*

Prompt: Write a summary of the information you read about Marco Polo.

Example Summary Plan

Planning Box
(topic) *Marco Polo*
① (detail) – *traveled with his father to China*
② { (detail) – *the khan hired the Polos*   (detail) – *Marco Polo served as a diplomat*
③ (detail) – *the khan liked Marco's stories and didn't want him to leave*
④ (detail) – *Marco Polo returned to Venice, where he told stories of Asia*
⑤ (detail) – *met Rustichello in prison*
⑥ { (detail) – *Rustichello wrote down Marco Polo's stories*   (detail) – *people used his book as a travel handbook*
⑦ (detail) – *information has been verified by scholars*

ACTIVITY G *Expository Writing—Summary*

Example Summary

Marco Polo is one of the most famous travelers of all time. He traveled to China with his father. There, Marco was hired by the ruling khan and served as a diplomat. The khan liked Marco and his storytelling and didn't want him to leave China. However, Marco Polo did return to Venice, where he told his stories of Asia. During a war, Marco Polo was imprisoned and met Rustichello, a famous writer. Rustichello recorded Marco Polo's stories and published a book that was used as a handbook by other travelers. Scholars have since verified the truthfulness of the information provided in the book.

ACTIVITY A *Vocabulary*

List 1: Tell

1. **pirate**   *n.* ▶ (a person who robs on the high seas)
2. **privateer**   *n.* ▶ (a crew member of a privately owned ship who attacks enemies on behalf of a government)
3. **buccaneer**   *n.* ▶ (a pirate who attacked Spanish ships)
4. **circumnavigate**   *v.* ▶ (to sail completely around the earth)

List 2: Strategy Practice

1. **romanticize**
   or **romanticize**   *v.* ▶ (to make romantic)
2. **plunder**   *v.* ▶ (to take things by force)
3. **jurisdiction**   *n.* ▶ (territory ruled by a government)
4. **intention**   *n.* ▶ (purpose)
5. **sponsorship**
   or **sponsorship**   *n.* ▶ (the act of assuming responsibility for a person or thing)
6. **nutrition**   *n.* ▶ (the process by which the body takes in and uses food)
7. **engagement**
   or **engagement**   *n.* ▶ (an encounter, conflict, or battle)
8. **international**   *adj.* ▶ (concerning two or more countries)
9. **regulation**   *n.* ▶ (a rule or law)
10. **intensity**   *n.* ▶ (strength)

ACTIVITY A *Vocabulary*

List 3: Word Families

Family 1	**inspire**	*v.*	▶ (to influence; to fill with courage)
	inspiration	*n.*	
	inspirational	*adj.*	

Family 2	**class**	*n.*	▶ (a grouping of things together that are alike)
	classify	*v.*	
	classification	*n.*	

Family 3	**theory**	*n.*	▶ (an idea that explains an event)
	theoretical	*adj.*	
	theoretically	*adv.*	

Family 4	**adventure**	*n.*	▶ (a thrilling or exciting experience)
	adventurous	*adj.*	
	adventuresome	*adj.*	

Family 5	**democracy**	*n.*	▶ (a government run by the people)
	democratic	*adj.*	
	democratically	*adv.*	

ACTIVITY B *Spelling Dictation*

1. **inspire**	4. **democracy**
2. **inspiration**	5. **democratic**
3. **inspirational**	6. **democratically**

(from Application Lesson 3)

Overhead 11

ACTIVITY G *Expository Writing—Summary*

Prompt: Write a summary of the most important information about pirates and piracy.

Example Summary Plan

Planning Box
(topic) *Pirates and Piracy*
① (detail) – *17th and 18th centuries were the Golden Age of Piracy*
② (detail) – *different types of pirates*
③ { (detail) – *pirates were sailors who attacked other ships to rob them* / (detail) – *took things for their own private gain*
④ (detail) – *privateers worked for a specific government or company*
⑤ (detail) – *had a Letter of Marque, which gave privateers permission to act*
⑥ (detail) – *Letters of Marque did not protect privateers from punishment*
⑦ (detail) – *buccaneers targeted Spanish ships*
⑧ (detail) – *life on a ship was difficult and dangerous*
⑨ (detail) – *ships had rules of conduct*
⑩ (detail) – *piracy still occurs today*

ACTIVITY G *Expository Writing—Summary*

Example Summary

Pirates and piracy have always existed. However, the 17th and 18th centuries were known as the Golden Age of Piracy. Then, there were different kinds of pirates. In general, pirates were sailors who attacked other ships to steal things for their own gain. Another type of pirate, the privateer, was hired by a specific government or company. Privateers had a Letter of Marque, which gave them permission to act on behalf of their employer. But they were still punished by the people they attacked or stole from. Buccaneers stole mainly from Spanish ships. Life on the pirate ships was difficult and dangerous. Each ship had its own rules of conduct. Piracy continues to happen today.

Overhead 13

ACTIVITY A *Vocabulary*

List 1: Tell

1. **Britain**   *n.* ▶ (an island nation in Europe; Great Britain, England)

2. **empire**   *n.* ▶ (a group of countries ruled by one country)

3. **mercantile**   *adj.* ▶ (relating to merchants)

4. **mercantilism**   *n.* ▶ (an economic system developed in France and Britain that stressed government control of the economy and trade)

List 2: Strategy Practice

1. **exploration**   *n.* ▶ (the act of traveling to an unknown place to learn about the place)

2. **acquisition**   *n.* ▶ (something you get that becomes your own)

3. **territory**   *n.* ▶ (any large area of land)
   or **territory**

4. **possession**   *n.* ▶ (a territory that is under the rule of a foreign country)

5. **culminate**   *v.* ▶ (to reach the final point)

6. **independence**   *n.* ▶ (the state of not being ruled by another country)

7. **autonomy**   *n.* ▶ (independence or freedom)

8. **individual**   *adj.* ▶ (single and distinct)

9. **prevalent**   *adj.* ▶ (widespread)

10. **deposit**   *n.* ▶ (a natural layer of minerals in the earth)

ACTIVITY A *Vocabulary*

List 3: Word Families

Family 1	value	n.	▶ (usefulness or importance)
	valuable	adj.	
	invaluable	adj.	
Family 2	inhabit	v.	▶ (to live in an area)
	inhabitant	n.	
	inhabitable	adj.	
Family 3	imperial	adj.	▶ (relating to an empire)
	imperialism	n.	
	imperialist	n.	
Family 4	expand	v.	▶ (to make larger)
	expansion	n.	
	expansive	adj.	
Family 5	colony	n.	▶ (a territory under the rule of another country)
	colonize	v.	
	colonization	n.	

ACTIVITY B *Spelling Dictation*

1. **value**	4. **imperial**
2. **valuable**	5. **imperialism**
3. **invaluable**	6. **imperialist**

Overhead 15

ACTIVITY G *Expository Writing—Summary*

Prompt: Write a summary of the information on the British Empire.

Example Summary Plan

Planning Box
(topic) *The British Empire*
① { (detail) – *empire began with trade*   (detail) – *looked for resources in other lands*
② (detail) – *established colonies where the resources were*
③ (detail) – *acquired land through wars*
④ (detail) – *established British culture in the acquired lands*
⑤ (detail) – *resources made Britain wealthy*
⑥ (detail) – *empire declined*
⑦ (detail) – *colonies wanted independence*
⑧ (detail) – *some countries fought for it*
⑨ (detail) – *Britain granted independence to some countries*

ACTIVITY G *Expository Writing—Summary*

Example Summary

   Great Britain spread its power by establishing the British Empire throughout the world. The British Empire started with trade because Britain wanted resources from other lands. When they found desired resources, they established colonies in the new lands. They also got new lands through wars. Britain introduced British culture to their new lands. The resources it gained made Britain very wealthy. Eventually, the empire declined. The countries and people wanted to be independent of Britain. In some cases, they had to fight for that independence. But in other cases, Britain gave people the independence they sought.

ACTIVITY A *Vocabulary*

List 1: Tell

1. **Mohandas Gandhi**   *n.* ▶ (a great human rights leader from India)
2. **Mahatma**   *n.* ▶ (a title given to Gandhi that means "great-souled one")
3. **campaign**   *n.* ▶ (a series of activities for some specific purpose)

List 2: Strategy Practice

1. **compassion**   *n.* ▶ (sympathy for and a desire to help suffering people)
2. **inferior**   *adj.* ▶ (lower in rank or importance)
3. **compartment**   *n.* ▶ (an enclosed space, such as a room on a train)
4. **passengers**   *n.* ▶ (people who travel in a vehicle)
5. **incident**   *n.* ▶ (an event)
6. **reputation**   *n.* ▶ (how people think of someone)
7. **obligation**   *n.* ▶ (something a person must do)
8. **comply**   *v.* ▶ (to act as requested)
   or **comply**
9. **relinquish**   *v.* ▶ (to give up)
10. **associate**   *v.* ▶ (to connect in thought or memory)
    or **associate**
    or **associate**

ACTIVITY A *Vocabulary*

List 3: Word Families

Family 1	**justice**	*n.*	▶ (fairness)
	injustice	*n.*	
	justification	*n.*	

Family 2	**conduct**	*v.*	▶ (to lead or guide)
	conductor	*n.*	
	conductible	*adj.*	

Family 3	**prosecute**	*v.*	▶ (to carry out a legal action against a person in a court of law)
	prosecution	*n.*	
	prosecutor	*n.*	

Family 4	**equal**	*adj.*	▶ (the same as)
	equality	*n.*	
	inequality	*n.*	

Family 5	**dedicate**	*v.*	▶ (to devote oneself to a purpose or person)
	dedication	*n.*	
	dedicator	*n.*	

ACTIVITY B *Spelling Dictation*

1. **justice**	4. **prosecute**
2. **injustice**	5. **prosecution**
3. **justification**	6. **prosecutor**

ACTIVITY G *Expository Writing—Extended Response*

Prompt: Describe some of the parts of Gandhi's life that led him to be a great leader for peace.

Example Extended Response Plan

Planning Box
(position) *Many factors in Gandhi's life led him to be a great leader for peace.*
(reason) *– ~~lived throughout the British Empire~~*
(explain) *– ~~born in India~~*
– ~~also lived in South Africa and Great Britain~~
① (reason) *– knew what it was like to be a racial outcast*
(explain) *– conductor told him to sit with other dark-skinned people in third-class section on the train*
– thrown off the train when he refused
② (reason) *– responded to violence with nonviolence*
{ (explain) *– hit repeatedly on the stagecoach*
– refused to fight back
③ (reason) *– organized people who disagreed with the government*
{ (explain) *– wrote pamphlets and petitions*
– made speeches
– people became more aware of what was happening

ACTIVITY G *Expository Writing—Extended Response*

Example Extended Response

Many factors in Gandhi's life led him to become a great leader for peace. First, he knew what it was like to be a racial outcast. On one trip, he was told to sit with other dark-skinned people in third class, even though he had a first-class ticket. When he refused, he was thrown off the train. Another factor is that he responded to violence with nonviolence. He was once hit repeatedly for refusing to move onto the footboard of a stagecoach, but he would not fight back. Finally, Gandhi organized people who disagreed with the government. He wrote pamphlets and petitions, and he made speeches. He made people more aware of what was happening in regard to the government and civil rights.

Overhead 21

ACTIVITY A *Vocabulary*

List 1: Tell

1.	Sybil Ludington	*n.* ▶	(a 16-year-old who warned neighbors)
2.	Susanna Boiling	*n.* ▶	(a teenager who crossed a river alone)
3.	Lydia Barrington Darragh	*n.* ▶	(a woman who warned George Washington)
4.	Anne Kennedy	*n.* ▶	(a woman who organized an attack)
5.	Margaret Warne	*n.* ▶	(a woman doctor who didn't charge a fee to patients)
6.	Prudence Wright	*n.* ▶	(a woman who commanded a regiment)
7.	Paul Revere	*n.* ▶	(a man who warned of British attack)
8.	General Lafayette	*n.* ▶	(an army general)

List 2: Strategy Practice

1.	invasion	*n.* ▶	(the entrance of an army into a country)
2.	regiment	*n.* ▶	(a military unit of an army)
3.	occupation	*n.* ▶	(a job; a profession)
4.	declaration	*n.* ▶	(a formal statement; an announcement)
5.	representation	*n.* ▶	(the function of speaking for a group of people)
6.	disobedience	*n.* ▶	(failure to follow an order)
7.	commandeer *or* commandeer	*v.* ▶	(to take; to seize)
8.	capture	*v.* ▶	(to take by force)
9.	official	*adj.* ▶	(relating to an office or position of duty)
10.	capacity	*n.* ▶	(a position; a function; a role)

Overhead 22

ACTIVITY A *Vocabulary*

List 3: Word Families

Family 1	**independent**	*adj.* ▶	(not controlled by others)
	independently	*adv.*	
	independence	*n.*	

Family 2	**colony**	*n.* ▶	(territory under the control of another country)
	colonial	*adj.*	
	colonist	*n.*	

Family 3	**produce**	*v.* ▶	(to make)
	product	*n.*	
	production	*n.*	

Family 4	**participate**	*v.* ▶	(to take part in an activity)
	participated	*v.*	
	participation	*n.*	

Family 5	**revolt**	*v.* ▶	(to break away from or rise up against an authority)
	revolution	*n.*	
	revolutionary	*adj.*	

ACTIVITY B *Spelling Dictation*

1. **independent**	4. **participate**
2. **independently**	5. **participated**
3. **independence**	6. **participation**

Overhead 23

ACTIVITY G *Expository Writing—Extended Response*

Prompt: Explain why women's roles were as important as men's roles in defeating the British during the Revolutionary War.

Example Extended Response Plan

Planning Box
(position) *Women's roles were as important as men's roles in defeating the British.*
① (reason) – *women saw things and warned other people*
(explain) – *Sybil Ludington witnessed attack on supply house and warned neighbors*   – *Susanna Boiling, teenager, crossed river and warned General Lafayette*
② (reason) – *women supported war efforts with supplies for colonial troops*
(explain) – *provided food, candles, soap, shelter*   – *raised money to purchase boots, gunpowder*
③ (reason) – *women protected crops and homes*
(explain) – *burned crops, Anne Kennedy attacked British on her land*
(reason) – ~~*women were nurses and soldiers*~~
(explain) – ~~*one nurse for every ten patients*~~   ~~*fought alongside husbands, dressed like men*~~

ACTIVITY G *Expository Writing—Extended Response*

Example Extended Response

   During the Revolutionary War, women's roles were as important as men's roles in defeating the British. Women, both young and old, witnessed attacks and meetings and found ways to warn people who were in danger. Sybil Ludington and Susanna Boiling, two teenagers, went out at night alone and warned others of impending attacks. Other women contributed to the war efforts by providing necessary supplies to the colonial troops. The women produced supplies such as food, candles, and soap, and gave shelter. They also raised money to purchase important supplies such as boots and gunpowder. Finally, many women protected their families' crops and homes while the men were off fighting. Some burned crops, while others, like Anne Kennedy, organized attacks against the British who were trying to take their homes and land.

Overhead 25

ACTIVITY A *Vocabulary*

List 1: Tell

1. the Senate | *n.* | ▶ (the upper house of the U.S. Congress that has two people from each state)
2. senators | *n.* | ▶ (members of the U.S. Senate)
3. Supreme Court | *n.* | ▶ (the highest court in the U.S.)
4. justices | *n.* | ▶ (the Supreme Court judges)
5. agencies | *n.* | ▶ (governmental offices that help run things)
6. system | *n.* | ▶ (a set of beliefs, facts, rules, and laws)
7. notifying | *v.* | ▶ (letting someone know about something)
8. democracy | *n.* | ▶ (a government ruled by the people, even if through representation)

List 2: Strategy Practice

1. comprise | *v.* | ▶ (to include or consist of)
2. population | *n.* | ▶ (the number of people living in an area)
3. Constitution | *n.* | ▶ (the document outlining the plan for the U.S. government)
4. unconstitutional | *adj.* | ▶ (not in keeping with the U.S. Constitution)
5. nominate | *v.* | ▶ (to appoint to a job or office)
6. limitation | *n.* | ▶ (something that keeps something else from happening)
7. responsibility | *n.* | ▶ (a job or duty)
8. impeachment | *n.* | ▶ (the act of bringing a formal charge against someone to remove that person from office)
9. similarly | *adv.* | ▶ (like something else)
10. presidential | *adj.* | ▶ (having to do with the president of a country or organization)

ACTIVITY A Vocabulary

List 3: Word Families

Family 1 legislate   *v.*   ▶ (to make a law)
             legislative   *adj.*
             legislation   *n.*

Family 2 execute   *v.*   ▶ (to carry out; to accomplish)
             executive   *n.*
             execution   *n.*

Family 3 judge   *n.*   ▶ (someone who hears and decides cases in a court of law)

             judicial   *adj.*
             judiciary   *n.*

Family 4 govern   *v.*   ▶ (to rule by right of authority)
             governor   *n.*
             government   *n.*

Family 5 represent   *v.*   ▶ (to serve as the speaker for others)
             representative   *n.*
             representation   *n.*

ACTIVITY B Spelling Dictation

1. **govern**	4. **represent**
2. **governor**	5. **representative**
3. **government**	6. **representation**

ACTIVITY G *Expository Writing—Extended Response*

Prompt: If you could choose a job in one branch of the U.S. government, tell which branch and why.

Example Extended Response Plan

Planning Box
(position) *If I could choose a job, I would choose the legislative branch.*
① (reason) – *makes more difference than other branches*
(explain) – *makes laws that are enforced by executive branch and judged by judicial branch*
(reason) – ~~has lots of opportunities~~
(explain) – ~~many representatives and senators~~
② (reason) – *important to people in 50 states*
{ (explain) – *represent people of state* – *focus on state issues*
③ (reason) – *many different issues would be considered*
(explain) – *environment, social issues, foreign affairs*

ACTIVITY G *Expository Writing—Extended Response*

Example Extended Response

If I applied for a U.S. government job, I would want it to be in the legislative branch for a number of reasons. First, the legislative branch makes the most difference. This branch makes laws that the executive branch must carry out and the judicial branch must judge. Second, the legislative branch is very important to individual states. The legislators and senators represent their states on critical issues. Finally, many different issues would be considered in the legislative branch. We would discuss the environment, social welfare, foreign affairs, and other issues.

Overhead 29

ACTIVITY A *Vocabulary*

List 1: Tell

1. guarantee   *v.* ▶ (to promise that something will happen)
2. aliens   *n.* ▶ (people who are not citizens of the country in which they are living)
3. privileges   *n.* ▶ (special rights)
4. society   *n.* ▶ (a group of people)
5. allegiance   *n.* ▶ (loyalty to a government)

List 2: Strategy Practice

1. automatically   *adv.* ▶ (done without a person's control)
   or automatically
2. citizen   *n.* ▶ (a person born in a country or one who chooses to become a member of a country by law)
3. citizenship   *n.* ▶ (the state of having the rights and duties of a citizen)
   or citizenship
4. opportunity   *n.* ▶ (a good chance to advance oneself)
5. territory   *n.* ▶ (a part of the United States that does not have the status of a state)
   or territory
6. nationals   *n.* ▶ (people who are members of a nation)
7. democratic   *adj.* ▶ (believing all people are politically equal)
8. generally   *adv.* ▶ (in most cases; usually)
9. circumstances   *n.* ▶ (events that affect other events)
10. particular   *adj.* ▶ (specific)

ACTIVITY A *Vocabulary*

List 3: Word Families

Family 1	natural	*adj.* ▶	(belonging to from birth)
	naturalized	*adj.*	
	naturalization	*n.*	

Family 2	immigrate	*v.* ▶	(to enter a country in which one was not born in order to make a home)
	immigrants	*n.*	
	immigration	*n.*	

Family 3	responsible	*adj.* ▶	(having a job or duty)
	responsibility	*n.*	
	responsibilities	*n.*	

Family 4	apply	*v.* ▶	(to make an application or request for a position or job)
	applicant	*n.*	
	application	*n.*	

Family 5	volunteer	*v.* ▶	(to do something of one's own free will)
	voluntary	*adj.*	
	voluntarily	*adv.*	

ACTIVITY B *Spelling Dictation*

1. **immigrate**	4. **responsible**
2. **immigrants**	5. **responsibility**
3. **immigration**	6. **responsibilities**

ACTIVITY G *Expository Writing—Extended Response*

Prompt: Pretend that you are trying to convince an alien to become an American citizen. What reasons would you use to support that position?

Example Extended Response Plan

Planning Box
(position) *I think you should become an American citizen.*
① (reason) – *more rights*
(explain) – *right to vote*
– *right to apply for government jobs*
– *right to run for certain offices*
– *get a U.S. passport*
② (reason) – *can request that family members come to the U.S.*
(explain) – ~~*close family members might be living in another country*~~
– *would like having loved ones close*
③ (reason) – *participate more fully in American democracy*
(explain) – *serve on juries*

ACTIVITY G *Expository Writing—Extended Response*

Example Extended Response

There are many reasons why you should become an American citizen. First, you would have more rights. You would be able to vote, apply for government jobs, run for certain offices, and get a U.S. passport. Next, you could request that family members be allowed to come to the United States. Wouldn't it be nice to have your grandmother, uncle, and cousin close to you in the United States? Finally, you would be able to more fully participate in American democracy. For example, you would be able to serve on juries.

ACTIVITY A *Vocabulary*

List 1: Tell

1.	ratify	*v.* ▶	(to approve)
2.	relieve	*v.* ▶	(to reduce or lighten pain, anxiety, etc.)
3.	migrant	*n.* ▶	(a person who moves from one region to another)
4.	refugees	*n.* ▶	(people who leave their homes because of danger)
5.	weary	*adj.* ▶	(tired; worn out)
6.	drought	*n.* ▶	(a long period of dry weather; lack of rain)

List 2: Strategy Practice

1.	according to	*adj.* ▶	(as stated in a document)
2.	international	*adj.* ▶	(concerning two or more countries)
3.	security	*n.* ▶	(protection from danger)
4.	centralize *or* centralize	*v.* ▶	(to organize under one point of control)
5.	inception	*n.* ▶	(beginning)
6.	dispute	*n.* ▶	(a fight or an argument)
7.	economic	*adj.* ▶	(having to do with money)
8.	impoverish	*v.* ▶	(to make very poor)
9.	environmental	*adj.* ▶	(having to do with the environment)
10.	sustainable	*adj.* ▶	(able to keep up or maintain over time)

Overhead 34

ACTIVITY A *Vocabulary*

List 3: Word Families

Family 1	**organize**	*v.*	▶	(to provide a structure; to arrange in an orderly way)
	organizing	*v.*		
	organization	*n.*		

Family 2	**moderate**	*v.*	▶	(to preside over something, such as a meeting; to referee)
	moderated	*v.*		
	moderation	*n.*		

Family 3	**diplomacy**	*n.*	▶	(the conducting of relations between or among nations; two or more countries talking to each other)
	diplomatic	*adj.*		
	diplomatically	*adv.*		

Family 4	**universe**	*n.*	▶	(all that exists)
	universal	*adj.*		
	universally	*adv.*		

Family 5	**observe**	*v.*	▶	(to watch closely)
	observation	*n.*		
	observational	*adj.*		

ACTIVITY B *Spelling Dictation*

1. **organize**	4. **observe**
2. **organizing**	5. **observation**
3. **organization**	6. **observational**

Overhead 35

ACTIVITY G *Expository Writing—Summary*

Prompt: Write a summary of the information contained in *The United Nations* article.

Example Summary Plan

Planning Box
(topic) *The United Nations*
① (detail) – *United Nations established in 1945*
② (detail) – *U.N. charter describes its purposes*
③ (detail) – *U.N. acts as a central organization for many nations*
④ (detail) – *tries to create and maintain international peace*
⑤ { (detail) – *works to relieve poverty in poor nations*   (detail) – *addresses other economic and social issues*
⑥ (detail) – *provides disaster relief*
⑦ { (detail) – *created a Universal Declaration of Human Rights*   (detail) – *makes sure countries uphold human rights*
⑧ { (detail) – *creates international laws*   (detail) – *laws provide a way for many nations to cooperate*

ACTIVITY G *Expository Writing—Summary*

Example Summary

The United Nations is a very important world organization. It was established in 1945. It has a charter that describes the purpose of the U.N. The U.N. acts as a central organization for many nations. One of the things the U.N. does is try to create and maintain peace among nations. It also works to relieve poverty in poor nations and addresses other social and economic issues. The U.N. also provides disaster relief. The United Nations created a Universal Declaration of Human Rights and makes sure that countries follow it. The U.N. creates international laws, which promote cooperation among nations of the world.

Overhead 37

ACTIVITY A *Vocabulary*

List 1: Tell

1. **barrier**   *n.* ▶ (something that blocks the way)
2. **elite**   *n.* ▶ (a part of a group regarded as the finest, best, or most powerful)
3. **neutral**   *adj.* ▶ (not belonging to any specific group)
4. **pamphlet**   *n.* ▶ (a short book with a paper cover)
5. **brochure**   *n.* ▶ (a small pamphlet)
6. **pseudonym**   *n.* ▶ (a fake name)
7. **Esperanto**   *n.* ▶ (an international language created by Lazar Zamenhof)
8. **Esperantists**   *n.* ▶ (people who speak Esperanto)

List 2: Strategy Practice

1. **different**   *adj.* ▶ (not the same as; unlike one another)
2. **education**   *n.* ▶ (the process of gaining knowledge or skill, especially by schooling)
3. **conversation**   *n.* ▶ (talk between or among people)
4. **particular**   *adj.* ▶ (belonging to a specific group)
5. **affiliate**   *v.* ▶ (to join together; unite)
   or **affiliate**
   or **affiliate**
6. **construct**   *v.* ▶ (to make or build)
7. **experience**   *n.* ▶ (something that a person has done)
   or **experience**
8. **necessity**   *n.* ▶ (something that is needed)
9. **universal**   *adj.* ▶ (shared by all)
10. **actively**   *adv.* ▶ (full of action)

ACTIVITY A *Vocabulary*

List 3: Word Families

Family 1	**receive**	*v.*	▶ (to get)
	recipient	*n.*	
	receptive	*adj.*	

Family 2	**distribute**	*v.*	▶ (to divide and give out in shares)
	distribution	*n.*	
	distributive	*adj.*	

Family 3	**communicate**	*v.*	▶ (to share thoughts or feelings)
	communication	*n.*	
	communicator	*n.*	

Family 4	**complicate**	*v.*	▶ (to make difficult or hard to understand)
	complicated	*adj.*	
	complication	*n.*	

Family 5	**grammar**	*n.*	▶ (rules of a language)
	grammatical	*adj.*	
	grammatically	*adv.*	

ACTIVITY B *Spelling Dictation*

1. **receive**	4. **communicate**
2. **recipient**	5. **communication**
3. **receptive**	6. **communicator**

ACTIVITY G *Expository Writing—Extended Response*

Prompt: Tell why Esperanto would make a good international language.

Example Extended Response Plan

Planning Box
(position) *Esperanto would make a good international language.*
① (reason) – *easy to learn*
{ (explain) – *simple grammatical rules*
– *can master in a year*
② (reason) – *a neutral language*
{ (explain) – *does not belong to one group of people*
– *not part of any political group*
③ (reason) – *used to communicate*
(explain) – *original books and Web pages in Esperanto*
– *some radio stations broadcast in Esperanto*
④ (reason) – *a community of people support Esperanto*
(explain) – *a Universal Congress is held each year*
– ~~*United Nations recognizes Esperanto*~~
– *popular in central and eastern Europe, eastern Asia, and parts of South America*

ACTIVITY G *Expository Writing—Extended Response*

Example Extended Response

Esperanto would be a good international language. One reason is that it is easy to learn. It has simple grammatical rules, and a person can master the language in a year. Another reason is that it is a neutral language. No single political or social group owns the language. In addition, Esperanto is already being used to communicate. People write books and Web pages in Esperanto. Some radio stations broadcast in Esperanto. Finally, there is a worldwide community of people who support the use of Esperanto. People gather at a yearly conference to discuss Esperanto. People speak the language in central and eastern Europe, eastern Asia, and some areas of South America.

Overhead 41

ACTIVITY A *Vocabulary*

List 1: Tell

1. **kanji**   *n.* ▶ (Chinese characters made from lines and brush strokes)
2. **Korea**   *n.* ▶ (a country in Asia)
3. **Taiwan**   *n.* ▶ (an island close to China)
4. **Roman**   *adj.* ▶ (of Rome)
5. **Qin Dynasty**   *n.* ▶ (rulers from the Qin family)
6. **scholars**   *n.* ▶ (learned people; people who spend quite a bit of time studying and learning)
7. **characters**   *n.* ▶ (drawings or pictures)

List 2: Strategy Practice

1. **historians**   *n.* ▶ (people who study the past)
2. **divination**   *n.* ▶ (a type of fortune-telling)
3. **eventually**   *adv.* ▶ (finally; in the end)
4. **informal**   *adj.* ▶ (made for everyday use)
5. **represent**   *v.* ▶ (to look like)
   or **represent**
6. **pronunciation**   *n.* ▶ (how something is said)
7. **standardize**   *v.* ▶ (to make the same or uniform)
8. **normalize**   *v.* ▶ (to make normal)
9. **mandatory**   *adj.* ▶ (must be done)
   or **mandatory**
10. **literate**   *adj.* ▶ (able to read and write)
    or **literate**

ACTIVITY A *Vocabulary*

List 3: Word Families

Family 1	interpret	*v.*	▶ (to tell the meaning of)
	interpreter	*n.*	
	interpretation	*n.*	

Family 2	origin	*n.*	▶ (the beginning of)
	originate	*v.*	
	original	*adj.*	

Family 3	simple	*adj.*	▶ (easy to understand)
	simplified	*v.*	
	simplification	*n.*	

Family 4	memory	*n.*	▶ (things learned and remembered)
	memorize	*v.*	
	memorization	*n.*	

Family 5	pronounce	*v.*	▶ (to say a word correctly)
	pronounceable	*adj.*	
	pronunciation	*n.*	

ACTIVITY B *Spelling Dictation*

1. **origin**	4. **interpret**
2. **originate**	5. **interpreter**
3. **original**	6. **interpretation**

ACTIVITY G *Expository Writing—Summary*

Prompt: Write a summary of the information on kanji presented in this article.

Example Summary Plan

Planning Box
(topic) *Kanji*
① (detail) – *a system of writing*   (detail) – *originated in China around 2000 B.C.*   (detail) – *recorded interpretations of cracks in bones and turtle shells*
② (detail) – *drawings given informal definition and pronunciation*
③ (detail) – *standardized around 221 B.C., then introduced in Japan*
④ (detail) – *grew to about 30,000 characters—too many to memorize*
⑤ (detail) – *during 20th century, both countries simplified kanji*   (detail) – *now, basic set of kanji for daily life*

ACTIVITY G *Expository Writing—Summary*

Example Summary

   Kanji is the writing system used in many Asian countries. Kanji is a system of writing that originated in China around 2000 B.C., as a record of interpretations of cracks in bones and turtle shells. Drawings were given informal definitions and pronunciations. Kanji characters were standardized around 221 B.C. and then introduced in Japan. The number of characters grew to about 30,000, and people had a hard time memorizing them. So, during the 20th century both China and Japan simplified their kanji and now have a basic set for daily life.

Overhead 45

ACTIVITY A *Vocabulary*

List 1: Tell

1. Mozambique   *n.* ▶ (an island country off the coast of Africa)
2. continent   *n.* ▶ (a large landmass)
3. Europe   *n.* ▶ (a continent across the Atlantic Ocean)
4. Asia   *n.* ▶ (the largest continent)
5. Eurasia   *n.* ▶ (Europe and Asia as one continent)
6. Kenya   *n.* ▶ (a country in Africa)
7. sodium carbonate   *n.* ▶ (a chemical for making glass and soap)
8. Lake Magadi   *n.* ▶ (a lake in Kenya)
9. Lake Naivasha   *n.* ▶ (a lake in Kenya)

List 2: Strategy Practice

1. enormous   *adj.* ▶ (very large)
2. geography   *n.* ▶ (the natural features of a particular place or region)
3. collision   *n.* ▶ (coming together with force)
4. economy   *n.* ▶ (the use of money, goods, and services)
5. concentration   *n.* ▶ (a large amount of a substance gathered in one place, resulting in increased strength or density)
6. altitude   *n.* ▶ (the height of land)
   or altitude
7. carnations   *n.* ▶ (a type of flower)
8. geothermally   *adv.* ▶ (having to do with heat from the earth)
9. commodity   *n.* ▶ (something that can be bought and sold)
10. speculate   *v.* ▶ (to predict)

ACTIVITY A *Vocabulary*

List 3: Word Families

Family 1	geology	n.	▶ (the study of the earth's history and formation)
	geologist	n.	
	geological	adj.	

Family 2	preserve	v.	▶ (to maintain or keep)
	preservation	n.	
	preservationist	n.	

Family 3	vary	v.	▶ (to change or make different)
	variety	n.	
	various	adj.	

Family 4	popular	adj.	▶ (liked by a lot of people)
	populate	v.	
	population	n.	

Family 5	aqua	n.	▶ (water)
	aquarium	n.	
	aquatic	adj.	

ACTIVITY B *Spelling Dictation*

1. **preserve**	4. **popular**
2. **preservation**	5. **populate**
3. **preservationist**	6. **population**

(from Application Lesson 12)

Overhead 47

ACTIVITY G *Expository Writing—Summary*

Prompt: Write a summary of the information about the Great Rift Valley.

Example Summary Plan

Planning Box
(topic) *The Great Rift Valley*
① (detail) – *stretches from northeastern Africa to Mozambique*
② (detail) – *crack in earth's crust created by collision of continents*
③ (detail) – *volcanoes give mountainous appearance*
③ (detail) – *deep lakes with unusual fish and aquatic life*
④ (detail) – *variety of climates*
④ (detail) – *variety of plant and animal life*
⑤ (detail) – *economy driven by natural resources, including sodium carbonate, rich soil, geothermal energy, oil, fish, wildlife*
② (detail) – *continuing to widen*

ACTIVITY G *Expository Writing—Summary*

Example Summary

The Great Rift Valley is a fascinating location on the African continent. It stretches from the northeastern part of Africa down to Mozambique. It was formed by a crack in the earth's crust that was caused by the collision of continents, and the crack is slowly widening. Several volcanoes give the valley a mountainous appearance, with several deep lakes that contain unusual fish and other aquatic life. A variety of climates also support many different animals and plant life. A number of natural resources, including sodium carbonate, rich soil, geothermal energy, oil, fish, and wildlife drive the economy of the Great Rift Valley.

ACTIVITY A *Vocabulary*

List 1: Tell

1. **Nepal** — *n.* ▶ (a small country in eastern Asia)
2. **Mt. Everest** — *n.* ▶ (the highest mountain in the world, located in Nepal)
3. **Sherpas** — *n.* ▶ (people who live in the mountains of Nepal)
4. **Khumbu Valley** — *n.* ▶ (south of Mt. Everest)
5. **Tibet** — *n.* ▶ (a country next to Nepal)
6. **Nangpa La** — *n.* ▶ (a mountain pass between Tibet and Nepal)
7. **Buddhism** — *n.* ▶ (a religion based on the teachings of Buddha)
8. **Nyingmapa Buddhism** — *n.* ▶ (a type of Buddhism)
9. **Tengboche Monastery** — *n.* ▶ (a religious gathering place located on Mt. Everest)
10. **Chomolungma** — *n.* ▶ (the Sherpa name for Mt. Everest)

List 2: Strategy Practice

1. **prowess** — *n.* ▶ (great ability or skill)
2. **expedition** — *n.* ▶ (a trip or journey for a definite purpose)
3. **fertilizer** — *n.* ▶ (something added to the soil to help things grow)
4. **alienate** *or* **alienate** — *v.* ▶ (to cause to be unfriendly)
5. **occupation** — *n.* ▶ (the seizure and control of a country by military force)
6. **prosperity** *or* **prosperity** — *n.* ▶ (success, wealth)
7. **substantial** *or* **substantial** — *adj.* ▶ (important)
8. **spirituality** — *n.* ▶ (concern with things of the spirit or soul)
9. **deforestation** — *n.* ▶ (the result of cutting down forests or trees)
10. **heritage** — *n.* ▶ (something passed down through families)

Overhead 50

ACTIVITY A *Vocabulary*

List 3: Word Families

Family 1 **mountain**   *n.* ▶ (land rising to a great height)

mountainous *adj.* ▶

mountaineers *n.* ▶

Family 2 **comprehend**   *v.*   ▶ (to understand)

comprehension *n.*   ▶

comprehensible *adj.* ▶

Family 3 **prosper**   *v.*   ▶ (to have success, wealth)

prosperous *adj.* ▶

prosperity *n.*   ▶

Family 4 **industry**   *n.*   ▶ (a manufacturing business)

industrial   *adj.* ▶

industrious *adj.* ▶

Family 5 **tradition**   *n.*   ▶ (a continued pattern of doing something the same way as it was done in the past)

traditionally *adv.* ▶

traditionalist *n.*   ▶

ACTIVITY B *Spelling Dictation*

1. **industry**	4. **tradition**
2. **industrial**	5. **traditionally**
3. **industrious**	6. **traditionalist**

Overhead 51

ACTIVITY G *Expository Writing—Extended Response*

Prompt: Describe how a Sherpa's life is different from your own.

Example Extended Response Plan

Planning Box
(position) *A Sherpa's life is different from my life.*
① (reason) – *food is different*
(explain) – *we purchase our food*
– *they grow or raise their food*
– *they eat yak meat, yak milk, yak cheese*
– *we both eat a similar food: potatoes*
② (reason) – *yaks are important to their lives*
(explain) – *we don't rely on yaks at all*
– *yaks provide food, clothing, and shoe leather*
③ (reason) – *our religions may differ*
(explain) – *they practice a form of Buddhism*
– *they believe that mountains are homes of gods*
④ (reason) – *our languages differ*
(explain) – *they speak a language similar to Tibetan*
– *theirs is not a written language*

ACTIVITY G *Expository Writing—Extended Response*

Example Extended Response

My life compared to the life of a Sherpa is different in many ways. First, the food I eat is very different. My family shops at grocery stores or goes to restaurants for food. The Sherpas grow or raise most of their food. They eat yak meat, yak milk, and yak cheese. People of both cultures eat potatoes. Next, yaks are very important to the life of a Sherpa. My family doesn't rely on yaks at all. The yaks provide food, clothing, and shoe leather for the Sherpas. In addition, we may have different religious beliefs and practices. The Sherpas practice a form of Buddhism. They also honor the mountains as homes of gods. Another major difference is our language. While I speak English, the Sherpas speak a language that is similar to the language of Tibet. While their language is spoken, there is no written form of the language.

ACTIVITY A *Vocabulary*

List 1: Tell

1.	Rapa Nui	*n.*	▶ (another name for Easter Island)
2.	Chile	*n.*	▶ (a country on the west side of South America)
3.	intrigue	*v.*	▶ (to make someone be curious about)
4.	archaeological	*adj.*	▶ (having to do with how people lived in the past)
5.	Polynesian	*adj.*	▶ (of islands in the Pacific, between Hawaii and New Zealand)
6.	revere	*v.*	▶ (to feel deep respect for)
7.	Peru	*n.*	▶ (a country north of Chile)
8.	Incas	*n.*	▶ (Indian people of Peru)
9.	Moai	*n.*	▶ (stone head statues on Easter Island)
10.	quarry	*n.*	▶ (a place where stone is cut)

List 2: Strategy Practice

1.	integrate	*v.*	▶ (to make whole by bringing parts together)
2.	overpopulate *or* overpopulate	*v.*	▶ (to have too many people living in a certain area)
3.	conclusion	*n.*	▶ (a final decision or opinion reached after some thought)
4.	massive	*adj.*	▶ (very large)
5.	elongate	*v.*	▶ (to make longer)
6.	inhabitants	*n.*	▶ (people who live in a place)
7.	ceremonial	*adj.*	▶ (related to a ceremony)
8.	destination	*n.*	▶ (a place to which a person is going)
9.	fascinate	*v.*	▶ (to hold the attention of by being very interesting)
10.	primitive	*adj.*	▶ (at an earlier stage of development)

Overhead 54

(ACTIVITY A) *Vocabulary*

List 3: Word Families

Family 1	explore	v.	▶	(to travel in order to learn about places)
	explorer	n.	▶	
	exploration	n.	▶	

Family 2	discover	v.	▶	(to learn about for the first time)
	discoverer	n.	▶	
	discovery	n.	▶	

Family 3	migrate	v.	▶	(to move from one place to another)
	migration	n.	▶	
	immigration	n.	▶	

Family 4	navigate	v.	▶	(to steer or direct the course of a ship or aircraft)
	navigator	n.	▶	
	navigation	n.	▶	

Family 5	explain	v.	▶	(to make clear and understandable)
	explanatory	adj.	▶	
	explanation	n.	▶	

(ACTIVITY B) *Spelling Dictation*

1. **explore**	4. **explain**
2. **explorer**	5. **explanatory**
3. **exploration**	6. **explanation**

ACTIVITY G *Expository Writing—Summary*

Prompt: Write a summary of the information you read in the *Easter Island* article.

Example Summary Plan

Planning Box
(topic) *Easter Island*
① (detail) – *Easter Island is located west of Chile, in the South Pacific Ocean*
② (detail) – *people have lived there since A.D. 700*
③ { (detail) – *they may have come from other Polynesian Islands*   (detail) – *islanders used a double canoe to navigate the ocean*
(detail) – ~~*scientists are unsure about the origins of Easter Islanders*~~
④ (detail) – *Easter Island has many large stone statues of heads called Moai*
⑤ (detail) – *the statues are all made of volcanic rock*
⑥ { (detail) – *the statues are very large and heavy*   (detail) – *no one knows how the statues were moved*
(detail) – ~~*today, Easter Island is a national park of Chile*~~
⑦ (detail) – *people travel there to see the statues*
⑧ (detail) – *people want to know why the statues were carved*

ACTIVITY G *Expository Writing—Summary*

Example Summary

Easter Island is a land of great mystery. It is located in the South Pacific Ocean, west of Chile. People have lived on the island since about A.D. 700. They may have come from other Polynesian Islands in double canoes, which were used to navigate the ocean. Easter Island has many carved stone heads, called Moai. They are carved out of volcanic rock. Some are extremely large and heavy, and no one knows how the native people moved them. People travel to Easter Island to see the statues. People are still trying to learn why the statues were carved.

ACTIVITY A *Vocabulary*

List 1: Tell

1.	Egypt	*n.*	▶ (a country in northeastern Africa)
2.	Cairo	*n.*	▶ (a city in Egypt)
3.	Giza	*n.*	▶ (a place near Cairo)
4.	Khufu	*n.*	▶ (a ruler of ancient Egypt)
5.	Babylon	*n.*	▶ (an ancient city in the Middle East)
6.	Nebuchadnezzar	*n.*	▶ (a ruler of Babylon)
7.	Euphrates River	*n.*	▶ (a river near Babylon)
8.	Zeus	*n.*	▶ (a Greek god)
9.	Phideas	*n.*	▶ (a Greek sculptor)
10.	Ephesus	*n.*	▶ (an ancient city in Turkey)
11.	Mausolus	*n.*	▶ (an ancient king)
12.	Halicarnassus	*n.*	▶ (an ancient city in Turkey)
13.	Aegean Sea	*n.*	▶ (a sea between Greece and Turkey)
14.	Helios	*n.*	▶ (the Greek sun god)
15.	Auguste Bartholdi	*n.*	▶ (a French sculptor)
16.	Alexandria	*n.*	▶ (a city in northern Egypt)

List 2: Strategy Practice

1.	monument	*n.*	▶ (something [often a statue] set up to keep alive the memory of a person or event)
2.	tribute	*n.*	▶ (something done as a sign of respect)
3.	pyramid	*n.*	▶ (a stone structure with a square base and four sides that come up to a peak)
4.	approximately *or* approximately *or* approximately	*adv.*	▶ (nearly)
5.	complicate	*v.*	▶ (to make difficult or hard to understand)
6.	commission	*v.*	▶ (to pay for work to be done)
7.	foundation	*n.*	▶ (the base or bottom)
8.	practical	*adj.*	▶ (showing good sense)
9.	Colossus	*n.*	▶ (a statue of Helios, the sun god)
10.	description	*n.*	▶ (a statement of how something looks)

ACTIVITY A *Vocabulary*

List 3: Word Families

Family 1	history	*n.*	▶ (a record of the past)
	historical	*adj.*	
	historian	*n.*	
Family 2	architecture	*n.*	▶ (the design, plan, and construction of buildings or other structures)
	architectural	*adj.*	
	architect	*n.*	
Family 3	compile	*v.*	▶ (to collect and put together)
	compiler	*n.*	
	compilation	*n.*	
Family 4	construct	*v.*	▶ (to make or build)
	construction	*n.*	
	deconstruct	*v.*	
Family 5	sculpture	*n.*	▶ (art figures and forms made of wood, stone, or clay)
	sculpt	*v.*	
	sculptor	*n.*	

ACTIVITY B *Spelling Dictation*

1. **history**	4. **construct**
2. **historical**	5. **construction**
3. **historian**	6. **deconstruct**

ACTIVITY G *Expository Writing—Extended Response*

Prompt: What three modern inventions do you think have made the most difference in the world and why?

Example Extended Response Plan

Planning Box
(position) *Three modern inventions have made the most difference in the world.*
① (reason) – *telephone improved communication*
(explain) – *letters take days or weeks*
– *people can communicate instantly*
– *hear voices of friends and family*
② (reason) – *refrigerator made food last longer*
(explain) – *possible to transport food or keep it in storage longer*
– *things spoil less easily*
③ (reason) – *computer made difficult tasks simpler*
(explain) – *math-based tasks, like bookkeeping, take less time*
– *people share information easily with disks and e-mail*

ACTIVITY G *Expository Writing—Extended Response*

Example Extended Response

   I believe that the telephone, the refrigerator, and the computer are the three inventions that have made the most difference in the world. First of all, the telephone improved communication. People used to have to send letters, which take days or weeks to deliver. The telephone helps them communicate instantly. People can also hear the voices of friends and family members. Secondly, the refrigerator made food last longer. Food can be transported farther and put into storage longer. It does not spoil as easily. Lastly, the computer has made difficult tasks simpler. Math-based tasks, like bookkeeping, take much less time on a computer than by hand. People can also share information more easily, using computer disks and e-mail.

Rubric— Summary	Student or Partner Rating		Teacher Rating	
1. Did the author state the topic and the main idea in the first sentence?	Yes	Fix up	Yes	No
2. Did the author focus on important details?	Yes	Fix up	Yes	No
3. Did the author combine details in some of the sentences?	Yes	Fix up	Yes	No
4. Is the summary easy to understand?	Yes	Fix up	Yes	No
5. Did the author correctly spell words, particularly the words found in the article?	Yes	Fix up	Yes	No
6. Did the author use correct capitalization, capitalizing the first word in the sentence and proper names of people, places, and things?	Yes	Fix up	Yes	No
7. Did the author use correct punctuation, including a period at the end of each sentence?	Yes	Fix up	Yes	No

Rubric— Extended Response	Student or Partner Rating		Teacher Rating	
1. Did the author tell his/her position in the first sentence?	Yes	Fix up	Yes	No
2. Did the author include at least three **strong, logical** reasons for his/her position?	Yes	Fix up	Yes	No
3. Did the author provide a **strong, logical** explanation for each of his/her reasons?	Yes	Fix up	Yes	No
4. Is the response easy to understand?	Yes	Fix up	Yes	No
5. Did the author correctly spell words, particularly the words found in the article?	Yes	Fix up	Yes	No
6. Did the author use correct capitalization, capitalizing the first word in the sentence and proper names of people, places, and things?	Yes	Fix up	Yes	No
7. Did the author use correct punctuation, including a period at the end of each sentence?	Yes	Fix up	Yes	No

Appendix A

Reproducibles

Reproduce the following student strategies and reference chart. Distribute the copies to students during the indicated lessons.

Reproducible	Lesson
Reproducible 1 REWARDS Strategies for Reading Long Words (This is also found in the back of the *Student Book*.)	Review Lesson 1 or Application Lesson 1
Reproducible 2 Prefixes, Suffixes, and Vowel Combinations Reference Chart (This is also found in the back of the *Student Book*.)	Review Lesson 1 or Application Lesson 1
Reproducible 3 Comprehension Strategy—Multiple Choice	Application Lesson 2
Reproducible 4 Writing Strategy—Summary	Application Lesson 3
Reproducible 5 Comprehension Strategy—Short Answer	Application Lesson 5
Reproducible 6 Writing Strategy—Extended Response	Application Lesson 7

REWARDS Strategies for Reading Long Words

Overt Strategy

1. Circle the prefixes.

2. Circle the suffixes.

3. Underline the vowels.

4. Say the parts of the word.

5. Say the whole word.

6. Make it a real word.

Example:

re con struc tion

Covert Strategy

1. Look for prefixes, suffixes, and vowels.

2. Say the parts of the word.

3. Say the whole word.

4. Make it a real word.

Prefixes, Suffixes, and Vowel Combinations Reference Chart

Prefixes

Decoding Element	Key Word	Decoding Element	Key Word	Decoding Element	Key Word
a	above	**com**	compare	**mis**	mistaken
ab	abdomen	**con**	continue	**multi**	multiage
ac	accommodate	**de**	depart	**over**	overpopulate
ad	advertise	**dis**	discover	**per**	permit
af	afford	**en**	entail	**pre**	prevent
ap	appreciate	**ex**	example	**pro**	protect
ar	arrange	**hydro**	hydrothermal	**re**	return
as	associate	**im**	immediate	**sub**	submarine
at	attention	**in**	insert	**trans**	translate
auto	automatic	**ir**	irregular	**un**	uncover
be	belong	**micro**	microscope		

Suffixes

Decoding Element	Key Word	Decoding Element	Key Word	Decoding Element	Key Word
able	disposable	**ful**	careful	**ness**	kindness
age	courage	**ible**	reversible	**or**	tailor
al	final	**ic**	frantic	**ous**	nervous
ance	disturbance	**ing**	running	**s**	birds
ant	dormant	**ion**	million	**ship**	ownership
ary	military	**ish**	selfish	**sion**	mission
ate	regulate	**ism**	realism	**sive**	expensive
cial	special	**ist**	artist	**tial**	partial
cious	precious	**ity**	oddity	**tion**	action
ed	landed	**ize**	criticize	**tious**	cautious
ence	essence	**le**	cradle	**tive**	attentive
ent	consistent	**less**	useless	**ture**	picture
er	farmer	**ly**	safely	**y**	industry
est	biggest	**ment**	argument		

Vowel Combinations

Decoding Element	Key Word	Decoding Element	Key Word	Decoding Element	Key Word
ai	rain	**ou**	loud	**a–e**	make
au	sauce	**ow**	low, down	**e–e**	Pete
ay	say	**oy**	boy	**i–e**	side
ea	meat, thread	**ar**	farm	**o–e**	hope
ee	deep	**er**	her	**u–e**	use
oa	foam	**ir**	bird		
oi	void	**or**	torn		
oo	moon, book	**ur**	turn		

Comprehension Strategy—Multiple Choice

Comprehension Strategy—Multiple Choice

Step 1: Read the item.

Step 2: Read all of the choices.

Step 3: Think about why each choice might be correct or incorrect. Check the article as needed.

Step 4: From the possible correct choices, select the best answer.

Writing Strategy—Summary

Writing Strategy—Summary

Step 1: LIST (List the details that are important enough to include in the summary.)

Step 2: CROSS OUT (Reread the details. Cross out any that you decide not to include.)

Step 3: CONNECT (Connect any details that could go into one sentence.)

Step 4: NUMBER (Number the details in a logical order.)

Step 5: WRITE (Write your summary.)

Step 6: EDIT (Revise and proofread your summary.)

Comprehension Strategy—Short Answer

Comprehension Strategy—Short Answer

Step 1: Read the item.

Step 2: Turn the question into part of the answer and write it down.

Step 3: Think of the answer or locate the answer in the article.

Step 4: Complete your answer.

Writing Strategy—Extended Response

Writing Strategy—Extended Response

Step 1: LIST (List the reasons for your position. For each reason, explain with details.)

Step 2: CROSS OUT (Reread your reasons and details. Cross out any that you decide not to include.)

Step 3: CONNECT (Connect any details that could go into one sentence.)

Step 4: NUMBER (Number the reasons in a logical order.)

Step 5: WRITE (Write your response.)

Step 6: EDIT (Revise and proofread your response.)

Appendix B

Optional Vocabulary Activities

The following activities were constructed for each lesson and can be used as part of each lesson or for any lesson that the teacher chooses. These activities can be used to provide additional in-class practice with lesson vocabulary, to stimulate discussion, or to assign as homework.

Yes/No/Why Activity

The format of this activity provides students the opportunity to demonstrate their depth and breadth of knowledge of selected vocabulary words. In this activity, students respond to the question by answering "Yes" or "No," and then provide a reason for their answer. Providing a reason (a "Why") for an answer requires students to logically assess the question, think of possible exceptions, and weigh alternatives.

Because of the difficulty of this task, we recommend initially modeling a number of activity items, stressing critical-thinking skills. The modeling might be similar to the following, which is based on the Application Lesson 1 activity.

1. Read the first item with me: *Would most **productions** have **protagonists**?*
2. I would answer "Yes" to this question, and here is my reason. Productions are plays, movies, and videos. All of these would have main characters, so I concluded that most productions would have protagonists.
3. Write your answer and your reason for your answer in the space provided. Look up when you are done.
4. Read item 2 with me: *Can **dialogue** ever be a **chorus**?*
5. After thinking about it, I would answer "No," because dialogue refers to conversation in a play. While members of a chorus might have a conversation, they cannot **be** the conversation because they are a group of people.
6. Write your answer and your reason for your answer in the space provided. Look up when you are done.
7. Read item 3 with me: *Are all **traditions religious**?*
8. I would answer "No" to this question. My reason is that although many traditions are religious, many have no religious base. For example, the traditions around birthday parties—giving gifts, eating cake, and blowing out candles—are not religious.
9. Write your answer and your reason for your answer in the space provided. Look up when you are done.

Note 1: You may want to ask students to share their answers and their reasons for those answers with partners or with the class.

Once students are familiar with the format, this vocabulary activity can be conducted in many ways. As a class activity, students read the item, record a "Yes" or "No" independently, and then share their answers and reasons with classmates. Alternatively, groups of students might be assigned to discuss one of the items and prepare a response. As groups share their responses with classmates, a lively discussion will often emerge. This vocabulary activity could also be independently completed (in writing) in class or as homework. If you wish, class discussion could occur the following day.

Completion Activity

This activity promotes linkage between vocabulary words and background knowledge. Definitions from word lists are provided for each word. Students then complete a sentence stem that contains the vocabulary word. This activity is structured for students to complete in writing and is ideal to assign as homework or an in-class assignment.

As with the previous activity items, modeling is useful. The model might be similar to the following, which is again based on the Application Lesson 1 activity.

1. Read the first definition with me: ***appreciate:** to like something.*
2. Now, read the sentence stem: *You might appreciate . . .*
3. When I think about things that I appreciate or like, I think about appreciating a good meal, the company of my friends, and special holidays.
4. Think of things that you might appreciate.
5. Next, I complete the item by adding the things I appreciate to the sentence stem.
6. Let's do another one together. Read the second definition with me: ***compete:** to strive against others; to try to win.*
7. Read the sentence stem: *People could compete in sports such as . . .*
8. I can think of a number of sports in which people compete, including football, soccer, and tennis.
9. Think of sports in which people compete, and add the names of some of those sports to the sentence stem.

Note 2: You may want to ask students to share their answers and their reasons for those answers with partners or with the class.

Application Lesson 1

Yes/No/Why Activity

1. Would most **productions** have **protagonists**? _____
   _____

2. Can **dialogue** ever be a **chorus**? _____
   _____

3. Are all **traditions religious**? _____
   _____

Completion Activity

1. **appreciate:** to like something

   You might appreciate _____
   _____ .

2. **compete:** to strive against others; to try to win

   People could compete in sports such as _____
   _____ .

3. **tradition:** doing something the same way it was done in the past

   Some traditions on birthdays are _____
   _____ .

4. **visible:** can be seen

   Some things visible in the sky include _____
   _____ .

5. **audience:** a group of people gathered to see a production

   An audience might be watching _____
   _____ .

Application Lesson 2

Yes/No/Why Activity

1. Could **skepticism** encourage **conversation?** _____

_____

2. Are all **merchants established?** _____

_____

3. Are **diplomatic** relations always **respectful?** _____

_____

Completion Activity

1. **information:** something told; items of knowledge

   You can get information about national and international events, entertainment

   options, and the latest styles from _____

   _____.

2. **voyage:** a trip, usually by ship

   I would really like to take a voyage to _____

   _____.

3. **translate:** to change into another language

   Languages you may want to translate into English include _____

   _____

   _____.

4. **establish:** to set up permanently

   People often establish _____

   _____.

5. **extensively:** large in amount

   Subjects that I extensively know about, or would like to know about, include

   _____.

Application Lesson 3

Yes/No/Why Activity

1. Would a **privateer** have **sponsorship**? _____

   _____

2. Do **jurisdictions** have **regulations**? _____

   _____

3. Can **intentions** have **intensity**? _____

   _____

Completion Activity

1. **inspirational:** causing influence or courage

   Inspirational ideas often come from _____

   _____ .

2. **adventure:** a thrilling or exciting experience

   My best adventure was _____

   _____ .

3. **nutrition:** the process by which the body takes in and uses food

   People who practice good nutrition habits always _____

   _____ .

4. **democracy:** a government run by the people

   To live in a democracy is important because _____

   _____ .

5. **international:** concerning two or more countries

   An international incident or crisis might occur if _____

   _____ .

Application Lesson 4

Yes/No/Why Activity

1. Do **territories** that are **possessions** have **autonomy**? _____
   _____

2. Can **deposits** be **prevalent** in **territories**? _____
   _____

3. Does **exploration** ever lead to **acquisition**? _____
   _____

Completion Activity

1. **expand:** to make larger

   These items expand when heated: _____

   _____ .

2. **value:** usefulness or importance

   Items of value include _____

   _____ .

3. **inhabitant:** a person who lives in an area

   Inhabitants of other countries may live in _____

   _____ .

4. **acquisition:** something you get that becomes your own

   The computer expert's latest acquisitions were _____

   _____ .

5. **independence:** the state of not being ruled by another country

   We celebrate our country's independence by _____

   _____ .

Application Lesson 5

Yes/No/Why Activity

1. Can **incidents** cause **compassion**? _____

_____

2. Do people always **comply** with their **obligations**? _____

_____

3. Could a person **relinquish** his or her **reputation**? _____

_____

Completion Activity

1. **conductor:** a person who leads or guides

   One job a train conductor might have is _____

   _____ .

2. **associate:** to connect in thought or memory

   I always associate summer with _____

   _____ .

3. **reputation:** how people think of someone

   Having a good reputation is considered important because _____

   _____

   _____ .

4. **prosecute:** to carry out a legal action against a person in a court of law

   Lawyers often prosecute people who _____

   _____ .

5. **obligation:** something a person must do

   On a job, a person's obligations might include _____

   _____ .

Application Lesson 6

Yes/No/Why Activity

1. Would a **regiment** ever **commandeer** a place? _____

_____

2. Is an **invasion** always **official**? _____

_____

3. Could a **regiment** participate in **disobedience**? _____

_____

Completion Activity

1. **participate:** to take part in an activity

   In school, I like to participate in _____

   _____ .

2. **colony:** territory under the control of another country

   A country might want a colony because _____

   _____ .

3. **occupation:** a job; a profession

   Occupations that are often thought to be heroic are _____

   _____ .

4. **disobedience:** failure to follow an order

   In the armed forces, disobedience may result in _____

   _____ .

5. **product:** something made

   Things that are products include _____

   _____ .

Application Lesson 7

Yes/No/Why Activity

1. Could a **presidential** act ever be **unconstitutional**? _____

_____

2. Can **democracy** be a **limitation**? _____

_____

3. Are **justices nominated** to the Supreme Court? _____

_____

Completion Activity

1. responsibility: a job or duty

After-school responsibilities might include _____

_____ .

2. population: the number of people living in an area

The population of an area can affect _____

_____ .

3. government: the body that rules by right of authority

The government has control over _____

_____ .

4. notify: to let someone know about something

The local newspaper notifies its readers about _____

_____ .

5. comprise: to include or consist of

A healthy diet may be comprised of _____

_____ .

Application Lesson 8

Yes/No/Why Activity

1. Do **citizens** have **responsibilities**? _____

   _____

2. Can **circumstances** create an **opportunity**? _____

   _____

3. Do **democratic societies guarantee** certain rights? _____

   _____

Completion Activity

1. **application:** a request for a position or job

   You might put in an application for _____

   _____ .

2. **volunteer:** to do something of one's own free will

   People volunteer to _____

   _____ .

3. **privileges:** special rights

   Things that can be privileges include _____

   _____ .

4. **automatically:** done without a person's control

   When the air filled with dust, I automatically _____

   _____ .

5. **allegiance:** loyalty to a government

   People show their allegiance by _____

   _____ .

Yes/No/Why Activity

1. Can **migrants** be **refugees**? _____
   _____

2. Are **disputes** always **economic**? _____
   _____

3. Is **international security sustainable**? _____
   _____

Completion Activity

1. **drought:** a long period of dry weather; lack of rain

   Effects of a drought might include _____
   _____.

2. **observe:** to watch closely

   To observe things at a distance, you might use _____
   _____.

3. **diplomatic:** effective type of discussion between two or more people or countries

   A diplomatic solution to a problem might avoid _____
   _____.

4. **weary:** tired; worn out

   I become very weary from _____
   _____.

5. **universe:** all that exists

   The universe includes all of the _____
   _____.

Application Lesson 10

Yes/No/Why Activity

1. Is getting a good **education** a **necessity**? _____

_____

2. Can **experience** be a **barrier**? _____

_____

3. Can the **elite affiliate**? _____

_____

Completion Activity

1. **pseudonym:** a fake name

   Writers often use pseudonyms because _____

   _____ .

2. **construct:** to make or build

   Things that are constructed include _____

   _____ .

3. **brochure:** a small pamphlet

   Different groups often send out brochures that tell about _____

   _____ .

4. **complicated:** difficult or hard to understand

   The most complicated thing I've ever done was _____

   _____ .

5. **receive:** to get

   People may receive an award for _____

   _____ .

Application Lesson 11

Yes/No/Why Activity

1. Are all **scholars historians**? _____

_____

2. Is it **mandatory** to be **literate**? _____

_____

3. Does **interpretation** require **memorization**? _____

_____

Completion Activity

1. **standardize:** to make the same or uniform

   Things that are standardized include _____

   _____.

2. **memorize:** the act of learning and remembering

   People often memorize _____

   _____.

3. **eventually:** finally; in the end

   An example of an activity that happens eventually is _____

   _____.

4. **informal:** made for everyday use

   At the informal school dance, students wore _____

   _____.

5. **pronounce:** to say a word correctly

   I was at a loss when I had to pronounce _____

   _____

Application Lesson 12

Yes/No/Why Activity

1. Can you **speculate** on the price of a **commodity**? _____

_____

2. Is the U.S. **economy enormous?** _____

_____

3. If you studied **geography**, could you learn about **altitudes**? _____

_____

Completion Activity

1. **Lake Magadi:** a lake in Kenya

   Lake Magadi is found on the continent of _____

   _____ .

2. **geography:** the natural features of a particular place or region

   The geography of North America includes _____

   _____ .

3. **preserve:** to maintain or keep

   People who are concerned about the environment often work to preserve

   _____

   _____ .

4. **collision:** coming together with force

   Traffic collisions may be caused by _____

   _____ .

5. **geologist:** a person who studies the earth's history and formation

   People who are geologists often _____

   _____ .

Yes/No/Why Activity

1. Would **expeditions** to **Mt. Everest** be somewhat dangerous? _____

_____

2. Could a military **occupation alienate** certain people? _____

_____

3. Is **prosperity** gained only as a part of a **heritage**? _____

_____

Completion Activity

1. **tradition:** doing something the same way as it was done in the past

   Family traditions include _____

   _____ .

2. **industry:** a manufacturing business

   Local industries include _____

   _____ .

3. **deforestation:** the result of cutting down forests or trees

   An example of why deforestation occurs would be _____

   _____ .

4. **spirituality:** concern with things of the spirit or soul

   People show their spirituality by _____

   _____ .

5. **prowess:** great ability or skill

   People could have prowess in _____

   _____ .

Application Lesson 14

Yes/No/Why Activity

1. Can **Chile** be a **destination**? _____

_____

2. Can a **quarry** be **massive**? _____

_____

3. Would **primitive** people **fascinate archaeologists**? _____

_____

Completion Activity

1. **primitive:** at an earlier stage of development

   The primitive computer game could not _____

   _____ .

2. **ceremonial:** related to a ceremony

   At graduation, ceremonial activities include _____

   _____ .

3. **intrigue:** to make someone be curious about

   I was intrigued by _____

   _____ .

4. **conclusion:** a final decision or opinion reached after some thought

   You could reach a conclusion about _____

   _____ .

5. **inhabitants:** people who live in a place

   The inhabitants of an island need _____

   _____ .

Application Lesson 15

Yes/No/Why Activity

1. Is a **monument** always a **tribute**? _____

   _____

2. Do **pyramids** have **foundations**? _____

   _____

3. Could an **architectural** plan lead to **construction**? _____

   _____

Completion Activity

1. **compile:** to collect and put together

   Things that can be compiled include _____

   _____ .

2. **practical:** showing good sense

   An example of a practical decision is _____

   _____ .

3. **approximately:** nearly

   Each year, you go to school for approximately this many weeks. _____

4. **foundation:** the base or bottom

   Most foundations of buildings are made out of _____

   _____ .

5. **historian:** a person who studies the past

   A historian would be interested in _____

   _____ .

Appendix C

Fluency Graph: Correct Words Per Minute

In each of the Application Lessons, students engage in repeated readings of Activity D articles in order to increase their reading fluency. A Fluency Graph for recording the student's first timing (Cold Timing) and last timing (Hot Timing) is found on the last page of the *Student Book*. A reproducible version of the Fluency Graph is included on the following page so that you can continue to conduct repeated reading activities after *REWARDS Plus* is completed.

Fluency Graph

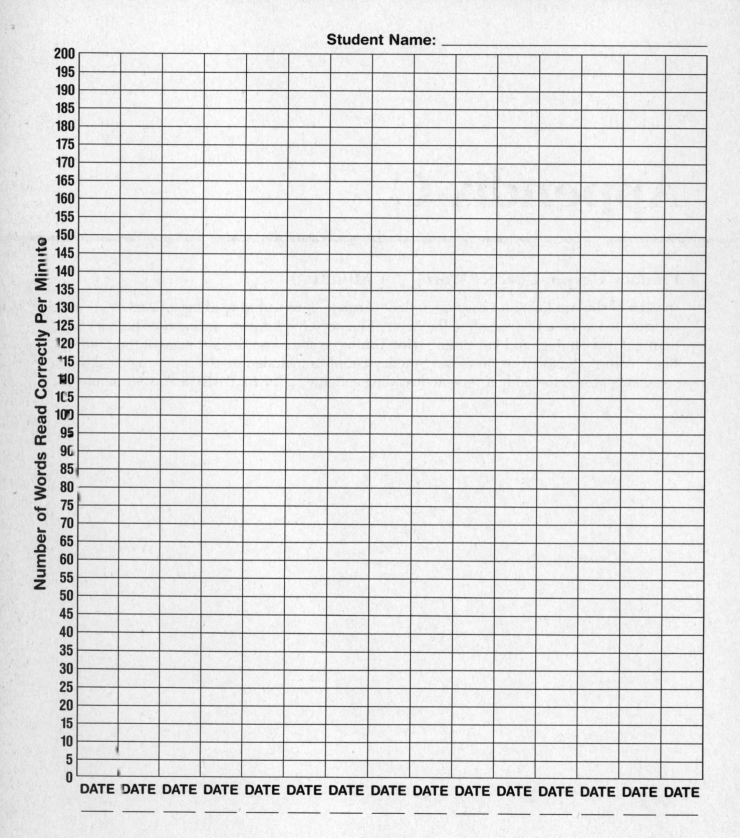

Student Name: _____

Number of Words Read Correctly Per Minute

200
195
190
185
180
175
170
165
160
155
150
145
140
135
130
125
120
115
110
105
100
95
90
85
80
75
70
65
60
55
50
45
40
35
30
25
20
15
10
5
0

DATE DATE DATE DATE DATE DATE DATE DATE DATE DATE DATE DATE DATE DATE DATE

____ ____ ____ ____ ____ ____ ____ ____ ____ ____ ____ ____ ____ ____ ____

Appendix D

Incentive/Grading System

In some cases, classes will profit from an additional incentive/grading system. This will provide a structured way to give students feedback on their behavior and academic progress. During each lesson, award points for each segment of the lesson as shown in the Review Lessons Chart and the Application Lessons Chart. These points can be used to determine a lesson grade and an overall grade. You may wish students to earn access to special events (e.g., popcorn party, free reading period, video viewing) or prizes (e.g., a book, school supplies, treats) as incentives. Procedures for awarding points during the Review Lessons and Application Lessons are outlined on the following pages.

You may reproduce the Review Lessons and Application Lessons Charts found on the following pages. However, you may also choose to have students use the charts found at the back of the *Student Book*.

Incentive/Grading System for Review Lessons

1. Before conducting the first Review Lesson, copy and distribute the Review Lessons Chart (see next page) to students.
2. After students complete Activities A–C, then Activities D and E, in the *Student Book*, award **Participation Points.** If students have followed your behavioral guidelines, paid attention, participated, and responded accurately, award **4 points.** If students perform below your expectations, award **0**, **1**, **2**, or **3** points. Have students record their points on the Review Lessons Chart throughout each lesson.
3. For the Reading Check, ask each student to read one sentence in Activity F. If the student makes no errors, award **4 Performance Points.** Award **3 points** if one error is made, **2 points** if two errors are made, and **0 points** if more than two errors are made.
4. At the end of the Review Lesson, have students add their points to find a subtotal.
5. Award **Bonus Points** for excellent reading and/or behavior.
6. Then, have students total their points.
7. You may wish to award a grade for each Review Lesson. Use the guidelines at right in determining the lesson grade.
8. The total points earned can be used to determine an overall grade for this portion of your reading program. A proposed grading scale is provided at right.

Daily Review Lesson Grade (Possible Points: 12)

11–12 points	A
9–10 points	B
8 points	C
7 points	D
Less than 7 points	F

Overall Review Lessons Grade (Possible Points: 72)

65–72 points	A
54–64 points	B
48–53 points	C
42–47 points	D
Less than 42 points	F

Review Lessons Chart

Name _____   Teacher _____

	Activities A–C (4 possible Participation Points)	Activities D and E (4 possible Participation Points)	Activity F Reading Check (4 possible Performance Points)	SUBTOTAL POINTS (12 possible points)	BONUS POINTS	TOTAL POINTS	LESSON GRADE
Review Lesson 1							
Review Lesson 2							
Review Lesson 3							
Review Lesson 4							
Review Lesson 5							
Review Lesson 6							

Participation Points (Possible Points: 4)

- Following behavioral guidelines
- Paying attention
- Participating
- Responding accurately

Performance Points (Possible Points: 4)

No errors	**4 points**
1 error	**3 points**
2 errors	**2 points**
More than 2 errors	**0 points**

Incentive/Grading System for Application Lessons

1. Before conducting the first Application Lesson, copy and distribute the Application Lessons Chart (see next page) to students.
2. During the lesson, award **Participation Points** as well as **Performance Points** as listed below.
3. After reading Lists 1 and 2 in Activity A, award **Participation Points**. If students have followed behavioral guidelines, paid attention, carefully practiced the words, and responded accurately, award **4 points.**
4. After the Oral Vocabulary exercise, in which students circle the number of the vocabulary word you give clues about, have students record their tally points (**5 Performance Points** possible).
5. After reading List 3 in Activity A, award **Participation Points**. If students have followed behavioral guidelines, paid attention, carefully practiced the words, and responded accurately, award **4 points**.
6. After the Activity B Spelling exercise, have students record **Performance Points** for the number of correct words (**6 points** possible).
7. After the Activity D Passage Reading, award **Participation Points**. If students have followed behavioral guidelines, paid attention, carefully read the passage, and responded accurately to the Comprehension Questions, award **4 points.**
8. After the Activity E Fluency exercise, award **Performance Points**. If a student's fluency increases from the Cold Timing to the Hot Timing, award **4 Bonus Performance Points**.
9. After the Activity F Multiple Choice exercise, award **4 Performance Points** for correct responses.
10. After the Activity F Short Answer exercise, award **4 Performance Points** for correct responses. (Although this exercise is not included in Application Lessons 1, 2, and 3, these points are given to all students on the Application Lessons Chart.)
11. After the Activity G Writing exercise, award **7 Performance Points** corresponding to the attributes of the rubrics.
12. At the end of the Application Lesson, have students add their points to find a subtotal.
13. Award **Bonus Points** for excellent work and/or behavior.
14. Then, have students total their points.
15. You may wish to award a grade for each Application Lesson. Use the guidelines below in determining the lesson grade.
16. The total points earned can be used to determine an overall grade for this portion of your reading program. A proposed grading scale is provided below.

Daily Application Lesson Grade (Possible Points: 42)

38–42 points	A
34–37 points	B
30–33 points	C
25–29 points	D
Less than 25 points	F

Overall Application Lessons Grade (Possible Points: 630)

570–630 points	A
510–569 points	B
450–509 points	C
375–449 points	D
Less than 375 points	F

Name _____

Teacher _____

	Activity A List 1 and List 2 (4 possible Participation Points)	Oral Vocabulary Tally (5 possible Performance Points)	Activity A List 3 (4 possible Participation Points)	Activity B Spelling (6 possible Performance Points)	Activity D Passage Reading (4 possible Participation Points)	Activity E Fluency (4 possible Performance Points)	Activity F Multiple Choice (4 possible Performance Points)	Activity F Short Answer (4 possible Performance Points)	Activity G Writing (7 possible Performance Points)	SUBTOTAL POINTS (42 possible points)	BONUS POINTS	TOTAL POINTS	LESSON GRADE
Application Lesson 1								4					
Application Lesson 2								4					
Application Lesson 3								4					
Application Lesson 4													
Application Lesson 5													
Application Lesson 6													
Application Lesson 7													
Application Lesson 8													
Application Lesson 9													
Application Lesson 10													
Application Lesson 11													
Application Lesson 12													
Application Lesson 13													
Application Lesson 14													
Application Lesson 15													

Other Incentives

Group Incentives

You may select to have special events to encourage participation and accurate reading. Oftentimes, it is easier to offer group incentives rather than individual incentives, thus encouraging students to support the academic and behavioral efforts of their peers. Group incentives could be one of the following: popcorn party, ten minutes to visit, a word game, or a special edible treat.

While you may determine your own criteria for awarding group incentives, the following plan can be used:

- Set a goal of all A's or B's in five lessons.
- At the end of each lesson, examine the Point/Grade columns to determine if all students received an A or B. If so, record a group point in a prominent place (e.g., on a bulletin board).
- When all students have earned A's or B's in five lessons, celebrate with the selected treat or event.

Individual Incentives

If you are teaching a small group that includes students with learning challenges, you may wish to award individual prizes when a certain number of A's or B's are earned. For example, an individual student could earn a special treat for five lessons of A or B grades.

Appendix E

Pronunciation Guide for Unique Words

The following pages contain uncommon vocabulary words—along with their phonetic pronunciations—that are found in **Activity A, Lists 1 and 2,** of the designated Application Lessons. In two- or three-word entries, the underlined word is phonetically illustrated.

A Pronunciation Key (*Webster's New World College Dictionary*, 4th ed.) is provided for your convenience.

PRONUNCIATION KEY

Vowel Sounds

Symbol	Key Words
a	at, cap, parrot
ā	ape, play, sail
ä	cot, father, heart
e	ten, wealth, merry
ē	even, feet, money
i	is, stick, mirror
ī	ice, high, sky
ō	go, open, tone
ô	all, law, horn
oo	could, look, pull
yoo	cure, furious
$\overline{oo}$	boot, crew, tune
y$\overline{oo}$	cute, few, use
oi	boy, oil, royal
ou	cow, out, sour
u	mud, ton, blood, trouble
ʉ	her, sir, word
ə	ago, agent, collect, focus
'l	cattle, paddle
'n	sudden, sweeten

Consonant Sounds

Symbol	Key Words
b	bed, table, rob
d	dog, middle, sad
f	for, phone, cough
g	get, wiggle, dog
h	hat, hope, ahead
hw	which, white
j	joy, badge, agent
k	kill, cat, quiet
l	let, yellow, ball
m	meet, number, time
n	net, candle, ton
p	put, sample, escape
r	red, wrong, born
s	sit, castle, office
t	top, letter, cat
v	voice, every, love
w	wet, always, quart
y	yes, canyon, onion
z	zoo, misery, rise
ch	chew, nature, punch
sh	shell, machine, bush
th	thin, nothing, truth
th	then, other, bathe
zh	beige, measure, seizure
ŋ	ring, anger, drink

APPLICATION LESSON 1

Dionysus	/dī´ə nī´səs/
Thespis	/thes´pis/
Pisistratus	/pi sis´trə təs/
dithyramb	/dith´ə ram´/
theatrical	/thē a´tri kəl/
protagonist	/prō tag´ə nist/

APPLICATION LESSON 2

Venetian	/ve nē´shən/
Genoa	/jen´ə wə/
Genoese	/jen´ə wēz´/
khan	/kän/

APPLICATION LESSON 3

privateer	/prī´və tir´/

APPLICATION LESSON 4

mercantile	/mʉr´kən tēl/
mercantilism	/mʉr´kən tel iz´em/
autonomy	/ô tän´ə mē/

APPLICATION LESSON 5

Mohandas Gandhi	/gän´dē/
Mahatma	/mə hät´mə/

APPLICATION LESSON 6

General Lafayette	/laf´ē et´/

APPLICATION LESSON 10

pseudonym .... /sōō´də nim´/

Esperanto .... /es´pə rän´tō/

Esperantists .... /es´pə´ rän tists/

APPLICATION LESSON 12

Mozambique .... /mō´zem bēk/

Lake Magadi .... /mä gä´dē/

Lake Naivasha .... /nī vä´shä/

APPLICATION LESSON 13

Nepal .... /nə pôl´/

Sherpas .... /sher´pəs/

Khumbu Valley .... /koom´ boo/

Nangpa La .... /nuŋ´pə lə/

Nyingmapa Buddhism .... /nyiŋ´mä pä/

Tengboche Monastery .... /tuŋ´bôchä/

Chomolungma .... /chō´mō luŋ mə/

APPLICATION LESSON 14

Rapa Nui .... /rä´pä nōō´ē/

archaeological .... /är´kē əläj´i kəl/

Polynesian .... /päl´i nē´zhən/

revere .... /ri vir´/

Incas .... /iŋ´kəs/

Moai .... /mō´ī/

APPLICATION LESSON 15

Cairo .... /kī´rō/

Giza .... /gē´zə/

Egyptian pharaoh Khufu .... /fār´ō/

Nebuchadnezzar .... /neb´ə kəd nez´ər/

Euphrates River .... /yо͞о frāt´ēz/

Zeus .... /zо͞оs/

Phideas .... /fid´ē əs/

Ephesus .... /ef´i səs/

Mausolus .... /mô´sə lus/

Halicarnassus Mausoleum .... /hal´ə kär nas´əs mô´zəlē´əm/

Aegean Sea .... /ē jē´ən/

Helios .... /hē´lē äs´/

Auguste Bartholdi .... /bär thôl´dē/

Alexandria .... /al´ig zan´drē ə/

Appendix F

Word List for *REWARDS Plus*

The following alphabetized list contains all **Activity A** words that were presented in the Application Lessons. (Additional words found in the social studies articles are not included in this list.)

Appendix G

Pretest/Posttest Fluency and Writing Assessment Procedures

The following procedures can be used to assess students' oral reading fluency and summary writing skills before and after participating in the *REWARDS Plus* program.

Fluency Assessment Procedure

1. Administer the following fluency measure to each student before they begin the *REWARDS Plus* program.
2. Make copies of the passage on the next page (one copy for each student for recording data and one copy for students to read).
3. Ask each student to read the passage as quickly and as carefully as possible.
4. Have the student read for one minute. Use a stopwatch or timer.
5. Record data as the student reads.
   - Underline all mispronunciations
   - If the student immediately corrects a mispronunciation, give credit for the word.
   - If the student reverses the order of words, both words are errors.
   - Cross out words that are omitted. They will not be counted.
   - Write in all additions. However, these will not be counted.
6. When the minute is complete, ask the student to stop.
7. Determine the total number of words read. Subtract any mispronunciations. Determine the number of words read in a minute.

Upon completion of *REWARDS Plus*, follow the above procedures with the same passage to ascertain progress in oral reading fluency.

Writing Assessment Procedure

Pretest

1. After teaching Activities A through F of Lesson 2, ask students to write a short summary of the Marco Polo passage on a separate piece of paper. Be sure students have completed their summaries before proceeding to Activity G in the lesson.
2. Say to students "Write a summary of the information you read about Marco Polo. Be sure that your first sentence tells the topic and the main idea. The rest of your sentences should include important details."
3. Use the Rubric for Summary found on page 344 for scoring students' summaries.

Writing Assessment Procedure

Posttest

1. After teaching Activities A through F of Lesson 14, ask students to write a short summary of the Easter Island passage on a separate piece of paper. Be sure students have completed their summaries before proceeding to Activity G in the lesson.
2. Say to students "Write a summary of the information you read in the Easter Island article. Be sure that your first sentence tells the topic and the main idea. The rest of your sentences should include important details."
3. Use the Rubric for Summary found on page 344 for scoring students' summaries.

ACTIVITY D *Passage Reading and Comprehension*

Pirates and Piracy

What Are Pirates?

3   Pirates are familiar characters. Books and movies like *Peter Pan* or *Treasure*
15   *Island* have romanticized them. But real pirates are criminals, known especially
26   for attacking ships and stealing their cargo while on the high seas. Piracy is
40   different from other types of robbery because it occurs outside the jurisdiction
52   of any one government. Although pirates existed in Roman times and still do
65   today, the ones who inspired the famous images in the movies lived in the 17th
80   and 18th centuries. This era is known as the "Golden Age of Piracy." (#1)

93   Several different kinds of pirates sailed the seas, stealing goods from other
105 ships. Because they came from various countries and differed in their intentions,
117 they were called pirates, privateers, buccaneers, or marooners. (#2)

125 **Pirates**
126 The term *pirates* refers to a general classification of sailors who used their
139 skills to attack other ships. The pirates attacked any ship that seemed to have
153 something worth stealing, whether it was gold, precious cargo, or the ship itself.
166 Unlike other types of pirates, these sailors plundered ships from all nations
178 strictly for their private gain. Bartholomew Roberts, known more commonly as
189 Black Bart, was probably the most successful pirate ever. He captured more
201 than 400 ships in less than four years, traveling the coasts of South America,
215 North America, the Caribbean, and the Bahamas. (#3)

222 **Privateers**
223 A privateer traveled on a ship that carried official papers from a government
236 or company. These papers were called a *Letter of Marque.* The Letter of
249 Marque gave the ship permission to act on behalf of a specific government or
263 company. For example, if England was at war with Spain, the English
275 government sponsored privateers to attack and plunder Spanish ships.
284 Theoretically, the Letter of Marque protected the privateers from punishment.
294 But frequently they were tried and punished by the nations they were
306 "permitted" to attack. Sir Francis Drake, famous for being the first Englishman
318 to circumnavigate the globe, was a privateer for England. His ship attacked and
331 looted Spanish ships as he traveled in the name of Queen Elizabeth. (#4)

Rubric— Summary	Student or Partner Rating		Teacher Rating	
1. Did the author state the topic and the main idea in the first sentence?	Yes	Fix up	Yes	No
2. Did the author focus on important details?	Yes	Fix up	Yes	No
3. Did the author combine details in some of the sentences?	Yes	Fix up	Yes	No
4. Is the summary easy to understand?	Yes	Fix up	Yes	No
5. Did the author correctly spell words, particularly the words found in the article?	Yes	Fix up	Yes	No
6. Did the author use correct capitalization, capitalizing the first word in the sentence and proper names of people, places, and things?	Yes	Fix up	Yes	No
7. Did the author use correct punctuation, including a period at the end of each sentence?	Yes	Fix up	Yes	No

References

The following references provide the research base and validation of the strategies presented in *REWARDS* (Archer, Gleason, & Vachon, 2005). For more information and a synopsis of the validation research, please see Appendix G in the *REWARDS* Teacher's Guide, pp. 351–358.

Adams, M. J. (1990). *Beginning to read: Thinking and learning about print.* Cambridge, MA: MIT Press.

Anderson, R. C., Hiebert, E., Scott, J. A., & Wilkinson, I. A. G. (1985). Conceptual and empirical bases of readability formulas. In G. Green & A. Davison (Eds.), *Linguistic complexity and text comprehension* (pp. 23–54). Hillsdale, NJ: Erlbaum.

Archer, A. L. (1981). *Decoding of multisyllabic words by skill deficient fourth and fifth grade students.* Unpublished doctoral dissertation, University of Washington.

Archer, A. L., Gleason, M. M., Vachon, V., & Hollenbeck, K. (2006). *Instructional strategies for teaching struggling fourth and fifth grade students to read long words.* Manuscript submitted for review.

Canney, G., & Schreiner, R. (1977). A study of the effectiveness of selected syllabication rules and phonogram patterns for word attack. *Reading Research Quarterly, 12,* 102–124.

Cunningham, P. (1998). The multisyllabic word dilemma: Helping students build meaning, spell, and read "big" words. *Reading & Writing Quarterly: Overcoming Learning Difficulties, 14,* 189–219.

Just, M. A., & Carpenter, P. A. (1987). *The psychology of reading and language comprehension.* Boston: Allyn & Bacon.

Lenz, B. K., & Hughes, C. A. (1990). A word identification strategy for adolescents with learning disabilities. *Journal of Learning Disabilities, 23,* 149–158, 163.

Nagy, W. E., & Anderson, R. C. (1984). How many words are there in printed school English? *Reading Research Quarterly, 19,* 302–330.

Perfetti, C. A. (1985). *Reading ability.* New York: Oxford University Press.

Perfetti, C. A. (1986). Continuities in reading acquisition, reading skill, and reading disability. *Remedial and Special Education, 7,* 11–21.

Rayner, K., & Pollatsek, A. (1989). *The psychology of reading.* Englewood Cliffs, NJ: Prentice Hall.

Samuels, S. J., LaBerge, D., & Bremer, C. D. (1978). Units of word recognition: Evidence for developmental changes. *Journal of Verbal Learning and Verbal Behavior, 17,* 715–720.

Share, D., & Stanovich, K. (1995). Cognitive processes in early reading development: Accommodating individual differences into a mode of acquisition. *Issues in Education: Contributions from Educational Psychology, 1,* 1–57.

Shefelbine, J. (1990). A syllabic-unit approach to teaching decoding of polysyllabic words to fourth- and sixth-grade disabled readers. In J. Zutell & S. McCormick (Eds.), *Literacy Theory and Research: Analysis from multiple paradigms. Thirty-ninth yearbook of the National Reading Conference* (pp. 223–229). Fort Worth, TX: Texas Christian University Press.

Shefelbine, J., & Calhoun, J. (1991). Variability in approaches to identifying polysyllabic words: A descriptive study of sixth graders with highly, moderately, and poorly developed syllabication strategies. In J. Zutell & S. McCormick (Eds.), *Learner factors/teacher factors: Issues in literacy research and instruction. Fortieth yearbook of the National Reading Conference* (pp. 169–177). Fort Worth, TX: Texas Christian University Press.

Stanovich, K. E. (1986). Matthew effects in reading: Some consequences of individual differences in the acquisition of literacy. *Reading Research Quarterly, 21,* 360–407.

Stanovich, K. E. (1991). Word recognition: Changing perspectives. In R. Barr, M. L. Kamil, P. B. Mosenthal, & P. D. Pearson (Eds.), *Handbook of reading research* (Vol. 2) (pp. 418–452). New York: Longman.

Vachon, V., & Gleason, M. M. (2006). *The effects of mastery teaching and varying practice contexts on middle school students' acquisition of multisyllabic word reading strategies.* Manuscript in preparation.

Woodcock, R. W. (1973). *Woodcock reading mastery tests.* Circle Pines, MN: American Guidance Service.

Woodcock, R. W. (1987). *Woodcock reading mastery tests* (revised). Circle Pines, MN: American Guidance Service.